Library of
Davidson College

CAPITOL HILL MANUAL

CAPITOL HILL MANUAL

by

FRANK CUMMINGS

With a Foreword by

SENATOR JACOB K. JAVITS

THE BUREAU OF NATIONAL AFFAIRS, INC. • WASHINGTON, D.C.

Copyright © 1976
The Bureau of National Affairs, Inc.
Washington, D.C. 20037

Library of Congress Cataloging in Publication Data

Cummings, Frank.
   Capitol Hill manual.

   Includes index.
   1. Legislation—United States. 2. United States. Congress. I. Title.
KF4945.C9   328.73'05   76-608060
ISBN 0-87179-226-5

Printed in the United States of America
International Standard Book Number: 0-87179-226-5

To Jill, Peter, and Maggie

"The actually possible in this world is vastly narrower than all that is demanded; and there is always a *pinch* between the ideal and the actual which can only be got through by leaving part of the ideal behind. There is hardly a good which we can imagine except as competing for the possession of the same bit of space and time with some other imagined good. Every end of desire that presents itself appears exclusive of some other end of desire. Shall a man drink and smoke, or keep his nerves in condition?—he cannot do both. Shall he follow his fancy for Amelia, or for Henrietta?—both cannot be the choice of his heart. Shall he have the dear old Republican party, or a spirit of unsophistication in public affairs?—he cannot have both, etc. So that the ethical philosopher's demand for the right scale of subordination in ideals is the fruit of an altogether practical need. Some part of the ideal must be butchered, and he needs to know which part. It is a tragic situation, and no mere speculative conundrum, with which he has to deal."

William James
The Moral Philosopher and the Moral Life, an address to the Yale Philosophic Club, 1891

FOREWORD

To most people, including many members of Congress and their staffs, the rules by which each House operates remain a puzzle. Often constituents have watched proceedings in the Senate, observing only six or seven Senators on the floor passing legislation and wondering if this is what the legislative process is all about.

In addition, for those working in the Congress and for those who wish to have an impact on the actions of the Congress, it is vitally important to understand the rules and procedures by which each body operates. On Capitol Hill procedure often means substance and failure to understand that has resulted in the defeat of much important legislation.

Given these facts of life on Capitol Hill, Frank Cummings' *Capitol Hill Manual* can play a vital role in helping journalists, lobbyists, students, interested observers, and even participants to better understand the legislative process and its operation in both Houses of Congress. *Capitol Hill Manual* tells the reader how the elementary task of introducing a bill is performed, but it also points out the hidden problems encountered along the way such as which committee a bill should be referred to, how referral to a given committee may be determined by the drafting of the bill, and how to contest a referral to a given committee.

Capitol Hill Manual also looks at the power centers in the Congress and reviews many of the recent reforms made in both Houses but particularly in the House of Representatives where there were drastic changes. Many progressive members of Congress believe that the recent reforms will do much to make the Congress more responsive to the people in this modern age of greater accountability. In the Senate for the first time in almost 60 years the filibuster rule was significantly modified to make it more difficult for a willful minority to block the actions of a large majority. The filibuster rule was responsible for years of delay in the enactment of meaningful civil rights legislation, and this reform should play an important role in helping the Senate meet its modern responsibilities. In the House, great efforts were made to reform the method of selecting committee chairmen and to dilute the power of two committees, the Rules Committee and the Ways and Means Committee, which had operated in such a way that members often felt frustrated and chagrined. I believe that these reforms and others will make the House and Senate more responsive to the needs of the people and will help to provide more confidence in government. This book will bring the reader up to date on all of these changes and put them in an historical context.

Capitol Hill Manual should prove indispensable to Senators, House members, and their staffs since it contains much information in convenient form which will be useful in handling the day-to-day legislative work. Because so much of the information needed to legislate in Congress is gained through experience it has been difficult in the past to find a useful primer dealing with the legislative process. I believe this book fulfills that function admirably.

Finally a personal note about the author. Frank Cummings is ideally situated to write a manual about the operations of Congress. He served as Minority Counsel on the Senate Labor and Public Welfare Committee and also served as Administrative Assistant in my Senate office. Based on intimate knowledge, I know that Frank Cummings has an outstanding grasp of the legislative process and has much to impart to the readers of this manual. It should be required reading for all who wish to understand and make use of congressional rules and procedures.

Senator Jacob K. Javits
R-N.Y.

PREFACE

This is a manual on federal legislative technique. The ground rules of legislative technique appear only partly in the statutes, resolutions, and rules of Congress. What is technically permitted by the rules may not be appropriate or customary. And what is appropriate or customary often can be accomplished by a request for unanimous consent or permission, despite rules to the contrary.

So what is needed is a concise manual or handbook to provide an effective means of learning one's way through the labyrinth of rules and customs by which Congress operates. Obviously, the senators and representatives themselves, who are vested with constitutional powers, have a basic need to understand how Capitol Hill "works." And yet it may take years for a representative or senator to master the system, if experience is the only guide. Of equal importance is mastery of legislative technique by newly appointed legislative aides —whose tenure tends to be brief.

Among those outside of Congress who need to know how laws are passed are lobbyists, the press, and special interest groups, to name just a few. Lobbyists and special interest groups may suffer from inadequate knowledge of techniques for accomplishing procedurally their substantive objectives. And the press may on occasion report congressional developments in a misleading way, not deliberately but because of inadequate procedural understanding.

This manual is not an "evaluation" of Congress as an institution. Such evaluations already abound—some, unfortunately, based on insufficient knowledge of how the institution actually works. In certain sections I have made personal judgments about Congress, but only in regard to its practical working. This manual is a *"how* to," not a *"what* to" book. It is a modest undertaking, but I hope it will prove a useful tool for those engaged in grander enterprises.

The Organization of This Manual

The major parts of this manual are: *first*, an outline of steps in the legislative process; *second*, an analysis of the power centers in Congress; *third*, consideration of money bills and the federal budget process; and *fourth*, a review of nonlegislative activities which take place in Capitol Hill offices. Finally, a number of appendices contain material pertinent to the legislative process, such as House and Senate rules, a lobbyist registration form, and excerpts from the Legislative Reorganization Act.

After dividing this manual into its major parts, inevitably I would have liked to have had *each* part come first. One would like to review and explain power centers before explaining legislative steps to make the legislative steps more meaningful in light of the power realities. On the other hand, one would like first to review legislative steps in order to give more meaning to the explanation of power centers. One would like to interweave a discussion of the nonlegislative activities on Capitol Hill because they necessarily affect legislation and take place within a framework of power centers. And, underlying it all, one would like to review the budget and financing process, because it is money which, in the end, counts.

Frustrating as it is, we take these items up one by one, hopefully with the understanding that there are interrelationships, and that a broader comprehension is necessary in order really to understand how Capitol Hill works.

A Note on the Equality of the Sexes

I hope I am no male chauvinist. In editing this manuscript, at one point I began to insert the words "or she" every time I found the word "he," and the word "congresswoman" every time I found the word "congressman," and so on and on. It just became unmanageable. So I left all the male pronouns in, and I apologize in advance for falling back upon the age-old lawyer's cop-out—that whenever the context makes it appropriate, the male shall include the female, the singular shall include the plural, and vice versa.

Acknowledgements

Much of this manual was drawn from personal experiences working on Capitol Hill, or working with Capitol Hill people while practicing law privately. I could not possibly acknowledge all the many officials on the Hill and elsewhere who have helped me, not so much in the writing of the book itself as in learning what it takes to operate effectively in or around Congress.

Yet there are a few public and private people without whose assistance I could never have begun and never have finished. Senator Jacob K. Javits is a master legislative tactician. To work with him is to learn the Hill, and I am deeply indebted to him for having given me the opportunity to see from the inside what is so difficult to understand from the outside. His staff, likewise, is filled with superb congressional aides—among the most skillful and dedicated staff on the Hill. That staff, and particularly Chuck Warren, a masterful legislative assistant, were most helpful.

In the private sector, two young associates in my law office—Peter Turza and Sheldon Stein—were most helpful. Both were able to draw on their Capitol Hill experiences and helped greatly in completing the text, especially those sections dealing with recent congressional reforms.

TABLE OF CONTENTS

FOREWORD *by Senator Jacob K. Javits*	ix
PREFACE	xi

Part I. An Outline of the Legislative Process

DRAFTING A MEASURE	3
Type of Measure	3
Bill	4
Joint Resolution	4
Concurrent Resolution	7
Resolution	7
Amendment	7
Drafting Techniques and Problems	8
Filling in the Blanks on the Form	8
Specificity Versus Delegation—Definitions	16
Delegations of Discretion	17
Programmatic and Regulatory Statutes	18
Retaining Congressional Power Not Subject to Veto	19
Sources of Constitutional Authority	20
Preemption	21
Jurisdictional Overlaps	22
Labelling the Parts of a Bill	22
Judicial Review	23
Effective Dates	23
Sources of Drafting Assistance	23
Legislative Counsel	24
Committee Staff	25
Interest Groups and Lobbyists	26
Executive Departments	28
The Parliamentarian	30
Academic Assistance	31
SPONSORSHIP AND INTRODUCTION OF A BILL	33
Choice of Sponsor and/or Cosponsor(s)	33
Sponsor and/or Cosponsor of a Bill	33
Sponsor and/or Cosponsor of an Amendment	34
Introductory Remarks to a Bill	35
Publicizing the Bill—Using the Congressional Record Reprint of Introductory Remarks	36
Referral to Committee	36

The Role of the Parliamentarian 36
Referral by Unanimous Consent 37
Pre-Introduction Conference With the
  Parliamentarian 37
Choice of "Target" Committee 38
COMMITTEE CONSIDERATIONS 39

Hearings 39
  Power of Chairmen 39
  Other Ways of Moving a Bill 40
  Purpose and Effect of Hearings 41
  Subject Matter of Hearings 43
  Witnesses and Statements 44
  Open and Closed Hearings 45
Executive Sessions of Subcommittees and Committees
  (Markups) 45
  Open and Closed Markup Sessions 46
  Rules, Quorum, Proxies, and Votes 47
  Function of Staff 48
  Press Coverage 49
  Offering Amendments—Finalizing a Bill 49
Reporting a Bill and the Committee Report 51
  Time of Filing 52
  Committee Report 53
  Drafting the Committee Report 53
  Printing and Submission of Minority Views 54
  Contents of the Committee Report 55
  Significance of Separate or Other Views 55
  Choice of a Floor Manager 57

FLOOR AND CONFERENCE COMMITTEE CONSIDERATION ... 59

Bringing a Bill to the House Floor 59
  Resolutions From the House Rules Committee ... 60
  Consent Calendar 60
  Suspension of the Rules 61
  Privileged Committees 61
Calendars 62
  Senate Calendars 62
  House Calendars 62
  Senate "Consent Calendar" and "Holds" 63
Filibusters 64
  Extended Debate and Procedural Delay 64
  Cloture 65
  Wearing Down a Filibuster 65
Floor Debate and Voting 65
  "Rules" for House Floor Debate 65

Unanimous Consent Agreements in the Senate	66
Debate, Amendments, and the "Third Reading"	66
Points of Order and Motions on the Previous Question	66
Voting	67
Paired Votes	68
Motion to Reconsider (and to Table)	68
Position of Staff Members (on the Floor)	68
Press Coverage	69
Germaneness Under the House Rules	69
Conference Committee Consideration	72
Conference Committee and Conference Report	72
Request for and Agreement to a Conference	72
Selection of Managers	73
Open and Closed Conferences	73
Authority of the Conferees—Matters in Disagreement	73
Presidential Action and Congressional Post-Veto Reaction	74

Part II. Power Centers in Congress

THE HOUSE	77
Recent Reforms	78
Criterion for Chairmanship	79
"Choice" Committee Assignments	79
Open Markups	79
The Hansen Substitute (H. Res. 988)—Committees and Subcommittees	79
December 1974 Democratic Caucus Rule Changes	80
Committees	81
Chairmen of Full Committees	81
Subcommittee Chairmen	82
Ranking Minority Members	83
Committee Members	83
The Ways and Means Committee and the Rules Committee	83
Democratic Caucus—Power on Substantive Issues	84
The Leadership	85
Democratic Steering and Policy Committee	85
Democratic Study Group	86
Other Groups	86
THE SENATE	87
Reforms	87
Open Markups	87
Staffing for Less Senior Senators	89

Selecting Chairmen	89
Filibuster Reform	89
Committees	90
Chairmen of Full Committees	90
Subcommittee Chairmen	91
Ranking Minority Members	91
Committee Members	91
The Majority Party	92
The Majority Leader	92
Democratic Conference	92
Democratic Steering Committee	93
Democratic Policy Committee	93
Other Groups	93

Part III. Money Bills

FUNDING LEGISLATIVE PROGRAMS	97
Constitutional Priority of the House	97
The Relationship of Authorizations and Appropriations	98
Open-Ended Authorizations	99
Continuing Resolutions	99
Special Parliamentary Conditions Applying to Appropriations Bills	100
THE FEDERAL BUDGET	102
The President's Budget	102
Congress' Pre-1974 Response to the President's Budget	102
The Impoundment Controversy	103
Congressional Budget and Impoundment Control Act of 1974	103
Budget Committees	104
Congressional Budget Office	104
Change in the Fiscal Year	104
Timetable for Development of the Congressional Budget	105
Impoundments	106

Part IV. Nonlegislative Activities in Capitol Hill Offices

THE STRUCTURE OF A CONGRESSMAN'S OFFICE	109
Staff Breakdown	110
Administrative Assistants	111
Legislative Assistants	112
A Congressman's Personal Secretary	113
Caseworkers and Secretaries	114
Press Secretary	115

TABLE OF CONTENTS

Relationship of Committee Staff to Personal Staff 116
Officers of the Congress and Other Capitol Hill
    Officials 117
    Secretary of the Senate and Clerk of the House 117
    Sergeant at Arms 118
    House Doorkeeper 118
    Majority and Minority Secretaries in the Senate and
      the House 118
    Parliamentarian 119
    Legislative Counsel 119
    Librarian of Congress and Congressional Research
      Service 119
CONGRESSIONAL RELATIONSHIPS WITH THE ADMINISTRA-
    TION, LOBBYISTS, AND CONSTITUENTS 120
    Dealing With Executive Departments and
      Independent Agencies 120
    Normal Relationships 120
    Ethical Considerations—Quasi-Judicial Matters ... 120
    Conflicts of Interest 121
    Congress and Federal Jobs 122
    Federal Employment Patronage 122
    "Advice and Consent" Nominees, Clearance 123
    Lobbying 123
    The Need for Lobbyists 123
    Registration Under the Lobbying Act 124
    Congressional Offices Seeking Lobbyists' Advice ... 124
    Pros and Cons of Accepting a Lobbyist's Assistance. 125
    The Lobbyist's Expertise: "Know Who" and
      "Know-How" 125
    The Congressman's Appointment Calendar 128
APPENDICES
    1. Resume of Congressional Activity of the
       Ninety-Third Congress 131
    2. Lobbyist Registration Form 133
    3. Standing Rules of the Senate (Ninety-Fourth
       Congress) 135
    4. House Rules (Ninety-Fourth Congress) 192
    5. Model Committee Caucus and Committee Rules
       Prepared by the Democratic Study Group 233
    6. House Democratic Caucus Rules and Manual 260
    7. Extracts From the Legislative Reorganization Acts
       of 1946 and 1970 266
GLOSSARY 315
TOPICAL INDEX 321

PART I

AN OUTLINE OF THE LEGISLATIVE PROCESS

DRAFTING A MEASURE

Before getting into nonlegislative, administrative, and political activities of representatives and senators, one ought first to understand the primary function of the legislator, which is, after all, the enactment and amendment of law. Part I of this book therefore deals with steps in the legislative process.

The first step in the process is the choice, by the originator of the legislation, of the type of measure best suited to his needs—bill, resolution, joint resolution, concurrent resolution, or amendment. The next step is drafting. Then comes the choice of a sponsor or cosponsor. One would think the "choice" is unnecessary if it is made by the author of a bill—he sponsors it himself. But even then he has the problem of selecting and soliciting cosponsors. And from the outside looking in, a lobbyist with a bill in hand is very often in search not only of cosponsors but also of a primary sponsor. He has, one might say, a "book in search of an author."

Once a bill is drafted and sponsors are lined up, the actual introduction of the bill and introductory remarks concerning it come next. The bill is then referred to committee and undergoes hearings, executive sessions, and "markups" in subcommittee and committee. Finally, a committee report is prepared.

Now the bill moves to the floor, where floor procedure governs. Thereafter, the bill moves to the opposite House, and finally to conference committee and enactment or veto.

Type of Measure

A senator or representative may sponsor—introduce or cosponsor (add his name to)—five different kinds of measures: bills, resolutions, concurrent resolutions, joint resolutions, and amendments of other measures. Each is a proposal, usually in writing (except for amendments in the House), to

- create a new law
- or amend an existing law
- or amend a proposal to create or amend a law
- or create or amend legislative rules
- or create or amend some policy not rising to the level of a law but expressing the sense of the congressional body which passes the measure.

Without diminishing in any way the significance of a bill or other measure, one may say that it is nothing but a proposal, and a proposal of no one but its sponsor. There are tens of thousands of bills, resolutions, and amendments introduced every year, and only a tiny fraction of them is ever enacted (see Appendix 1). Ninety-nine percent go nowhere. And yet every one has some significance, for each records in writing the ideas and proposals of elected officials and may very well have some influence on the thinking of congressmen and upon other measures which do pass.

Of the five principal types of measures, four stand in their own right, and one, the amendment, stands only as a rider to some other measure.

Bill

By far the most common type of measure, a bill,* if passed by both Houses of Congress and signed by the President (or passed over his veto), becomes a law—ordinarily a public law, except in a few instances in which "private bills" † for the relief of particular persons are passed.

Joint Resolution

A joint resolution, although captioned differently, must meet the same requirements as a bill, and if passed becomes a law with fully the same legal effect (if such effect is sought) as a bill. As a matter of practice, however, a bill generally is used for laws of general application, whereas a joint resolution generally is used for laws of limited and short-term application or for special purposes. For example, the Internal Revenue Code or the National Labor Relations Act would be amended by passage of a bill. In contrast, a national railroad strike would be terminated statutorily or "National

---

* See Exhibit A, page 5, for the format of the first page of a bill.
† See Exhibit B, page 6, extract from the *Congressional Record*.

Exhibit A

90TH CONGRESS
1ST SESSION
S. 830

Indication of Congress, Session, and Bill Number — "S." for Senate and "H.R." for House of Representatives (whichever is the originating body)

IN THE SENATE OF THE UNITED STATES

FEBRUARY 3, 1967

Mr. YARBOROUGH (for himself, Mr. BIBLE, Mr. CANNON, Mr. CLARK, Mr. KENNEDY of Massachusetts, Mr. LONG of Missouri, Mr. MORSE, Mr. RANDOLPH, Mr. SMATHERS, and Mr. WILLIAMS of New Jersey) introduced the following bill; which was read twice and referred to the Committee on Labor and Public Welfare

Date of introduction

Sponsor (and co-sponsors)

Reference to Committee (ordinarily inserted by the Parliamentarian)

A BILL

To prohibit age discrimination in employment.

General statement of purpose

1 *Be it enacted by the Senate and House of Representa-*
2 *tives of the United States of America in Congress assembled,*

Enacting clause

3 That this Act may be cited as the "Age Discrimination
4 in Employment Act of 1967."

Short title (the words beginning "That" are really Section 1, but are not numbered)

5   STATEMENT OF FINDINGS AND PURPOSE

6   SEC. 2. (a) The Congress hereby finds and declares
7 that—

8   (1) in the face of rising productivity and affluence,
9   older workers find themselves disadvantaged in their

(2)

Exhibit B

May 10, 1976   CONGRESSIONAL RECORD — SENATE   S 6717

showed Mr. Ford and Henry Kissinger in dinner jackets, grinning with satisfaction.

A year later the cheers have mocking echoes. For the costs of the American action in the Mayaguez affair were heavy, and they are easy enough to see now—the casualties in lives, truth, diplomacy and law.

The Mayaguez had a crew of 39. The operations ordered by Mr. Ford cost the lives of 41 American servicemen, plus another 50 wounded—casualties that the Administration did its best to hide.

And it was all unnecessary. If the United States had allowed even a modest time for a response to its warnings and its diplomatic efforts, the Mayaguez and its crew would have been returned without the loss of a single American life. That is plain from the official record and timetable of what happened.

It was 5:03 A.M. on May 12, 1975, Eastern Daylight Time, when Washington first heard of the seizure. The President was told at 7:40. At 2 that afternoon the White House announced the news and demanded the ship's release, saying that otherwise there would be "the most serious consequences." At 4:30 an attempt was made to send a diplomatic note to Cambodia through the Chinese.

The first American air attack, made to prevent what was thought to be an effort to move the Mayaguez, sank a Cambodian gunboat at 8:30 P.M. May 13. That was just 30½ hours after the first White House statement, 28 hours after the first diplomatic move.

At 7:07 P.M. the next day, May 14, the Cambodian Government broadcast that it was ready to return the ship and crew. But two minutes later, at 7:09, before Washington knew of the broadcast, the costly Marine attack began. At 10.23 that night a U.S. destroyer sighted the Mayaguez crew being returned in a boat with a white flag. But after that, and even after the crew was in American hands, U.S. planes bombed targets on the mainland.

In the clearest of situations it would be unwise to take such hasty and massive military action over the seizure of a ship. And in this case just about everything was unclear: the reason for the seizure, the degree of control by Cambodia's new Khmer Rouge Government, even its awareness of the American diplomatic notes. Accounts published in the last year in fact indicate that the Mayaguez was seized in a confused local situation without the knowledge of Phnom Penh.

But Mr. Ford and his men were not interested in the facts—or in the lives they might lose. They were interested in flexing American muscles. They wanted to use the occasion for a show of "strength." That is why they used a sledgehammer, hastily, to crack a peanut.

The glory faded pretty fast after the four days of the Mayaguez, and some who regretted being swept up in the jingo emotions of the moment hoped, at least, that the episode would have no lasting import. Unfortunately, it had and continues to have much significance.

The lesson of lawlessness is the worst of all. A specific statute, passed in 1973 and still on the books, flatly forbids "combat activities by U.S. military forces in or over or from off the shores of North Vietnam, South Vietnam, Laos or Cambodia." President Ford did not mention that statute in ordering action that, on its face, violated the law. Hardly anyone else raised an eyebrow either—just after Vietnam and Watergate.

The spinelessness of Congress when a President took aggressive action of dubious legality made all the talk about curbing Executive abuse of power seem just that: talk. The precedent of the Mayaguez almost certainly encouraged Mr. Ford and Mr. Kissinger in their secret intervention in Angola. Senator Frank Church cheered the Mayaguez; why should he be surprised now when he has trouble convincing his colleagues that they should restrain intelligence activities?

"What I did in the case of the Mayaguez," Mr. Ford said in Wilkesboro, N.C., last March, "is a good example of the decisiveness that I can act with when we are faced with a problem. I would do it again."

But the ironic thing is that the authors of the overkill have gained nothing from their cynical bravado. Poor Gerald Ford is now desperately trying to lecture Ronald Reagan about the duty of a great power to be restrained and reasonable. As for Henry Kissinger, the man who wanted to use B-52's to punish Cambodia over the Mayaguez, his most bloodthirsty policies have made him no friends on the right.

CONSIDERATION OF CERTAIN MEASURES ON THE CALENDAR

Mr. MANSFIELD. Mr. President, I ask unanimous consent that the Senate proceed to the consideration of Calendar No. 739 through Calendar No. 757.

The ACTING PRESIDENT pro tempore. Without objection, it is so ordered.

DR. CRISPIN E. SEE

The bill (S. 2318) for the relief of Dr. Crispin E. See, was considered, ordered to be engrossed for a third reading, read the third time, and passed, as follows:

Be it enacted by the Senate and House of Representatives of the United States of America in Congress assembled, That, for the purposes of the Immigration and Nationality Act, Doctor Crispin E. See, A19 778 692 shall be held and considered to have been lawfully admitted to the United States for permanent residence as of the date of the enactment of this Act upon payment of the required visa fee. Upon the granting of permanent residence to such alien as provided for in this Act, the Secretary of State shall instruct the proper officer to reduce by the required number, during the current fiscal year or the fiscal year next following, the total number of immigrant visa and conditional entries which are made available to natives of the country of the alien's birth under paragraphs (1) through (8) of section 203(a) of the Immigration and Nationality Act.

CANDIDO BADLUA

The bill (H.R. 2776) for the relief of Candido Badlua, was considered, ordered to a third reading, read the third time, and passed.

JENNIFER ANN BLUM

The bill (H.R. 4038) for the relief of Jennifer Ann Blum, was considered, ordered to a third reading, read the third time, and passed.

FRANK M. RUSSELL

The bill (H.R. 5227) for the relief of Frank M. Russell, was considered, ordered to a third reading, read the third time, and passed.

RANDY E. CRISMUNDO

The bill (H.R. 8863) for the relief of Randy E. Crismundo, was considered, ordered to a third reading, read the third time, and passed.

KYONG CHU STOUT

The Senate proceeded to consider the bill (S. 1404) for the relief of Kyong Chu Stout, which had been reported from the Committee on the Judiciary with an amendment to strike out all after the enacting clause and insert the following:

That, in the administration of the Immigration and Nationality Act, Mrs. Kyong Chu Stout, the widow of a citizen of the United States, shall be held and considered to be within the purview of section 201(b) of that Act and the provisions of section 204 of such Act shall not be applicable in this case.

The amendment was agreed to.

The bill was ordered to be engrossed for a third reading, read the third time, and passed.

The title was amended so as to read:

A bill for the relief of Mrs. Kyong Chu Stout.

SOVIET SPACE PROGRAMS, 1971-75

The concurrent resolution (S. Con. Res. 113) authorizing the printing of additional copies of the committee print entitled "Soviet Space Programs, 1971–75", was considered and agreed to, as follows:

Resolved by the Senate (the House of Representatives concurring), That there be printed for the use of the Senate Committee on Aeronautical and Space Sciences one thousand five hundred additional copies each of volumes 1 and 2 of its committee print entitled "Soviet Space Programs, 1971-1975", Ninety-fourth Congress, second session, prepared by the Congressional Research Service with the cooperation of the Law Library, Library of Congress.

STANDING RULES OF THE SENATE

The resolution (S. Res. 156) authorizing and directing the Committee on Rules and Administration to prepare a revision of the Standing Rules of the Senate was considered and agreed to, as follows:

Resolved, That the Committee on Rules and Administration is authorized and directed to prepare a comprehensive codification and revision of the Standing Rules of the Senate which will—

(1) provide for an orderly and logical arrangement of the standing rules,

(2) incorporate therein rules of the Senate which presently are not, but properly should be, part of the standing rules, and

(3) omit provisions which are no longer applicable to the procedures and practices of the Senate.

Such revision shall not make any substantive change in the standing rules, or any other rule of the Senate incorporated therein, or make other change which is inconsistent with the procedures and practices of the Senate.

SEC. 2. The committee shall report the revision prepared pursuant to this resolution to the Senate as soon as practicable.

EDWARD P. FERRETER

The resolution (S. Res. 440) to pay a gratuity to Edward P. Ferreter, was considered and agreed to, as follows:

Resolved, That the Secretary of the Senate hereby is authorized and directed to pay, from the contingent fund of the Senate, to Edward P. Ferreter, widower of Eileen F. Fer-

Baseball Week" would be declared, typically, by joint resolution.

Concurrent Resolution

A concurrent resolution must pass both Houses of Congress, but requires *no approval* by the President, and *does not become law* or affect law except for that relating to the internal affairs of Congress (housekeeping matters affecting both Houses of Congress—that is, internal budgets and the like). One exception to this description would be an instance in which a previous law (a bill or joint resolution signed by the President) authorizes it own "termination" by concurrent resolution. For example, Section 3 of the "Gulf of Tonkin Resolution," which was passed by joint resolution, authorized its own "termination" by concurrent resolution (see pages 17, 19). More commonly, however, concurrent resolutions are confined to internal congressional "housekeeping" business, and occasionally are used for expressing the "sense of the Congress."

Resolution

A resolution (either a Senate resolution or a House resolution) passes only one House and is ordinarily used for the internal business of that House or for expressing the "sense of the Senate" or the "sense of the House." It does not have the effect of law, except insofar as the Senate or the House makes the "law" for its own internal business (for example, its own rules), or except when a previous law gives the resolution legal effect (e.g., disapproval of a "presidential reorganization plan," if such plan was authorized by the Reorganization Act, subject to veto by either House of Congress) (see page 19).

Amendment

Finally, an amendment may be offered to any other measure—a bill, joint resolution, concurrent resolution, or resolution. The introduction of an amendment merely results in the amendment being printed (in the Senate only) and referred to whatever committee* has jurisdiction of the measure it

---

* An amendment may also be offered in committee without any prior "introduction" on the floor, or may be introduced on the floor, to amend a measure pending on the floor. See pages 14, 66–72.

seeks to amend. The introduction of an amendment does not "amend" the measure it is aimed at: it merely presents the text of an amendment which the introducing senator or representative *intends* to offer. Having been introduced, an amendment must still be called up, offered, and voted upon. If passed, it is incorporated into the measure it originally sought to amend.

An amendment may be in the first or second degree. A second-degree amendment is an amendment to another pending amendment.

Drafting Techniques and Problems

Before getting into the substance of a measure, the draftsman of a measure must go through certain purely formal steps to prepare the measure for introduction.

Filling in the Blanks on the Form

Exhibits C through G are duplicates of the blank forms used in the Senate for the introduction of bills and other measures (comparable forms are used in the House). Each illustration is marked by identifying codes (circled numbers) 1 through 7, an explanation of which follows.

Codes 1 and 2 identify the Congress and session in which the introduction of the measure takes place. In 1975, for example, one would insert "94th" in the space following code 1, and "1st" in the space following code 2.

Code 3 is the number assigned to a bill or resolution upon introduction. The introducer leaves this space blank, and the bill clerk assigns a number—the next unused number for the measure in question. Bills, joint resolutions, concurrent resolutions, and resolutions have separate series of numbers.

Amendments are handled somewhat differently. An amendment in the Senate does receive an "Amendment Number," which is stamped on by the bill clerk (at the *bottom* of the first page). But the amendment is an amendment *to* some bill or resolution which has already been introduced and which already *has* a number. Accordingly, on introduction of an amendment to a pending measure, the introducer should insert in the space for code 3 the number of the measure he proposes to amend.

Exhibit C

① CONGRESS
② SESSION

S. ③

(NOTE.—Fill in all blank lines except those provided for the date, number, and reference of bill.)

IN THE SENATE OF THE UNITED STATES

Mr. ④

introduced the following bill; which was read twice and referred to the Committee on ⑤

A BILL

⑥

(Insert title of bill here)

Be it enacted by the Senate and House of Representatives of the United States of America in Congress assembled, ⑦

Exhibit D

① CONGRESS
② SESSION

S. ③
H. R.

IN THE SENATE OF THE UNITED STATES

Referred to the Committee on ⑤ and ordered to be printed.

Ordered to lie on the table and to be printed.

AMENDMENT

Intended to be proposed by Mr. ④

(Insert title of bill below)

to S. ⑥ , a bill ⑥A

H.R. , an Act

⑦ viz: On page , line , insert the following:

Amdt. No.

Exhibit E

① ___ CONGRESS
② ___ SESSION

S. RES. ③

(NOTE.—Fill in all blank lines except those provided for the date, number, and reference of resolution.)

IN THE SENATE OF THE UNITED STATES

Mr. ④ ___

submitted the following resolution; which was ⑤ ___

RESOLUTION
⑥
(Insert title of resolution here)

Resolved, ⑦

Exhibit F

① CONGRESS
② SESSION

S. J. RES. ③

(NOTE.—Fill in all blank lines except those provided for the date, number, and reference of resolution.)

IN THE SENATE OF THE UNITED STATES

Mr. ④

introduced the following joint resolution; which was read twice and referred to the Committee on ⑤

JOINT RESOLUTION
⑥
(Insert title of joint resolution here)

Resolved by the Senate and House of Representatives of the United States of America in Congress assembled, ⑦

Exhibit G

① CONGRESS
② SESSION

S. CON. RES. ③

(NOTE.—Fill in all blank lines except those provided for the date, number, and reference of resolution.)

IN THE SENATE OF THE UNITED STATES

Mr. ④

submitted the following concurrent resolution; which was ⑤

CONCURRENT RESOLUTION

⑥
(Insert title of concurrent resolution here)

Resolved by the Senate (the House of Representatives concurring), ⑦

In code 4, the introducer inserts his own name, as well as the name of any cosponsor. The names of the cosponsors are inserted in parentheses, as follows: "Mr. Williams (for himself, Mr. Bible and Mr. Cannon)."

Code 5 is the space for the Parliamentarian to insert the "reference" of the measure. The space is left blank by the introducer, and is filled in by the bill clerk. A bill is ordinarily referred to a committee on advice of the Parliamentarian. But, in any event, an amendment follows the bill it amends: If the bill is in committee, the amendment will be referred there; if a bill is pending on the floor, the amendment will be "ordered to lie on the table and to be printed"—that is, it remains, without referral, awaiting call-up on the floor.

It is useful to remember that an amendment once referred to a committee and not adopted there will not be reported out of the committee automatically when the bill is reported out. Accordingly, if a senator wishes an amendment to be circulated on the floor together with a pending bill, he should *reintroduce* it *after* the bill has been reported out and placed upon the floor calendar so that that amendment will be reprinted with the appropriate calendar number on it and circulated on the floor.

Code 6 is inserted by the person introducing the bill, and is the official title of the measure, e.g.:

"A BILL"

"To prohibit age discrimination in employment."

The introducer is free to devise the title of his own bill, but may wish to seek and consider the advice of the Parliamentarian or other expert, because a title may influence reference to the desired committee—particularly where the bill falls within the possible jurisdiction of two committees and could go either way. The title of the bill should not be confused with the "short title" discussed below (code 7).

An exception to the discretion that the introducer may exercise in devising a title occurs in the case of an amendment. An amendment itself has no title, but the form (see Exhibit D) requires insertion of the title of the measure being amended. On the amendment form under code 6 the introducer should insert the number of the bill being amended, and under code 6A, the title of the measure being amended. Note that in the Senate, for example, a bill with an "S." number is one which has not yet passed the House and is, therefore, referred to as a *"bill* to prohibit age discrimination in employment" (italics added), whereas a bill with an "H.R." number is one which has already passed the House and is, therefore, referred to as an "*Act* to prohibit age discrimination in employment" (italics added).

Code 7 denotes the beginning of the actual text of the bill or resolution. Section 1 of any bill is rarely numbered as such, but begins with the word "That." This section is most frequently used to provide a short title for the measure. For example:

> "Be it enacted by the Senate and House of Representatives of the United States of America in Congress assembled
>
> That this Act may be cited as the "Age Discrimination in Employment Act of 1967."

Everything beginning with the word "that" is section 1 of the bill, and the next section will be section 2.

An exception to this rule occurs in the introduction of an amendment, where code 7, while it begins the text of the proposal, is not designated explicitly or implicitly with a number but instead denotes the placement of the proposed amendment. The printed form after the word "viz" provides for an insertion: "On page   , line   ." This particular form is useful, however, only if the page and line referred to are at the very end of the pending bill to be amended. Otherwise, in order to make an insertion, one ordinarily must first strike out the existing material being supplanted by the amendment. The typical form is as follows:

> "Viz: On page 5, strike out lines 5 through 10, and insert, in lieu thereof, the following:"

or:

> "Viz: On page 5, line 5, strike out the word 'never' and insert, in lieu thereof, the word 'always'."

If one wishes to insert an addition to a bill *without* deleting any other provision of the bill a good device is to find the end of a title or section of the bill (for example, page 5, line 10) and have the amendment provide:

> "On page 5, between lines 10 and 11, insert the following:"

One can insert any number of lines or even pages "between lines 10 and 11 on page 5," and this device will still be satisfactory.

Specificity Versus Delegation—Definitions

While not all measures are of sufficient complexity to warrant the development of detailed definitions, at least *some* definitions are useful in most measures. Their incorporation avoids the necessity of repeating lengthy qualifications of the use of a particular term.

Definitions may be made applicable to the use of a term throughout a bill, or in a particular title or chapter, or even in a single section of a bill which has a number of subsections. The initial question arising in the development of definitions is whether a term should be defined in detail in the law itself or whether the agency administering the particular law should be given discretion to define it.

The Internal Revenue Code contains examples of each approach and also examples which combine both approaches. For instance, in Section 401 of the Internal Revenue Code, which deals with qualified pension plans, the Code contains a definition of "owner-employee," a term which is used in the sections of the Code permitting so-called Keogh plans for partnerships and sole proprietorships. The definition is as follows:

"(3) Owner-employee.—The term "owner-employee" means an employee who—
(A) owns the entire interest in an unincorporated trade or business, or
(B) in the case of a partnership, is a partner who owns more than 10 percent of either the capital interest or the profits interest in such partnership.
To the extent provided in regulations prescribed by the Secretary or his delegate, such term also means an individual who has been an owner-employee within the meaning of the preceding sentence."

Note that the definition starts out by telling you what the term "means" and not just what it "includes."

In contrast, Section 401 also includes a definition of the word "employee" as follows:

"(1) Employee.—The term "employee" includes, for any taxable year, any individual who has earned income (as defined in paragraph (2)) for the taxable year. To the

extent provided in regulations prescribed by the Secretary or his delegate, such term also includes, for any taxable year—
> (A) an individual who would be an employee within the meaning of the preceding sentence but for the fact that the trade or business carried on by such individual did not have net profits for the taxable year, and
> (B) an individual who has been an employee within the meaning of the preceding sentence for any prior taxable year."

Here the definition is not exhaustive; it merely gives an example. But in both cases, additional discretion is specifically granted to the Secretary of the Treasury ("or his delegate") to provide, by regulations, for further inclusion or exclusion from the coverage of the term in question.

Delegations of Discretion

Particularly when the Congress and the executive branch are controlled by different political parties, the inventive genius of legislative draftsmen tends to give birth to a variety of devices to control the extent to which legislative or administrative power is delegated.

The advantages of delegation are obvious. Congress needs to know much less about a particular issue in order to delegate authority to deal with it than it would if it had to legislate the issue itself. It can draft broad principles and leave the details to the executive branch. Delegation allows for changes in policy, which can be accomplished more easily by revising regulations than by amending statutes in Congress. Delegation can leave exempting power to the executive branch. It also can leave to the executive branch the determination of which penalty shall apply. And it can do so with or without retaining a "string" (congressional veto power), such as in the War Powers Act (see pages 7, 19).

When both the executive branch and the legislative branch are controlled by the same political party, on the other hand, the issue of delegation tends to arise much less frequently. If past experience is any guide, this is so because committee chairmen tend to take their orders from "downtown." One might also ask why the President would ask Congress to retain power over him.

Delegations to independent agencies differ somewhat from delegations to political departments, although the definition of an "independent agency" has become increasingly ambiguous. Heretofore, the classic independent agency—for example, the National Labor Relations Board—was one operating under the Administrative Procedure Act, with hearing examiners, lawyers, briefs, decisions, and judicial review in the court of appeals. The members of independent agencies such as the NLRB typically hold office for fixed terms (staggered) and are much less subject to political influence than cabinet officers (serving at the pleasure of the President) and their subordinates. With the development of agencies like the Federal Energy Administration whose officials all serve at the pleasure of the President, the denomination "independent" has much less meaning. But, conversely, while a typical independent agency is in no position to "lobby" Congress, a more political agency such as the FEA *can* and does lobby, and in fact the whole White House apparatus lobbies for it.

Programmatic and Regulatory Statutes

While all statutes ought to be equally well drafted, programmatic legislation has tended in recent years to lack the precision which is required of regulatory legislation.

Regulatory laws ordinarily are written with an eye toward litigation, since they can involve disputes either between private parties or between the government and private parties. Such laws often end up in court where ambiguities inevitably result in litigation.

Programmatic legislation—the authorization of grants, loans and other forms of federal assistance—is much less likely to generate litigation, and therefore tends to be written in more general terms, leaving to the government the discretion to administer the program in the interest of certain stated congressional objectives. On the other hand, when it comes to the allocation of money, particularly allocation among the states (or even cities), programmatic legislation may become very precise, since representatives and senators pinpoint specific dollar amounts which must be allocated to their constituencies.*

---

* The best known example is the so-called Hill-Burton formula for the allocation of hospital assistance money.

Retaining Congressional Power Not Subject to Veto

Increasingly, Congress is urged to grant discretion to the executive branch but fears that it will have no way of checking an abuse of executive discretion, since the executive branch could veto any effort to overrule an unacceptable interpretation of the statute or exercise of executive power. One device frequently used to retain congressional power even after the executive branch has received its authorization is the "reorganization plan." Under 5 U.S.C. § 901–913, the President was given authority to reorganize the Federal Government by transferring, for example, the whole or part of any agency to any other agency. He could accomplish this objective by issuing a "reorganization plan" and submitting that plan to Congress. Once the plan was submitted, it became effective and had the effect of law *unless*, within 60 days, either House of Congress passed a resolution disapproving the plan (5 U.S.C. § 906). Thus, under the reorganization-plan device, a simple resolution of either House could have the effect of law, not in its own right, but because a previous act of Congress said so.

Another device to retain congressional power may be seen in the so-called Gulf of Tonkin resolution, which (arguably) gave President Johnson authority to carry on the Viet Nam war. That resolution provided, by its own terms, that the authority granted under it could be terminated by concurrent resolution (see page 7) of the Congress (which would not be subject to veto by the President).

Finally, the War Powers Act* constitutes a classic example of Congress' attempt to hold a "string" on power delegated to the executive branch. In this Act, Congress codified the circumstances under which the President could use his discretion to commit armed forces to combat but provided that the exercise of that discretion expired automatically if Congress did nothing after a stated number of days. This is the reverse of the old presidential reorganization plan. Under the reorganization plan, the President could reshuffle parts of the executive branch, and the reshuffling *became effective* if Congress did *nothing* after a stated number of days. Under the War Powers Act, the President can act, but his power to act *terminates* after a stated number of days if Congress does

---
* Public Law 93–148.

nothing. The latter device is, in effect, a congressional recognition of its own impotence. Congress understood perfectly well its inclination to engage in endless debate and put the burden on the "action minded" members to get further authorization, lest whatever Presidential action had occurred would come to a halt automatically.*

Sources of Constitutional Authority

Most Acts of Congress are an exercise of the commerce power—"to regulate commerce with foreign nations, and among the several States" (Article I, Section 8, Clause 3). The commerce power is the broadest of congressional powers, at least under Supreme Court interpretations since the mid-1930s. Yet the Internal Revenue Code has its own source of constitutional authorization in the 16th Amendment, and the War Powers Act is based upon Article I, Section 8 ("to make rules for the government and regulation of the land and naval forces").

While the source of power is not always spelled out in legislation, more often than not statutes begin with a statement of congressional findings and policy. Why? The conventional wisdom is that, since Congress requires a constitutional jurisdictional base, one needs to find an effect upon, for example, interstate commerce in order to exercise the congressional commerce power. This conclusion is not as obvious as it appears. Most legislation regulating commerce or businesses engaged in commerce would be sustained constitutionally even without such findings. So why include them?

The advantage of congressional findings is that they help assure a proper constitutional foundation. The disadvantage is that they may become the basis for variations in statutory interpretation. Give a lawyer a losing case, and he will search the "findings" for grounds to win it. He will find some statement of policy to stretch or shrink the statute.

If there is any moral in this, it is that findings are probably inevitable, and sometimes necessary, but they should not be used as a way of launching into a philosophical dissertation unnecessary to accomplish the legislative and constitutional objective.

In unusual and special cases congressional findings some-

---

* A complete list of "legislative veto" provisions appears in H. Doc. No. 416, 93d Cong., 2d Sess. 753 (1975).

times must be introduced. One recent example involved an interplay between the tax power and the commerce power in the drafting of the 1974 pension reform bill.* Two versions of the bill had been developed, one originating in the tax-writing committees of Congress, and another in the committees on labor. The resolution of the controversy combined the Treasury's jurisdiction over taxes with the Labor Department's jurisdiction over other forms of enforcement. Since ordinarily a tax law cannot "preempt" state regulatory laws, the pension reform bill was revised to include a finding that the conduct sought to be regulated affected commerce; on that basis, the law contains a provision specifically stating that it is Congress' intent under the commerce power to preempt the field and nullify all state laws on the subject.

Preemption

A federal law in and of itself nullifies state laws on a subject only if they *conflict* with the federal law, in violation of the supremacy clause of the Constitution (Article VI). True "preemption" involves the nullification of *all* state laws on a subject, whether they conflict with, add to, or agree with federal law. Such preemption can be accomplished by specifically so providing, or it can be negated by so providing. *The worst draftsmanship is silent on preemption* and keeps everybody guessing until a court decides the question.

As an example of explicit preemption, the Pension Reform Act, Public Law 93–406, § 514, provided that, with certain exceptions, the provisions of Titles I and IV of that Act "shall supersede any and all State laws insofar as they may now or thereafter relate to any employee benefit plan. . . ." Conversely, in the earlier Welfare and Pension Plans Disclosure Act, Public Law 85–836, § 16(b), Congress stipulated that the provisions of that Act (with certain exceptions) "shall not be held to exempt or relieve any person from any liability, duty, penalty or punishment provided by any present or future law of the United States or any State. . . ."

Note that there is a way to go about drafting a preemption provision. And there are certain specific issues which must be dealt with. Do you preempt or don't you? Are there any exceptions to the preemption? Do you preempt both state and federal law? And so on.

---

* Public Law 93–406 (1974).

Note further that preemption is ordinarily substantive, not procedural, unless it is stated otherwise. Questions of jurisdiction are different from questions of preemption. Which court has jurisdiction? Are there alternatives? A state court, for example, can try a federal question (though such a case may be subject to removal to federal court at the discretion of a party). Mere preemption does not settle the matter. The drafter may intend that the federal courts or federal boards or commissions have exclusive jurisdiction, but if he wants that result, he should say so.

Jurisdictional Overlaps

The worst of all possible worlds is to have the same set of facts give rise to proceedings before more than one agency. For example, as things now stand if a union excludes blacks or women from membership, and if membership is a condition of employment, an almost ludicrous array of proceedings before all sorts of commissions and courts can be generated: an unfair labor practice proceeding before the NLRB, discrimination proceedings before the EEOC and before state and local fair employment practices commissions, cases in the federal courts under the old civil rights statute (42 U.S.C. 1981), as well as government contract matters under the applicable executive order, and arbitrations pursuant to labor-management arbitration agreements—and these situations do not exhaust the possibilities.

Nor is it any kindness to the plaintiffs in such cases to give them so many bites at the apple. All you assure is that no compromise or settlement is likely because the court or agency in which the case is being tried has no settlement jurisdiction over other possible proceedings.

Labelling the Parts of a Bill

Many lengthy statutes cannot be read intelligently by anyone; they often need to be explained by someone who was on hand during the legislative process and who understood whatever it was Congress had in mind. Such people, unfortunately, have a way of disappearing; and, therefore, the good legislative draftsman will write a statute which stands on its own feet.

The moral: Err on the side of including headings, subheadings, sub-subheadings, and cross-references. If a draftsman is worried about the possibility that the heading may be misused and result in a misconstruction of the statute, he may say in the statute itself that a heading is not part of the statute and shall not be used to construe it. But at the very least headings can be used to help readers find their way through the legislative labyrinth.

Judicial Review

In recent years, more and more statutes which remain silent on judicial review of executive action have generated litigation not only over the substance of the statute but also over the proper forum in which the substance may be litigated. It makes no sense whatever to ignore the question of judicial review, for a forum will always be found in which the case can be heard, and orderly government is advanced by specifically designating the appropriate judicial forum. Even if Congress is inclined to limit judicial review, one does not accomplish that objective by remaining silent. A careful draftsman ought to say where the case is to be heard, how the case is to be heard, and what the criteria for judicial review ought to be. Examples of legislation covering judicial review abound, and the alternatives in wording are as varied as the ingenuity of legislative draftsmen.

Effective Dates

The drafting problem with regard to effective dates is not serious, unless one ignores dates altogether. Statutes ought to say when they shall be effective. If a bill remains silent, it will be effective when the President signs it. This may sound reasonable, but it is not if the bill involves a program necessitating a bureaucracy which does not even exist and cannot even exist until some time after the President signs the law authorizing its existence. Reasonable "lag dates" are essential, particularly when it comes to new programs, and only a lazy or sloppy draftsman leaves them out. It should be noted that different provisions in the same statute may be effective on different dates.

Sources of Drafting Assistance

A senator or representative (or a lobbyist, once he has found a congressman willing to introduce a measure) has an infinite variety of sources of assistance upon which he may call, depending upon the circumstances, and depending upon his willingness to rely upon the expertise, opinions, and competence of others.

The six most common and useful sources of drafting assistance in the preparation of a bill, resolution, or amendment are: the Office of Legislative Counsel (in either the House or the Senate); professional staff members in the employ of committees; experts in the employ of interest groups; experts in the executive branch of the government; the Parliamentarians of the Senate or the House; and academic resources (law school faculties for example).

Each of these sources has advantages and disadvantages, and each can be of use at some time or another. But each can also be a disaster if the nature of the source is not understood and its advice is taken uncritically.

Legislative Counsel

With a few exceptions, lawyers on the professional staff of the Office of Legislative Counsel of the Senate or the House are good draftsmen but not experts on legislative substance or content. And good but contentless drafting can be worse than inexpert drafting by someone who at least understands the subject matter at hand.

The big "plus" in Legislative Counsel is that these lawyers are at least familiar with the most common drafting mistakes—common to any bill—and usually will avoid them. "Program legislation" must have certain components (language authorizing the appropriation of money, for example), and Legislative Counsel, given the right dollar figures, will draft these components into a bill with consummate expertise. Likewise, Legislative Counsel will review the first draft of a bill and at least seek to assure internal consistency, proper definitions of terms, and the like. Thus, even if the lobbyist-draftsman of a bill is a top expert in his own field, it is to his advantage to have the sponsoring Congressman check with Legislative Counsel.

But Legislative Counsel rarely "conceives" an idea, and is rarely quite certain of what the author has in mind, what objectives he seeks, what substantive problems have or have not been anticipated. Because intent is sometimes unclear initially, there is a tremendous advantage in having a first draft of a bill put together by a professional (preferably a lawyer) on the staff of the senator or representative who will introduce the legislation and who has *conceived* the idea, or if a lobbyist originates the idea, then by the lobbyist himself or his own counsel.

In sum, one ought *never* to rely exclusively on Legislative Counsel, but one ought *always* to give Legislative Counsel an opportunity to review legislation in draft in order to avoid purely technical drafting mistakes. An exception to this rule might be made where the law is already well codified, where codes have been amended many times, and where there are experts on the staff of Legislative Counsel who are proficient not only in drafting but also in *substance* (for example, on amendments to the Internal Revenue Code).

Committee Staff

A second source of assistance in the preparation of legislation is found in professionals (usually lawyers) on the staffs of the substantive committees that have jurisdiction of the subject matter affected by the proposed bill. Tax experts, for example, can be found on the staffs of the House Ways and Means Committee, the Senate Finance Committee, and the Joint Committee on Internal Revenue Taxation; labor experts can be found on the staffs of the House Education and Labor Committee and the Senate Labor and Public Welfare Committee; and so on.

Two factors must be taken into consideration in use of these professionals, however: First, they may not be experts at all; and, second, they may be either unavailable in a practical sense or useless in an ideological sense.

The professional staff of a committee ordinarily is appointed by the senior members of the committee. The chairman appoints most of the majority staff, and the ranking minority member appoints most of the minority staff.* Ideally, the representatives and senators making these appointments ought to pick persons who are experts in their fields, with due

---

* Recent rules changes have given each senator one professional staff appointment on each of his committees. These appointees are not likely to be the real experts, however, since they lack the variety and length of experience which develops from being in charge of *all* bills passing through a committee.

consideration, obviously, for ideological compatibility. But that is not always the case (indeed, I wonder if it is even ordinarily the case). Too often, one finds in these high-paid professional positions either personal acquaintances of the senator or representative, or persons who are retained on staff or payroll for reasons other than subject matter expertise (for example, political operatives, experts in other fields, or speechwriters generally).

Interest Groups and Lobbyists

Another major source of expert assistance in the preparation of proposed legislation is offered by the infinite variety of lobbyists and interest groups, particularly those with offices in Washington, D.C. The catalogue of lobbyists and interest groups is almost endless, and the resources on which they draw are equally substantial.

There is nothing really insidious about the presence of lobbyists in Washington—at least not *inherently* insidious. There are, to be sure, representatives of large organizations whose lobbying activity is the best known and often the most controversial. Among the well-known interest groups are the AFL-CIO, the National Association of Manufacturers, the Chamber of Commerce of the United States, the American Medical Association, even the National Rifle Association. There are also lobbying organizations with varying degrees of real or purported altruism: Common Cause, the various Ralph Nadar organizations, the National Education Association, various ecological organizations, even representatives of local and state governments (the Governors' Conference), and so on. On a narrower scale, there are lobbying groups with special interests and special expertise: the American Association of Retired Persons, the various societies of professional engineers, the American Library Association, and the like.

And there are lawyers and other professionals in Washington who, though not regularly on the payroll of any particular interest group, have been retained by one or several groups over a period of time, during which they have developed expertise in various fields.

I say that there is nothing inherently insidious about the existence of these lobbyists because, in my view, lobbies are *absolutely essential to the effective conduct of government, particularly in the legislative branch.* How else will the chairman of the Veterans' Committee learn what the interests of veterans are—or at least are supposed to be—unless he asks the American Legion or a similar organization? How else will the chairman of an Education Subcommittee learn the interests of teachers and educational institutions unless he asks the organizations which represent those interests?

This is not to say that lobbyists do not have an "ax to grind." They certainly do. They will be looking out for their own interests, and they may not be terribly concerned with the general public welfare. But an effective congressman can distill the wisdom of an expert and avoid being carried along with the expert's undisclosed concerns, insofar as they are inconsistent with the public interest. A case in point occurred during the drafting of pension reform legislation. The senators involved could not possibly avoid the use of highly technical language and concepts developed in the actuarial profession. Most of the professional actuaries, however, were opposed to pension legislation. At the outset, many of them insisted that the terms which they used every day in their professional work could not be defined with sufficient precision to permit legislative drafting. If one had taken their initial advice on drafting, no progress could have been made at all. On the other hand, if one had proceeded to draft legislation without their professional help, the exercise might have been utterly futile. The dilemma was resolved by submitting a first draft to a group of professional actuaries (most of whom insisted that no legislation could be intelligently drafted in this field), and by telling them that, unless the definitions and technical language of the bill were refined by the professionals, the bill would be introduced, nevertheless, in a very short time. As a consequence of this approach a number of professional actuaries decided that it was better to have well-drafted regulation than poorly drafted legislation, the option of no legislation having been eliminated. Thus, a great deal of indispensable technical help was received from opponents of the legislation itself.

The above case is not an isolated instance. The same sort of thing occurs year in and year out in technical fields such as banking, insurance, taxation, and the like.

Executive Departments

While in recent times the Congress has been in the control of one political party and the Administration in the control of another, the system works quite differently when both Houses of Congress and the Presidency are controlled by the same political party, or at the very least the Presidency and one House of Congress are controlled by the same party.

With common party control, the resources in Congress needed to generate new legislation tend to atrophy. No congressional staff has yet been able to match the resources of the Administration. In 1975, for example, the entire staff of the Senate Committee on Labor and Public Welfare was about 100 people, which was dwarfed by the endless resources of the Department of Labor (with its Bureau of Labor Statistics and its far-flung legal staff) and the Department of Health, Education, and Welfare. Since the Administration possesses such resources, when the chairman of a committee is a member of the same party as the President, he commonly has developed a close working relationship with the legislative affairs branch in the Cabinet department involved with a particular piece of legislation. If a technical question needs to be answered, even if the chairman asks his legal assistant for the answer, the easy way out is to place a call "downtown" and get the answer.

Likewise, in the development of legislative proposals, the usual procedure has been for the proposal to be developed in the executive department involved, cleared through the Office of Management and Budget (which coordinates the various departments), delivered to Capitol Hill accompanied by an appropriate message from the President, and introduced by the chairman of the committee having legislative jurisdiction over it. Indeed, the introductory speech delivered by the chairman has frequently been written "downtown," although undoubtedly it has been cleared in some cursory fashion with the legislation's sponsoring senator or representative.

When Congress is controlled by one party and the Presidency by another, the working relationship between Congress and the Administration breaks down. The natural suspicions of representatives and senators that proposals of the Administration would work to the political *dis*advantage of a congressman in the opposite party necessarily prevail. Indeed, a chairman working to pass the President's proposal is necessarily working for a proposal which will be a credit to the President, and thus, perhaps, a disadvantage to the congressman's own presidential candidate in the next election.

That does not mean that technical information cannot be obtained from particular agencies on specific questions, but legislative proposals formulated in the agencies often are looked upon with suspicion by congressmen in the opposite political party, and even technical information may become suspect when a congressman surmises that the information may be "shaded" to support an Administration proposal and not the congressman's own proposal.

Apart from the problem of working relationships between Congress and executive departments, there is the problem of delay. Assuming a congressman wishes to coordinate his own legislative initiatives with those of the Administration—whether the Administration is in the same party or the opposite party—the problems of timing are formidable. With only rare exceptions, Administration proposals must be cleared through a vast federal bureaucracy even though a proposal is initiated at the agency level and eventually supported by a Cabinet officer. The clearance medium is the Office of Management and Budget. Indeed, the standard statement of position of any Cabinet officer or agency head, when delivering written comments to a committee chairman concerning pending legislation, contains the following notation, in substantially the following form: "The Office of Management and Budget advises that there is no objection to this report, and that the enactment of S.   would be in accord with the program of the President."

This simple notation takes only a moment to type and sign, but it frequently takes months if not years to obtain through the vast federal bureaucracy the clearances necessary so that an individual Cabinet member can say that a particular position is "in accord with the President's program." Consequently, while the technical expertise of the executive branch of government may be available quickly to an individual senator or representative, the *support* of the Administration is often so difficult to obtain and involves such a time-consuming process that the representative or senator may not want to bother.

An exception to this rule often occurs, however, when amendments to an important piece of legislation are being offered on the Senate or House floors, or when a bill is in a Senate-House conference and a compromise is being struck. Under these circumstances, White House lobbyists in the hall or outside the conference committee meeting room are frequently authorized to make what amount to snap judgments, because the alternative is to make no judgment at all and to let the matter go by default.

The Parliamentarian

Ordinarily, referral of a bill or resolution to the appropriate committee, whether in the House or Senate, is "decided" by the presiding officer on the basis of committee jurisdictions as spelled out in the rules. (On disputes over the assignment of measures to the appropriate committees, see pages 36–38.) But the real "decision" is made by a little-known officer of the Senate or House who advises the presiding officer on parliamentary questions—the Parliamentarian.

It is a good idea to seek the advice of the Parliamentarian before introduction of a bill in order not to leave matters of reference to the uncertainty of a decision made after the bill has been introduced. While the rules of each House define the jurisdiction of the various committees in general terms (see Appendices 3 and 4), many a bill or resolution falls within or in-between two committees' jurisdiction, or may fall within the jurisdiction of both. In such instances, the sponsoring senator or representative may wish to be assured in advance that his measure will be referred to a particular committee—ordinarily a committee of which he is a member or chairman—so that he will be in a better position to move it along at the committee level and to prevent it from being bottled up by inaction.

To obtain such assurance, the sponsoring congressman is well advised to show the Parliamentarian a draft of his bill and ask his opinion as to how the matter will be referred. Not infrequently the Parliamentarian will note that it is a close question as to which of two committees the measure will be referred to (see pages 36–37). In such circumstances, the

Parliamentarian can be asked what features of the bill would tend to move it one way or the other. Upon identifying those features, the sponsor may be able either to eliminate them or to modify them, thus assuring a favorable reference. Even if those features are deemed essential to the legislation, the sponsor may be willing to delete them for purposes of introduction and reference. Later he can move to amend the legislation to reinsert the necessary features, either at the committee level or when the bill reaches the House or Senate floor. If the amendment is added at the committee level, there is always the possibility that the objectionable amendment might result in a motion to rerefer the bill after it is reported from committee. But even that eventuality can be avoided if the sponsor withholds his amendment and offers it only when the bill or resolution reaches the floor.

Academic Assistance

Many a representative or senator has discovered a goldmine of technical assistance in the universities of his home state and elsewhere. Many law schools have legislative drafting departments which are only too pleased to assign faculty experts and students to the preparation of legislative material. In addition, there are certain areas, for instance, tax law and constitutional law, in which the most highly trained specialists are found in universities. It is not at all unusual for senators and representatives to call upon the deans or faculties of universities for assistance, much of which is available to a congressman without cost.

Academic assistance ought to be approached with caution. This statement in no way is meant to demean the caliber of such assistance. It should be noted, however, that rarely will a university faculty member, regardless of his field of expertise, be qualified to make the kind of political judgments which are often necessary for legislative success. So there must be an interplay. The senator or representative asks the faculty member for a draft of a proposal seeking certain stated objectives. If the draft comes back in a form which the representative or senator deems too extreme or otherwise offensive to significant legislative factions, a redraft may be necessary.

In short, academic assistance, like other forms of assistance, has its pros and cons. It can be used effectively, provided the congressman does not operate in utter ignorance of its disadvantages.

SPONSORSHIP AND INTRODUCTION OF A BILL

Choice of Sponsor and/or Cosponsor(s)

Among the most important factors which determine the fate of a legislative proposal is sponsorship. The right sponsor (or cosponsor) can set the tone of debate, can place his knowledge and prestige behind a measure, and may assure favorable action at one level or another, and in some cases throughout the legislative process. The wrong sponsor may add nothing and may even assure *un*favorable consideration in some circumstances.

Sponsor and/or Cosponsor of a Bill

A lobbyist seeking introduction of a bill, or the President or the Administration seeking introduction of a bill, or, indeed, a congressman seeking maximum momentum behind a bill will seek out a primary sponsor, and/or cosponsors, depending upon how he wishes to proceed.

The primary sponsor is the person who actually introduces the bill, and whose name appears first upon it (see page 5). Ordinarily, a bill will achieve maximum momentum if its primary sponsor is at least a member, and at most the chairman, of the committee (or the key subcommittee of the committee) to which the Parliamentarian will refer the bill.

A bill can be made into a "bipartisan" measure, or at least given a bipartisan flavor, if it is cosponsored by the ranking member of the same committee in the opposite political party from the sponsor. Or it can be made a partisan but nevertheless a high-powered measure by making the chairman the principal sponsor and having all the members of the majority party on that committee join as cosponsors, thus indicating on the face of the measure that it has the support of a majority of the committee to which it will be referred.

Ideally, of course, a measure sponsored by *all* the members of the committee involved would produce evidence not

only of majority support but also of bipartisan support, and of the absence of any controversy over it in that committee.*
Alternatively, the measure may be sponsored by the chairman of the *sub*committee to which the measure will be referred for hearings, and perhaps be cosponsored by the members of that subcommittee.

Sponsor and/or Cosponsor of an Amendment

The choice of a sponsor of an *amendment* involves somewhat different factors than the choice of a sponsor of a bill. If a bill originally was introduced by a chairman and the chairman could have been persuaded to adopt or offer a particular amendment, he simply would have modified the bill before introducing it. Occasionally amendments will be offered by members of the majority party who are not in complete agreement with the views of the chairman or principal sponsor of the measure involved.

At the committee or subcommittee level, an amendment may be offered by a "minority" group, and such amendment may accrue majority support and pass despite the opposition of the chairman. Indeed, the chairman may even "accept it," although, for political reasons, he would not incorporate it into his own bill voluntarily before introduction. He would have to go through the exercise of having it offered by a member of another party so that he could accept it "reluctantly." Thus, most amendments to a chairman's bill are offered by members of the minority party. Obviously the best choice of sponsor is the ranking minority member, and, after that, minority members in order of seniority.

If amendments to a bill have been offered and voted down in subcommittee and/or full committee, once the bill is voted out of committee, the sponsors of those amendments typically will write and have printed with the committee report "individual views," "supplemental views," or "minority views" (see pages 55–57). These separate views set forth the position of the senators or representatives on amendments which they offered and which were voted down in committee and alert

---

* In the Senate, there is no limit on the number of cosponsors of a bill, while in the House each bill may have no more than 25 cosponsors. If a measure is supported by more than 25 representatives, the additional supporters not allowed to sponsor the primary bill can sponsor identical bills which have different numerical designations but the same contents as the primary bill.

the members of the House or Senate to what is likely to happen on the floor—that is, a reoffering of these same amendments. Indeed, although the senator or representative who reoffers amendments on the floor will have an opportunity to explain his position later on the floor, the views he sets forth at the end of the committee report have a bigger audience than his explanation on the floor, as any spectator in the House or Senate gallery will soon discover (most speeches are actually heard by only a handful of congressmen).

Amendments on the floor can be written out in longhand, typed, or introduced or "read into" the record at least a day before being called up and, thus, can be printed. The choice of a sponsor for a floor amendment involves somewhat different factors than the choice of a sponsor for a committee amendment. The senior members of a committee (or subcommittee) usually become "conferees" to resolve any differences between the House version and the Senate version of a bill. Ordinarily, if an amendment is offered—and even adopted—on the floor by a senator or representative *who is not a member of the committee of origin* (indeed, who is not a member of the *subcommittee* of origin), its sponsoring congressman *will not be a conferee*, and therefore will not be able to protect his amendment should the chairman wish to "trade it off" in conference. For this reason alone, it is highly desirable to have amendments offered on the floor by members of the subcommittee of origin, or at least have a subcommittee member as a prime cosponsor of any amendment so offered, so that he can protect the amendment when and if the bill, as amended, goes to conference.

Introductory Remarks to a Bill

Any member of the House or Senate may introduce a bill simply by handing it to the clerk without any explanation. Thus introduced, a bill will be printed (a relatively limited printing) and referred to the committee having jurisdiction of it under the rules of that chamber.

There are great advantages in printing "introductory remarks" in the *Congressional Record*, and, indeed, under the Senate's rules there are advantages in having the full text of the bill printed in the *Congressional Record* (by unanimous consent—routinely granted) at the end of the introductory remarks. In so doing, the sponsor is able to circulate the text of his bill to the thousands of *Congressional Record* subscribers in and out of government.

In his introductory remarks, the sponsor may explain his reasons for introducing the bill, the meaning of it, the segments of the population and organizations who support it and will benefit by it, and so on. By printing the text of the bill in the *Congressional Record*, he accomplishes a circulation of that text far beyond any circulation derived from the routine limited printing of the bill upon introduction (Copies of the bill from such printing must still be requested individually by interested persons and organizations.)

Publicizing the Bill—Using the Congressional Record Reprint of Introductory Remarks

There is another important advantage to inclusion of a bill in the *Congressional Record*. The sponsor (or interest group backing the sponsor's proposal) may have a copy of the *Congressional Record* photo-offset and reprinted in thousands or tens of thousands of copies for circulation as he sees fit, and, because of the small type used in the *Congressional Record*, he can make a mailing of his reprint at considerably less expense than would be involved in trying to duplicate the typewritten explanation of the bill, together with copies of the bill text itself as printed.

Finally, if a senator can arrange it, under Senate rules, he may be able to have a group of supporting or sponsoring senators appear on the Senate floor with him in a "round robin" colloquy in praise of the bill, and thus be able to include colloquy remarks in his reprint, which will produce a document showing broad support for the measure.

Referral to Committee

The Role of the Parliamentarian

A critical point in the legislative process is the referral of a bill to committee. Most measures are referred to committee on recommendation of the Parliamentarian (who advises the presiding officer) (see pages 37–38). But novel measures frequently fall into uncertain areas or combine matters within the jurisdiction of more than one committee. If the matter is left to the Parliamentarian, he ordinarily will decide on the basis of "primary emphasis." One most notable exception seems to be a precedent in the House that the Parliamentarian will refer to the Committtee on Ways and Means not only all bills with primary emphasis on tax, but also all bills of any kind which amend the Internal Revenue Code even incidentally. Thus, a bill of 80 pages containing one paragraph amending the Internal Revenue Code and otherwise exclusively within the jurisdiction of another committee could nevertheless be referred to the Committee on Ways and Means in the House.

Referral by Unanimous Consent

But the choice of committee can be changed by unanimous consent. Thus, a senator introducing a bill which normally would go to the Senate Finance Committee (which covers tax matters) can have the bill referred to another committee if the sponsoring senator stands up on the floor and asks unanimous consent that the bill be referred to another committee—provided no other senator objects. But a wise course would be to clear the matter in advance with the chairman and the ranking minority member of the committee which would *otherwise* get the bill. If another member objects, the chair will rule. The ruling of the chair can then be appealed to the floor, and a rollcall vote obtained. Rarely, however, will the members of either party overrule the Parliamentarian and the presiding officer on a question of referral.

Pre-Introduction Conference With the Parliamentarian

Still another way to influence referral is to have a pre-introduction conference with the Parliamentarian. Sometimes, as a result, the text of a measure can be slightly modified to achieve a simple referral without a unanimous consent request. For example, in the 80-page measure mentioned above, the simple deletion of the one paragraph amending the Internal Revenue Code would free the Parliamentarian to refer the matter to another committee. After the measure has been referred, the paragraph could be offered as an amendment (either in committee or on the floor) to restore the text to its original form. Such an amendment has a greater chance of being retained when it is offered on the floor. If it is adopted in committee, the amended bill, once reported out, may be subject to a motion to rerefer to the committee having jurisdiction of the amendment. On the other hand, if the amendment is offered on the floor, it normally will not be subject to rereferral, except on the ground that no hearings were held on it. (This argument has no bearing on jurisdiction.)

Choice of "Target" Committee

As indicated in the previous sections, there are drafting techniques and other parliamentary devices which can materially affect the choice of the committee to which a bill will be referred. Why pick a particular committee as a target? The principal reasons are these: First, the members of one committee and/or its chairman, may be more sympathetic (as to broad ideology or narrow legal impact) to what the author of a measure has in mind. Second, the target committee already may have announced its intention to hold hearings on a specific subject matter not limited to any particular bill. Referral of a bill to that committee automatically may mean a hearing for that bill. Or third, the sponsor of a measure may want to offer his proposal as an amendment to another bill that the target committee may be marking up.

But one may go too far. He may ask unanimous consent, and even get it, for a referral of a bill to a committee which ordinarily would not have jurisdiction of it. Why would anyone object, when 95 percent of all bills die at the moment of their introduction? (See Appendix 1.) But when the bill springs forth from that committee, that is quite another story, and the entire measure may be subject to motions to recommit, or rerefer, to another committee.

COMMITTEE CONSIDERATIONS

Congressional action (as distinguished from the individual action of designing and introducing a bill) begins at the committee level. Conversely, of course, *inaction* also begins in committee.

Hearings

Power of Chairmen

Hearings are the first step in the legislative process after a bill has been introduced. More importantly, the *absence* of hearings is the first step in the *"nonlegislative"* process— the process of "killing" a bill. And most bills—indeed, almost all bills—are killed this way. Although the rules of many committees suggest that a majority can initiate hearings on a bill without the acquiescence of the chairman, as a practical matter the Congress, as presently structured, vests in the chairmen of its committees and subcommittees general power to decide which bills will be given hearing, and when.

That is not to say that members (of both parties) are without influence in attempting to persuade a chairman to hold hearings on a particular measure. In the House the full committee chairmen cannot ignore the pressures of the Democratic Caucus nor can the subcommittee chairmen thwart the wishes of the Democratic caucuses of committees without facing the danger of being deposed. Nonetheless, on matters of critical importance on which they do *not* wish to act, committee chairmen can ordinarily resist those pressures, particularly in the Senate.

Thus, for example, the great panoply of measures introduced every year by representatives and senators who wish to restrict the power of organized labor are regularly referred to the Labor committees, then to the Labor subcommittees, and then to oblivion, provided the chairmen of the respective committees and subcomittees are sufficiently friendly to organized labor (as they ordinarily are) to refuse to hold any hearings on those measures. And the same route to oblivion is followed in areas under other chairmen of other committees.

Even when the politics of the situation demand a hearing on a bill to which the chairman is unsympathetic, the chairman's power over *timing* may send a bill to the wastebasket. Thus, where the Congress is in the control of one party and the Presidency in the control of another, many Presidential bills are sent up to the Hill with the support and endorsement of the entire Administration but are never given hearings. Even if they are given hearings, chairmen frequently arrange to hold such hearings so late in a Congress that they can say, after the hearings are over, that there is simply "no time left" to hold executive markup sessions, report the bills to the floor, and pass them.

Setting aside any Machiavellian motives, many committees simply have too much active business to permit hearings, markups, and reports on all the bills which the chairmen would like to act upon. So a chairman's choice of priorities is critical. He *may*, among other things, operate by consensus within the majority party members of the committee (or on occasion a consensus of all members of the committee). This procedure appeared to be growing more prevalent in the House after the wave of recent reforms (see pages 78–81).

Other Ways of Moving a Bill

Even lacking action by the chairman, there are other ways of moving a bill. Most committees, upon receipt of a bill on reference after introduction, enter the bill upon their legislative calendar and send routine requests for comments to interested or affected executive departments or agencies. These agencies receive hundreds if not thousands of such requests for comments, and they know that, in most instances, the bills involved probably will never receive a hearing. So they usually do not respond to these requests for comments at all.

One way of moving a legislative proposal is to follow up requests for comments with indications to the agencies that the bill is a "live bill" on which hearings are likely to be held, or an important bill on which hearings will be urged, and the requests for comments should be taken seriously (particularly if the sponsor of the bill has reason to believe that the comments would be favorable).

Another approach in moving a bill out of limbo is to offer it as an amendment to some other piece of legislation which is already on the move. The dialectic involved sometimes runs as follows: (1) The sponsor reintroduces his bill as an amendment to a measure already in markup or otherwise on the move. (2) The chairman or manager of the live bill resists the amendment, believing that it would complicate and hinder his own bill, and argues that the amendment ought not to be accepted because no hearings have been held on it. (3) The sponsor of the amendment says that he understands and that he will withdraw the amendment, if the chairman will assure him that a hearing will be held on his own measure at a specific time. (4) As a result, a hearing is scheduled on the amendment (in the form of a separate bill), which otherwise might never have been scheduled.

There are, of course, many other stratagems which may be used in moving an otherwise dormant measure into active consideration, among them, persuasion, coalitions, lobbying, and so forth. Suffice it to say that a chairman ordinarily can hold hearings on anything he wants, and markups and votes as well. Other members, and particularly members of the minority party, must keep their wits about them and be alert to "vehicles" which they may use to "hitch a ride." But they must also be sensitive to the fact that the vehicle may be important in itself, and ought not to be overloaded. Not infrequently, a small but important bill becomes everyone's favorite vehicle, and is nicknamed a "Christmas tree" on which all members of the Congress attempt to attach their own special ornaments. The result, on occasion, is that the Christmas tree tips over from sheer weight, destroying not only the tree, but all the ornaments as well.

Purpose and Effect of Hearings

What are the hearings for, and what difference do they make? They make a little difference, sometimes even a great difference, but too often interest groups unfamiliar with congressional procedure overemphasize the significance of hearings—or at least hearings alone.

The ordinary quorum rules (see Senate Rule V, House Rule XV, in Appendices 3 and 4, respectively) rarely apply in hearings, particularly legislative hearings, and on many occasions only the chairman (or a designated acting chairman) and perhaps one or two other members of the committee will be present throughout a legislative hearing. Indeed, it is not at all uncommon to have more spectators, witnesses, and representatives of the press present in the hearing room than members of the committee.

So who is listening (besides the reporters)? Hardly anyone—sometimes not even the chairman. This is particularly true in "routine" hearings on noncontroversial bills. But it is certainly not true when a hearing is held on a "hot topic" of national interest.

To add to the boredom, it is not at all uncommon for witness after witness to appear and each read 20 or 30 pages of prepared statement, droning on for hours on end. The statement has already been supplied to the members of the committee, so they need not listen to the recitation; and the press has already received its copies and filed its reports, if any were deemed appropriate. A good chairman ought not to allow that practice. Instead, he should insist that the full text of the prepared statement be printed in the hearing record, and that the witness summarize and emphasize his position in no more than 10 minutes. Most chairman *urge* this procedure, but very few *insist* upon it; and very few witnesses respond to mere urging. Indeed, even a written summary is a waste of time from the witness' point of view.

A witness preparing for testimony before a committee ought to assume that the chairman and members of the committee, as well as members of the press, will be bored by either a recitation *or* a summary of prepared testimony. An effective witness will speak completely extemporaneously, with his major objective being to *wake up* the committee, make it pay attention, and make it *care* about what is being said. A big booming voice, gestures, large charts or other exhibits—anything out of the ordinary—will be a welcome relief to the members of the committee and the press, particularly if the hearings are televised. Watch the 7 o'clock news. *That* is what the editors clip out and televise.

When all is said and done, a hearing rarely will result in any amendment or change of position on legislation by anyone. There are too many other things going on. Often spectators see the spectacle (rarely reported in the media) of a representative or senator sitting behind the rostrum in a legislative hearing reading and signing his mail, even reading the newspaper, whispering to his colleagues and members of his staff, and wandering in and out to take phone calls, or to go to other committee meetings if he is a member of more than one committee or subcommittee which is meeting at the same time.

Hearings are essential *to make a record* and, on occasion, to pursuade; but standing alone they are of very little significance. So every legislative position reflected in testimony before a hearing *must*, to be effective, be followed up by personal contact with members of the committee and their staffs (see pages 49, 126–128).

Subject Matter of Hearings

A hearing may be held on a general topic (like energy) or may focus on the provisions of a particular bill or set of bills. Select, special, and joint committees can hold *non-legislative* hearings, such as the well-known Senate "Watergate" hearings, and standing committees may hold "oversight hearings." A Senate or House committee may also hold hearings on a measure already passed by the other chamber. This frequently occurs in the Senate Finance and Appropriations Committees where the House counterparts control the origination of taxing and spending bills.

While true oversight hearings have been rare, under the recent Hansen substitute (H. Res. 988) as amended by H. Res. 5, each House committee with over 20 members is now required to establish one oversight subcommittee. The House Government Operations Committee is required by the resolution to submit a report to the House on the oversight plans of the various standing committees. The purpose of oversight hearings is to investigate the operations of government agencies under the jurisdiction of particular committees to see if federal laws are being properly executed. Seven committees in the House have special oversight duties which allow their oversight subcommittees to investigate agencies not specifically under the full committees' jurisdiction. It is still not clear whether an "activist" Congress will carry on extensive oversight investigations or whether the heavy legislative calendars of standing committees (in contrast to special committees such as those investigating the C.I.A. in 1975) will once again relegate oversight activities to the back burner.

Witnesses and Statements

The decisions as to who will testify and in what order are generally made by committee staff subject to the approval of the chairman who will preside at the hearings. If the Administration wishes to send a representative, or if the committee requests the comments of an executive agency, the Administration's representative will usually testify first. Other witnesses on a bill may include representatives of concerned interest groups (for example, the AFL-CIO, National Association of Manufacturers, and the Chamber of Commerce of the United States), representatives of "public interest" groups, expert witnesses, representatives of professional associations (such as the American Bar Association and the American Medical Association) and even senators and representatives who are not members of the committee receiving testimony. Sometimes individuals whose unfortunate experiences have stimulated legislative action are asked to testify. For example, in 1971, at hearings on pension reform before the Subcommittee on Labor, workers who lost their retirement benefits testified about their personal misfortunes and the inadequacies they saw in private pension programs.

Witnesses generally are required to submit written statements before they testify. Extemporaneous oral comments usually are made while summarizing written statements or after reading prepared remarks, particularly in response to questions of committee members. Witnesses are generally permitted to correct and to make additions to the transcript of their testimony prior to publication.

The opening statements and questions of committee members are usually prepared by staff aides, who frequently accompany their senators or representatives to hearings and who give advice and suggest comments as the hearings progress. And in some cases, a "Q & A" is "planted," with the exact text of both the question and the answer written out in advance, though designed to appear spontaneous. (Ordinarily, a Q & A would be arranged between a witness or lobbyist and a member or his key staff aide.)

Open and Closed Hearings

In the House hearings are open to the public unless the committee votes on the day of the hearing to close the proceeding. Open hearings may be given radio and television coverage.

Senate committee hearings are governed by § 112(a) of the Legislative Reorganization Act of 1970 (2 U.S.C. §190 a-1(b)), which provides that hearings shall be open to the public except when the committee determines that testimony may relate to a matter of national security, may tend to reflect adversely on the character or reputation of the witness or any other individual, or may divulge matters deemed confidential under other provisions of law or government regulation. The statute also provides that an open hearing may be broadcast by radio or television, or both, under such rules as the committee may adopt.

The television networks generally will cover only hearings on controversial or well-publicized matters and then will tape only the more important witnesses.

Executive Sessions of Subcommittees and Committees (Markups)

The *real* legislative activity of a committee takes place in executive session—where bills are amended and redrafted ("marked up"), voted upon, and reported. While these meetings are often informal, they are nevertheless the subject of various sets of rules and customs concerning quorum, proxies, votes, timetable, and so forth (see pages 47–48). And they are heavily influenced by staff members, who frequently are closer to the legislation than their respective senators and representatives. Markup sessions may be closed or open to the public (increasingly the latter, particularly in the House). If a markup is closed, the public and the press is excluded, but the press usually manages to get considerable information about what goes on nevertheless. The results of a closed markup are reflected in committee reports; but dissenting views may also be printed, disclosing the nature of the controversy, if any, which took place.

Open and Closed Markup Sessions

In the name of "reform," "democracy," and other apple-pie objectives, the Congress in recent years has leaned toward holding its executive sessions open to the public.

Do open markups really make a difference? Well, obviously, they make some, since they give the public and interested parties some insight into what is going on. Further, to a degree Congress will behave in a more responsible manner when conducting its business in public view subject to comment from the press. But the kind of give and take which has been characteristic of closed sessions is not likely to occur in open sessions. Thus, the principal consequences of opening executive sessions may turn out to be: (1) that the efficiency and speed of such sessions will be lessened; (2) that more time will be devoted to speech making and other plays to the grandstands; and (3) that the *real* business of legislative compromise may, to some extent, take place elsewhere—in private.

This is not to say that the process of legislative compromise will not be affected by the changed rules. Compromise will somehow take place, that is, will take place in private discussion, and what takes place in public will merely be a performance of a script (or at least a trade) already made elsewhere.

The script itself, however, may be somewhat different than what it would have been had it been both written and performed in a full committee meeting behind closed doors. In effect, the process of compromise will be "pushed back" a step to some other time at some other place, but the same *dramatis personae* will not be present at that time and place. More than likely the real business of legislative compromise will be conducted in caucuses; and those will be *party* caucuses, the Democratic members of a given committee or subcommittee in one caucus and the Republican members in another, in contrast to the nonpartisan groupings which formed in committee sessions where a majority or consensus could be reached combining members of *both* parties.

The resulting compromise may, therefore, be different. Only when the majority party is unable to reach any consensus at all in its own caucus will members of that caucus be likely to seek alliance with some of the minority members to produce a majority of the full committee.

In consequence, one might suspect that the influence of the minority members in the shaping of legislation may be substantially diminished under the new House* rules because the "deal" will already have been made in the majority caucus, before the committee ever meets in its open markup session.

It will take some time, of course, to determine what new procedural patterns will develop. But one thing is certain: The kind of "off-the-record" horse trading which has long been characteristic of closed door legislative markups simply cannot take place in formal executive sessions under the new rules.

Rules, Quorum, Proxies, and Votes

Before 1970, many committees had no rules whatsoever. Those that did have rules frequently never published them, so that it was impossible or at least difficult to find out what the rules were.

Section 133B of the Legislative Reorganization Act of 1970 (2 U.S.C. 190 a-2) required each committee of the Senate to adopt rules "not inconsistent with the standing rules of the Senate or with those provisions of law having the force and effect of standing rules of the Senate" and further required the publication of such rules in the *Congressional Record* not later than March 1 of each year.

In the House, committees are directed only to adopt written rules, and the Joint Committee on Congressional Operations now publishes a pamphlet containing the rules of all committees in both Houses, except those which for some reason have not complied with the statute or with the custom of the House.

---
* A similar trend developed in the Senate late in 1975.

The most fundamental House and Senate rules concern quorum and the use of proxies. Only rarely will a committee find a 100-percent turnout of its membership in executive session. Often a representative or senator will be out of town, or necessarily detained, or even committed to some other committee or subcommittee meeting at the same time. Accordingly, many committees have adopted a rule which permits a quorum of less than 50 percent for the conduct of most business, except a final vote to report a bill.

Many committees also permit the use of proxies. Rules on the use of these proxies vary. In the Senate, some committees require written proxies and some require specific proxies on specific issues while others permit a general proxy. In the House, each committee decides whether to permit proxies, but, where permitted, the proxies must be in writing to a specific representative on a specific provision, except for procedural matters on which general proxies are permitted.

It is a frustrating matter indeed, however, for a senator or representative to present a proposed amendment to a bill in executive session and find one or two other members present, each holding a half dozen proxies. The proxies may very well be cast against the amendment, even though the members whose proxies are being cast have no real knowledge of the issue and might very well have voted the other way had they been there in person to hear arguments.

About the only way to forestall misuse of proxies is to give ample notice to committee members and to their staffs about a pending vote *and* the arguments to be made. But a partial solution would be to outlaw the "general proxy" on substantive matters (as the House has done) and permit the voting of proxies only where the written proxy states specifically on its face the exact vote in which it is to be cast. The trouble with this solution, however, is that a specific proxy is not very useful, since a minor alteration of an amendment might nullify it.

Function of Staff

Whatever the rule on proxies may be, as a practical matter it is the staff which often casts the proxy—at least in the Senate. Two members may be sitting in committee side by side, with their respective assistants sitting directly behind them. One leaves in the middle of the meeting and says to his colleague: "You have my proxy. Please cast it whatever way my assistant tells you." The Senate committee's chairman will not recognize the assistant, but the senator who remains may be really nothing but a mouthpiece for the staff member of the absent senator.

Press Coverage

When closed executive sessions are taking up matters of substantial national interest, it is not at all uncommon to find the press lined up in the hall waiting for the committee meeting to "break"—the doors open, senators walk out, and a flood of questions comes on. Indeed, frequently network television cameras are set up in the hall, flood lights and all, and as the chairman or other key senator walks out of the session the lights go on and the interview begins.

But that is the exception, not the rule. Ordinarily there is little or no press coverage of executive sessions; thus these sessions present ideal opportunities to kill legislation in a way which will not attach political responsibility to the senator or representative who does the dirty deed.

Press coverage, therefore, can be used as a means of insuring that legislation will not be killed surreptitiously. When an objecting representative or senator *knows* that a key member of the press is attending an open executive session or monitoring a closed one, he also knows that, whatever happens, session results *will* make the evening TV news and the next day's morning press.

Offering Amendments—Finalizing a Bill

Many a routine bill comes out of committee after a brief discussion in executive session and a voice vote with no dissent. The bill is never examined line by line by each member of the committee, and no one sees the "report" which will accompany the bill because no such report has been written yet. But when controversy arises and attention is focused, routine inspection gives way to more rigorous standards.

The focal point of any executive session is the offering and disposition of amendments. While rules may vary, general parliamentary principles apply to the sequence of votes on amendments. Amendments in the first and second degree are in order, but amendments in the third degree are not permitted. If an amendment is offered to a pending bill (that is, an amendment in the first degree), an amendment may be offered to the pending amendment (an amendment in the second degree). The vote on the amendment in the second degree occurs first.

If a substitute amendment is offered and adopted, no further amendments to the substitute are in order. Accordingly, the offering of a substitute forces members who have modifications or alternatives under consideration to offer them, before the vote on the substitute, as amendments to the substitute. In addition, while the substitute is pending, "perfecting" amendments may be offered to the original text of the bill. This principle is well justified on the ground that, if a single vote on a substitute is to decide the outcome, the bill which is about to be stricken out in favor of the substitute ought to be allowed to be perfected as best it can be before the choice between the two alternatives is made.

Those are the general ground rules; but, as often as not, practical alternatives will develop. One member of a committee hearing another member offer an amendment which would be controversial will suggest a compromise that might satisfy the sponsor of the amendment and be acceptable to the author of the bill.

Alternatively, the chairman may say that he objects to the specific language of the amendment, although he accepts the principle of the amendment, and he may suggest a redraft. On many occasions, the chairman will accept the idea of the amendment but object to its inclusion in the text of the bill as such. He may prefer instead to agree to include specific language in the accompanying committee report stating that it is the understanding of the committee that the qualification proposed by the sponsor of the amendment be considered part of the legislative history of the bill. This device is less than binding as a matter of law, but may very well create legislative history which would put a binding interpretative gloss on some language that might otherwise be ambiguous in the text of the bill.

One might ask why a chairman sponsoring a bill would wish to accommodate himself to a minority senator when the chairman knows he has the votes to defeat any amendment. The answer is that he may have the votes in committee, but he may not have them on the floor; so he will try very hard to bring his bill out of committee by unanimous vote of the members and perhaps get it passed without controversy on the floor. To accomplish this, he must forestall the inclusion of any dissenting views with the committee report. Or he may feel he has the votes on the floor but lacks the time as Congress draws to the close of its session to bring up a controversial matter. In this situation, if he can assure the leadership that the matter can be disposed of in a few hours on the floor without controversy, he will be able to squeeze his bill through in the closing days of the Congress. Another reason he may wish to avoid controversy is that his bill may be headed for a Senate-House conference, where it will face the version of the other chamber passed overwhelmingly. The chairman may feel that his position in conference will be untenable unless his alternative version also passes his chamber overwhelmingly, so he will accommodate the minority even though he has the votes to defeat floor amendments, but less than overwhelmingly. And in the House, even though a representative may have the votes to get his bill out of his own committee, he may fear difficulty with the House Rules Committee, which could be surmounted if his bill were less controversial.

All these reasons, and more, generate a good deal of give and take in executive sessions of congressional committees. Inevitably, they require that members be well briefed and well staffed, because it is almost certain that at least one member will be well briefed and well staffed—the sponsor of the bill being marked up.

Reporting a Bill and the Committee Report

After a bill has been amended as the majority wishes, the committee votes to "report" it. When we speak of "committee reports," of the fact that the "committee" reported a bill, or of the fact that the "committee adopted an amendment to the bill," we are speaking jurisdictionally, and we ought to distinguish the jurisdictional activity of the committee, which in fact is done by the committee as a whole, from the actual work of the committee, which is not always an act of the whole committee.

The committee, *as a committee*, does one thing—it votes. Just about everything else is done by *individuals*—individual representatives and senators (usually the chairman) and their individual staff members.

Time of Filing

The vote on reporting a bill ordinarily does not take place on the day the bill is actually reported. The committee votes merely to have the bill "ordered reported." At this point, several steps usually are missing:

- The bill itself has not been typed up (or printed in page proof) in final form with the amendments inserted. (Instead, they are lying around on slips of paper, having been submitted by individual members of the committee and voted up or down.)
- The final draft has not been examined carefully by members of the technical staff to make sure that all the parts fit together, that amended sections or titles have been properly renumbered and properly cross-referenced, and so forth.
- There is not in existence at this point, ordinarily, anything remotely resembling a "committee report" to accompany the bill.
- No representative or senator has been selected as the person who actually "reports" the bill.
- And dissenting senators and representatives have not had the opportunity to prepare and file separate views, individual views, minority views, dissenting views, or whatever they wish to call their statement of position as distinguished from that set forth in the "committee report."

All these steps take time. Accordingly, when the committee votes to have the bill "ordered reported," it is the common practice to allow time for their completion, with instructions as to when various deadlines are to be met.

Committee Report

What exactly is a "committee report"? Notwithstanding the fact that the courts, in construing legislation, consider the views expressed in a committee report as forceful legislative history expressing the interpretation placed upon legislation by the committee which drafted it, a committee report is usually not the report of a committee at all. On the contrary, it is frequently written by one senator or representative and his staff, and very frequently is seen by no one else but that individual until it is printed as a government document. It shows on its face what it is: "Mr. Jones, from the Committee on _____, submitted the following report." Who is this Mr. Jones? Most often he is the chairman of the subcommittee which held the hearings; he is the principal sponsor of the bill; and he will be the "floor manager" when the bill reaches the floor. None of this is coincidence. Much of the discretion which had to be exercised to bring this bill to the floor was vested in the subcommittee chairman. How did it happen that the bill got a hearing at all? It happened because the subcommittee chairman, in selecting the bills on which to hold a hearing, picked his own. How did it happen that he became the floor manager? It happened, of course, because he picked himself as floor manager, or he asked the chairman of the full committee to pick him. How did it happen that he was the draftsman of the committee report? It happened because the author of the bill and the person who ran the hearings and the person who will have to defend the bill on the floor are one and the same individual. And if the bill is finally enacted into law, it will be known not by its public law number or its bill number, but by its nickname, which will be its author's name, sometimes coupled with the name of the person holding the same position in the opposite chamber of Congress (note, for example, the Taft-Hartley Act, the Norris-LaGuardia Act, the Celler-Kefauver Act).

Drafting the Committee Report

Who drafts the committee report? If the bill is really a "Presidential Bill," accompanied by a message from the President of the United States and devised by technicians in one of the Cabinet departments, there is a great bureaucratic structure standing behind it. And in circumstances in which the chairman is a member of the same political party as the President, it is not at all uncommon for the technical work, including the drafting of the committee report, to be done by the legal staff of the Cabinet department which originally devised the bill—Labor, Justice, or whichever.

But in circumstances in which the Congress is controlled by one party and the White House held by another, cooperation between the executive and legislative branches is often missing, and the chairman or other manager of the bill is left to his own devices, which means his personal staff and the professional staff of the committee of which he is the chairman. Either way, the basic outlines of the committee report are traditional (examine almost any report, at random, for the headings), though to some extent they are controlled by the rules of the House or Senate and of the committee of which the floor manager is a member or chairman, and even by the terms of the Legislative Reorganization Act.

Printing and Submission of Minority Views

Section 133 (e) of the Legislative Reorganization Act of 1946, as amended, required that each member of the Senate who so requests be given no less than three calendar days in which to file supplemental, minority, or additional views on a bill or resolution, and that if he complies with that time limit the committee report itself shall include, printed in a single document, those views. In practice, however, a good deal more than three days is ordinarily taken in the preparation of the report itself, as well as the views of individual senators (and House members, since the same practice is followed in the House). The extra time is *not* regularly provided simply to permit the dissenting member to read the document he is dissenting from. With only some exceptions, the dissenting member never sees the committee report from which he is dissenting until it is printed simultaneously with the dissenting views!

There are a few chairmen who have followed the practice of circulating a draft or galley proof of the committee report to permit members of the committee to make suggestions or comments, which, incidentally, permits dissenting senators to pinpoint the terms of their dissent by learning the content of the "majority" report. But prior circulation of the report is far from the universal practice, and it is not required by the rules or by the Reorganization Act. Indeed, a number of chairmen have said that that practice precipitates endless and unnecessary delay by permitting a large number of individual senators to generate crosscurrents of debate on small technical points which might not otherwise occur if the draft report were kept in the pocket of one person until actually filed.

Contents of the Committee Report

Be that as it may, however, the report ordinarily contains the following elements:

- an *introduction*, which attempts to summarize the origin of the bill, its objective, and generally what it does
- a *summary* of the hearings and other steps taken by the committee in the legislative process
- frequently, a *section-by-section analysis*, which purports to describe in layman's terms what the technical language of each section of the bill provides (But all too frequently in recent times, the section-by-section analysis simply paraphrases, or even quotes verbatim, the language of each section which it purports to be "analyzing.")
- a *discussion* of the amendments to the bill adopted by the subcommittee and the full committee, and pursuant to recent changes in the rules, the votes of the committee, at least on final passage
- a so-called *Ramsayer* or *Cordon* print showing changes made by the bill, or which would be made by the bill, in existing law
- finally, *individual, minority,* and *supplemental views* on the legislation, if submitted in accordance with the rules and in time so that they may be printed together with the report.

Significance of Separate or Other Views

Assuming that a representative or senator cannot see the actual language of the report from which he is dissenting, how can he write separate views, and why should he bother?

Obviously, a senator or representative who offered amendments or took positions in committee which were voted down and who wishes to renew his efforts on the House or Senate floor has a reason to write a dissent from the report. He is not so much dissenting from the report as from the bill or a part of the bill which the report accompanies. What a member does in his individual or separate views (as distinguished from "supplemental views," which simply endorse the bill for reasons other than the reasons of the principal sponsors) is to explain that the bill differs from what he had in mind, and why he was right and the committee wrong. The member knows, without seeing the majority report, that it will endorse positions which differ from those which he took in committee.

Why bother? The answers are several. Most importantly, the dissenting representative or senator puts all of his colleagues (not just colleagues who are members of the same committee and who are already on notice) on notice that this legislation has a controversial aspect to it and that amendments may be offered on the floor. In effect, the member puts the leadership of the House or Senate on notice that this is not "consent calendar" business, which can be passed by unanimous consent with no real debate. He also tells his colleagues what the amendments offered on the floor will be. The member puts the staffs of individual representatives or senators on notice that they will have to study a question and advise their congressmen which way they ought to vote, consistent with their own philosophies and political positions.

Obviously, there are other ways—speeches, letters, floor statements, press releases, etc.—to alert the Congress to the controversial aspects of a measure beside filing a dissenting view as part of the committee report, and those other ways may even be supplements to the filing of individual or separate views. But it is the committee report itself which is printed, which is distributed, which is an operative legislative document, and which cannot be ignored by congressional leaders and their staffs when legislation is scheduled and when determinations are made as to whether a measure can pass by unanimous consent or must be treated as debatable and controversial legislation.

Who drafts individual views? An individual representative or senator can and may. More likely, the staff member who worked on the legislation will do so. Indeed, in a Congress in which the chairman is a member of one party and the President another, if the bill as reported differs from the proposal which is part of the President's program, the appropriate Cabinet department or staff of that department may very well participate in the drafting of individual views of representatives or senators who are "minority members" of the committee but members of the President's party representing his views within the committee.

Choice of a Floor Manager

As noted above, the floor manager of a bill and the senator or representative who reported it are often one and the same person—the chairman of the subcommittee of origin. But there are exceptions.

Many subcommittees have such broad jurisdiction that not all or even most legislation originating in them is authored by their chairmen. However, little if any legislation is reported out of any committee of the Congress which is not authored by some member of the majority party. Indeed, even if a member of the minority party comes up with a bill which the majority party would like to see enacted into law, the bill which finally comes out of committee will be a version of the orginal idea, redrafted by, reintroduced by, and named after the chairman of the subcommittee—sometimes nicknamed with hyphenated authors to include the member of the minority party who originated the idea (see page 53).

But when a really hot issue arises and a true champion is needed on the floor of the House or the Senate to fend off an expected massive attack upon the legislation, it is not unusual for the committee as a whole to decide that a particular member of the committee—chosen not necessarily by seniority but, rather, because of familiarity with the legislation and tactical skill in floor maneuver—shall be the "floor manager." The person selected ordinarily writes and files the committee report. The late Senator Wayne Morse of Oregon, though not the chairman of the Senate Labor Subcommittee, frequently was selected to report the most controversial of labor legislation simply because he had gained a reputation as an authority in the field, a forceful advocate on the floor, and a skillful tactician under the Senate rules. He was also known as a friend of the labor movement and a supporter (in most cases) of the views its leaders advocated.

The "minority floor manager" is chosen much like the majority floor manager. Usually the senior minority member of a committee will initiate or represent amendments which were defeated in committee by the majority party. He naturally falls into the position of the minority floor manager, though on occasion a compromise will be reached at the committee level which will enable the two floor managers—the minority floor manager and the majority floor manager (titles which are not statutory but merely customary)—to share responsibilities, since they are both supporters of the legislation which has reached the floor.

When time for debate on a bill or amendment is limited, either by resolution originating in the House Rules Committee and adopted as a "rule" by the House or by unanimous consent agreement in the Senate, ordinarily the allocation of that time is the result of a division between the minority and majority managers—or between the floor manager and the author of an amendment, if the minority floor manager does not support the amendment. The two senators or representatives who control the allotted time in turn "yield" portions of that time to those wishing to speak in behalf of or in opposition to the bill or an amendment to the bill. Thus, while the position of the majority floor manager of a bill is more critical than the position of minority floor manager, each has a function which will affect to some extent the course of a measure after it reaches the floor.

FLOOR AND CONFERENCE COMMITTEE CONSIDERATION

"No one is to speak impertinently or beside the question, superfluously, or tediously. . . ." (*Annotation by House Parliamentarian:* "[N]either by rule nor practice has the House ever suppressed superfluous or tedious speaking. . . .")

"No one is to disturb another in his speech by hissing, coughing, spitting. . . ."

Jefferson's Manual

The procedures in the two Houses of Congress differ sharply when a measure comes to the floor. The differences are largely a result of the fact that there are over 400 members in the House and only 100 in the Senate. Debate in the Senate is unlimited, and individual members have more rights during debate. The House lodges much greater power in the leadership and in its Rules Committee, limiting the rights of individual members (particularly those not members of the committee reporting the bill) to voting.

Bringing a Bill to the House Floor

There are a number of alternative methods of bringing a bill to the House floor. Excluding special procedures of limited interest (such as special days for calling up District of Columbia business), the four most significant procedures for bringing a bill to the House floor are:

- a report of a bill from the substantive committee with jurisdiction of it, plus a "rule" (that is, resolution governing floor debate) from the House Rules Committee
- a report from the substantive committee, plus successful passage after placing the bill on the "consent calendar"
- a report of the bill from the substantive committee, plus passage on suspension of the rules, and
- a report of the bill from a substantive committee with privilege to report the bill and call it up without a rule.

The following sections discuss each of these procedures briefly and attempt to explain their interrelationship.

Resolutions From the House Rules Committee

A resolution or rule from the House Rules Committee is the most common method of bringing a measure to the floor. A rule is the means by which a bill may be taken from its position on a floor calendar and moved directly to the floor for consideration. The chairman and interested members of the substantive committees reporting the bill appear before the Rules Committee and make their arguments as to why the particular bill should receive immediate floor consideration. If the Rules Committee agrees that the bill should be moved quickly, it will report a resolution to the House that the bill be considered. Such resolutions or rules are generally adopted by the House, though some are controversial and occasionally one is defeated.

A rule will provide the amount of time for debate; who will control the time; whether amendments will (open rule) or will not (closed rule) be allowed from the floor; and, every now and then, whether points of order which might be raised against a particular bill or amendment will be waived.

Consent Calendar

House Rule XIII, Clause 4, provides:

> After a bill has been favorably reported and shall be upon either the House or Union Calendar any Member may file with the Clerk a notice that he desires such bill placed upon a special calendar known as the "Consent Calendar". On the first and third Mondays of each month immediately after the reading of the Journal, the Speaker shall direct the Clerk to call the bills in numerical order, which have been for three legislative days upon the "Consent Calendar". Should objection be made to consideration of any bill so called, it shall be carried over on the calendar without prejudice to the next day when the "Consent Calendar" is again called, and if objected to by three or more Members, it shall immediately be stricken from the calendar, and shall not thereafter during the same session of that Congress be placed again thereon; *Provided*, that no bill shall be called twice on the same legislative day."

In essence the consent calendar in each house serves to expedite the passage of noncontroversial measures of all kinds.

In the House the consent calendar formalizes the procedure for calling up a bill. In the Senate this is accomplished informally by the calling of the regular calendar (see pages 63–64). The principal difference is that in the House it takes three members to object to passage off the consent calendar, whereas in the Senate a single member may object. And in the House, once objection is made on two days, the bill is off the consent calendar for good, whereas in the Senate consent may be attempted any number of times.

By practice, House passage on the consent calendar ordinarily requires that a bill be of relatively minor importance, not involving expenditure of more than a million dollars, and not making fundamental changes in policy or involving opposition to the program of the President.

Suspension of the Rules

House Rule XXVII provides that on the first and third Mondays of a month, and on the Tuesdays immediately following those days, and during the last six days of the session, the Speaker may entertain motions to suspend the rules, which require passage by a two-thirds vote. Debate on these motions is limited to 40 minutes (Clause 3). Because recognition for purposes of these motions is in the absolute discretion of the Speaker, this procedure, which on its face is a democratization of House Rules, is subject to some very severe limits.

Privileged Committees

Under House Rule XI, Clause 22, certain committees are authorized to report bills on certain stated subjects at any time, and to obtain their immediate consideration without first obtaining a rule from the Rules Committee. Ordinarily, these subjects are appropriations, revenue bills from the Ways and Means Committee, rules from the Rules Committee, certain Interior Committee measures, certain Rivers and Harbors bills from the Committee on Public Works, and pension bills from the Veterans' Committee. But the privilege is not without its drawbacks, for consideration of a measure without first obtaining a rule sidesteps the possibility of a "closed rule" and other limitations of debate. So some committees, most notably the Ways and Means Committee, ordinarily obtain a rule (a closed rule) from the Rules Committee before bringing bills such as tax measures to the House floor, even though they could be brought up under the privilege. Another reason to go to the Rules Committee, even if a committee is authorized to bring a privileged bill to the floor directly, is that the Rules Committee "rule" may immunize a measure from points of order which might otherwise be fatal to the bill.

Calendars

Senate Calendars

There is only one legislative calendar * in the Senate, and all bills reported from any committee—whether authorizing bills or appropriations bills—are placed upon that calendar in the order in which they are reported.

House Calendars

In the House there are a number of calendars. The "House Calendar" includes all bills except money bills. The "Union Calendar" contains all appropriations bills and all revenue raising bills. The "Consent Calendar" includes noncontroversial bills which can pass by consent. The "Private Calendar" includes nonpublic bills affecting only one individual (for example, bills permitting the immigration of a person not otherwise eligible for immigration under laws of general application). And the "Discharge Calendar" includes motions to remove stalled bills from the consideration of committees. Again, it should be noted that bills placed on these different calendars in the House would be placed on the single legislative calendar of the Senate if reported from a committee in the Senate.

In addition to their purely legislative functions, these calendars also serve certain other purposes. The House calendar contains not only listings of the bills but also brief legislative histories of the principal bills coming before the House. The back page of both House and Senate calendars contains a run-down of the status of all appropriations bills, giving a quick overview of the entire budget.

---

* There is a separate calendar called the "executive calendar," which exists only in the Senate, for actions in which only the Senate has constitutional authority—the ratification of treaties and the confirmation of Presidential appointments requiring the advice and consent of the Senate.

FLOOR AND CONFERENCE COMMITTEE CONSIDERATION 63

The consent calendar in the House is called only on specified days of the month. If on the first call a measure is objected to by one member, the bill is held over until the next call. If on the second call three or more members object, the measure is struck from the calendar. If less than three members object on the second call and the measure is not passed over by request, the bill will be passed by unanimous consent without debate. Both parties have "objectors" on the House floor who closely watch the calendar and who object to controversial or complex measures which should be not passed by consent.

Senate "Consent Calendar" and "Holds"

In the Senate, which has only a single calendar and no consent calendar, the leadership will, from time to time, "call the consent calendar," which simply involves reading down the list of bills which have been reported since the last time the calendar was called to see if anyone objects. Typically, a notation appears in the calendar after the last bill which was subject to the last consent-calendar call.

Ordinarily, when the consent calendar is called in the Senate, the majority leader will check with the minority leader, who in turn will check with the members of the various interested committees, to see whether legislation on the calendar is controversial or is likely to encounter any opposition, or whether any amendments will be offered. If there are announced plans to offer any amendments, or if any senator says he plans to speak against a particular bill, the Minority Leader will object at the call of the calendar, and the bill ordinarily will not be subject thereafter to a consent calendar call, unless objection is later withdrawn. If a majority senator wishes to object, he will then notify the Majority Leader, who will simply pass over the bill when he comes to it on the consent-calendar call.

On occasion in the Senate, however, a single senator or small group of senators, while not wishing to block passage by consent for some indefinite period, seeks further information or otherwise wishes to delay consent passage. Under these circumstances, the senator calls his respective Minority or Majority leader and places a "hold" on the bill, which will prevent its passage by unanimous consent for some stated period of time, until an ambiguity is resolved.

A senator may place a hold not only on a consent-calendar bill but also on a controversial measure or nomination. In 1973 the Democratic Policy Committee (which plays an important role in determining the party's legislative program) decided that once a bill or nomination was placed on the Senate calendar, no hold would be honored for more than three days of the session, unless it was a committee hold.* An initial hold on a measure or nomination would exhaust the right of any other member to place a further hold on the matter. The Policy Committee refrained from extending the three-day hold limitation to nominations to offices, particularly judgeships, with duties confined within the boundaries of a particular state.

Filibusters

Because of the size of its membership, the House has restricted floor debate and has curbed the use of the filibuster. In contrast, the Senate, with only 100 members, has continued its tradition of unlimited debate and has become the filibuster's home.

Extended Debate and Procedural Delay

The filibuster is the final weapon of those senators who are in the minority on a particular measure and who are strongly opposed to it. The tactic involves the use of extended debate and parliamentary procedures to stall and finally obstruct consideration of the opposed measure.

A filibuster will be most effective near the end of a legislative session because it will eat up precious time which is needed for the consideration of other pending legislation. A filibuster earlier in the session can succeed where there are enough energetic supporters or where it is delaying passage of urgently needed legislation.

The most important element of a filibuster is the continuation of debate by its supporters. The delay from extended debate can be supplemented by such parliamentary tactics as demanding quorum calls, demanding rollcall votes on unnecessary or similar motions, and making frequent points of order.

---

* 121 Cong. Rec. S23610 (Daily Ed. December 20, 1973).

Cloture

In recent years the best and most frequently used weapon against the filibuster has been cloture, which is the ending of debate by vote of the Senate. Rule 22, which contains the cloture provision, was first adopted in 1917, and provided that debate could be terminated by a vote of two thirds of the senators present and voting. In 1949, Rule 22 was amended to require the vote of two thirds of all senators, but was changed back to its original form in 1959.

In 1975 after a lengthy and at times bitter struggle over amending Rule 22, "liberals" and "moderates" reached a compromise with "conservative" forces to require a vote of three fifths of all senators (60 senators) for cloture on all measures except a change in the Standing Rules, which will require a vote of two thirds of the senators present and voting.

The adoption of the three-fifths cloture rule marked the culmination of a 20-year effort by senate "liberals" to alter the two-thirds rule, which was used successfully for many years by conservatives to thwart civil rights legislation. But whether the result was to the advantage of the "liberals" remains to be seen. With much of civil rights legislation behind us, recent debates suggest that a small band of liberals seeking to block certain legislation (such as that dealing with strip mining, the S.S.T., busing, etc.) may have had more use for the old filibuster rule than the conservatives ever did!

Wearing Down a Filibuster

If there are not enough votes for cloture, filibuster opponents may attempt to wear down the filibustering senators by holding extended all-night sessions in the hope of eventually exhausting debate. The tactic rarely succeeds, and the current leadership opposes it, though on occasion uses it as a "gesture," only to abandon it when it fails.

Floor Debate and Voting

"Rules" for House Floor Debate

Procedures for bringing a measure to the floor are more informal in the Senate than in the House. In the House, the resolutions of the Rules Committee generally control such matters as when a bill will be considered, how much time will be spent in debate, who will have control of the allotted time, whether amendments will be allowed, whether the five-minute rule will apply to amendments, and so forth.

Unanimous Consent Agreements in the Senate

In the Senate, such matters are generally worked out by the leadership of both parties with the participation of interested senators. The result of this informal negotiation process is called a unanimous consent agreement, which, as indicated by its name, requires the consent of all senators. Such an agreement establishes the scenario for handling most important legislation.

Debate, Amendments, and the "Third Reading"

In the absence of a unanimous consent agreement, a bill may be debated in the Senate for any length of time because of the Senate's unlimited debate rule, although a senator may not speak more than twice on any one question in the same day without leave of the Senate—a rule with no teeth at all.* Unlike procedure in the House, according to which a period for making germane amendments to bills follows a period of general debate, procedure in the Senate allows amendments to be offered at any time a bill is under consideration, and amendments *need not be germane*, except for those to a general appropriation bill.

When no amendments are pending and no member is seeking recognition, the bill is read for a third time. (Both "first reading" and "second reading" are regularly accomplished before a measure is referred to committee, and no further "reading" occurs until the "third reading" just before a final vote on the floor.) Once the bill has been read a third time, no amendments may be offered except by unanimous consent, unless the bill is reconsidered. Third reading is the prelude to a final vote—up or down.

Points of Order and Motions on the Previous Question

Rule 22 of the Senate's Standing Rules provides that a point of order, which is an objection that the Senate's rules

---

* By offering a different amendment each time, he speaks on a different question each time.

are not being followed, may be raised at any time except when the Senate is dividing. (On "division," a form of vote, see the section immediately following.) But the rules themselves may be suspended *by vote* (as distinguished from unanimous consent) under Rule 40, provided that one day's written notice is given and a two-thirds vote of the senators present is obtained. Unlike the House rules, which allow closing of debate pursuant to a "rule" adopted by majority vote, or by majority vote for a motion on "the previous question" (see page 218), the Senate rules contain no such provision because of the Senate's policy of unlimited debate.

Voting

There are four methods of voting in the Senate.

- A measure may be voted on by *consent:* When debate ends, if no objections are heard, the bill is passed.
- A bill or resolution may be voted on by *voice vote*, with the senators answering affirmatively or negatively as a group, and the presiding officer announcing the result.
- A measure may be voted on by a *division vote*, which involves a count either of raised hands or those senators who stand.
- Finally, a measure may be voted on by *rollcall vote* which occurs if the "Yeas and Neas" are called for by one fifth of the senators present. The rollcall vote is the only method by which a record is made of how a senator voted on a particular issue.*

In the House, five voting methods may be used: voice vote, division vote, teller vote, recorded vote, and yea and nay vote.

- The *voice* and *division* votes are like those in the Senate.
- The *teller vote* is used upon the request of one fifth of the quorum and requires congressmen to pass observers or "tellers" who count their votes but do not record how they vote.

---

* In the Senate, a "yea or nay" vote is obtained by having sufficient "seconds"—one fifth of those voting on the last vote, or one fifth of those present on the basis of a "presumptive quorum," i.e., one fifth of 51, or 11 seconders (See Riddick, *Senate Procedure*, S. Doc. No. 93–21, 93d Cong., 1st Sess. 899 (1974)).

- The *recorded vote* also requires a request by one fifth of the quorum and entails the recording of members' votes by an electronic device. This method substitutes for and is backed up by the teller method of voting, in which tellers record members' votes.
- The *yea and nay method* is not used in the Committee of the Whole, but is used in the full House.

Paired Votes

A "pair" refers to two members who have agreed that neither will vote. Both the Senate and the House allow members to be excused from voting when their votes are paired. A "live pair" arises when one member is absent and the other, who is present, will not vote because of the pairing. A "general pair" or "dead pair" (common in the House) arises when the votes of two absent members are paired. Paired votes are not counted when votes are totaled.

It should be noted that a "dead pair" makes no difference, while a "live pair" does. In my view, a live pair is inexcusable, particularly if the one vote of the nonvoting but present member would have changed the outcome. I have seen the leadership pressure some members to accept a live pair to alter the outcome. Only rarely does the press, watching in the gallery, note the event. Responsible and alert journalism should do better.

Motion to Reconsider (and to Table)

After a vote, it is customary for victorious senators to move to reconsider the matter just voted on and then for a cooperating victorious member to move to table the motion to reconsider, thereby finalizing the initial vote. It is also customary to seek and obtain permission to make technical corrections after the passage of a bill or resolution.

Position of Staff Members (on the Floor)

Senate Rule XXIII provides that no person shall be admitted to the Senate floor except certain listed individuals, including "[c]lerks to Senate committees and clerks to Senators when in the actual discharge of their official duties." When a senator is a floor manager for a bill or a key participant in the floor debate, he is usually accompanied by his legislative aide in charge of the bill or by committee staff under his control (patronage). The principal aide will frequently sit next to his senator during the debate, while secondary assistants may sit on a few corner couches.

Press Coverage

Reporters are not allowed on the Senate or House floors, but certain observer galleries are reserved for use by the press. (As this manual is being written, it is expected that Congress will consider a proposal to allow live television coverage of floor proceedings in both the House and the Senate.) In addition, each house provides galleries for press, TV, and radio, where calls are received, interviews are conducted and recorded, and reports and stories are written. Each gallery has a table reserved for piles of press releases from congressional offices—and *that* table is where most "news" of Capitol Hill originates.

Germaneness Under the House Rules

Unlike the Senate, where nongermane amendments to pending legislation are acceptable except for an appropriation bill, the House requires germaneness—for legislation coming up through committees, legislation returning from the Senate with Senate amendments, and legislation in conference committee.

Germaneness, however, may be waived one way or another. For example, a bill returning from Senate-House conference may include Senate amendments not germane to the original House bill (amendments which, if offered originally in the House, would have been subject to a point of order).

Rule XVI, Clause 7, of the House Rules provides that "no motion or proposition on a subject different from that under consideration shall be admitted under color of amendment." But because the Senate has no germaneness rule, the House frequently passes nongermane Senate amendments, and so House Rule XXVIII, Clause 4, provides:

> "4. (a) With respect to any report of a committee of conference called up before the House containing any matter which would be in violation of the provisions of clause 7 of Rule XVI if such matter had been offered as an amendment in the House, and which—

(1) is contained in any Senate amendment to that measure (including a Senate amendment in the nature of a substitute for the text of that measure as passed by the House) accepted by the House conferees or agreed to by the conference committee with modification; or

(2) is contained in any substitute agreed to by the conference committee;

it shall be in order, at any time after the reading of the report has been completed or dispensed with and before the reading of the statement, to make a point of order that such nongermane matter, as described above, which shall be specified in the point of order, is contained in the report.

"(b) If such point of order is sustained, it then shall be in order for the Chair to entertain a motion, which is of high privilege, that the House reject the nongermane matter covered by the point of order. It shall be in order to debate such motion for forty minutes, one-half of such time to be given to debate in favor of, and one-half in opposition to, the motion.

"(c) Not withstanding the final disposition of any point of order made under paragraph (a), or of any motion to reject made pursuant to a point of order under paragraph (b), of this clause, it shall be in order to make further points of order on the ground stated in such paragraph (a), and motions to reject pursuant thereto under such paragraph (b), with respect to other nongermane matter in the report of the committee of conference not covered by any previous point of order which has been sustained.

"(d) If any such motion to reject has been adopted, after final disposition of all points of order and motions to reject under the preceding provisions of this clause, the conference report shall be considered as rejected and the question then pending before the House shall be whether to recede and concur with an amendment which shall consist of that portion of the conference report not rejected. If all such motions to reject are defeated, then, after the allocation of time for debate on the conference report as provided in clause 2(a) of this Rule, it shall be in order to move the previous question on the adoption of the conference report."

The germaneness rule, like so many other rules, is not as absolute as it might seem. Bills and conference reports are called up under rules normally originating in the House Rules Committee, and, among other matters, these rules control germaneness. For example, in a vote on a military procurement bill returning from conference, the "rule" recommended by the House Rules Committee was as follows:

"H. RES. 601"

"*Resolved*, That upon the adoption of this resolution it shall be in order to consider the conference report on the bill (H.R. 9286) to authorize appropriations during the fiscal year 1974 for procurement of aircraft, missiles, naval vessels, tracked combat vehicles, torpedoes, and other weapons, and research, development, test, and evaluation for the Armed Forces, and to prescribe the authorized personnel strength for each active duty component and of the Selected Reserve of each reserve component of the Armed Forces, and the military training student loads, and for other purposes, and *all points of order against the said conference report are hereby waived.*" [Italics supplied.]

The rule was defeated on a rollcall vote. Thus the key vote was not on the conference report but on the rule, because, in the absence of a rule such as H. Res. 601 under which "all points of order against the said conference report are hereby waived," a call-up of the conference report would have been ineffective, since the nongermane amendments would each have been subject to a point of order.

There are many ins and outs in the interplay between legislation and rules in the House. Here it is sufficient to note that the House Rules prohibit nongermane amendments, but an individual rule (resolution) may waive points of order; and, while it is difficult in many cases to obtain such a waiver, it is not impossible. So the germaneness rule of the House typically does not deter the Senate from attaching nongermane riders to House legislation.

Another way out of the possible impasse created by the House germaneness rules is through separate votes on each nongermane amendment. In consideration of a recent conference report on a Treasury/Post Office appropriation bill the House conferees held their ground and came in with a conference report which compromised all germane questions and reported continuing disagreement on all amendments which would have been or had been subject to a point of order when the bill first was considered in the House. In this instance, some 51 amendments in disagreement were taken upon the House floor. In each case, the manager of the bill moved, for example, as follows.

"MOTION OFFERED BY MR. STEED"

Mr. STEED. 'Mr. Speaker, I offer a motion.'

"The Clerk read as follows:
'Mr. STEED moves that the House recede from its disagreement to the amendment of the Senate numbered 46 and concur therein.'
"The motion was agreed to.
"The SPEAKER. 'The Clerk will report the next amendment in disagreement.' " *

Conference Committee Consideration

Where there are minor differences between the House and Senate versions of a bill, one chamber will often accept the other's version without requesting a conference. But where one chamber has added important amendments to the other's bill and neither chamber is willing to accept the other's version, the only way for the bill to get to the President is by way of a conference committee.

Conference Committee and Conference Report

A conference committee is composed of representatives or managers from the Senate and the House who negotiate the differences in the two chambers' bills and who eventually produce, if all goes well, a conference report, which is generally a compromise bill with a chance of being accepted by both houses. A conference report (which is a bill, not a committee report) is accompanied by a statement of managers or a joint explanatory statement—the equivalent of a committee report. There are no minority views in the statement of managers.

Request for and Agreement to a Conference

Either chamber may request a conference on the provisions in dispute in a bill. The requesting chamber, however, must have physical possession of the "papers" (the bill with indorsements). Either chamber may of course agree to a conference.

The significance of being the requesting or agreeing chamber is that the *requesting* chamber acts last on the report and has the final say in approving or killing the report. The conference report is first sent to the agreeing chamber. If the agreeing chamber rejects the report, it can be sent back to conference by a majority vote. In contrast, if the requesting

---

* *Congressional Record*, p. H9082 (Daily Edition, 10/16/73).

chamber rejects the report after it has been approved by the agreeing chamber, the report is dead unless both chambers by concurrent resolution vote to send the bill back to conference.

Selection of Managers

In the Senate, the managers for a conference are elected by the full chamber, although the committee chairmen play the major role in selecting the conferees. In the House, conferees are officially selected by the Speaker; but, again, the committee chairmen exercise great influence. Generally, the managers of a bill include the chairman, the ranking minority member, and the senior members (both majority and minority) of the subcommittee of origin.

Open and Closed Conferences

The trend toward opening congressional meetings to the public reached a high point in the passage of S. Res. 9 in late 1975. Under the resolution, conference committee meetings must be held in public (assuming House concurrence) except when a majority of the conferees of either the Senate or the House vote in open session to close the conference for the day.

Authority of the Conferees—Matters in Disagreement

Both Senate and House floor managers have authority to negotiate only those matters in disagreement between the two Houses. The managers cannot introduce provisions into the committee report which are not germane to the matters in disagreement. But where the second chamber has amended the first chamber's bill by striking the entire contents thereof and by substituting its own measure, the conferees will be free to insert new provisions dealing with the same subject because there will be *total disagreement* between the two chambers.

The "strike and insert" technique is subject to vast—and frequent—abuse. Suppose one chamber seeks only to change one word in a 10-page bill. If it strikes out the one objectionable word and substitutes another word, then *only* that word is conferrable. But if, instead, the second chamber strikes out the *whole* text of the bill and substitutes its own bill, the *whole* bill is conferrable, even if the "new" bill is identical in all respects to the "original' bill except for that one word!

Once a conference report is written and submitted to the two Houses, it is not subject to amendment. Since the two chambers are faced with a take-it-or-leave-it situation, the Senate and House conferees ordinarily strike compromises they believe palatable to their respective chambers.

Presidential Action and Congressional Post-Veto Reaction

After a bill has gone through conference (if necessary) and has been approved by both chambers, it is enrolled and delivered to the White House. The President has 10 days within which to act on the bill. If the President signs the bill or fails to sign it within 10 days of delivery, the bill becomes law. If the President vetoes the bill, it is returned with a veto message to the chamber where it originated. If the Congress adjourns within the 10-day period, the President may refrain from signing the bill and thereby pocket veto the measure.

Congress can override a Presidential veto by a two-thirds vote of those present and voting in each house. If the veto is overriden, the bill becomes law; but if the override attempt fails, the bill dies.

PART II
POWER CENTERS IN CONGRESS

THE HOUSE

This manual is not a tract in political philosophy, and the analysis of power centers which follows in this and the next chapter is not an attempt to analyze or reconcile the relationship between what happens and what should happen in a democracy. I limit myself largely to how the Capitol Hill power structure functions for the information of those working on the Hill, or with the Hill. On occasion, I have not been able to resist the temptation to inject my own views of how it *ought* to work, but I believe those instances have been clearly identified (and can be discounted at the option of the reader). With this injunction in mind, we begin by examining the *de jure* and *de facto* power centers on Capitol Hill because any legislative plan not tailored to deal with such power centers may turn out to be worthless.

In the House more than in the Senate, unofficial or semi-official bodies not having any direct standing or status under applicable laws or rules may nonetheless constitute real and substantial centers of power. In theory, the only "laws" governing the Congress are the Constitution, statutes such as the Legislative Reorganization Act, and the rules of each chamber adopted by resolution in each chamber. But in practice, voting blocs have been developed, with varying degrees of formality and voting discipline. The most obvious of these, and the strongest, are the party caucuses.

The power premise of any unofficial or semi-official bloc is *voting discipline*, and this is particularly so if the voting bloc is the majority party caucus. Assume, for purposes of discussion, that the majority caucus includes 60 percent of the membership of the House. A vote within that caucus on an issue may divide 51 percent to 49 percent, and thus the "policy" of the majority is established by less than a majority of the House itself—51 percent of a 60 percent caucus is the vote of only 30.6 percent of the membership of the House. But if the caucus exerts universal discipline upon its membership, when an issue goes to the House floor, every member of the majority caucus (clearly a majority of the House) will vote for a decision reached in the caucus. In effect, then, by use of a caucus a small percentage of the House can control the House—and sometimes, though only rarely, it does.

Much of the discussion below focuses on the rules, procedures, and customs of unofficial or semi-official bodies such as the caucus. And principally upon such bodies within the *majority* party, because there is no way in which the majority of a *minority* party can exert the sort of power under consideration here.

As suggested above, I am not inclined to expand very much upon the ideological implications of caucus rule. One might consider, however, what the alternatives are (and have been). The power of the caucus in its current historical framework is an alternative to the power of individual leaders—the Speaker, the chairman of the Rules Committee, the chairman of the Ways and Means Committee, and the like. In this sense, caucus power is a democratization. Nonetheless, caucus rule is essentially undemocratic in a constitutional sense. Any time a majority of the majority—which results in less than a majority of the whole House—rules the House, the true majority is not at work. At the very least, the caucus system tends to block cross-party coalitions which might constitute an absolute majority of the House *but for* the exercise of voting discipline by the caucus.

One ought to keep in mind, however, that rarely has this sort of discipline been exerted on *substantive* issues. It seems to work absolutely on the election of committee chairmen and some purely procedural matters. It probably will work on the removal of a chairman who fails to abide by certain decisions of the caucus. It probably will not work on decisions of the caucus on particular measures, or amendments to particular measures, of a substantive nature.

Recent Reforms

During 1971-1975, procedural reforms in the House generally reduced the power of committee chairmen and increased the power of subcommittee chairmen, committee members, the Democratic Caucus, and the House leadership.

THE HOUSE

Criterion for Chairmanship

One important reform was the decision of the Democratic (majority) Caucus to subject committee chairmen to election by the Caucus ostensibly without regard to seniority. Of course, the Caucus has no power by statute or rule to elect a chairman, but the Caucus' designation of a member as a candidate for a chairmanship is tantamount to election, provided that, once the Caucus picks its committee chairmen, the party membership votes together on the floor to confirm the actions of the Caucus. The election of committee chairmen "ostensibly without regard to seniority" did in fact make a difference when the Caucus deposed three senior committee chairmen at the start of the 94th Congress.

"Choice" Committee Assignments

A second early reform was the change in the Democratic Caucus Rules limiting the number of committees on which a member could serve. This limitation provided more choice committee assignments to junior members.

Open Markups

In March 1973, H. Res. 259 was passed, providing, among other things, that meetings for the transaction of business, including markup sessions and voting on bills in executive session, would be open to the public, except when the committee or subcommittee, in open session with a quorum present, decided by rollcall vote to close the meeting to the public. In preparation for the 94th Congress, the Democratic Caucus decided that the vote to close a markup session must be taken on the day of the session and not sooner.

The Hansen Substitute (H. Res. 988)—Committees and Subcommittees

The most sweeping reforms were implemented in late 1974. On October 8 of that year, the House passed the "Hansen substitute" (a Democratic Caucus committee proposal) to the Bolling resolution (H. Res. 988, a measure drafted by a bipartisan select committee), thereby approving milder procedural reforms and less drastic committee jurisdictional changes than those contained in the Bolling resolution.

The Hansen substitute contained, among others, the following reforms:

- the requirement that committees with over 15 members (changed to 20 by H. Res. 5) establish a minimum of four subcommittees
- the requirement that committees with over 15 members (changed to 20 by H. Res. 5) establish an oversight subcommittee
- the increase in committee staff from six professional and six clerical employees to 18 professional and 12 clerical employees and the grant of control to the minority party of one third of those employees (subsequently changed to a committee staff total of 42, of which the minority will control 16)
- the grant of control to the minority of one third of the investigative funds used to supplement committee staffs (subsequently voided)
- the authorization of the Speaker to make dual or sequential referrals of bills to various committees, with the Speaker having the power to split bills and send parts to different committees
- the requirements of inflation impact statements in committee reports and statements in Appropriations Committee reports indicating any changes in existing law
- the requirement that Congress return in December of election years to prepare for the next Congress
- and the abolition of proxy voting (subsequently modified so that each committee decides whether to permit proxies; where permitted, proxies must be in writing to a particular congressman on a specific provision or amendments thereto, except for procedural matters on which general proxies are permitted).

December 1974 Democratic Caucus Rule Changes

The reforms of H. Res. 988 were followed in December of 1974 by important changes in the Democratic Caucus rules. The Caucus weakened the House Ways and Means Committee and its chairman by transferring that committee's power to make committee assignments to the Democratic Steering and Policy Committee and by increasing the size of Ways and Means from 25 to 37 members. The Caucus authorized the

Speaker to nominate all members of the Rules Committee for approval by the Caucus and required that all Appropriations subcommittee chairmen be elected by the Caucus. The Caucus also required that all committees have a Democratic two-to-one plus one majority. These and other reforms have resulted in power shifts in the House which have altered to some extent the process of passing a bill or amendment through the House.

Committees

Even though the Democratic Caucus and the leadership may have greater influence than the committees on broad matters of policy and politics, the committees are still the key centers for the day-to-day work of writing and reporting bills. To move a measure toward enactment, generally step one is to convince the chairman (or at least a member) of the pertinent committee or subcommittee to sponsor or cosponsor the measure. A bill introduced by a congressman *not* a member of the committee with jurisdiction is, in most cases, a sure-fire way to run up printing costs and nothing much else.

Chairmen of Full Committees

Before the recent reforms, full committe chairmen generally exercised unilateral and almost absolute *negative* power. A bill or amendment could ordinarily be buried by a chairman, acting alone. And under House procedures such as the germaneness rule and "closed rules," a committee chairman could exclude provisions from his bill, even on the floor.

But the Democratic Caucus rules (the Caucus' Standing Rules and the manual of the Caucus) now provide that full committee chairmen are nominated by the Committee on Committees (which in 1975 was the Democratic Steering and Policy Committee), and not necessarily according to seniority. The Caucus votes on all nominations. A secret ballot is taken if one fifth of those present at the Caucus meeting demand a secret vote. As noted above, this election procedure was utilized by the members of the 94th Congress to depose three senior chairmen. The shock waves from this action have apparently affected the surviving chairmen, who now seemingly try to operate by consensus and in accordance with the wishes of the Caucus.

Increases in the rights and powers of subcommittee chairmen have also lessened the once autocratic power of some full committee chairmen, as has the limitation on the number of subcommittee chairmanships a full committee chairman may hold. Yet despite the decrease in their power, the full committee chairmen are generally still important figures—indeed, still the *most* important figures—who influence legislation.

Subcommittee Chairmen

Under the present Caucus rules, the subcommittee chairmen have been strengthened relative to full chairmen and lately have been made more responsive to committee members. Instead of being selected by full chairmen, subcommittee chairmen are selected by a process in which Democratic committee members bid for subcommittee chairmanships in the order of full committee seniority or seniority on the subcommittee concerned, as the Democratic caucus on *the committee* determines. Any such bid is subject to the approval of a majority of those present and voting in the Democratic caucus *on the committee.* An exception to this procedure is the selection of Appropriations subcommittee chairmen, who must be approved by the full Democratic Caucus.

The Caucus rules provide that insofar as practicable full chairmen shall permit subcommittee chairmen to handle on the floor legislation that has been reported by subcommittees. The subcommittee chairman is entitled to select at least one staff member for the subcommittee, subject to the approval of a majority of the Democratic members of the full committee. Instead of the full chairman establishing the number and jurisdiction of subcommittees, the Democratic caucus of the committee will make those decisions.

The Caucus rules authorize each subcommittee to meet, hold hearings, and report bills, with the subcommittee chairman setting the meeting dates. Unlike previous practice in which a full chairman could bypass a troublesome subcommittee simply by not referring a particular bill to the subcommittee, the Caucus rules provide that all legislation shall be referred to the appropriate subcommittee within two weeks unless a majority of the Democrats on the full committee vote for full committee consideration. The Caucus rules also provide that each subcommittee shall have an adequate budget which shall be subject to the overall control not of the full chairman but of a majority of the Democratic caucus on the committee.

By having the power to call or not to call hearings on a bill, the subcommittee chairman holds both negative and positive power—he controls which bills will move and which will die. Of course, a subcommittee chairman is answerable to the Democratic members of the committee, and if strong interest is expressed by committee members in holding a hearing on a bill, the subcommittee chairman ordinarily will call a hearing.

Ranking Minority Members

The influence of a ranking minority member of a committee or subcommittee will generally result from the personal relationship between the ranking member and the chairman, as well as the leadership qualities of the ranking member which enable him to speak for and influence other minority members. The ranking member's power will also vary depending on whether the minority party controls the White House and whether the President has a sustainable veto power. The gain in minority control of staff under the Hansen substitute appears to have increased to a limited extent minority input into the legislative process.

Committee Members

The decrease in the full chairmen's power, the increase in the subcommittee chairmen's power, and the increase in the role of the Democratic caucus of the various committees has heightened the influence of individual committee members. Thus, a lobbyist interested in the passage of a measure now needs to pay somewhat more attention to obtaining the support of members of the committee (and subcommittee) with jurisdiction, not just the chairmen.

The Ways and Means Committee and the Rules Committee

Two of the most powerful committees in the House were and still are the Ways and Means Committee and the Rules Committee. Recent reforms have decreased the power of these two bodies, but they still continue as power centers. Ways and

Means, Rules, and Appropriations are still "exclusive" committees under the Democratic Caucus rules: No member of an exclusive committee may also serve on another "exclusive," "major," or "nonmajor" committee.

The great power of the Ways and Means Committee was somewhat reduced by a number of recent reforms. The Committee's power of assigning committee memberships was transferred to the Democratic Steering and Policy Committee, and a new chairman was elected to succeed the formerly powerful Wilbur D. Mills. The formerly cohesive and relatively conservative membership of the Committee was diluted by increasing the membership from 25 to 37. In addition, the Committee, which previously functioned only as a full committee, was required to establish at least four subcommittees.

The power of the Rules Committee was reduced by 1975 changes in the Caucus rules, which now provide that chairman and members of the committee are to be nominated by the Speaker and approved by the Democratic Caucus. The Caucus rules also provide that if, within four legislative days following notice by a chairman that he or she will seek a closed rule, 50 or more Democrats give notice that they wish to offer a germane amendment, the Rules Committee shall not act on the closed rule until the Democratic Caucus has decided whether the amendment should be allowed. In February 1975, the Caucus instructed the Democratic members of the Rules Committee to allow oil depletion allowance amendments to a Ways and Means tax bill, which eventually resulted in the repeal of that allowance for large companies. In former days, Wilbur Mills routinely would have obtained a closed rule, and if Mills' bill did not repeal the allowance, no floor amendments could have been offered to accomplish that objective.

Democratic Caucus—Power on Substantive Issues

Many of the important procedural reforms in the House were brought about by the Democratic (majority) Caucus. The combination of a large "liberal" freshman class with the House members of the Democratic Study Group produced enough votes to lessen the power of the full committee chairmen and to give individual members greater influence.

At the present time, it is still not clear (but probably

unlikely) that the Caucus will become "King Caucus," dictating positions which members must take on particular issues. On March 12, 1975, one day before a House committee was to vote on an Administration bill providing funds for military aid to Indochina, the Caucus adopted a nonbinding, sense-of-the-Caucus resolution opposing such funding. The committee voted to adjourn without taking action on the bill. Many members were disturbed by this action, and it appears that the role of the Caucus regarding particular substantive issues has yet to be fully defined.

The Leadership

The recent procedural reforms in the House have increased the power of the Speaker and his assistants. The Speaker's power of dual or sequential referral of bills and his power to split bills gives him influence over the passage of legislation. The Speaker's power to nominate the chairman and members of the Rules Committee gives him influence over that committee. The Speaker's position as chairman of the Democratic Steering and Policy Committee, which nominates the chairmen and members of other committees, gives the Speaker some influence over all House members. And the decrease in power of the committee chairmen has by comparison made the Speaker a more powerful figure.

Democratic Steering and Policy Committee

The Democratic Steering and Policy Committee is composed of the Speaker, the Majority Leader, the Caucus chairman, 12 members elected from 12 equal regions, and eight members appointed by the Speaker. For the 94th Congress, five of the eight appointees had to be the Whip and the four Deputy Whips; the Speaker was authorized to appoint one additional member to the Committee.

The Caucus rules state that the Steering Committee shall "make recommendations regarding party policy, legislative priorities, scheduling of matters for House or Caucus action, and other matters as appropriate to further Democratic programs and policies." In addition, the Steering Committee functions as the Committee on Committees, making nominations for committee chairmanships and memberships.

Some have referred to the Steering Committee as the executive committee of the Caucus. At least it has great potential influence, and it could serve as a power base for a Speaker seeking expanded power for himself.

Democratic Study Group

The Democratic Study Group (DSG) was a major force in bringing about the recent procedural reforms in the House. Organized in the late 1950s the DSG is a legislative coordinating and research organization consisting of "liberal" and "moderate" Democratic House members. The DSG evidently sees its primary function as mobilizing liberal strength on important issues. It also prepares research materials on issues before the Congress, conducts briefings for members and staff, and operates a whip system for key votes. And it has a campaign fund which provides financial and research assistance. But now that the procedural reforms which the DSG advocated have been implemented and its members have attained positions of power "inside" the congressional system, it remains to be seen whether the DSG will maintain its vitality as a source of influence or whether its former leaders will shift the focus of "liberal" power to their new institutional positions.

Other Groups

In addition to the institutional and political power centers mentioned previously, there exist groups which focus on promoting the welfare of a particular interest group. Examples which come to mind include, among others, the Black Caucus, the farm bloc, and the labor bloc, and the "Wednesday Clubs." The influence of any such group obviously depends upon the size of its membership and the moral or other influence it may have over its own members as well as over other less aligned members of the House.

THE SENATE

Unlike the House, the Senate has instituted relatively few recent changes in its power structure. Institutional power centers such as the chairmanships of the committees remain essentially unchanged, and semi-official or unofficial bodies like the Democratic Conference (equivalent to the Democratic Caucus in the House) and the Democratic Policy Committee presently appear to lack the renewed vitality of their counterparts in the House.

One reason for the fewer Senate reforms is the fact that only one third of the Senate's members are up for election at any one time. With greater continuity in membership, the Senate is less susceptible than the House to such freshmen-induced change as occurred in the House prior to the 94th Congress.

With fewer members, the Senate has had the luxury of conducting its affairs with relatively greater informality than the House. Rather than controlling floor debate by binding "rules" passed by a rules committee, the Senate uses unanimous consent agreements which are reached through negotiation. The relationships between the various power centers in the Senate, as, for example, between full committee and subcommittee chairmen, are controlled less by formal rules than by practice, tradition, and accommodation.

Reforms

Open Markups

Senate Rule XXV 7(b) was amended in 1973 to provide that meetings of the Senate's standing committees, other than hearings, would be open to the public except during closed sessions for bill markups, for voting, or when the majority of the committee votes for a closed session. Any closed session may be opened to the public by rule or by majority vote of the committee. Prior to the passage of S. Res. 9 in 1975, the

Senate's approach to open meetings contrasted with that of the House and resulted in more closed markups.

In July, 1975, the Senate Government Operations Committee reported out S.5, the "Government in the Sunshine Act." The bill, as reported, repealed Rule XXV 7(b) of the Senate's Standing Rules and provided that committee and subcommittee meetings in both the Senate and the House (excluding hearings, which in the Senate are covered by Section 112 (a) of the Legislative Reorganization Act of 1970, 2 U.S.C. § 190 a-1 (b)) shall be open to the public except in specifically enumerated situations. Title I of the bill was referred to the Senate Rules and Administration Committee because it affected Senate procedures. The Committee struck Title I from the measure and substituted an amended S. Res. 9, which provided that each committee could adopt its own rules on open meetings at the start of each new Congress. On November 5, 1975, the committee substitute was rejected by the full Senate.

S. Res. 9 as finally adopted by the Senate provides that each standing, select, and special committee or subcommittee of the Senate shall hold all of its meetings in public except when a majority of the committee or subcommittee votes in open session to close the meeting or set of meetings for not more than 14 days. The resolution provides that meetings can be closed only for matters which must be kept secret for national defense reasons, which relate to committee staff, which involve criminal or other charges, which reveal the identity of law enforcement agents or informers that should be kept secret, which reveal trade secrets or financial or commercial information if the law requires that the information be kept secret or if the government obtained the information on a confidential basis, or which reveal "matters required to be kept confidential under other provisions of law or government regulation."

S. Res. 9 also provides that conference committee meetings shall be public except when a majority of the conferees of either the Senate or the House vote in open session to close the conference for the day. All committees, including conference committees, must prepare a transcript of each meeting except when a committee majority votes otherwise. On the motion of a member which is seconded, a committee may meet privately to discuss whether a session should be closed, but a vote to close the session must be in public. A committee chairmen may close a meeting when the public audience is disorderly or engages in a demonstration. S. Res. 9 also permits radio and television coverage of open committee meetings in accordance with committee rules.

The Senate approval of S. Res. 9 was followed by the adoption of S. Res. 5, which requires that independent federal agencies hold most of their meetings in public. S. 5, the bill itself, was being considered by the House as this book went to press.

Staffing for Less Senior Senators

A second recent reform implemented by S. Res. 60 (94th Congress) provided increased staffing for less senior senators to aid them in meeting their committee responsibilities. The new staffers will be part of each senator's personal office, although they will have the responsibility of keeping up with committee matters and will have certain rights to information from the official committee staff. The staff increases will probably lessen to some extent the power of committee chairmen since they will give committee members a chance of keeping abreast of committee activities and of having a greater input into the legislative process.

Selecting Chairmen

Another potentially significant reform is the Democratic Conference's approval of secret balloting for committee chairmen when one fifth of the Conference so requests. The reform was not applicable to the selection of chairmen for the 94th Congress but will be applicable to any future selections. A secret ballot will be held two days after a successful request for it in order to give the chairmen time to organize resistance to any challenge.

Filibuster Reform

A hard fought battle was waged early in the 94th Congress to change the voting requirement for ending a filibuster from two thirds of the Senators voting and present to three fifths of all senators (60 senators). This procedural reform was eventually implemented and is treated in greater detail in the section on filibusters (see pages 64–65).

Committees

Without power transfers to entities like the leadership and the Democratic Conference as in the House, the Senate legislative committees are still *the* undiminished key legislative power centers. An interested member or lobbyist generally must convince both the full committee and the subcommittee chairmen to support or at least not to oppose the measure he is promoting. One way of getting a measure through committee is to convince a member of the committee (preferably a member of the pertinent *sub*committee) who has an interest in supporting the measure to sponsor it. This senator may then lobby the full and subcommittee chairmen to act on the proposal. If both chairmen are not persuaded of the merits of a measure, it will be almost impossible or at least most difficult to move a measure to the Senate floor for a vote. As in the House, a measure whose prime sponsor is not a member of the committee with jurisdiction will rarely see the light of day.

Chairmen of Full Committees

Full committee chairmen in the Senate generally have not had the supreme power which their House counterparts once had. A chairman's committee can be bypassed by referring a House-passed measure directly to the Senate floor (as was done with the 1975 Voting Rights Act). Since nongermane amendments are in order except for general appropriation bills, *any* senator thwarted by a committee chairman may offer *any* proposal as a floor amendment to almost *any* bill.

Yet, full chairmen in the Senate have great power. A full chairman can call committee meetings, thereby exercising the power to block or allow committee consideration of bills.* The chairman may refuse to refer a bill to a subcommittee, keeping the bill at the full committee level. Of course, if a

---

* The chairman's power to call (and to refuse to call) meetings has been circumscribed to a minor extent by Section 133(a) of the Legislative Reorganization Act of 1946, as amended, which provides that committees shall fix regular meeting days and that a special meeting shall be held when three committee members request such a meeting and a majority of the committee members support their request.

chairman abuses his referral power, the committee may intercede to stop the practice. The full chairman appoints subcommittee chairmen, although there are often enough subcommittees so that each majority committee member may chair one subcommittee. But full chairmen have been known to chair more than one subcommittee. And full chairmen also control staffing, determine who the floor manager of a bill will be, and greatly influence the selection of the conferees on a bill.

Subcommittee Chairmen

The two most important powers of the subcommittee chairman are the power to hold hearings on bills and the power to schedule subcommittee markups. The subcommittee chairman, in other words, has the power to move bills referred to his subcommittee or to let them die.

If a full chairman disagrees with a subcommittee chairman over a particular measure, the full chairman can subtly influence the subcommittee chairman through his power to appoint the latter and his control of staffing. But the decision to hold hearings is usually that of the subcommittee chairman, and much depends upon the personalities and the issues involved. In practice, impasses between full and subcommittee chairman rarely arise.

Ranking Minority Members

As with House ranking members, the influence of a Senate ranking member of a committee or subcommittee ordinarily depends upon the relationship of the ranking member and the chairman and upon the ranking member's ability to speak for and influence his minority colleagues on the committee. Whether the minority party controls the White House and whether the President has a sustainable veto will also affect the authority of ranking members.

Committee Members

Although not as important as a full or subcommittee chairman, a committee member still has influence, particularly in the Senate where every vote counts and nongermane floor amendments are always available alternatives. Committee members may sometimes influence chairmen to hold or not to hold hearings and markups, and no sponsor or lobbyist, if he is serious in his legislative purpose, should neglect trying to obtain the support of every possible committee member on both sides of the aisle.

The Majority Party

The Majority Leader

More influential than the institutional leaders of the Senate (the Vice President and the President Pro Tempere) is the Majority Leader. The Majority Leader is the key figure in moving the majority party's legislative program through the Senate. He has great influence over activities on the Senate floor, and he functions as a central source of information. The Majority Leader may influence members on particular bills, but whether he will do so depends upon the style of the particular Leader. For example, as Majority Leader, Lyndon Johnson played a very active and powerful role in passing legislation. His successor, Senator Mike Mansfield, appears more as a conciliator and guardian of the rights of individual Democratic senators. In fact, he rarely tries to influence members on a particular bill and, reportedly, generally will not see lobbyists except on matters which involve him as a senator representing the state of Montana.

In addition to being the Democratic floor leader, the Majority Leader chairs the Democratic Conference, the Democratic Policy Committee, and the Democratic Steering Committee (which makes committee assignments).

Democratic Conference

Unlike the House Democratic Caucus, the Democratic Conference in the Senate has not implemented important procedural reforms affecting the various power centers. One exception, though, may turn out to be the institution of a secret ballot for the election of committee chairmen when one fifth of the Conference so requests.

In addition to voting on committee chairmen, the Democratic Conference votes on the committee assignments of the Democratic Steering Committee and on the policy resolutions of the Democratic Policy Committee. But without voting discipline on the floor, policy resolutions are of very limited effect.

Democratic Steering Committee

The Democratic Steering Committee nominates the chairmen and members of the Senate's committees. These nominations are sent to the Democratic Conference and then to the floor for approval. The Majority Leader is the chairman of the Committee and appoints members. Membership on the Committee is assumed to provide some influence over other senators although its degree of influence in an individualistic body like the Senate is doubtful.

Democratic Policy Committee

During the administrations of Presidents Kennedy and Johnson, the Democratic Policy Committee functioned primarily to schedule bills for floor action. Since the Republican Presidency in 1969, the committee has set forth party positions on major issues on which substantial agreement exists among Democrats. The Committee meets regularly and by a two-thirds vote of those present passes draft resolutions or motions expressing party policy. Such resolutions may be reinforced by submission to the Democratic Conference for approval. The Committee's resolutions do not bind Democratic senators and do not infringe upon the jurisdiction of the legislative committees. Members of the Committee are selected by the leadership, subject to the concurrence of the Democratic Conference, on various bases, such as maintaining a balance of the geographic and philosophic representation of the Democratic members of the Senate.

Other Groups

As in the House, various influence groups (the farm bloc, the labor bloc, the "Wednesday Club," etc.) exist in the Senate. Their power depends upon the size of their memberships and the moral or other influence they may have over nonmember senators.

PART III
MONEY BILLS

FUNDING LEGISLATIVE PROGRAMS

While substantive legislation originating from various legislative committees almost always contains authorization for the appropriation of money, mere authorization produces no money in the Treasury or budget of the United States for the funding of a program. All that the authorization does is *permit* the appropriation of a sum of money *not more than* the amount authorized (and frequently it turns out to be a good deal less).

Within the limits set by authorizing legislation, the appropriations committees of the two Houses "fund" these authorizations. Appropriations bills, therefore, occupy a very central position in the programmatic legislation coming out of Congress (subject, however, to actions of the Budget Committees, etc., discussed at pages 104–106.)

Constitutional Priority of the House

While authorizing legislation originating in the substantive committees of the Congress may start in a committee of either House, the Constitution has been read as requiring that appropriations bills originate in the House of Representatives. Every appropriations bill has an "H.R." number on it, and each passes the House of Representatives before it is voted on in the Senate (although it may be subject to hearings and discussions in the Senate in anticipation of action by the House.)

The House priority on appropriations bills does not mean that specific appropriations which were not included in a House-passed bill cannot be added in the Senate. An appropriations bill, like any other bill, may be amended in the second chamber which considers it, and the differences can be resolved in conference. But the bill—the vehicle in which the appropriation is carried—always originates in the House.

The Relationship of Authorizations and Appropriations

There is a certain rationality in dividing the authorizing and appropriating responsibility in legislation—though it is frequently frustrating to members of the authorizing committees who are unable to secure adequate appropriations to fund their favorite programs. A member of the Labor and Public Welfare Committee, for example, may have concentrated for a long time on a single program—a manpower or health program—and have concluded that a proper and adequate funding of that program to achieve all the objectives of the authorizing legislation will require a stated number of dollars. He need not concern himself with the overall state of the United States budget in order to reach that figure. Indeed, the hearings and other information available to him in his capacity as a member of the authorizing committee would be inadequate for him to make *any* kind of a reasoned determination of the impact upon the budget of the United States of the particular dollar figure which he inserts in his authorizing legislation.

Appropriations bills, as opposed to single authorization bills, are not pinpointed to single programs authorized by single bills. They are rarely even pinpointed to a single department. Commonly one appropriations bill will fund all of the programs for several Cabinet departments. For example, the "Labor-HEW appropriations bill" will fund in a single measure all of the authorized programs administered by two entire Cabinet departments, plus a number of independent regulatory agencies.

Within each appropriations committee, there will be a number of subcommittees specializing in the programs in particular fields and under particular Cabinet departments. All too often the appropriations committees, whose membership is based chiefly on seniority, will not be composed of congressmen with interests akin to those promoting the legislation to be funded. And the tension between the advocates of programs and the expenditure-resisting senators on these appropriations committees and subcommittees has at times been explosive. On the other hand, it has sometimes been charged that programs which have popular appeal but which are known to be unworkable have been passed—with the support on occasion of the President—but with a tacit understanding that they would not be funded, leaving them as mere rhetoric and a program for disappointed expectations.

Open-Ended Authorizations

Conversely, there has in the past been a practice, which has diminished in recent years, of enacting substantive programs with "open-ended" authorizations, thereby leaving the entire funding process to the appropriations committee, without any numerical guidance from the committee which enacted the program. The typical language is: "There is hereby authorized to be appropriated such sums as may be appropriated for the operation of the program authorized by this act." Use of open-ended clauses is an easy way out for the authorizing committee, but it is an abdication of its responsibilities; and a number of senators in recent years have refused to vote for any authorizing legislation with such open-ended money authorizations included.

There are variants, however. On occasion, when a new program is created, it is anticipated that a number of fiscal years will be required before the program is fully structured, staffed up, and under way. Indeed, the program may begin half way through a fiscal year, when very little authorization is required. Accordingly, it is not at all uncommon in such circumstances to include in the authorizing language a small money authority for the first (partial) fiscal year, a slightly larger one for the second, with increases in the third and fourth—and *then* an open-ended authorization for fiscal years thereafter. The final authorization has the advantage of keeping the program in existence, subject to adequate appropriations, and of not requiring the Administration to seek renewal of the authorizing legislation before appropriations can be passed. On the other hand, it has the disadvantage of foregoing an automatic legislative oversight which would result from the demand for a new authorizing bill after a stated period of time.

Continuing Resolutions *

In recent years, to a greater or lesser extent depending upon the calendar situation, Congress has failed to pass the

---
* This section may become increasingly obsolete under the new Congressonal Budget Act (see pages 103–106.)

necessary appropriations bills by the start of a fiscal year. Congress, of course, runs on a calendar year convening in January. The executive branch, on the other hand, has operated on a fiscal year with its appropriation legislation expiring at the end of June. This has meant that, at the start of a new Congress (every other year), Congress has had only six months to pass all its appropriations bills; otherwise, on July 1, some branches of the Federal Government will run out of money, just about entirely. As a result of the lapse of appropriations at the end of June, it has become a familiar practice for Congress to pass "continuing resolutions" permitting the affected departments to spend, for a brief period of time, money at the same rate as authorized in the previous year under appropriations just expired. In the early 1970s the practice became so common that a number of departments went through a substantial part of their fiscal years operating only under continuing resolutions.

"Continuing resolutions" are *laws*, not mere concurrent resolutions of two Houses of Congress—they must be passed by the House and the Senate, and require the signature of the President. Typically, however, they are framed as "joint resolutions" rather than as "bills."

Special Parliamentary Conditions Applying to Appropriations Bills

The House has long had a "rule of germaneness" under which, if amendments are allowed at all, the amendments to a bill must be germane to the subject matter of the bill itself. The Senate, on the other hand, has never had a rule of germaneness, unless it is imposed on an ad hoc basis by a unanimous consent agreement or order (see page 66).

There is an exception* in the Senate to which a rule of germaneness has always applied under the Senate's own rules, and that is appropriations bills. This prevents, for example, the addition of a State Department appropriation to a bill reported from the Senate Appropriations Committee dealing with Labor-HEW funding.

---

* Another exception involves amendments voted after cloture has been adopted.

One of the strictures imposed by parliamentary procedure beside the rule of germaneness is the rule that "legislation" in an appropriations bill is subject to a point of order. That is to say, the appropriations bill itself cannot restructure the program which it is funding. But there are ingenious devices to get around the foregoing rule, the most common of which is to attach a condition to the expenditure of the money being appropriated. The Parliamentarians have their own rules of thumb to determine whether such conditions should be deemed "legislation" in appropriations bills or not. By and large, the principal rule of thumb is a determination as to whether the condition inserted in the bill requires that a person in the executive branch of government *make a qualitative determination* instead of merely counting. If it gives him any discretion, it is legislation.

It should be understood that these parliamentary restrictions are merely openings to a point of order: If no one objects, all kinds of substantive legislation can be added to an appropriations bill. And if someone does object, a point of order, even if sustained by the chair, can be overruled by a vote of the entire body. Indeed, the point of order can be avoided altogether by the familiar technique, often employed by authors of nongermane amendments, of raising a "question of germaneness" *before* a point of order is ruled on, and asking for a vote on the question of germaneness. This puts the question to a vote of the full Senate *without* a prior ruling of the presiding officer. While the ruling of the presiding officer on the point of order could be appealed to the full Senate in any event, the prior posing of a question of germaneness gets the issue to a vote and gives the proposer of the "nongermane" amendment an opportunity to have his colleagues vote *for* the amendment without being forced to vote *against* the prior ruling of a colleague—the presiding officer. And, while the amendment may technically be nongermane, once the majority vote "for" the sponsor on the question of germaneness, the amendment satisfies the rule and is no longer subject to a point of order.

Thus, a variety of devices are available to accomplish "legislation on an appropriations bill." Such legislation is not ordinarily enacted, but it can be, if the members decide to go that way.

THE FEDERAL BUDGET

The President's Budget

The development of the President's budget, before it is submitted to Congress, is the result of a complex interaction between the President's office, the Office of Management and Budget, and the various government agencies and departments. After development of guidelines within the Administration, each agency and department formulates its budget, which is submitted to the Office of Management and Budget and thence to the President. Individual agency budgets are modified at the White House level and then integrated into one document, which constitutes the overall federal budget, for submission to Congress. It should be noted here that the federal budget is not an authorization to do anything. It is a program, subject to congressional authorization and appropriation.

Congress' Pre-1974 Response to the President's Budget

Prior to the Congressional Budget and Impoundment Control Act of 1974 (which will be fully implemented in 1976), Congress never voted on the President's budget as a whole. Rather, it made individual authorizations for individual programs and made appropriations within the limits of those authorizations.

The only Capitol Hill committee which attempted to address itself directly to the budget as a whole was the Joint Economic Committee, consisting of members of both Houses, which annually held hearings on the President's budget. But the Joint Economic Committee never had legislative jurisdiction to *do* anything about the budget except talk about it.

The General Accounting Office and its chief, the Comptroller General, were of little assistance to the Congress on the budget; but of course the General Accounting Office was not responsible for the budget as such. It was, and still is, re-

THE FEDERAL BUDGET   103

sponsible for monitoring the *execution* of spending laws on behalf of Congress, seeing to it that money is not expended in violation of specific appropriations and authorizations of Congress.

The Impoundment Controversy

In early 1973, a considerable controversy arose over whether or not the President had the obligation to spend up to the limits of congressional appropriations, as distinguished from his obligation *not* to spend monies in excess of those limits. The controversy arose over the President's practice of "impounding" (refusing to spend) funds authorized and appropriated by Congress for programs with which the President either disagreed or at least took issue as to the amount appropriated.

The President, on his side, argued that he had the obligation to impound funds, because only he and the Office of Management and Budget had an overview of the entire budget system, whereas Congress appropriated and authorized money piecemeal, without regard for the total funds appropriated in a fiscal year and the effect that such appropriations might have on the fiscal soundess of government.

In a nutshell, the issue was what content to give to the adage "Congress holds the purse strings." The Congress took the position that the power of the purse meant the right both to prevent the expenditure of money and to compel the expenditure of money. The President, it seems, took the position that the purse power merely involved the right to pull the string and shut off the money, but not to open the purse and force expenditure. The courts have generally agreed with Congress' position. The Congress dealt with the impoundment problem as well as other budget difficulties by passing the Congressional Budget and Impoundment Control Act of 1974.

Congressional Budget and Impoundment Control Act of 1974

The Congressional Budget and Impoundment Control Act of 1974 is designed to provide Congress with the procedures, organization, and information necessary to detemine (and control) each year how much money the government has, how much it should take in, and how much it should spend. The Act has created certain entities which may alter the "money bill" terrain heretofore dominated by the taxing and appropriations committees of Congress.

Budget Committees

The Act creates a Senate Budget Committee (which presently has 16 members) and a similar House committee (with 23 members). The committees are to function as the focal points for all information and analyses relating to the formulation of fiscal policies and budget priorities. Membership in the House Committee is on a rotating basis, while membership on the Senate committee is permanent. Thus, the Senate committee very likely will become the more influential of the two committees.

It remains to be seen how much power the two budget committees will accrue as they interact with their older and more powerful relatives, House Ways and Means, Senate Finance, House Appropriations, and Senate Appropriations. The principal functions of the new committees and their related entities are explained below.

Congressional Budget Office

The Act establishes a Congressional Budget Office (CBO) with a director and deputy director appointed for a four-year term by the Speaker of the House and the President Pro Tem of the Senate. The CBO will assist the Budget Committees and provide information and services on the budget to other committees and members of Congress. One of the prime functions of the CBO will be to analyze the budget proposals of the Office of Management and Budget (the executive branch's budgetary arm).

Change in the Fiscal Year

The Act changes the beginning of the federal fiscal year from July 1 to October 1, effective October 1, 1976. The change is designed to eliminate one of the most serious budgetary problems of the Congress—having to run the country on continuing resolutions from July until the appropriations process is completed—by giving Congress enough time (in theory) to complete its work on the budget before the new fiscal year begins.

Timetable for Development of the Congressional Budget

Under the Act's provisions, a detailed timetable is established for the development of a congressional budget and for the completion of congressional action on budget matters.

In brief, the timetable is as follows:

November 10	President submits current service budget.
January 18 (or 15 days after Congress reconvenes)	President submits his budget.
March 15	Budget Committees receive budget reports from other congressional committees.
April 1	CBO reports to Budget Committees.
April 15	Budget Committees report out first concurrent budget resolution.
May 15	Congressional committees report bills and resolutions authorizing new budget authority.
May 15	Congress completes action on first budget resolution.
Seven days after Labor Day	Congress completes action on bills and resolutions providing new budget authority and new spending authority.
September 15	Congress completes action on second concurrent budget resolution.
September 25	Congress completes action on reconciliation bill or resolution, or both, implementing second concurrent budget resolution.
October 1	Fiscal year begins.

As under prior law, the President is required to submit his budget to Congress 15 days after Congress reconvenes in January. In addition, the President must submit to Congress a current service budget by November 10 of the previous year. The current service budget will show estimated expenditures and proposed appropriations as if all existing programs and activities were to be carried on for the ensuing fiscal year at existing levels with no policy change.

Congress' first budget resolution (by May 15) will establish overall spending levels and recommended subtargets for functional categories as well as appropriate levels and projected and desirable surpluses and debts. The second budget resolution (by September 15) will either restate or change the target of the first budget resolution in light of the most recent economic data and congressional actions on individual spending and revenue measures. If it is necessary for congressional actions on appropriations and taxing measures to be reconciled with the second budget resolution, Congress may not recess for more than three days until a reconciliation bill has been enacted.

Impoundments

The Act limits the President's ability to impound funds. In addition to deleting the "other developments" clause of the Anti-Deficiency Act (which was used to justify many impoundments), the Act requires the President to request and both houses of Congress to pass a recision bill in order for the President to terminate or cancel a program or to delay the obligation of a one-year appropriation to the end of the fiscal year in which it is available.

The Act also delegates to the President a limited authority to defer the obligation of appropriated funds for a period not to exceed the expiration of the fiscal year in which they are deferred. The President must notify Congress that he proposes to defer funds, and the deferral will be subject to the disapproval of either chamber by adoption of an impoundment resolution. If either chamber passes an impoundment resolution, the President is required to make the funds available for obligation.

PART IV

NONLEGISLATIVE ACTIVITIES IN CAPITOL HILL OFFICES

THE STRUCTURE OF A CONGRESSMAN'S OFFICE

A congressional office has a personality all its own. Its character is to a large degree an extension of the personality of the individual member who occupies it. Variations in offices are much greater in the Senate than in the House because there are more variables in the Senate—staffs are much larger and senators have a much larger number of committee and subcommittee assignments. Since the variations are important, what follows is more true for senators than for representatives.

If one would draw a flow chart of authority, or table of organization, for an executive agency or a business, one would place a single box at the top for the President (or director, or Cabinet member) and under that a small number of boxes for Vice President (or Assistant Secretaries, etc.) and under those a larger number of boxes for various subsidiary offices, and so on down to the "line" assignments. This flow chart would form a pyramid of authority, with decisions made at the top and executed at the bottom.

The structure of a legislative office is, however, quite the opposite. If one sees the principal executive power of a legislative office as being exercised in the act of voting, which cannot be delegated, then there is very little to "execute" there.

True, much can be written in a senator's or representative's name—letters which go out over his signature though he never sees them; speeches and press releases which are mailed out well in advance of delivery; telephone calls made by staff in the name of the senator or representative, though the member does not necessarily know the call is or has been made; and so on. Still, the only significance of these letters, speeches, telephone calls, and other communications lies in the fact that they *purport* to emanate from the senator or representative himself. *No one cares* what a staff member thinks except to the extent that he speaks *for* his senator or representative, or to the extent that he is understood to have the senator's or representative's "ear" so that his advice may be expected to be taken.

Accordingly, if one were to draft an organization chart of a large staff for a senator or representative, one might, to a certain extent, have a pyramid, but that would be only for ministerial tasks—with secretaries and file clerks responsible to professional staff members, who in turn are responsible to the senator or representative. But when it comes to *substantive* acts and *decision making*, the actual structure of the office is a wheel, with the senator or representative at the hub and staff as spokes about him, each staff member giving advice and taking instructions.

How can such a system work? It would be unworkable in the executive sense, but if one views the function of a legislator in terms of his own priorities—which involve efficiency to some extent, but primarily involve "being right" even at the expense of efficiency—the wheel structure is the only one which is possible.

The foregoing excludes certain nonlegislative functions—casework, answering the mail, proper scheduling of appointments, "ombudsman" functions, and so on—where efficiency may indeed be a central question. But in a purely legislative sense, it takes very little efficiency to cast a vote—the problem is to be "right."

Staff Breakdown

Senators typically have much larger staffs than representatives, and among senators staff sizes vary greatly according to the size of the state from which the member is elected. On the House side, on the other hand, congressional districts are more nearly of uniform size; and so staffs of individual representatives tend to be about the same size—normally a few professional staff members and a half dozen clerks at most.

But in either case, a senior senator or a senior representative who has achieved either a ranking minority position or a chairmanship of a committee or subcommittee can greatly augment his operation once he obtains the appointive power over positions on committee payrolls. Ordinarily the chairman of a committee appoints all the majority staff of that committee; and the ranking minority member appoints the minority staff—in each case subject to the willingness of either to permit second-ranking members or chairmen of subcommittees to appoint their own staff members.*

Very frequently, moreover, staff members appointed to committee payrolls serve dual functions. In addition to performing responsibilities assigned to them in their capacity as staff members of a committee, professional staff members and even clerical staff members perform a great many functions which are, arguably, personal to the senator or representative who is their patron. The result is that it is frequently impossible to determine from looking at a directory who the key staff member is for a particular senator or representative on an issue in which an outsider is interested. The best way to find out is to ask the administrative assistant of the senator involved.

The most obvious "titles" on a senator's or representative's staff are: administrative assistant, legislative assistant, personal secretary, caseworker, and press secretary. And on the committee staffs there are "professional staff members" (who often use the title "counsel" or "minority counsel" when they are lawyers) and clerical staff members.

Administrative Assistants

By custom, the chief of staff of a senator or representative is called the administrative assistant, and there is ordinarily one such person on any member's staff. The "AA" traditionally has two principal roles—chief of staff and principal political advisor. When a senator or representative runs for reelection, most frequently his AA turns out to be the campaign manager.

From a lobbyist's point of view the AA may not be the most knowledgeable staff person on any particular subject—indeed, he is frequently the least knowledgeable. *And yet many lobbyists believe that the AA is the only person to see. Why?* Because the AA has the senator's or representative's ear—he sees the member every day, and his suggestions are

---

* The House Democratic Caucus Rules guarantee that a subcommittee chairman shall be entitled to select at least one staff member.

most likely to be accepted. A specialist on the staff, on the other hand, may be the person nominally in charge of a particular piece of legislation or a particular matter; but his influence with the representative or senator, the number of times he sees the "boss," and his ability to get things done in a hurry may be very limited.

Another principal function typically under the control of an AA is handling endorsements and political clearances of executive branch appointments—that is, letters from a senator or representative to the President or another official of the executive branch of government endorsing a particular candidate for appointment to a high-level position. Finally, an AA may be the key person for a reporter who wants the "inside" story on something confidential going on in a representative's or senator's office.

Legislative Assistants

Legislative Assistants (LAs), as their name implies, supposedly are responsible for all facets of a senator's or representative's legislative activity. However, depending upon the degree of confidence which a representative or senator has in his administrative assistant and legislative assistant, the LA may or may not be the "top legislative staff" in a Capitol Hill office. That is to say, many AA's are purely political, or purely administrative, or purely press, but they may have little or nothing to do with legislation. If so, then when a lobbyist contacts a representative's or senator's LA, he has seen the top legislative staff member. On the other hand, some AA's "skim off" the critical legislative issues; and in those cases, seeing the LA without also seeing the AA may be insufficient.

But while the LA is supposed to deal solely with legislative matters, he seldom stops there. The LA is concerned with the drafting of bills, amendments, and the like for the member and also with keeping the member informed on issues and legislation proposed by other members which may be of concern. Yet inevitably an LA has, at the very least, regular contact with the departments and agencies downtown that have a direct interest in pending legislation. Indeed, the LA's contact downtown may be at a much higher level than the contact regularly made by lower level caseworkers and clerical staff. Accordingly, if a constituent is seeking to exert congressional pressure upon an executive agency, even though routine matters would be handled by a caseworker, a better route may turn out to be through the LA. (Of course, an even better route may turn out to be through the AA, if the AA is in regular contact with the top political officials in the agency or department).

I make these comments, hopefully, without any invidious or insidious overtones with respect to such matters as "improper influence" or the like. It is of course possible for a representative or senator to exert improper influence upon a political official in the executive branch (and vice versa). But it is equally possible for the legislator, through staff or directly, to exert completely proper influence in the public interest upon an official of the executive branch. The "ombudsman" congressional function has, as far as I know, never been considered improper, and is in fact essential to the effective operation of government.

Other duties of the LA include acting as the conduit either to muster cosponsors for the boss' bill, or, conversely, to influence his boss to cosponsor legislation with a colleague. An LA's contact with other members' staffs and with others interested in various pieces of legislation (such as lobbyists) is usually quite extensive, so that the LA can be effective for his boss by being informed of the legislation and its implications.

If the member has no committee staff under his patronage, the LA must also attend committee hearings, brief the member on the issues involved, prepare questions for the member to ask at the hearing, write testimony if the member is a witness, and even correct the member's testimony in the transcript. Finally, in addition to answering constituent mail, the LA is usually called upon to write speeches which the senator or representative gives to various groups on legislative and even nonlegislative issues.

A Congressman's Personal Secretary

The *Congressional Directory* lists the home addresses of only two members of a representative's or senator's staff—the AA and the personal secretary—and with good reason. As staff members go, while the AA is supposed to be the "boss" of the office, actually in most Capitol Hill offices the member's personal secretary is the one who really knows the most about what the member is doing.

Knowledge is power. To the extent that the personal secretary makes and keeps the congressman's appointment schedule, the secretary can make it possible (or almost impossible) for a visitor "to get to see the boss." The personal secretary can get messages through in detail with a sense of urgency, can slow them down or bury them, or can remind the member of the importance of something, or can ignore it.

One ought to keep in mind that a senator's or representative's office is deluged with phone calls and mail. Almost all of it is addressed to the member himself. Ninety-nine percent of it does not, ordinarily, get through to the member. And while the mail room personnel and other staff assistants may exercise varying degrees of filtering power, it is the congressman's personal secretary who ordinarily has the final say as to what gets through.

No generalities will work. Unless one learns otherwise, one ought to treat the representative's or senator's personal secretary with exactly the same respect and attention that one would give the congressman himself. To do otherwise is an exercise in Russian roulette.

Caseworkers and Secretaries

Most congressional offices have more caseworkers and secretaries than any other type of employee, and it is sometimes difficult to distinguish one from the other. A caseworker is a person assigned to solve particular constituent problems. Generally, he will refer each problem to the appropriate agency or department, under the cover of the senator's or representative's name (through the use of a simple "buck slip"*). When matters are resolved, the caseworker will inform the constituent of the outcome.

A secretary, on the other hand, is purely clerical by definition but may have other responsibilities, including case-

---

* Typically a buck slip forwards the constituent's inquiry to the department or agency, asks what's going on, and requests return of the original letter with a report in duplicate so that the member can forward one copy back to the constituent.

work, besides clerical work. Many a caseworker or secretary on the Hill will claim possession of the real power in the office, and to some extent this is so. The sheer volume of minor (nonlegislative) matters coming through a congressional office inevitably leads to delegation of most routine matters to caseworkers and secretaries.

How is it possible for a clerical assistant to exert any influence upon a high official or any other official of the executive branch? It is simply a question of credibility. To the extent that an official of the executive branch believes that a Capitol Hill clerical assistant "has the ear" of a member and in fact speaks for the member, to that extent the executive branch must respond substantially as it would respond to a phone call directly from the member. And while there are many clerical assistants on Capitol Hill who have not established that kind of credibility, there are many who have. The trick is to know one from the other.

Press Secretary

The power of a representative or a senator is often largely the power of the press. What, after all, does a congressman do for a living, and for his constituents? He votes, but that takes less than 1 percent of his time, and one vote is at most a tiny fraction of a consensus. The rest of the time the member *speaks*, writes, argues, and voices his feelings or those of his constituents. But to whom? His choice is between talking to the wall, to a few colleagues, or to the world. And his power is assured in large part by the size of his audience, which in turn is controlled by his ability to "make news." That is his press secretary's job.

The press secretary's functions are difficult to describe and vary from office to office. At the least he is responsible for the preparation and timely issuance of press releases This involves knowing what statements have news potential, writing them up in a way which is likely to "make news," and getting them to the press gallery and into the hands of appropriate reporters well before press deadlines. It involves deciding whether a release should be made generally to the press, or whether a particular reporter should be given an "exclusive" in the hope of building up a larger story in one journal. It involves deciding what paragraph and what line should be extracted from the text of a speech and moved "up top" or put into a special "cover release" to attract press interest. And it involves talking with reporters and correspondents on a daily basis, and giving them material "on background" or "off the record" to build up interest in a story.

It also involves certain negative functions—making sure that erroneous and adverse stories are killed (if killing is possible); making sure that, if there is to be an adverse story, at least the "other side of the story" is also printed; and knowing how to keep confidences without giving an inquiring reporter an adverse inference. And all of this involves knowing just about everything which is going on in the office, in order to make sure that erroneous adverse stories are not given out by accident.

Suppose, for example, the boss gets a case—some agency in the executive branch has taken a course of action which, if publicized, would generate a public sense of outrage against the agency involved. A mere letter from a representative or senator may or may not produce a result. On the other hand, a press release, well written and properly timed, followed up by a few key calls to columnists and network newsmen, can create a full-scale blast. Not every case deserves such press coverage, and not every case is even helped by it. But there are some cases where it works, provided the timing is right, the press secretary is effective, and the case is appropriate for "human interest stories" or the like.

Relationship of Committee Staff to Personal Staff

With very few exceptions, all jobs on Capitol Hill are "patronage jobs."* Every committee staff member is appointed by some representative or senator, serves at his or her pleasure, and can be removed without notice and without cause. Nonetheless, the rules provide that a committee staff member is supposed to do nothing but committee business. But what is committee business? The term has been interpreted expansively.

If a member is senior enough to appoint committee staff—ordinarily the chairman, subcommittee chairman, or

---

* By and large, legislative counsel and a few other jobs have been professionalized to the point where it may be impossible to identify a "patron."

ranking minority member *—he is going to receive a goodly volume of mail on the matters which are in the jurisdiction of his committee or subcommittee. Dealing with that mail, though it is nothing but constituent mail, is typically deemed "committee business" and the senator's or representative's office almost universally refers it to committee staff, if it is "their" committee staff. The same may be said of casework related to the committee's jurisdiction. Stretching a point, the same may be said of speech writing and preparation of press releases, maintenance of files, and a whole panoply of other matters which have to do, at least arguably, with the committee's jurisdiction.

But that is not all. Chairmen of committees have been known to give a particular committee staff member many other responsibilities, some having nothing whatever to do with the committee's jurisdiction. It may violate the rules, but it happens. From the outsider's point of view, it is enough to know that it does happen and that such happenings have to be taken into consideration when attempting to track down the person on a particular congressman's staff who is responsible for a particular matter or type of matter.

Officers of the Congress and Other Capitol Hill Officials

Secretary of the Senate and Clerk of the House

The Secretary of the Senate is an elected patronage position over which the majority leadership has great influence. The Secretary is responsible for, among other things, officially certifying bills passed by the Senate, maintaining the Senate Disbursement Office, and maintaining a wide variety of other files and functions, such as overseeing the bill clerks, etc.

The Clerk of the House is also elected; and as in the Senate, the majority party leadership has much to say about the candidate. The Clerk's duties are similar to those of the Secretary of the Senate.

---

* Under S. Res. 60 passed in the 94th Congress, junior senators will have the right to appoint some staff members (depending upon the committees involved) to help them in meeting their committee responsibilities. But most committee staff will remain under the control of senior members.

Sergeant at Arms

The Sergeant at Arms in the House is elected and is primarily responsible for maintaining order in the House areas of Capitol Hill. The Capitol Hill police on the House side are under the command of the House Sergeant at Arms. The Sergeant at Arms of the Senate, also elected, is in charge of Senate pages, Senate post office employees, and various other service employees, in addition to controlling the Capitol Hill police on the Senate side.

House Doorkeeper

The Doorkeeper of the House is in charge of House pages, doorkeepers, barbers, and other service employees. His job is also an elected patronage position.

Majority and Minority Secretaries in the Senate and the House

The Secretary for the Majority in the Senate is generally nominated by the Majority Leader and is approved by the Democratic Conference and the full Senate. The Secretary is in charge of majority activities in the Senate Chamber and the Democratic cloakroom, supervises telephone pages and messengers, and sets up meetings of the Democratic Conference and the Democratic Steering Committee. The Secretary also maintains the records of the Conference and the Steering Committee. Serving as a liaison between the majority leadership and Democratic senators, the Secretary briefs members on votes, keeps them informed of upcoming legislation, takes polls on important votes when directed, and monitors Senate appointments to boards and commissions.

The duties of the Senate Minority Secretary and the House Majority and Minority Secretaries are similar to those of the Senate Majority Secretary.

The Secretary to the Majority and the Secretary to the Minority are both information centers and *power centers*—particularly in the sense that "knowledge is power" in any legislative body. These two officials are frequently on (or near) the floor during debates and even during (or just before) votes, and exert considerable influence and guidance, since they are the repository and conduit of so much information held by the leadership of each party.

The Structure of a Congressman's Office

Parliamentarian

The Parliamentarians in both the House and the Senate are selected by the Senate and House leaders, but have traditionally served for extended periods of time. Their functions and influence are described elsewhere (see pages 36–38).

Legislative Counsel

In both the House and the Senate, Legislative Counsel offices are maintained to provide members with expert assistance in drafting legislation. Their functions are described elsewhere (see pages 24–25).

Librarian of Congress and Congressional Research Service

Appointed by the President and confirmed by the Senate, the Librarian of Congress oversees an organization with vast informational resources. Among other functions, the Librarian maintains the Congressional Research Service. At the request of members or staff the Service will analyze problems, prepare research papers, and put together lists and summaries of publications relevant to a problem. The Service has experts in many fields available for consultation. But expertise and time availability will vary, and one ought never to assume that a mere request to the Service for research on a minor but complex matter will necessarily produce a thorough result.

CONGRESSIONAL RELATIONSHIPS WITH THE ADMINISTRATION, LOBBYISTS, AND CONSTITUENTS

Dealing With Executive Departments and Independent Agencies

Every office on Capitol Hill is regularly in contact with a wide variety of executive departments and independent agencies. Such contact is the normal grist of the casework mill. Within this daily contact are both risks and opportunities.

Normal Relationships

Normal casework relationships between a Capitol Hill office and an executive department are based simply on inquiries about the status of cases. The effect of an inquiry varies from department to department; but in many departments the mildest inquiry about the status of a case at least insures that the case will not be treated capriciously, because the file in which the case is kept will be "flagged" to indicate that there has been a congressional inquiry, and, therefore, that whatever disposition is made, the representative or senator must be informed of it. Most congressional inquiries result in nothing more than such flagging, yet they are worthwhile if only to preclude or deter capricious or arbitrary executive action.

The next step beyond a mere status inquiry would be an expression of position on the pending matter. And beyond that, varying degrees of intensity can be applied, up to and including a visit by the congressman himself to the head of an agency or department, or a personal letter, or a phone call.

Ethical Considerations—Quasi-Judicial Matters

A clear distinction should be made between ordinary or political executive decisions on the one hand and quasi-judicial ones on the other. And a clear distinction should be made between an expression of interest in a matter of policy and an expression of interest in a case.

On a matter of policy the representative or senator may wish to write a letter to the Cabinet officer involved and release it to the press. On a case he would not normally wish to do that, though if the case raises an important issue of policy he might.

On the other hand, just as an *ex parte* communication to a judge concerning a pending case ordinarily is considered improper, so such a communication to quasi-judicial agencies such as the NLRB, the SEC, the FTC, the FPC, and so on ought also to be considered improper. But one ought to distinguish between the lawyers in a quasi-judicial agency and the "judges." Somewhat more freedom is allowable in dealing with lawyers in an agency (in its Office of General Counsel) who are in actuality "advocates" before their own agencies. The same might be said of the Justice Department with respect to pending enforcement matters.

Generally, a member of Congress probably should avoid contact with an executive agency unless he is willing to have it reported on the 7 o'clock network news. Beyond this injunction, the subtleties of executive/congressional relationships are too complex to cover in this brief manual.

Conflicts of Interest

As suggested above, casework always involves the risk of a conflict of interest. An unknowing caseworker could very well go to bat for a constituent without realizing that the constituent was a large contributor to the boss' last campaign. On the other hand, why should such a contributor be deprived of the normal ombudsman services available to all constituents? The dilemma requires some resolution, and the answers are as varied as the personalities in the House and Senate.

Conflict of interest is also possible when it comes to voting on legislation. A senator or representative with a financial interest in oil may vote on the depletion allowance. Suppose his interest coincides with the interest (as he perceives it) of his state: Should he not then vote the interest of his state?

But if he does, is he in a conflict-of-interest position? (Indeed, has he been "bribed"?) The same problem comes up for members who are practicing lawyers with clients who have an interest in legislation.

My own view (which I can say with confidence is *not* the majority view) is that a member ought to "recuse" himself and not vote on any matter in which he has a financial interest, or an attorney-client interest, or any other kind of personal interest, *even if* he perceives the interest of his state to coincide. An appearance of propriety is ordinarily more important than the outcome of a particular vote. In the long run, however, the better course would be to dispose of all such conflicts of interest in order not to deprive the state of an important vote. Of course opinions vary; and as yet the Congress has done precious little about adopting ethical rules to govern these situations.

Congress and Federal Jobs

Federal Employment Patronage

The system by which congressmen are involved in the appointment of federal executive officials varies from year to year, from administration to administration, and from case to case. Despite a good many exceptions, however, there are certain general guidelines. Obviously, any member may write to the President or any other federal official recommending anyone for a federal appointment. Ordinarily and by custom, an initial recommendation to fill an important vacancy ought only to be made by a representative or senator for the state or district where the job applicant resides. This is simply a matter of courtesy. A senator from Idaho may have a candidate from Idaho for a particular job and would feel a bit miffed on discovering that a senator from Utah was pushing another Idaho resident for the same job. It is not inappropriate, however, for a representative or senator to write letters of support for the appointment of nonresidents who have already been recommended by their own representative or senator.

"Patronage" in the congressional context is a term without precise meaning. Obviously it means appointing people. Political supporters, friends, and constituents all seek the support of their congressmen. Some such support is proper; some is improper and even may be unlawful.

"Advice and Consent" Nominees, Clearance

"Advice and consent" nominees go only to the Senate, where an elaborate system of Senate courtesy and even veto powers is involved. For example, take the category judgeships. Ordinarily the Senate Judiciary Committee will kill an appointment of any federal district judge strongly opposed by either senator from the state in which that judge will sit. Other advice and consent appointments may be killed by senators from the state of residence of the appointee. And even non-advice and consent appointments to regional posts in a senator's or representative's state may sometimes be killed by an individual member.

But objectionable advice and consent nominations ordinarily do not go that far before being stifled. Most administrations (the Nixon Administration was a notable exception) have gone through an elaborate system of "clearances" and courtesy calls to assure that even a member opposed to a particular appointment will not go as far as to put his foot down and attempt to defeat the nomination or confirmation of a particular constituent.

Lobbying

The Need for Lobbyists

While the legislative histories of the various statutes governing the practice of lobbying are full of case histories suggesting that somehow "lobbying" is a dirty word, there is nothing inherently underhanded or evil (or even unnecessary) about the practice of lobbying, provided it is conducted properly. Indeed, if lobbying were outlawed altogether, Congress might well be operating in a vacuum.

No representative or senator can be an expert in everything, and even the experts in Congress cannot remain constantly "current" on every aspect of their specialties. Nor can representatives or senators be expected to know how individual segments of the electorate or the economy feel about specific issues, unless persons representing those segments come forth and speak up. Ralph Nader, the most articulate spokesman in recent times for consumer interests, has called not for the abolition of lobbying but for its expert practice by consumers on their own behalf.

Registration Under the Lobbying Act

All that currently is required to set up as a lobbyist (and one hesitates to use the word "required" when the requirement is honored most often in its breach, ordinarily without penalty) is registration under the Lobbying Act. The text of the standard form used for registration under the Act is set forth in Appendix 2 at the back of this manual.

The registration form is a simple one. Very little disclosure is required*—simply the fact that a lobbyist is lobbying, what he is lobbying for, how much he is being paid for it, and what expenses are involved. Frequently, a lobbyist performs a number of services for his client—not all of which are reportable under the act—so that only a portion of his "fee" is disclosed. I sometimes wonder, in fact, whether some of the disclosures made in these registrations are not really to the advantage of the lobbyist; for lawyers (expert lobbyists, very often) are prohibited from most "advertising." And what better lawful way is there for a Washington lawyer to "advertise" than to "register" for dozens of clients under the Lobbying Act and have those registrations reprinted in the *Congressional Record* by the tens of thousands of copies?

Congressional Offices Seeking Lobbyists' Advice

A congressional office frequently does not await a call from a lobbyist but takes the initiative in order to find out what a particular group within the congressman's constituency would like to have done. Liberal senators on the Senate Labor Committee regularly contact the lobbyists for the AFL-CIO when a labor issue comes up, for example. Or they call the NAACP when a civil rights issue comes up. More business-oriented senators regularly call such organizations as the Chamber of Commerce of the United States and the National Association of Manufacturers on business issues.

---

* As this manual goes to press, Congress is considering amendments to lobbying disclosure legislation. The Senate passed S.2477 on June 15, 1976, and the House was marking up a companion bill, H.R. 15.

Pros and Cons of Accepting a Lobbyist's Assistance

The services of lobbyists include not only their position statements but also a good deal of technical expertise and assistance which can be obtained at no cost to a senator or representative, provided the member accepts those services with a critical eye. For example, suppose a senator or representative decides that he wants to deal with the problem of abandoned automobiles—suppose that he wants to create added incentive for their proper scrapping and recycling. No more logical place could be found for initial assistance in drafting that legislation, in making sure that the scheme is workable, than the trade association representing people in the recycling business. That trade association, in turn, can call its own technical and legal specialists to draft the legislation, write speeches in support of it, and collect economic data to support its necessity and workability.

But there are risks. The members of a lobbying group almost inevitably will have as their principal concern the success of their own businesses. They may come up with a workable plan, a plan profitable for the members of the group. But the plan also may incur a cost greatly in excess of what might be necessary to solve the problem some other way.

So there ought to be an interchange—contact with trade associations, consumer groups, officials of the interested departments and agencies of the executive branch of government, and others—before a draft of legislation and supporting economic data can be put together in a way which has a decent chance of passage and of being sensible and effective after enactment. No matter what formula is used for putting this package together—and there are risks in any formula—lobbyists are an essential ingredient of the legislative system.

The Lobbyist's Expertise: "Know Who" and "Know-How"

Who is an effective lobbyist? What does he know, and know how to do, that an "amateur" does not? The answer falls into two categories—"know-how" and "know who."

Any clever and careful person with an infinite amount of time can do anything a lobbyist can. But a skilled lobbyist, unlike an amateur, can accomplish a great deal in a very short period of time, and can avoid many mistakes possibly very damaging to the course of legislation he supports.

There is no directory which can point the average citizen in the direction of the congressman or the key staff member involved with a particular piece of legislation. The *Congressional Directory* lists the members of various committees and subcommittees in order of seniority, but it does not show which congressman has the controlling or highest interest in a particular type of legislation. Even less likely than such a directory would be a directory showing the ideology or the historical inclinations of a particular senator or representative so that a lobbyist could readily find a member of Congress who might be induced to introduce and support a particular amendment. No such directory could possibly be current enough or detailed enough to be an adequate guide. But a real "directory" of this sort does exist in the minds of individual lobbyists who spend a regular and substantial amount of time dealing with the Congress on specific issues and, ordinarily, with specific members of specific committees, so that they know, almost instinctively, which representatives and which senators on which committees can be expected to vote which way on a particular issue. In this sense, *the lobbyist is the "directory."* The amount of time that he can save an amateur simply in the search for the proper representative or senator is substantial.

Even if a written directory were available, many representatives and senators have substantial staffs (particularly in the Senate), and the real "approach" is made not so often (or only) to the representative or senator, but rather (or also) to the staff member responsible for the amendment in question.

There is at least one privately published, and very useful, staff directory which gives the titles and biographies of key staff members on Capitol Hill.* But even this directory gives little information as to the substantive legislative responsibilities of particular staff members. Indeed, when it comes to committee staff, one cannot determine from this directory who the "patron" of a particular staff member is. One might assume that the majority staff members of a committee are

---

* See Charles B. Brownson, *Congressional Staff Directory 1975* (Alexandria, Va.: The Congressional Staff Directory, 1975). See also *Bimonthly Directory of Key Congressional Aides* (Washington: The Congressional Monitor), initiated in 1975.

appointed by the chairman, and the minority staff members are appointed by the "ranking minority member" of a particular committee. But this is not always the case. The second and third senior members, or the chairmen of the various subcommittees, frequently have been allocated a certain number of professional staff members who work on legislation of interest to them, but who are not ordinarily identified as being responsible to them. Accordingly, the experienced lobbyist once again is the "directory" in the sense that he can be expected to know, or at least to know how to find out quickly, who the key staff member on a particular issue in a particular committee is and who the staff member's patron is. And knowledge such as this goes stale almost daily.

Once having determined whom to see, one turns next to the question of "know-how"—knowing how to approach a subject matter with a particular senator, representative, or staff member, and knowing which type of appeal and what type of supporting data and technical assistance would be most likely to get results. A few examples come quickly to mind. Some congressmen are particularly insistent upon technical expertise and supporting statistical and other information, and a lobbyist approaching such a congressman will come armed with that sort of material. Other representatives or senators are particularly concerned about particular segments of their own constituencies whose support has been weakening, and a lobbyist hoping to exploit this fact will come accompanied by a representative of such a group, if that group supports the position which the lobbyist wants to be taken, or at least will come in with information explaining how the representative or senator may use this position politically in appealing for the support of that group.

In an encounter with a lobbyist, the staff member or senator or representative is very likely to ask a certain series of obvious questions. How does the Administration feel about it? How does the chairman feel about it? How will the other members of my own party on this committee feel about it? The skilled lobbyist knows who the "opinion leaders" on a particular committee are and who the "followers" are, and he will not approach the followers first because he knows that if he can recruit the opinion leaders on a committee the followers can be won over later.

Or the lobbyist can take a different tack entirely. If the Administration can be induced to "ask for" something similar in an appropriate message to Congress (either the State of the Union message, or a specific legislative message), the lobbyist's game may be half won, particularly when the same party controls both the White House and the Congress.

An inventive lobbyist can devise "trade-offs" which will (or may have a chance to) appeal to the very opponents who might seem least accessible. Frequently a lobbyist can inject himself into an ideological confrontation between two ideologically warring senators, and, by suggesting a compromise between them not on the basis of ideology but on the basis of the particular technical program, gain the support of both sides—making his proposal almost invincible.

Finally, the lobbyist must be a parliamentarian, as well as a specialist in the field for which he is lobbying. He may find no support for his proposal on the committee which ordinarily would be expected to have jurisdiction of it. But if he knows his parliamentary ABC's, on occasion he may be able to find a basis for plugging his idea into the jurisdiction of some other committee where he *will* be able to find substantial support. The simple rephrasing of an idea, the changing of a few words in the preamble of a bill, or a slight shift in emphasis may induce referral of a measure to a committee other than the one which ordinarily would receive it, and may lodge the measure in the hands of a chairman and a committee membership much more sympathetic than the obvious one (and, conversely, a mistake in phrasing or emphasis may torpedo an idea which, if properly framed, would encounter no difficulty at all).

All these things the skilled lobbyist can do. His functions, viewed ministerially, are neither inherently "good" nor inherently "bad." But they are procedurally necessary, one way or the other, if Congress is to operate in a manner which is not completely isolated from the realities of national life and the various contexts in which our national and economic life is conducted.

The Congressman's Appointment Calendar

Appearances, speeches, appointments, and the like involve some of the most time-consuming work of a congressional office, and frequently have little to do with the business of legislation. A busy senator can arrange, and sometimes does arrange, 20 or 30 appointments in a single day. They are nothing but courtesy calls—strung out at five minute intervals in the afternoon—and are frequently held in a large reception room just off the Senate floor while the Senate is in session (or in the Speaker's Lobby off the House floor).

A busy member can give two or three speeches in a single day if they are all in Washington or all in a particular city he is visiting. He can arrange to have his photograph taken with literally hundreds of constituents, week after week, and that can be the best sort of publicity; for these photographs end up framed on walls all over his state, and some very important walls at that.

But there are risks. Obviously, the congressman does not want to turn loose upon the world (and perhaps upon the press) a photograph in which he is smiling and shaking hands with a top leader of an organized crime syndicate. And yet without careful screening of appointments, flash bulbs will pop from out of nowhere and the deed is done.

The same is true of speeches. A member is invited to give a speech at a meeting of some organization with a high-sounding name and a large number of members, only to discover later to his dismay that the organization has endorsed all sorts of positions which he opposes; that it discriminates against blacks, women, and Chicanos; or is on some kind of a subversive list.

There is not space here to detail the variety of systems which can be used to screen and control appearances, appointments, photographs, and endorsements; but many screening methods are available. The point is, a member's contacts with the public present both risks and opportunities.

But then, the very nature of politics is the combination of risks and opportunities. To take no risks is to seize very few opportunities and to accomplish very little. The question is: *What* risks, and for *what* opportunities? It is a question of *judgment*. But *judgment*, after all, is what we elect when we send someone to Capitol Hill. And good judgment, combined with skill, is the essential political ingredient.

APPENDIX 1
Resume of Congressional Activity—Ninety-Third Congress

United States of America — PROCEEDINGS AND DEBATES OF THE 93ᵈ CONGRESS, SECOND SESSION

Vol. 120   WASHINGTON, FRIDAY, JANUARY 10, 1975   No. 181

Daily Digest

RÉSUMÉ OF CONGRESSIONAL ACTIVITY OF NINETY-THIRD CONGRESS

	FIRST SESSION January 3 through December 22, 1973			SECOND SESSION January 21 through December 20, 1974		
	Senate	House	Total	Senate	House	Total
Days in session	184	175	..	168	159	..
Time in session	1,084 hrs., 13'	790 hrs., 18'	..	1,068 hrs., 09'	813 hrs., 04'	..
Congressional Record:						
Pages of proceedings	23,962	12,060	36,022	22,643	12,777	35,420
Extensions of Remarks	..	..	8,461	..	..	7,517
Public bills enacted into law	100	145	245	168	236	404
Private bills enacted into law	7	43	50	25	48	73
Bills in conference	5	3	..	6	6	..
Bills through conference	22	48	..	39	77	..
Measures passed, total	726	717	1,443	838	807	1,645
Senate bills	280	105	..	246	176	..
House bills	177	260	..	292	288	..
Senate joint resolutions	37	16	..	36	24	..
House joint resolutions	30	37	..	17	17	..
Senate concurrent resolutions	26	16	..	30	27	..
House concurrent resolutions	36	38	..	42	46	..
Simple resolutions	140	245	..	175	229	..
Measures reported, total	*676	*630	1,306	*748	*733	1,481
Senate bills	326	36	..	307	91	..
House bills	152	347	..	232	394	..
Senate joint resolutions	31	1	..	26	9	..
House joint resolutions	12	14	..	8	14	..
Senate concurrent resolutions	19	7	..	18	14	..
House concurrent resolutions	20	24	..	16	19	..
Simple resolutions	116	201	..	141	192	..
Special reports	33	40	..	27	65	..
Conference reports	13	78	..	41	125	..
Measures pending on calendar	20	39	..	9	86	..
Measures introduced, total	3,334	14,194	17,528	1,793	6,901	8,694
Bills	2,860	12,150	..	1,400	5,540	..
Joint resolutions	184	870	..	80	312	..
Concurrent resolutions	62	412	..	65	286	..
Simple resolutions	228	762	..	248	763	..
Quorum calls	26	185	..	34	190	..
Yea-and-nay votes	594	307	..	544	325	..
Recorded votes	..	234	..	..	212	..
Bills vetoed	5	5	10	6	23	29
Vetoes overridden	..	1	1	..	4	4

*These figures on measures reported include all placed on calendar or acted on by Senate even if there was no accompanying report. In the Senate 664 reports were filed during the first session and 763 in the second session; while the House filed 748 in the first session and 918 in the second session.

APPENDIX 1

D 1428   CONGRESSIONAL RECORD — DAILY DIGEST   *January 10, 1975*

DISPOSITION OF EXECUTIVE NOMINATIONS

These tables account for all nominations submitted to the Senate by the President for confirmation.

FIRST SESSION
January 3 through December 22, 1973

Army nominations, totaling 21,200, disposed of as follows:

Confirmed	19,987
Unconfirmed	1,212
Withdrawn	1

Navy nominations, totaling 18,740, disposed of as follows:

Confirmed	18,740
Unconfirmed	0

Air Force nominations, totaling 20,410, disposed of as follows:

Confirmed	20,409
Unconfirmed	1

Marine Corps nominations, totaling 4,483, disposed of as follows:

Confirmed	4,480
Unconfirmed	3

Civilian nominations, totaling 3,247, disposed of as follows:

Confirmed	3,201
Unconfirmed	37
Withdrawn	9

Summary

Total nominations received	68,080
Total confirmed	66,817
Total unconfirmed	1,253
Total withdrawn	10

SECOND SESSION
January 21 through December 20, 1974

Army nominations, totaling 17,706, disposed of as follows:

Confirmed	17,703
Unconfirmed	•
Withdrawn	1
Returned**	2

Navy nominations, totaling 17,887, disposed of as follows:

Confirmed	17,885
Unconfirmed	1
Returned**	1

Air Force nominations, totaling 19,556, disposed of as follows:

Confirmed	19,490
Unconfirmed	66

Marine Corps nominations, totaling 7,614, disposed of as follows:

Confirmed	5,887
Unconfirmed	1,727

Civilian nominations, totaling 3,541, disposed of as follows:

Confirmed	3,472
Unconfirmed	22
Withdrawn	4
Returned**	43

Summary

Total nominations received	66,304
Total confirmed	64,437
Total unconfirmed	1,816
Total withdrawn	4
Total returned**	46

**Returned to the President during the October-November recess in accordance with Senate Rule XXXVIII.

APPENDIX 2
Lobbyist Registration Form*

FILE ONE COPY WITH THE SECRETARY OF THE SENATE AND FILE TWO COPIES WITH THE CLERK OF THE HOUSE OF REPRESENTATIVES:
This page (page 1) is designed to supply identifying data; and page 2 (on the back of this page) deals with financial data.

PLACE AN "X" BELOW THE APPROPRIATE LETTER OR FIGURE IN THE BOX AT THE RIGHT OF THE "REPORT" HEADING BELOW:

"PRELIMINARY" REPORT ("Registration"): To "register," place an "X" below the letter "P" and fill out page 1 only.

"QUARTERLY" REPORT: To indicate which one of the four calendar quarters is covered by this Report, place an "X" below the appropriate figure. Fill out both page 1 and page 2 (on the back of this page) as many additional pages as may be required. The first additional page should be numbered as page "3," and the rest of such pages should be "4," "5," "6," etc. Preparation and filing in accordance with instructions will accomplish compliance with all quarterly reporting requirements of the Act.

Year: 19........

REPORT
PURSUANT TO FEDERAL REGULATION OF LOBBYING ACT

	QUARTER			
P	1st	2d	3d	4th

(Mark one square only)

NOTE on ITEM "A."—(a) IN GENERAL. This "Report" form may be used by either an organization or an individual, as follows:
 (i) "*Employee*."—To file as an "employee," state (in Item "B") the name, address, and nature of business of the "employer." (If the "employee" is a firm [such as a law firm or public relations firm], partners and salaried staff members of such firm may join in filing a Report as an "employee.")
 (ii) "*Employer*."—To file as an "employer," write "None" in answer to Item "B."
(b) SEPARATE REPORTS. An agent or employee should not attempt to combine his Report with the employer's Report:
 (i) Employers subject to the Act must file separate Reports and are not relieved of this requirement merely because Reports are filed by their agents or employees.
 (ii) Employees subject to the Act must file separate Reports and are not relieved of this requirement merely because Reports are filed by their employers.

A. ORGANIZATION OR INDIVIDUAL FILING
1. State name, address, and nature of business.
2. If this Report is for an Employer, list names of agents or employees who will file Reports for this Quarter.

NOTE on ITEM "B."—*Reports by Agents or Employees.* An employee is to file, each quarter, as many Reports as he has employers; except that:
(a) If a particular undertaking is jointly financed by a group of employers, the group is to be considered as one employer, but all members of the group are to be named, and the contribution of each member is to be specified; (b) if the work is done in the interest of one person but payment therefor is made by another, a single Report—naming both persons as "employers"—is to be filed each quarter.

B. EMPLOYER—State name, address, and nature of business. If there is no employer, write "None."

NOTE ON ITEM "C."—(a) The expression "in connection with legislative interests," as used in this Report, means "in connection with attempting, directly or indirectly, to influence the passage or defeat of legislation." The term 'legislation' means bills, resolutions, amendments, nominations, and other matters pending or proposed in either House of Congress, and includes any other matter which may be the subject of action by either House"—
(b) Before undertaking any activities in connection with legislative interests, organizations and individuals subject to the Lobbying Act are required to file a "Preliminary" Report (Registration).
(c) After beginning such activities, they must file a "Quarterly" Report at the end of each calendar quarter in which they have either received or expended anything of value in connection with legislative interests.

C. LEGISLATIVE INTERESTS, AND PUBLICATIONS in connection therewith:

1. State approximately how long legislative interests are to continue. If receipts and expenditures in connection with legislative interests have terminated, place an "X" in the box at the left, so that this Office will no longer expect to receive Reports.
2. State the general legislative interests of the person filing and set forth the *specific* legislative interests by reciting: (a) Short titles of statutes and bills; (b) House and Senate numbers of bills, where known; (c) citations of statutes, where known; (d) whether for or against such statutes and bills.
3. In the case of those publications which the person filing has caused to be issued or distributed, in connection with legislative interests, set forth: (a) description, (b) quantity distributed, (c) date of distribution, (d) name of printer or publisher (if publications were paid for by person filing) or name of donor (if publications were received as a gift).

(Answer items 1, 2, and 3 in the space below. Attach additional pages if more space is needed.)

4. If this is a "Preliminary" Report (Registration) rather than a "Quarterly" Report, state below what the nature and amount of anticipated expenses will be; and if for an agent or employee, state also what the daily, monthly, or annual rate of compensation is to be. If this is a "Quarterly" Report, disregard this Item "C" and fill out Items "D" and "E" on the back of this page. Do not attempt to combine a "Preliminary" Report (Registration) with a "Quarterly" Report.

State or Territory
_____ } ss:

AFFIDAVIT

I, the undersigned affiant, being duly sworn, say: (1) That I have examined the attached Report, numbered consecutively from page 1 through page _____ and the same is true, correct, and complete as I verily believe. (Be sure to fill in number of last page.)

[If the Report is for an individual, strike out paragraph "2."] ← (2) That I am _____ of the above-named organization, for whom this Report is filed, and that I am authorized to make this affidavit for and on behalf of such person.

[Print or type name below signature] (Signed) _____ Affiant
(Typed)

Subscribed and sworn to before me on _____, 19____

[Print or type name below signature] (Signed) _____ (Official authorized to administer oaths)
(Typed)

Issued 6-4-58 by the Secretary of the Senate and the Clerk of the House of Representatives. (Superseding Form issued 1-1-51.)

---

*As this manual goes to press, Congress is considering amendments to lobbying disclosure legislation. The Senate passed S. 2477 on June 15, 1976, and the House was marking up a companion bill, H.R. 15.

APPENDIX 2

NOTE on ITEM "D."—(a) IN GENERAL. The term "contribution" includes *anything of value*. When an organization or individual uses printed or duplicated matter in a campaign attempting to influence legislation, *money received* by such organization or individual—for such printed or duplicated matter—is a "contribution." "The term 'contribution' includes a gift, subscription, loan, advance, or deposit of money, or anything of value and includes a contract, promise, or agreement, whether or not legally enforceable, to make a contribution"—§ 302 (a) of the Lobbying Act.

(b) IF THIS REPORT IS FOR AN EMPLOYER.—(i) *In General.* Item "D" is designed for the reporting of all receipts from which expenditures are made, or will be made, in connection with legislative interests.

(ii) *Receipts of Business Firms and Individuals.*—A business firm (or individual) which is subject to the Lobbying Act by reason of expenditures which it makes in attempting to influence legislation—but which has no funds to expend except those which are available in the ordinary course of operating a business not connected in any way with the influencing of legislation—will have no receipts to report, even though it does have expenditures to report.

(iii) *Receipts of Multi-purpose Organizations.*—Some organizations do not receive any funds which are to be expended solely for the purpose of attempting to influence legislation. Such organizations make such expenditures out of a general fund raised by dues, assessments, or other contributions. The percentage of the general fund which is used for such expenditures indicates the percentage of dues, assessments, or other contributions which may be considered to have been paid for that purpose. Therefore, in reporting receipts, such organizations may specify what that percentage is, and report their dues, assessments, and other contributions on that basis. However, each contributor of $500 or more is to be listed, regardless of whether the contribution was made solely for legislative purposes.

(c) IF THIS REPORT IS FOR AN AGENT OR EMPLOYEE.—(i) *In General.* In the case of many employees, all receipts will come under Items "D 5" (received for services) and "D 12" (expense money and reimbursements). In the absence of a clear statement to the contrary, it will be presumed that your employer is to reimburse you for all expenditures which you make in connection with legislative interests.

(ii) *Employer as Contributor of $500 or More.*—When your contribution from your employer (in the form of salary, fee, etc.) amounts to $500 or more, it is not necessary to report such contributions under "D 13" and "D 14," since the amount has already been reported under "D 5," and the name of the "employer" has been given under Item "B" on page 1 of this report.

D. RECEIPTS (INCLUDING CONTRIBUTIONS AND LOANS)

Fill in every blank. If the answer to any numbered item is "None," write "NONE" in the space following the number.

Receipts (other than loans)

1. $--------- Dues and assessments
2. $--------- Gifts of money or anything of value
3. $--------- Printed or duplicated matter received as a gift
4. $--------- Receipts from sale of printed or duplicated matter
5. $--------- Received for services (e. g., salary, fee, etc.)
6. $--------- TOTAL for this Quarter (Add items "1" through "5")
7. $--------- Received during previous Quarters of calendar year
8. $--------- TOTAL from Jan. 1 through this Quarter (Add "6" and "7")

Loans Received—"The term 'contribution' includes a . . . loan . . ."—§ 302 (a).

9. $--------- TOTAL now owed to others on account of loans
10. $--------- Borrowed from others during this Quarter
11. $--------- Repaid to others during this Quarter
12. $--------- "Expense Money" and Reimbursements received this quarter.

Contributors of $500 or More (from Jan. 1 through this Quarter)
13. Have there been such contributors?
Please answer "yes" or "no": _____ ←
14. In the case of each contributor whose contributions (including loans) during the "period" from January 1 through the last day of this Quarter, total $500 or more:
Attach hereto plain sheets of paper, approximately the size of this page, tabulate data under the headings "Amount" and "Name and Address of Contributor"; and indicate whether the last day of the period is March 31, June 30, September 30, or December 31. Prepare such tabulation in accordance with the following example:

Amount	Name and Address of Contributor ("Period" from Jan. 1 through _____, 19____)
$1,500.00	John Doe, 1621 Blank Bldg., New York, N. Y.
1,785.00	The Roe Corporation, 2511 Doe Bldg., Chicago, Ill.
$3,285.00	TOTAL

NOTE on ITEM "E."—(a) IN GENERAL. "The term 'expenditure' includes a payment, distribution, loan, advance, deposit, or gift of money or anything of value and includes a contract, promise, or agreement, whether or not legally enforceable, to make an expenditure"—§ 302 (b) of the Lobbying Act.
(b) IF THIS REPORT IS FOR AN AGENT OR EMPLOYEE. In the case of many employees, all expenditures will come under telephone and telegraph (Item "E 6") and travel, food, lodging, and entertainment (Item "E 7").

E. EXPENDITURES (INCLUDING LOANS) in connection with legislative interests:

Fill in every blank. If the answer to any numbered item is "None," write "NONE" in the space following the number.

Expenditures (other than loans)

1. $--------- Public relations and advertising services
2. $--------- Wages, salaries, fees, commissions (other than Item "1")
3. $--------- Gifts or contributions made during Quarter
4. $--------- Printed or duplicated matter, including distribution cost
5. $--------- Office overhead (rent, supplies, utilities, etc.)
6. $--------- Telephone and telegraph
7. $--------- Travel, food, lodging, and entertainment
8. $--------- All other expenditures
9. $--------- TOTAL for this Quarter (add "1" through "8")
10. $--------- Expended during previous Quarters of calendar year
11. $--------- TOTAL from January 1 through this Quarter (add "9" and "10")

Loans Made to Others—"The term 'expenditure' includes a . . . loan . . ."—§ 302 (b).

12. $--------- TOTAL now owed to person filing
13. $--------- Lent to others during this Quarter
14. $--------- Repayments received during this Quarter

15. *Recipients of Expenditures of $10 or More*

In the case of expenditures made during this Quarter by, or on behalf of, the person filing: Attach plain sheets of paper approximately the size of this page and tabulate data as to expenditures under the following headings: "Amount," "Date or Dates," "Name and Address of Recipient," "Purpose." Prepare such tabulation in accordance with the following example:

Amount	Date or Dates—Name and Address of Recipient—Purpose
$1,750.00	7–11: Roe Printing Co., 3214 Blank Ave., St. Louis, Mo.—Printing and mailing circulars on the "Marshbanks Bill."
$2,400.00	7–15, 8–15, 9–15: Britten & Blatten, 3127 Gremlin Bldg., Washington, D. C.—Public relations service at $800.00 per month.
$4,150.00	TOTAL

APPENDIX 3

Standing Rules of the Senate*

Ninety-Fourth Congress

RULE I [1]

APPOINTMENT OF A SENATOR TO THE CHAIR

1. In the absence of the Vice President, the Senate shall choose a President pro tempore. [1.1]
[Jefferson's Manual, Sec. IX.]

On Mar. 12, 1890, the Senate agreed to the following:
Resolved, That it is competent for the Senate to elect a President pro tempore, who shall hold the office during the pleasure of the Senate and until another is elected, and shall execute the duties thereof during all future absences of the Vice President until the Senate otherwise order. (S. Jour. 165, 51-1, Mar. 12, 1890.)

2. In the absence of the Vice President, and pending the election of a President pro tempore, the Secretary of the Senate, or in his absence the Chief Clerk,[1] shall perform the duties of the Chair. [1.2]
[Jefferson's Manual, Sec. IX.]

3. The President pro tempore shall have the right to name in open Senate, or, if absent, in writing, a Senator to perform the duties of the Chair; but such substitution shall not extend beyond an adjournment, except by unanimous consent. [1.3]
[Jefferson's Manual, Sec. IX.]

4.[2] In event of a vacancy in the office of the Vice President,[3] or whenever the powers and duties of the President [1.4]

---

*Selected provisions taken from U.S., Congress, Senate, Committee on Rules and Administration, STANDING RULES OF THE UNITED STATES SENATE AND PROVISIONS OF THE LEGISLATIVE REORGANIZATION ACTS OF 1946 AND 1970 RELATING TO OPERATION OF THE SENATE, March 7, 1975. In the original, footnotes are numbered beginning with 1 on each page. In the following excerpts, only substantive footnotes have been included, and while the original footnote numbering has been retained, pagination differs.

shall devolve on the Vice President, the President pro tempore shall have the right to name, in writing, a Senator to perform the duties of the Chair during his absence; and the Senator so named shall have the right to name in open session, or in writing, if absent, a Senator to perform the duties of the Chair, but such substitution shall not extend beyond adjournment, except by unanimous consent.

[Jefferson's Manual, Sec. IX.

On Jan. 4, 1905, the Senate agreed to the following:
Resolved, That whenever a Senator shall be designated by the President pro tempore to perform the duties of the Chair during his temporary absence he shall be empowered to sign, as acting President pro tempore, the enrolled bills and joint resolutions coming from the House of Representatives for presentation to the President of the United States. (S. Jour. 47, 58–3, Jan. 4, 1905.)

[2]

RULE II

OATHS, ETC.

The oaths or affirmations required by the Constitution and prescribed by law shall be taken and subscribed by each Senator, in open Senate, before entering upon his duties.

OATH REQUIRED BY THE CONSTITUTION AND BY LAW TO BE TAKEN BY SENATORS UNDER RULE II

I, A B, do solemnly swear (or affirm) that I will support and defend the Constitution of the United States against all enemies, foreign and domestic; that I will bear true faith and allegiance to the same; that I take this obligation freely, without any mental reservation or purpose of evasion; and that I will well and faithfully discharge the duties of the office on which I am about to enter: So help me God. (5 U.S.C. 3331.)

[3]

RULE III

COMMENCEMENT OF DAILY SESSIONS

[3.1] 1. The Presiding Officer having taken the chair, and a quorum being present, the Journal of the preceding day shall be read, and any mistake made in the entries corrected. The reading of the Journal shall not be suspended unless by unanimous consent; and when any motion shall be made to

STANDING RULES OF THE SENATE—94TH CONGRESS   137

amend or correct the same, it shall be deemed a privileged question, and proceeded with until disposed of.

[Jefferson's Manual, Secs. VI, XLIX.]

2. A quorum shall consist of a majority of the Senators duly chosen and sworn. [Jefferson's Manual, Sec. VI. **[3.2]**

On Feb. 6, 1939, the Senate agreed to the following: **[3.3]**
Resolved, That the Chaplain shall open each calendar day's session of the Senate with prayer. (S. Jour. 93, 76-1, Feb. 5, 1939.)

On Feb. 29, 1960, the Senate agreed to the following:
Resolved, That during the session of the Senate when that body is in continuous session, the Presiding Officer shall temporarily suspend the business of the Senate at noon each day for the purpose of having the customary daily prayer by the Chaplain of the Senate. (S. Jour. 135, 86-2, Feb. 29, 1960.)

RULE IV **[4]**

JOURNAL

1. The proceedings of the Senate shall be briefly and accurately stated on the Journal. Messages of the President in full; titles of bills and joint resolutions, and such parts as shall be affected by proposed amendments; every vote, and a brief statement of the contents of each petition, memorial, or paper presented to the Senate, shall be entered. **[4.1]**

[Jefferson's Manual, Sec. VIII]

2. The legislative, the executive, the confidential legislative proceedings, and the proceedings when sitting as a Court of Impeachment, shall each be recorded in a separate book. [Jefferson's Manual, Sec. XLIX. **[4.2]**

RULE V **[5]**

QUORUM—ABSENT SENATORS MAY BE SENT FOR

1. No Senator shall absent himself from the service of the Senate without leave. [Jefferson's Manual, Sec. VIII. **[5.1]**

2. If, at any time during the daily sessions of the Senate, a question shall be raised by any Senator as to the presence of a quorum, the Presiding Officer shall forthwith direct the Secretary to call the roll and shall announce the result, and these proceedings shall be without debate. **[5.2]**

[Jefferson's Manual, Sec. VII.]

[5.3] 3. Whenever upon such roll call it shall be ascertained that a quorum is not present, a majority of the Senators present may direct the Sergeant at Arms to request, and, when necessary, to compel the attendance of the absent Senators, which order shall be determined without debate; and pending its execution, and until a quorum shall be present, no debate nor motion, except to adjourn, shall be in order.

[Jefferson's Manual, Secs. VII, VIII.

[6] RULE VI

PRESENTATION OF CREDENTIALS

[6.1] 1. The presentation of the credentials of Senators elect and other questions of privilege shall always be in order, except during the reading and correction of the Journal, while a question of order or a motion to adjourn is pending, or while the Senate is dividing; and all questions and motions arising or made upon the presentation of such credentials shall be proceeded with until disposed of.

[6.2] 2. The Secretary shall keep a record of the certificates of election of Senators by entering in a well-bound book kept for that purpose the date of the election, the name of the person elected and the vote given at the election, the date of the certificate, the name of the governor and the secretary of state signing and countersigning the same, and the State from which such Senator is elected.

[6.3] *On July 17, 1961, the Senate agreed to the following:*

Resolved, That, in the opinion of the Senate, the following are convenient and sufficient forms of the certificates of election of a Senator for a six-year term, or an unexpired term, or for the appointment of a Senator to fill a vacancy, to be signed by the executive of any State in pursuance of the Constitution and the statutes of the United States:

"CERTIFICATE OF ELECTION FOR SIX-YEAR TERM

"To the President of the Senate of the United States:

"This is to certify that on the — day of ——, 19—, A—— B—— was duly chosen by the qualified electors of the State of —— a Senator from said State to represent said State in the Senate of the United States for the term of six years, beginning on the 3d day of January, 19—.

"Witness: His excellency our governor ——, and our seal hereto affixed at ——— this — day of ——, in the year of our Lord 19—.
"By the governor:
"C—— D——,
"Governor.
"E—— F——,
"Secretary of State."

"CERTIFICATE OF ELECTION FOR UNEXPIRED TERM
"To the President of the Senate of the United States:
"This is to certify that on the — day of ——, 19—, A—— B—— was duly chosen by the qualified electors of the State of —— a Senator for the unexpired term ending at noon on the 3d day of January, 19—, to fill the vacancy in the representation from said State in the Senate of the United States caused by the —— of C—— D——.
"Witness: His excellency our governor ——, and our seal hereto affixed at ——— this — day of ——, in the year of our Lord 19—.
"By the governor:
"E—— F——,
"Governor.
"G—— H——,
"Secretary of State."

"CERTIFICATE OF APPOINTMENT [6.4]
"To the President of the Senate of the United States:
"This is to certify that, pursuant to the power vested in me by the Constitution of the United States and the laws of the State of ——, I, A—— B——, the governor of said State, do hereby appoint C—— D—— a Senator from said State to represent said State in the Senate of the United States until the vacancy therein, caused by the —— of E—— F——, is filled by election as provided by law.
"Witness: His excellency our governor ——, and our seal hereto affixed at —— this — day of ——, in the year of our Lord 19—.
"By the governor:
"G—— H——,
"Governor.
"I—— J——,
"Secretary of State."

Resolved, That the Secretary of the Senate shall send copies of these suggested forms and these resolutions to the executive and secretary of each State wherein an election is about to take place or an appointment is to be made in season that they may use such forms if they see fit. (S. Jour. 17, 73–2, Jan. 4, 1934; S. Jour. 547, 87–1, July 17, 1961.)

RULE VII [7]

MORNING BUSINESS

1. After the Journal is read, the Presiding Officer shall lay before the Senate messages from the President, reports and [7.1]

communications from the heads of Departments, and other communications addressed to the Senate, and such bills, joint resolutions, and other messages from the House of Representatives as may remain upon his table from any previous day's session undisposed of. The Presiding Officer shall then call for, in the following order:

The presentation of petitions and memorials.
Reports of standing and select committees.
The introduction of bills and joint resolutions.
Concurrent and other resolutions.

All of which shall be received and disposed of in such order, unless unanimous consent shall be otherwise given.

[Jefferson's Manual, Sec. XIV.

On Jan. 16, 1908, the Senate agreed to the following:
Resolved, That no communications from heads of departments, commissioners, chiefs of bureaus, or other executive officers, except when authorized or required by law, or when made in response to a resolution of the Senate, will be received by the Senate unless such communications shall be transmitted to the Senate by the President. (S. Jour. 122, 60-1, Jan. 16, 1908.)

On Dec. 17, 1885, the Senate agreed to the following:
Ordered, That until otherwise ordered, the Chair shall proceed with the call for resolutions to be newly offered before laying before the Senate resolutions which came over from a former day. (S. Jour. 102, 49-1, Dec. 17, 1885.)

[7.2] 2.[1][2] Senators having petitions, memorials, pension bills, or bills for the payment of private claims to present after the morning hour may deliver them to the Secretary of the Senate, endorsing upon them their names and the reference or disposition to be made thereof, and said petitions, memorials, and bills shall, with the approval of the Presiding Officer, be entered on the Journal with the names of the Senators presenting them as having been read twice and referred to the appropriate committees, and the Secretary of the Senate shall furnish a transcript of such entries to the official reporter of debates for publication in the Record.

---

[2] See also Sec. 131 of the Legislative Reorganization Act of 1946.

¹ It shall not be in order to interrupt a Senator having the floor for the purpose of introducing any memorial, petition, report of a committee, resolution, or bill. It shall be the duty of the Chair to enforce this rule without any point of order hereunder being made by a Senator.

3. Until the morning business shall have been concluded, [7.3] and so announced from the Chair, or until the hour of 1 o'clock has arrived, no motion to proceed to the consideration of any bill, resolution, report of a committee, or other subject upon the Calendar shall be entertained by the Presiding Officer, unless by unanimous consent; and if such consent be given, the motion shall not be subject to amendment, and shall be decided without debate upon the merits of the subject proposed to be taken up: ¹ *Provided, however,* That on Mondays the Calendar shall be called under Rule VIII, and during the morning hour no motion shall be entertained to proceed to the consideration of any bill, resolution, report of a committee, or other subject upon the Calendar except the motion to continue the consideration of a bill, resolution, report of a committee, or other subject against objection as provided in Rule VIII.

[Jefferson's Manual, Sec. XIV.

4. Every petition or memorial shall be referred, without [7.4] putting the question, unless objection to such reference is made; in which case all motions for the reception or reference of such petition, memorial, or other paper shall be put in the order in which the same shall be made, and shall not be open to amendment, except to add instructions.

[Jefferson's Manual, Sec. XIX.

5.² Every petition or memorial shall be signed by the [7.5] petitioner or memorialist and have indorsed thereon a brief statement of its contents, and shall be presented and referred without debate. But no petition or memorial or other paper signed by citizens or subjects of a foreign power shall be received, unless the same be transmitted to the Senate by the President.

[Jefferson's Manual, Sec. XIX.

[7.6] 6.[1] Only a brief statement of the contents, as provided for in Rule VII, paragraph five, of such communications as are presented under the order of business "Presentation of petitions and memorials" shall be printed in the Congressional Record; and no other portion of such communications shall be inserted in the Record unless specifically so ordered by vote of the Senate, as provided for in Rule XXIX, paragraph one; except that communications from the legislatures or conventions, lawfully called, of the respective States, Territories, and insular possessions shall be printed in full in the Record whenever presented, and the original copies of such communications shall be retained in the files of the Secretary of the Senate.

On Feb. 7, 1887, the Senate agreed to the following:
Ordered, That when petitions and memorials are ordered printed in the Congressional Record the order shall be deemed to apply to the body of the petition only, and the names attached to said petition or memorial shall not be printed unless specially ordered by the Senate. (S. Jour. 280, 49-2, Feb. 7, 1887.)

[7.7] 7.[2] The Presiding Officer may at any time lay, and it shall be in order at any time for a Senator to move to lay, before the Senate, any bill or other matter sent to the Senate by the President or the House of Representatives, and any question pending at that time shall be suspended for this purpose. Any motion so made shall be determined without debate.   [Jefferson's Manual, Sec. XIV.

[8] RULE VIII

ORDER OF BUSINESS

[8.1] 1. At the conclusion of the morning business for each day, unless upon motion the Senate shall at any time otherwise order, the Senate will proceed to the consideration of the Calendar of Bills and Resolutions, and continue such consideration until 2 o'clock; and bills and resolutions that are not objected to shall be taken up in their order, and each Senator shall be entitled to speak once and for five minutes only upon any question; and the objection may be interposed at any stage of the proceedings, but upon motion the Senate may continue such consideration; and this order shall commence immediately after the call for "concurrent and other resolutions," and shall take precedence of the unfinished business and other special orders. But if the Senate shall proceed with the consideration of any matter notwithstanding an objection, the foregoing provisions touching debate shall not apply. [Jefferson's Manual, Sec. XIV.

2.[1] All motions made before 2 o'clock to proceed to the consideration of any matter shall be determined without debate. [Jefferson's Manual, Sec. XIV. [8.2]

3.[2] At the conclusion of the morning hour or after the unfinished business or pending business has first been laid before the Senate on any calendar day, and until after the duration of three hours, except as determined to the contrary by unanimous consent or on motion without debate, all debate shall be germane and confined to the specific question then pending before the Senate. [8.3]

On August 10, 1888, the Senate agreed to the following:
Resolved, That after to-day, unless otherwise ordered, the morning hour shall terminate at the expiration of two hours after the meeting of the Senate. (S. Jour. 1266, 50–1, Aug. 10, 1888.)

RULE IX [9]

ORDER OF BUSINESS

Immediately after the consideration of cases not objected to upon the Calendar is completed, and not later than 2 o'clock if there shall be no special orders for that time, the Calendar of General Orders shall be taken up and proceeded with in its order, beginning with the first subject on the Calendar next after the last subject disposed of in proceeding with the Calendar; and in such case the following motions shall be in order at any time as privileged motions, save as against a motion to adjourn, or to proceed to the consideration of executive business, or questions of privilege, to wit:

First. A motion to proceed to the consideration of an appropriation or revenue bill.

Second. A motion to proceed to the consideration of any other bill on the Calendar, which motion shall not be open to amendment.

Third. A motion to pass over the pending subject, which if carried shall have the effect to leave such subject without prejudice in its place on the Calendar.

Fourth. A motion to place such subject at the foot of the Calendar.

Each of the foregoing motions shall be decided without debate and shall have precedence in the order above named, and may be submitted as in the nature and with all the rights of questions of order. [Jefferson's Manual, Secs. XIV, XXXIII.]

[10]
RULE X
SPECIAL ORDERS

[10.1] 1. Any subject may, by a vote of two-thirds of the Senators present, be made a special order; and when the time so fixed for its consideration arrives the Presiding Officer shall lay it before the Senate, unless there be unfinished business of the preceding day, and if it is not finally disposed of on that day it shall take its place on the Calendar of Special Orders in the order of time at which it was made special, unless it shall become by adjournment the unfinished business. [Jefferson's Manual, Secs. XVIII, XXXIII.]

[10.2] 2. When two or more special orders have been made for the same time, they shall have precedence according to the order in which they were severally assigned, and that order shall only be changed by direction of the Senate.

¹ And all motions to change such order, or to proceed to the consideration of other business, shall be decided without debate. [Jefferson's Manual, Secs. XVIII, XXXIII.]

[11]
RULE XI
OBJECTION TO READING A PAPER

When the reading of a paper is called for, and objected to, it shall be determined by a vote of the Senate, without debate. [Jefferson's Manual, Sec. XXXII.]

RULE XII

VOTING, ETC.

1. When the yeas and nays are ordered, the names of Senators shall be called alphabetically; and each Senator shall, without debate, declare his assent or dissent to the question, unless excused by the Senate; and no Senator shall be permitted to vote after the decision shall have been announced by the Presiding Officer, but may for sufficient reasons, with unanimous consent, change or withdraw his vote. No motion to suspend this rule shall be in order, nor shall the Presiding Officer entertain any request to suspend it by unanimous consent. [Jefferson's Manual, Sec. XLI.]

2. When a Senator declines to vote on call of his name, he shall be required to assign his reasons therefor, and having assigned them, the Presiding Officer shall submit the question to the Senate: "Shall the Senator, for the reasons assigned by him, be excused from voting?" which shall be decided without debate; and these proceedings shall be had after the roll call and before the result is announced; and any further proceedings in reference thereto shall be after such announcement. [Jefferson's Manual, Secs. XVII, XLI.]

3.[1] No request by a Senator for unanimous consent for the taking of a final vote on a specified date upon the passage of a bill or joint resolution shall be submitted to the Senate for agreement thereto until, upon a roll call ordered for the purpose by the Presiding Officer, it shall be disclosed that a quorum of the Senate is present; and when a unanimous consent is thus given the same shall operate as the order of the Senate, but any unanimous consent may be revoked by another unanimous consent granted in the manner prescribed above upon one day's notice.

RULE XIII

RECONSIDERATION

1. When a question has been decided by the Senate, any Senator voting with the prevailing side or who has not voted [1]

may, on the same day or on either of the next two days of actual session thereafter, move a reconsideration; and if the Senate shall refuse to reconsider, or upon reconsideration shall affirm its first decision, no further motion to reconsider shall be in order unless by unanimous consent. Every motion to reconsider shall be decided by a majority vote,[2] and may be laid on the table without affecting the question in reference to which the same is made, which shall be a final disposition of the motion. [Jefferson's Manual, Sec. XLIII.

[13.2] 2. When a bill, resolution, report, amendment, order, or message, upon which a vote has been taken, shall have gone out of the possession of the Senate and been communicated to the House of Representatives, the motion to reconsider shall be accompanied by a motion to request the House to return the same; which last motion shall be acted upon immediately, and without debate, and if determined in the negative shall be a final disposition of the motion to reconsider. [Jefferson's Manual, Sec. XLIII.

[14] RULE XIV

BILLS, JOINT RESOLUTIONS, AND RESOLUTIONS

[14.1] 1. Whenever a bill or joint resolution shall be offered, its introduction shall, if objected to, be postponed for one day. [Jefferson's Manual, Sec. XXIII.

[14.2] 2. Every bill and joint resolution shall receive three readings previous to its passage, which readings shall be on three different days, unless the Senate unanimously direct otherwise; and the Presiding Officer shall give notice at each reading whether it be the first, second, or third: [1] *Provided*, That the first or second reading of each bill may be by title only, unless the Senate in any case shall otherwise order. [Jefferson's Manual, Sec. XXII.

[14.3] 3. No bill or joint resolution shall be committed or amended until it shall have been twice read, after which it may be referred to a committee; bills and joint resolutions introduced on leave, and bills and joint resolutions from the

House of Representatives, shall be read once, and may be read twice, on the same day, if not objected to, for reference, but shall not be considered on that day [2] nor debated, except for reference, unless by unanimous consent.

[Jefferson's Manual, Sec. XXV.

4. Every bill and joint resolution reported from a committee, not having previously been read, shall be read once, and twice, if not objected to, on the same day, and placed on the Calendar in the order in which the same may be reported; and every bill and joint resolution introduced on leave, and every bill and joint resolution of the House of Representatives which shall have received a first and second reading without being referred to a committee, shall, if objection be made to further proceeding thereon, be placed on the Calendar. [Jefferson's Manual, Sec. XXV. [14.4]

5.[1] The Secretary of the Senate shall examine all bills, amendments, and joint resolutions before they go out of the possession of the Senate, and shall examine all bills and joint resolutions which shall have passed both Houses, to see that the same are correctly enrolled, and, when signed by the Speaker of the House and the President of the Senate, shall forthwith present the same, when they shall have originated in the Senate, to the President of the United States and report the fact and date of such presentation to the Senate. [14.5]

6.[1] All resolutions shall lie over one day for consideration, unless by unanimous consent the Senate shall otherwise direct. [Jefferson's Manual, Sec. XXV. [14.6]

RULE XV [2]   [15]

BILLS

1. When a bill or resolution shall have been ordered to be read a third time, it shall not be in order to propose amendments, unless by unanimous consent, but it shall be in order at any time before the passage of any bill or resolution to move its commitment; and when the bill or resolution shall again be reported from the committee it shall be placed on the Calendar. [Jefferson's Manual, Secs. XXVI, XXX. [15.1]

[15.2] 2. Whenever a private bill is under consideration, it shall be in order to move, as a substitute for it, a resolution of the Senate referring the case to the Court of Claims, under the provisions of the act approved March 3, 1883.

[16]
RULE XVI

AMENDMENTS TO APPROPRIATION BILLS

[16.1] 1. Al' general appropriation bills shall be referred to the Committee on Appropr ations,[1] and no amendments shall be received to any general appropriation bill the effect of which will be to increase an appropriation already contained in the bill, or to add a new item of appropriation, unless it be made to carry out the provisions of some existing law, or treaty stipulation, or act, or resolution previously passed by the Senate during that session; or unless the same be moved by direction of a standing or select committee of the Senate, or proposed in pursuance of an estimate submitted in accordance with law.

[16.2] 2.[2] The Committee on Appropriations shall not report an appropriation bill containing amendments proposing new or general legislation or any restriction on the expenditure of the funds appropriated which proposes a limitation not authorized by law if such restriction is to take effect or cease to be effective upon the happening of a contingency, and if an appropriation bill is reported to the Senate containing amendments proposing new or general legislation or any such restriction, a point of order may be made against the bill, and if the point is sustained, the bill shall be recommitted to the Committee on Appropriations.

[16.3] 3.[3] All amendments to general appropriation bills moved by direction of a standing or select committee of the Senate, proposing to increase an appropriation already contained in the bill, or to add new items of appropriation, shall, at least one day before they are considered, be referred to the Committee on Appropriations, and when actually proposed to the bill no amendment proposing to increase the amount stated in such amendment shall be received; in like manner, amendments proposing new items of appropriation to river and harbor bills, establishing post roads, or proposing new post roads, shall, before being considered, be referred to the Committee on Public Works. [Jefferson's Manual, Sec. XXXV.

4.[1] No amendment which proposes general legislation shall [16.4] be received to any general appropriation bill, nor shall any amendment not germane or relevant to the subject matter contained in the bill be received; nor shall any amendment to any item or clause of such bill be received which does not directly relate thereto; nor shall any restriction on the expenditure of the funds appropriated which proposes a limitation not authorized by law be received if such restriction is to take effect or cease to be effective upon the happening of a contingency; and all questions of relevancy of amendments under this rule, when raised, shall be submitted to the Senate and be decided without debate; and any such amendment or restriction to a general appropriation bill may be laid on the table without prejudice to the bill.
[Jefferson's Manual, Sec. XXXV.

5. No amendment, the object of which is to provide for [16.5] a private claim, shall be received to any general appropriation bill, unless it be to carry out the provisions of an existing law or a treaty stipulation, which shall be cited on the face of the amendment. [Jefferson's Manual, Sec. XXXV.

6.[1] (a) Three members of the following-named commit- [16.6] tees, to be selected by their respective committees, shall be ex officio members of the Committee on Appropriations, to serve on said committee when the annual appropriation bill making appropriations for the purposes specified in the following table opposite the name of the committee is being considered by the Committee on Appropriations:

Name of committee	Purpose of appropriation
Committee on Agriculture and Forestry.	For the Department of Agriculture.
[2] Committee on Post Office and Civil Service.	For the Post Office Department.

Committee on Armed Services_____	For the Department of War[3]; for the Department of the Navy.
Committee on the District of Columbia.	For the District of Columbia.
Committee on Public Works_____	For Rivers and Harbors.
Committee on Foreign Relations___	For the Diplomatic and Consular Service.
[4] Senate members of the Joint Committee on Atomic Energy (to be selected by said members).	For the development and utilization of atomic energy.
[5] Committee on Aeronautical and Space Sciences.	For aeronautical and space activities and matters relating to the scientific aspects thereof, except those peculiar to or primarily associated with the development of weapons systems or military operations.
[6] Committee on Finance_____	For the International Trade Commission.

(b) At least one member of each committee enumerated in subparagraph (a), to be selected by his or their respective committees, shall be a member of any conference committee appointed to confer with the House upon the annual appropriation bill making appropriations for the purposes specified in the foregoing table opposite the name of his or their respective committee. [Jefferson's Manual, Sec. XXXV.]

[16.7] 7.[1] When a point of order is made against any restriction on the expenditure of funds appropriated in a general appropriation bill on the ground that the restriction violates this rule, the rule shall be construed strictly and, in case of doubt, in favor of the point of order.

[16.8] 8.[2] Every report on general appropriation bills filed by the Committee on Appropriations shall identify with particularity each recommended amendment which proposes an item of appropriation which is not made to carry out the provisions of an existing law, a treaty stipulation, or an act or resolution previously passed by the Senate during that session.

---

[3] Name changed to Department of the Army by the National Security Act of 1947 (July 26, 1946, 61 Stat. 499; 5 U.S.C. Supp. 171).

RULE XVII

AMENDMENT MAY BE LAID ON THE TABLE WITHOUT PREJUDICE TO THE BILL

When an amendment proposed to any pending measure is laid on the table, it shall not carry with it, or prejudice, such measure.

RULE XVIII

AMENDMENTS—DIVISION OF A QUESTION

If the question in debate contains several propositions, any Senator may have the same divided, except a motion to strike out and insert, which shall not be divided; but the rejection of a motion to strike out and insert one proposition shall not prevent a motion to strike out and insert a different proposition; nor shall it prevent a motion simply to strike out; nor shall the rejection of a motion to strike out prevent a motion to strike out and insert. But pending a motion to strike out and insert, the part to be stricken out and the part to be inserted shall each be regarded for the purpose of amendment as a question; and motions to amend the part to be stricken out shall have precedence.

[Jefferson's Manual, Secs. XXXV, XXXVI.

RULE XIX

DEBATE

1. When a Senator desires to speak, he shall rise and address the Presiding Officer, and shall not proceed until he is recognized, and the Presiding Officer shall recognize the Senator who shall first address him. No Senator shall interrupt another Senator in debate without his consent, and to obtain such consent he shall first address the Presiding Officer, and no Senator shall speak more than twice upon any one question in debate on the same day without leave of the Senate, which shall be determined without debate.

[Jefferson's Manual, Secs. XVII, XXXIX.

2.[1] No Senator in debate shall, directly or indirectly, by any form of words impute to another Senator or to other

Senators any conduct or motive unworthy or unbecoming a Senator. [Jefferson's Manual, Sec. XVII.

[19.3] 3.¹ No Senator in debate shall refer offensively to any State of the Union.

[19.4] 4.² If any Senator, in speaking or otherwise, in the opinion of the Presiding Officer transgress the rules of the Senate the Presiding Officer shall, either on his own motion or at the request of any other Senator, call him to order; and when a Senator shall be called to order he shall take his seat, and may not proceed without leave of the Senate, which, if granted, shall be upon motion that he be allowed to proceed in order, which motion shall be determined without debate. Any Senator directed by the Presiding Officer to take his seat, and any Senator requesting the Presiding Officer to require a Senator to take his seat, may appeal from the ruling of the Chair, which appeal shall be open to debate.

[Jefferson's Manual, Sec. XVIII.

[19.5] 5. If a Senator be called to order for words spoken in debate, upon the demand of the Senator or of any other Senator, the exceptionable words shall be taken down in writing, and read at the table for the information of the Senate.

[Jefferson's Manual, Sec. XVII.

[19.6] 6.¹ Whenever confusion arises in the Chamber or the galleries, or demonstrations of approval or disapproval are indulged in by the occupants of the galleries, it shall be the duty of the Chair to enforce order on his own initiative and without any point of order being made by a Senator.

[19.7] 7.² No Senator shall introduce to or bring to the attention of the Senate during its sessions any occupant in the galleries of the Senate. No motion to suspend this rule shall be in order, nor may the Presiding Officer entertain any request to suspend it by unanimous consent.

[19.8] 8.³ Former Presidents of the United States shall be entitled to address the Senate upon appropriate notice to the Presiding Officer who shall thereupon make the necessary arrangements.

RULE XX [20]

QUESTIONS OF ORDER

1. A question of order may be raised at any stage of the [20.1] proceedings, except when the Senate is dividing, and, unless submitted to the Senate, shall be decided by the Presiding Officer without debate, subject to an appeal to the Senate. When an appeal is taken, any subsequent question of order which may arise before the decision of such appeal shall be decided by the Presiding Officer without debate; and every appeal therefrom shall be decided at once, and without debate; and any appeal may be laid on the table without prejudice to the pending proposition, and thereupon shall be held as affirming the decision of the Presiding Officer.

[Jefferson's Manual, Sec. XXXIII.]

2. The Presiding Officer may submit any question of order [20.2] for the decision of the Senate. [Jefferson's Manual, Sec. XXXIII.]

RULE XXI [21]

MOTIONS

1. All motions shall be reduced to writing, if desired by [21.1] the Presiding Officer or by any Senator, and shall be read before the same shall be debated. [Jefferson's Manual, Sec. XX.]

2. Any motion or resolution may be withdrawn or modi- [21.2] fied by the mover at any time before a decision, amendment, or ordering of the yeas and nays, except a motion to reconsider, which shall not be withdrawn without leave.

[Jefferson's Manual, Sec. XX.]

RULE XXII [22]

PRECEDENCE OF MOTIONS

1. When a question is pending, no motion shall be received [22.1] but—

    To adjourn.

    To adjourn to a day certain, or that when the Senate adjourn it shall be to a day certain.

To take a recess.
To proceed to the consideration of executive business.
To lay on the table.
To postpone indefinitely.
To postpone to a day certain.
To commit.
To amend.

Which several motions shall have precedence as they stand arranged; and the motions relating to adjournment, to take a recess, to proceed to the consideration of executive business, to lay on the table, shall be decided without debate.

[Jefferson's Manual, Sec. XXXIII.

[22.2] 2.[1] Notwithstanding the provisions of rule III or rule VI or any other rule of the Senate,[2] at any time a motion signed by sixteen Senators, to bring to a close the debate upon any measure, motion, other matter pending before the Senate, or the unfinished business, is presented to the Senate, the Presiding Officer shall at once state the motion to the Senate, and one hour after the Senate meets on the following calendar day but one, he shall lay the motion before the Senate and direct that the Secretary call the roll, and upon the ascertainment that a quorum is present, the Presiding Officer shall, without debate, submit to the Senate by a yea-and-nay vote the question:

"Is it the sense of the Senate that the debate shall be brought to a close?"

And if that question shall be decided in the affirmative by three-fifths of the Senators duly chosen and sworn—except on a measure or motion to amend the Senate rules, in which case the necessary affirmative vote shall be two-thirds of the Senators present and voting [1]—then said measure, motion, or other matter pending before the Senate, or the unfinished business, shall be the unfinished business to the exclusion of all other business until disposed of.

Thereafter no Senator shall be entitled to speak in all more than one hour on the measure, motion, or other matter

Standing Rules of the Senate—94th Congress 155

pending before the Senate, or the unfinished business, the amendments thereto, and motions affecting the same, and it shall be the duty of the Presiding Officer to keep the time of each Senator who speaks. Except by unanimous consent, no amendment shall be in order after the vote to bring the debate to a close, unless the same has been presented and read prior to that time. No dilatory motion, or dilatory amendment, or amendment not germane shall be in order. Points of order, including questions of relevancy, and appeals from the decision of the Presiding Officer, shall be decided without debate.

3. The provisions of the last paragraph [2] of rule VIII [22.3] (prohibiting debate on motions made before 2 o'clock)[1] shall not apply to any motion to proceed to the consideration of any motion, resolution, or proposal to change any of the Standing Rules of the Senate.

RULE XXIII [23]

PREAMBLES

When a bill or resolution is accompanied by a preamble, the question shall first be put on the bill or resolution and then on the preamble, which may be withdrawn by a mover before an amendment of the same, or ordering of the yeas and nays; or it may be laid on the table without prejudice to the bill or resolution, and shall be a final disposition of such preamble.   [Jefferson's Manual, Sec. XXVI.

RULE XXIV [24]

APPOINTMENT OF COMMITTEES

1. In the appointment of the standing committees, the [24.1] Senate, unless otherwise ordered, shall proceed by ballot to appoint severally the chairman of each committee, and then, by one ballot, the other members necessary to complete the same. A majority of the whole number of votes given shall

---

[2] Refers to second paragraph of rule VIII, which rule has since been amended by the addition of a third paragraph.

be necessary to the choice of a chairman of a standing committee, but a plurality of votes shall elect the other members thereof. All other committees shall be appointed by ballot, unless otherwise ordered, and a plurality of votes shall appoint. [Jefferson's Manual, Sec. XI.

[24.2] 2. When a chairman of a committee shall resign or cease to serve on a committee, and the Presiding Officer be authorized by the Senate to fill the vacancy in such committee, unless specially otherwise ordered, it shall be only to fill up the number of the committee.

[25] RULE XXV [1]

STANDING COMMITTEES

[25.1] 1. The following standing committees shall be appointed at the commencement of each Congress, with leave to report by bill or otherwise:

[25.1a] (a) [2] (1) **Committee on Aeronautical and Space Sciences,** to which committee shall be referred all proposed legislation, messages, petitions, memorials, and other matters relating primarily to the following subjects:

(A) Aeronautical and space activities, as that term is defined in the National Aeronautics and Space Act of 1958, except those which are peculiar to or primarily associated with the development of weapons systems or military operations.

(B) Matters relating generally to the scientific aspects of such aeronautical and space activities, except those which are peculiar to or primarily associated with the development of weapons systems or military operations.

(C) National Aeronautics and Space Administration.

(2) Such committee also shall have jurisdiction to survey and review, and to prepare studies and reports upon, aeronautical and space activities of all agencies of the United States, including such activities which are peculiar to or primarily associated with the development of weapons systems or military operations.

(b) **Committee on Agriculture and Forestry,** to which [25.1b] committee shall be referred all proposed legislation, messages, petitions, memorials, and other matters relating to the following subjects:

1. Agriculture generally.
2. Inspection of livestock and meat products.
3. Animal industry and diseases of animals.
4. Adulteration of seeds, insect pests, and protection of birds and animals in forest reserves.
5. Agricultural colleges and experiment stations.
6. Forestry in general, and forest reserves other than those created from the public domain.
7. Agricultural economics and research.
8. Agricultural and industrial chemistry.
9. Dairy industry.
10. Entomology and plant quarantine.
11. Human nutrition and home economics.
12. Plant industry, soils, and agricultural engineering.
13. Agricultural educational extension services.
14. Extension of farm credit and farm security.
15. Rural electrification.
16. Agricultural production and marketing and stabilization of prices of agricultural products.
17. Crop insurance and soil conservation.

(c)[1] **Committee on Appropriations,** to which committee [25.1c] shall be referred all proposed legislation, messages, petitions, memorials, and other matters relating to the following subjects:

1. Except as provided in subparagraph (r), appropriation of the revenue for the support of the Government.

2. Rescission of appropriations contained in appropriation Acts (referred to in section 105 of title 1, United States Code).

3. The amount of new spending authority described in section 401(c)(2) (A) and (B) of the Congressional Budget Act of 1974 provided in bills and resolutions referred to the

committee under section 401(b)(2) of that Act (but subject to the provisions of section 401(b)(3) of that Act).

4. New advance spending authority described in section 401(c)(2)(C) of the Congressional Budget Act of 1974 provided in bills and resolutions referred to the committee under section 401(b)(2) of that Act (but subject to the provisions of section 401(b)(3) of that Act).

[25.1d] (d)[1] **Committee on Armed Services,** to which committee shall be referred all proposed legislation, messages, petitions, memorials, and other matters relating to the following subjects:

1. Common defense generally.

2. The Department of Defense, the Department of the Army, the Department of the Navy, and the Department of the Air Force generally.

3. Soldiers' and sailors' homes.

4. Pay, promotion, retirement, and other benefits and privileges of members of the Armed Forces.

5. Selective service.

6. Size and composition of the Army, Navy, and Air Force.

7. Forts, arsenals, military reservations, and navy yards.

8. Ammunition depots.

9. Maintenance and operation of the Panama Canal, including the administration, sanitation, and government of the Canal Zone.

10. Conservation, development, and use of naval petroleum and oil shale reserves.

11. Strategic and critical materials necessary for the common defense.

12.[1] Aeronautical and space activities peculiar to or primarily associated with the development of weapons systems or military operations.

[25.1e] (e) **Committee on Banking, Housing and Urban Affairs,**[2] to which committee shall be referred all proposed legislation, messages, petitions, memorials, and other matters relating to the following subjects:

STANDING RULES OF THE SENATE—94TH CONGRESS   159

1. Banking and currency generally.
2. Financial aid to commerce and industry, other than matters relating to such aid which are specifically assigned to other committees under this rule.
3. Deposit insurance.
4. Public and private housing.
5. Federal Reserve System.
6. Gold and silver, including the coinage thereof.
7. Issuance of notes and redemption thereof.
8. Valuation and revaluation of the dollar.
9. Control of prices of commodities, rents, or services.
10.[3] Urban affairs generally.

(f) **Committee on Commerce,**[1] to which committee shall be referred all proposed legislation, messages, petitions, memorials, and other matters relating to the following subjects: [25.1f]

1. Interstate and foreign commerce generally.
2. Regulations of interstate railroads, busses, trucks, and pipe lines.
3. Communication by telephone, telegraph, radio, and television.
4. Civil aeronautics,[2] except aeronautical and space activities of the National Aeronautics and Space Administration.
5. Merchant marine generally.
6. Registering and licensing of vessels and small boats.
7. Navigation and the laws relating thereto, including pilotage.
8. Rules and international arrangements to prevent collisions at sea.
9. Merchant marine officers and seamen.
10. Measures relating to the regulation of common carriers by water and to the inspection of merchant marine vessels, lights and signals, lifesaving equipment, and fire protection on such vessels.
11. Coast and Geodetic Survey.
12. The Coast Guard, including lifesaving service, lighthouses, lightships, and ocean derelicts.

13. The United States Coast Guard and Merchant Marine Academies.

14. Weather Bureau.

15. Except as provided in paragraph (d), the Panama Canal and interoceanic canals generally.

16. Inland waterways.

17. Fisheries and wildlife, including research, restoration, refuges, and conservation.

18. Bureau of Standards, including standardization of weights and measures and the metric system.

[25.1g] (g) **Committee on the District of Columbia,** to which committee shall be referred all proposed legislation, messages, petitions, memorials, and other matters relating to the following subjects:

1. All measures relating to the municipal affairs of the District of Columbia in general, other than appropriations therefor, including—

2. Public health and safety, sanitation, and quarantine regulations.

3. Regulation of sale of intoxicating liquors.

4. Adulteration of food and drugs.

5. Taxes and tax sales.

6. Insurance, executors, administrators, wills, and divorce.

7. Municipal and juvenile courts.

8. Incorporation and organization of societies.

9. Municipal code and amendments to the criminal and corporation laws.

[25.1h] (h) **Committee on Finance,** to which committee shall be referred all proposed legislation, messages, petitions, memorials, and other matters relating to the following subjects[1]:

1. Except as provided in the Congressional Budget Act of 1974, revenue measures generally.[2]

2. Except as provided in the Congressional Budget Act of 1974, the bonded debt of the United States.[1]

3. The deposit of public moneys.

4. Customs, collection districts, and ports of entry and delivery.
5. Reciprocal trade agreements.
6. Transportation of dutiable goods.
7. Revenue measures relating to the insular possessions.
8. Tariffs and import quotas, and matters related thereto.
9. National social security.

(i) **Committee on Foreign Relations,** to which committee [25.1i] shall be referred all proposed legislation, messages, petitions, memorials, and other matters relating to the following subjects:

1. Relations of the United States with foreign nations generally.
2. Treaties.
3. Establishment of boundary lines between the United States and foreign nations.
4. Protection of American citizens abroad and expatriation.
5. Neutrality.
6. International conferences and congresses.
7. The American National Red Cross.
8. Intervention abroad and declarations of war.
9. Measures relating to the diplomatic service.
10. Acquisition of land and buildings for embassies and legations in foreign countries.
11. Measures to foster commercial intercourse with foreign nations and to safeguard American business interests abroad.
12. United Nations Organization and international financial and monetary organizations.
13. Foreign loans.

(j) (1) **Committee on Government Operations,**[1] to which [25.1j] committee shall be referred all proposed legislation, messages, petitions, memorials, and other matters relating to the following subjects:

>(A) Except as provided in the Congressional Budget Act of 1974, budget and accounting measures, other than appropriations.[2]

(B) Reorganizations in the executive branch of the Government.

(2) Such committee shall have the duty of—

(A) receiving and examining reports of the Comptroller General of the United States and of submitting such recommendations to the Senate as it deems necessary or desirable in connection with the subject matter of such reports;

(B) studying the operation of Government activities at all levels with a view to determining its economy and efficiency;

(C) evaluating the effects of laws enacted to reorganize the legislative and executive branches of the Government;

(D) studying the intergovernmental relationships between the United States and the States and municipalities, and between the United States and international organizations of which the United States is a member.

[25.1k] (k) **Committee on Interior and Insular Affairs,**[1] to which committee shall be referred all proposed legislation, messages, petitions, memorials, and other matters relating to the following subjects:

1. Public lands generally, including entry, easements, and grazing thereon.

2. Mineral resources of the public lands.

3. Forfeiture of land grants and alien ownership, including alien ownership of mineral lands.

4. Forest reserves and national parks created from the public domain.

5. Military parks and battlefields.[2]

6. Preservation of prehistoric ruins and objects of interest on the public domain.

7. Measures relating generally to the insular possessions of the United States, except those affecting their revenue and appropriations.[3]

8. Irrigation and reclamation, including water supply for

reclamation projects, and easements of public lands for irrigation projects.

9. Interstate compacts relating to apportionment of waters for irrigation purposes.

10. Mining interests generally.

11. Mineral land laws and claims and entries thereunder.

12. Geological survey.

13. Mining schools and experimental stations.

14. Petroleum conservation and conservation of the radium supply in the United States.

15. Relations of the United States with the Indians and the Indian tribes.

16. Measures relating to the care, education, and management of Indians, including the care and allotment of Indian lands and general and special measures relating to claims which are paid out of Indian funds.

(l) **Committee on the Judiciary,** to which committee shall be referred all proposed legislation, messages, petitions, memorials, and other matters relating to the following subjects: [25.11]

1. Judicial proceedings, civil and criminal, generally.

2. Constitutional amendments.

3. Federal courts and judges.

4. Local courts in the territories and possessions.

5. Revision and codification of the statutes of the United States.

6. National penitentiaries.

7. Protection of trade and commerce against unlawful restraints and monopolies.

8. Holidays and celebrations.

9. Bankruptcy, mutiny, espionage, and counterfeiting.

10. State and territorial boundary lines.

11. Meetings of Congress, attendance of Members, and their acceptance of incompatible offices.

12. Civil liberties.

13. Patents, copyrights, and trademarks.

14. Patent Office.
15. Immigration and naturalization.
16. Apportionment of Representatives.
17. Measures relating to claims against the United States.
18. Interstate compacts generally.

[25.1m] (m) **Committee on Labor and Public Welfare,** to which committee shall be referred all proposed legislation, messages, petitions, memorials, and other matters relating to the following subjects: [1]

1. Measures relating to education, labor, or public welfare generally.
2. Mediation and arbitration of labor disputes.
3. Wages and hours of labor.
4. Convict labor and the entry of goods made by convicts into interstate commerce.
5. Regulation or prevention of importation of foreign laborers under contract.
6. Child labor.
7. Labor statistics.
8. Labor standards.
9. School-lunch program.
10. Vocational rehabilitation.
11. Railroad labor and railroad retirement and unemployment, except revenue measures relating thereto.
12. United States Employees' Compensation Commission.
13. Columbia Institution for the Deaf, Dumb, and Blind[2]; Howard University; Freedmen's Hospital; and St. Elizabeths Hospital.
14. Public health and quarantine.
15. Welfare of miners.

[25.1n] (n) **Committee on Post Office and Civil Service,**[1] to which committee shall be referred all proposed legislation, messages, petitions, memorials, and other matters relating to the following subjects:

1. The Federal civil service generally.

---
[1] Now Gallaudet College. See Pub. Law 83-420, June 18, 1954, 68 Stat. 265.

2. The status of officers and employees of the United States, including their compensation, classification, and retirement.

3. The postal service generally, including the railway mail service, and measures relating to ocean mail and pneumatic-tube service; but excluding post roads.

4. Postal-savings banks.

5. Census and the collection of statistics generally.

6. The National Archives.

(o) **Committee on Public Works,** to which committee shall [25.1o] be referred all proposed legislation, messages, petitions, memorials, and other matters relating to the following subjects:

1. Flood control and improvement of rivers and harbors.

2. Public works for the benefit of navigation, and bridges and dams (other than international bridges and dams).

3. Water power.

4. Oil and other pollution of navigable waters.

5. Public buildings and occupied or improved grounds of the United States generally.

6. Measures relating to the purchase of sites and construction of post offices, customhouses, Federal courthouses, and Government buildings within the District of Columbia.

7. Measures relating to the Capitol Building and the Senate and House Office Buildings.

8. Measures relating to the construction or reconstruction, maintenance, and care of the buildings and grounds of the Botanic Gardens, the Library of Congress, and the Smithsonian Institution.

9. Public reservations and parks within the District of Columbia, including Rock Creek Park and the Zoological Park.

10. Measures relating to the construction or maintenance of roads and post roads.

(p) (1) **Committee on Rules and Administration,** to which [25.1p] committee shall be referred all proposed legislation, messages, petitions, memorials, and other matters relating to the following subjects:

(A) Matters relating to the payment of money out of the contingent fund of the Senate or creating a charge upon the same; except that any resolution relating to substantive matter within the jurisdiction of any other standing committee of the Senate shall be first referred to such committee.

(B) Except as provided in paragraph (o) 8, matters relating to the Library of Congress and the Senate Library; statuary and pictures; acceptance or purchase of works of art for the Capitol; the Botanic Gardens; management of the Library of Congress; purchase of books and manuscripts; erection of monuments to the memory of individuals.

(C) Except as provided in paragraph (o) 8, matters relating to the Smithsonian Institution and the incorporation of similar institutions.

(D) Matters relating to the election of the President, Vice President, or Members of Congress; corrupt practices; contested elections; credentials and qualifications; Federal elections generally; Presidential succession.

(E) [1] Matters relating to parliamentary rules; floor and gallery rules; Senate Restaurant; administration of the Senate Office Buildings and of the Senate wing of the Capitol; assignment of office space; and services to the Senate.

(F) Matters relating to printing and correction of the Congressional Record.[2]

(2) [3] Such committee shall also have the duty of assigning office space in the Senate wing of the Capitol and in the Senate Office Buildings.

[25.1q] (q) **Committee on Veterans' Affairs,**[4] to which committee shall be referred all proposed legislation, messages, petitions, memorials, and other matters relating to the following subjects:

1. Veterans' measures generally.
2. Pensions of all wars of the United States, general and special.

---

[2] The committee's general jurisdiction over matters relating to congressional printing is expressed in rule XXIX *infra*.

3. Life insurance issued by the Government on account of service in the armed forces.

4. Compensation of veterans.

5. Vocational rehabilitation and education of veterans.

6. Veterans' hospitals, medical care and treatment of veterans.

7. Soldiers' and sailors' civil relief.

8. Readjustment of servicemen to civil life.

9. National cemeteries.

(r)(1)[5] **Committee on the Budget,** to which committee shall [25.1r] be referred all concurrent resolutions on the budget (as defined in section 3(a)(4) of the Congressional Budget Act of 1974) and all other matters required to be referred to that committee under titles III and IV of that Act, and messages, petitions, memorials, and other matters relating thereto.

(2) Such committee shall have the duty—

(A) to report the matters required to be reported by it under titles III and IV of the Congressional Budget Act of 1974;

(B) to make continuing studies of the effect on budget outlays of relevant existing and proposed legislation and to report the results of such studies to the Senate on a recurring basis;

(C) to request and evaluate continuing studies of tax expenditures, to devise methods of coordinating tax expenditures, policies, and programs with direct budget outlays, and to report the results of such studies to the Senate on a recurring basis; and

(D) to review, on a continuing basis, the conduct by the Congressional Budget Office of its functions and duties.

2.[1] Except as otherwise provided by paragraph 6 of this [25.2] rule, each of the following standing committees shall consist of the number of Senators set forth in the following table on the line on which the name of that committee appears:

Committee	Members
Aeronautical and Space Sciences	10
Agriculture and Forestry	14
Appropriations	26

Committee	Members
Armed Services	16
Banking, Housing and Urban Affairs	13
Budget [2]	16
Commerce	18
Finance	18
Foreign Relations	17
Government Operations	14
Interior and Insular Affairs	14
Judiciary	15
Labor and Public Welfare	15
Public Works	14.

[25.3] 3.[1] Except as otherwise provided by paragraph 6 of this rule, each of the following standing committees shall consist of the number of Senators set forth in the following table on the line on which the name of that committee appears:

Committee	Members
District of Columbia	7
Post Office and Civil Service	9
Rules and Administration	8
Veterans' Affairs	9.

[25.4] 4.[2] The said committees shall continue and have the power to act until their successors are appointed.

[25.5] 5.[3] (a) Except as provided in paragraph (b) of this subsection, each standing committee, and each subcommittee of any such committee, is authorized to fix the number of its members (but not less than one-third of its entire membership) who shall constitute a quorum thereof for the transaction of such business as may be considered by said committee, subject to the provisions of section 133(d)[1] of the Legislative Reorganization Act of 1946.

(b) Each standing committee, and each subcommittee of any such committee, is authorized to fix a lesser number than one-third of its entire membership who shall constitute a quorum thereof for the purpose of taking sworn testimony.

[25.6] 6.[2] (a) Except as otherwise provided by this paragraph, each Senator shall serve on two and no more of the standing committees named in paragraph 2. Except as otherwise provided by this paragraph, no Senator shall serve on more than one committee included within the following classes: standing committees named in paragraph 3; select and special committees of the Senate; and joint committees of the Congress.

(b) Each Senator who on the day preceding the effective date of section 132 of the Legislative Reorganization Act of 1970 was serving as a member of any standing committee shall be entitled to continue to serve on each such committee of which he was a member on that day as long as his service as a member of such committee remains continuous after that day. Each Senator who (1) on that day was serving as a member of the Committee on Aeronautical and Space Sciences or the Committee on Government Operations, (2) on that date was entitled, under the proviso contained in the first sentence of paragraph 4 of this rule as such rule existed on that day, to serve on three committees named in that sentence, and (3) on June 30, 1971, is serving on three such committees, of which at least one is the Committee on Aeronautical and Space Sciences or the Committee on Government Operations, shall be entitled to continue to serve on each of the committees of which he is a member on June 30, 1971, so long as his service as a member of each such committee remains continuous thereafter. Each Senator who, on the day preceding the effective date of section 132 of the Legislative Reorganization Act of 1970, was a member of more than one committee of the classes described in the second sentence of subparagraph (a) shall be entitled to serve on each such committee of which he was a member on that day as long as his service as a member of that committee remains continuous after that day. Each Senator who on that day was a member of more than one committee of those classes may be assigned during the 92d Congress to other committees included within those classes, except that no Senator may serve on a number of committees of those classes greater than the number of such committees on which he was serving on the day preceding such effective date.[1] Notwithstanding the provisions of paragraphs 2 and 3, each committee of the Senate shall be temporarily increased in membership by such number as may be required to carry into effect the provisions of this subparagraph.

(c) By agreement entered into by the majority leader and the minority leader, the membership of one or more of the standing committees named in paragraph 2 or paragraph 3 of this rule may be increased temporarily from time to time by such number or numbers as may be required to accord to the majority party a majority of the membership of all standing committees. When any such temporary increase is necessary to accord to the majority party a majority of the membership of all standing committees, members of the majority party in such number as may be required for that purpose may serve as members of three standing committees named in paragraph 2. No such temporary increase in the membership of one or more standing committees under this subparagraph or subparagraph (b) shall be continued in effect after the need therefor has ended. No standing committee may be increased in membership under this subparagraph or subparagraph (b) by more than four members in excess of the number prescribed for that committee by paragraph 2 or paragraph 3 of this rule.

(d) Notwithstanding the limitations contained in subparagraph (a), a Senator may serve at any time on one additional committee included within the following classes: a temporary committee of the Senate or a temporary joint committee of the Congress which, by the terms of the measure by which it was established as initially agreed to, will not continue in existence for more than one Congress; or a joint committee of the Congress having jurisdiction with respect to a subject matter which is directly related to the jurisdiction of a committee named in paragraph 3 of which that Senator is a member.

(e) No Senator shall serve at any time on more than one of the following committees: Committee on Appropriations, Committee on Armed Services, Committee on Finance, and Committee on Foreign Relations. Notwithstanding the limitation contained in this subparagraph, a Senator who on the day preceding the effective date of section 132 of the Legislative Reorganization Act of 1970 was a member of more than one such committee may continue to serve as a member of each such committee of which he was a member on that day as long as his service on that committee remains continuous after that day.

(f) No Senator shall serve at any time as chairman of more than one committee included within the following classes: standing, select, and special committees of the Senate; and joint committees of the Congress except that—

(1) A Senator may serve as chairman of a joint committee of the Congress having jurisdiction with respect to a subject matter which is directly related to the jurisdiction of a committee named in paragraph 2 or paragraph 3 of which that Senator is the chairman;

(2) A Senator who on the day preceding the effective date of section 132 of the Legislative Reorganization Act of 1970 was serving as chairman of more than one committee included within the classes described in this subparagraph may continue to serve as chairman of each such committee of which he was chairman on that day as long as his service as chairman of that committee remains continuous after that day; and

(3) A Senator who is serving at any time as chairman of a committee included within the classes described in this subparagraph may at the same time serve also as chairman of one temporary committee of the Senate or temporary joint committee of the Congress which, by the terms of the measure by which it was established as originally agreed to, will not continue in existence for more than one Congress.

(g) No Senator shall serve at any time as chairman of more than one subcommittee of the same committee if that committee is named in paragraph 2. Notwithstanding the limitation contained in this subparagraph, a Senator who on the day preceding the effective date of section 132 of the Legislative Reorganization Act of 1970 was serving as chairman of more than one such subcommittee may continue to serve as chairman of each such subcommittee of which he was chairman on that day as long as his service as chairman of that subcommittee remains continuous after that day.

(h) For purposes of the first sentence of subparagraph (a), membership on the Committee on the Budget shall not be taken into account until that date occurring during the first session of the Ninety-fifth Congress, upon which the appointment of the majority and minority party members of the standing committees of the Senate is initially completed.

[25.7] 7.[2] (a)[3] No standing committee shall sit without special leave while the Senate is in session after (1) the conclusion of the morning hour, or (2) the Senate has proceeded to the consideration of unfinished business, pending business, or any other business except private bills and the routine morning business, whichever is earlier.

(b)[1] Meetings for the transaction of business of each standing committee of the Senate, other than for the conduct of hearings (which are provided for in section 112(a) of the Legislative Reorganization Act of 1970), shall be open to the public except during closed sessions for marking up bills or for voting or when the committee by majority vote orders a closed session: *Provided,* That any such closed session may

---

[2] As amended, S. Jour. 49, 88-2, Jan. 30, 1964; redesignated as par. 7 by Sec. 132(b) of Pub. Law 91-510, 84 Stat. 1165, Oct. 26, 1970. Effective Jan. 3, 1971, section 134(c) of the Legislative Reorganization Act of 1946, as amended by the Legislative Reorganization Act of 1970 (84 Stat. 1155, Oct. 26, 1970) and by Sec. 1(6) of Pub. Law 91-552, 84 Stat. 1440, Dec, 16, 1970, will be applicable to the Senate, as follows:

(c) Except as otherwise provided in this subsection, no standing committee of the Senate shall sit, without special leave, while the Senate is in session. The prohibition contained in the preceding sentence shall not apply to the Committee on Appropriations of the Senate. Any other standing committee of the Senate may sit for any purpose while the Senate is in session if consent therefor has been obtained from the majority leader and the minority leader of the Senate. In the event of the absence of either of such leaders, the consent of the absent leader may be given by a Senator designated by such leader for that purpose. Notwithstanding the provisions of this subsection, any standing committee of the Senate may sit without special leave for any purpose as authorized by paragraph 7 of rule XXV of the Standing Rules of the Senate.

[1] As amended, S. Jour. 173, 93-1, Mar. 6, 1973. Section 102(e) of the Congressional Budget Act of 1974 (Pub. Law 93-344, 88 Stat. 302, July 12, 1974) excludes the Senate Committee on the Budget from the provisions of paragraph 7(b) of rule XXV. However, section 102(d) of the same Act does carry special provisions relating to open or closed sessions of the Budget Committee.

STANDING RULES OF THE SENATE—94TH CONGRESS   173

be open to the public if the committee by rule or by majority vote so determines.

RULE XXVI [26]

REFERENCE TO COMMITTEES; MOTIONS TO DISCHARGE, AND REPORTS OF COMMITTEES TO LIE OVER

1. When motions are made for reference of a subject to a select committee, or to a standing committee, the question of reference to a standing committee shall be put first; and a motion simply to refer shall not be opened to amendment, except to add instructions.   [Jefferson's Manual, Secs. XXVII, XXXIII.]   [26.1]

2. All reports of committees and motions to discharge a committee from the consideration of a subject, and all subjects from which a committee shall be discharged, shall lie over one day for consideration, unless by unanimous consent the Senate shall otherwise direct.   [Jefferson's Manual, Sec. XXVII.]   [26.2]

RULE XXVII [27]

REPORTS OF CONFERENCE COMMITTEES

1. The presentation of reports of committees of conference shall always be in order, except when the Journal is being read or a question of order or a motion to adjourn is pending, or while the Senate is dividing; and when received the question of proceeding to the consideration of the report, if raised, shall be immediately put, and shall be determined without debate.   [Jefferson's Manual, Sec. XLVI.]   [27.1]

2.[1] Conferees shall not insert in their report matter not committed to them by either House, nor shall they strike from the bill matter agreed to by both Houses. If new matter is inserted in the report, or if matter which was agreed to by both Houses is stricken from the bill, a point of order may be made against the report, and if the point of order is sustained, the report shall be recommitted to the committee of conference.   [27.2]

174   APPENDIX 3

[28]   RULE XXVIII

MESSAGES

[28.1]   1. Messages from the President of the United States or from the House of Representatives may be received at any stage of proceedings, except while the Senate is dividing, or while the Journal is being read, or while a question of order or a motion to adjourn is pending.   [Jefferson's Manual, Sec. XLVII.

[28.2]   2. Messages shall be sent to the House of Representatives by the Secretary, who shall previously certify the determination of the Senate upon all bills, joint resolutions, and other resolutions which may be communicated to the House, or in which its concurrence may be requested; and the Secretary shall also certify and deliver to the President of the United States all resolutions and other communications which may be directed to him by the Senate.   [Jefferson's Manual, Sec. XLVII.

[29]   RULE XXIX

PRINTING OF PAPERS, ETC.

[29.1]   1. Every motion to print documents, reports, and other matter transmitted by either of the executive departments, or to print memorials, petitions, accompanying documents, or any other paper, except bills of the Senate or House of Representatives, resolutions submitted by a Senator, communications from the legislatures or conventions, lawfully called, of the respective States, and motions to print by order of the standing or select committees of the Senate, shall, unless the Senate otherwise order, be referred to the Committee on Rules and Administration.[1] When a motion is made to commit with instructions, it shall be in order to add thereto a motion to print.

[29.2]   2. Motions to print additional numbers shall also be referred to the Committee on Rules and Administration;[1] and when the committee shall report favorably, the report shall be accompanied by an estimate of the probable cost thereof; and when the cost of printing such additional numbers shall exceed the sum of five [2] hundred dollars, the concurrence of the House of Representatives shall be necessary for an order to print the same.

3. Every bill and joint resolution introduced on leave or reported from a committee, and all bills and joint resolutions received from the House of Representatives, and all reports of committees, shall be printed, unless, for the dispatch of the business of the Senate, such printing may be dispensed with. [29.3]

4.[1] Whenever a committee reports a bill or a joint resolution repealing or amending any statute or part thereof it shall make a report thereon and shall include in such report or in an accompanying document (to be prepared by the staff of such committee) (a) the text of the statute or part thereof which is proposed to be repealed; and (b) a comparative print of that part of the bill or joint resolution making the amendment and of the statute or part thereof proposed to be amended, showing by stricken-through type and italics, parallel columns, or other appropriate typographical devices the omissions and insertions which would be made by the bill or joint resolution if enacted in the form recommended by the committee. This subsection shall not apply to any such report in which it is stated that, in the opinion of the committee, it is necessary to dispense with the requirements of this subsection to expedite the business of the Senate. [29.4]

RULE XXX [30]

WITHDRAWAL OF PAPERS

1. No memorial or other paper presented to the Senate, except original treaties finally acted upon, shall be withdrawn from its files except by order of the Senate. But when an act may pass for the settlement of any private claim, the Secretary is authorized to transmit to the officer charged with the settlement the papers on file relating to the claim. [30.1]

---

[1] By Act of Apr. 19, 1949 (ch. 72, 63 Stat. 48), the limitation on printing extra copies was increased from $500 to $1,200.

[30.2] 2. No memorial or other paper upon which an adverse report has been made shall be withdrawn from the files of the Senate unless copies thereof shall be left in the office of the Secretary. [Jefferson's Manual, Sec. XVI.

[31]
RULE XXXI
REFERENCE OF CLAIMS ADVERSELY REPORTED

Whenever a committee of the Senate, to whom any claim has been referred, reports adversely, and the report is agreed to, it shall not be in order to move to take the papers from the files for the purpose of referring them at a subsequent session, unless the claimant shall present a petition therefor, stating that new evidence has been discovered since the report, and setting forth the substance of such new evidence.[1] But when there has been no adverse report it shall be the duty of the Secretary to transmit all such papers to the committee in which such claims are pending.

[32]
RULE XXXII
BUSINESS CONTINUED FROM SESSION TO SESSION

[32.1] 1.[2] At the second or any subsequent session of a Congress, the legislative business of the Senate which remained undetermined at the close of the next preceding session of that Congress shall be resumed and proceeded with in the same manner as if no adjournment of the Senate had taken place; and all papers referred to committees and not reported upon at the close of a session of Congress shall be returned to the office of the Secretary of the Senate, and be retained by him until the next succeeding session of that Congress, when they shall be returned to the several committees to which they had previously been referred. [Jefferson's Manual, Sec. LI.

[32.2] 2.[2] The rules of the Senate shall continue from one Congress to the next Congress unless they are changed as provided in these rules.

RULE XXXIII

PRIVILEGE OF THE FLOOR [1]

No person shall be admitted to the floor of the Senate while in session, except as follows:

The President of the United States and his private secretary.

The President elect and Vice President elect of the United States.[2]

Ex-Presidents and ex-Vice Presidents of the United States.

Judges of the Supreme Court.

Ex-Senators and Senators elect.

The officers and employees of the Senate in the discharge of their official duties.

Ex-Secretaries and ex-Sergeants at Arms of the Senate.[3]

Members of the House of Representatives and Members elect.[4]

Ex-Speakers of the House of Representatives.[5]

The Sergeant at Arms of the House and his chief deputy and the Clerk of the House and his deputy.

Heads of the Executive Departments.

Ambassadors and Ministers of the United States.[6]

Governors of States and Territories.

The General Commanding the Army.

The Senior Admiral of the Navy on the active list.

Members of National Legislatures of foreign countries.

Judges of the Court of Claims.

The Commissioner of the District of Columbia.[1]

The Librarian of Congress and the Assistant Librarian in charge of the Law Library.

The Architect of the Capitol.[2]

The Chaplain of the House of Representatives.[3]

The Secretary of the Smithsonian Institution.[2]

Clerks to Senate committees and clerks to Senators when in the actual discharge of their official duties. Clerks to Senators, to be admitted to the floor, must be regularly appointed and borne upon the rolls of the Secretary of the Senate as such.⁴

[34]
RULE XXXIV
REGULATION OF THE SENATE WING OF THE CAPITOL

[34.1] 1. The Senate Chamber shall not be granted for any other purpose than for the use of the Senate;⁵ no smoking shall be permitted at any time on the floor of the Senate, or lighted cigars be brought into the Chamber.

[34.2] 2. It shall be the duty of the Committee on Rules and Administration⁶ to make all rules and regulations respecting such parts of the Capitol, its passages and galleries, including the restaurant⁷ and the Senate Office Building, as are or may be set apart for the use of the Senate and its officers, to be enforced under the direction of the Presiding Officer. ¹They shall make such regulations respecting the reporters' galleries of the Senate, together with the adjoining rooms and facilities, as will confine their occupancy and use to bona fide reporters for daily newspapers and periodicals, to bona fide reporters of news or press associations requiring telegraph service to their membership, and to bona fide reporters for daily news dissemination through radio, wire, wireless, and similar media of transmission. These regulations shall so provide for the use of such space and facilities as fairly to distribute their use to all such media of news dissemination.

[35]
RULE XXXV
SESSION WITH CLOSED DOORS

On a motion made and seconded to close the doors of the Senate, on the discussion of any business which may, in the opinion of a Senator, require secrecy, the Presiding Officer shall direct the galleries to be cleared; and during the discussion of such motion the doors shall remain closed.

[Jefferson's Manual, Sec. XVIII.

---

⁴ See also "Regulations Controlling the Admission of Employees of Senators and Senate. Committees to the Senate Floor," adopted by the Committee on Rules and Administration on Jan. 25, 1956, and revised Feb. 4, 1971.

RULE XXXVI [36]
EXECUTIVE SESSIONS

1. When the President of the United States shall meet [36.1] the Senate in the Senate Chamber for the consideration of Executive business, he shall have a seat on the right of the Presiding Officer. When the Senate shall be convened by the President of the United States to any other place, the Presiding Officer of the Senate and the Senators shall attend at the place appointed, with the necessary officers of the Senate.

2. When acting upon confidential or Executive busi- [36.2] ness,[1] unless the same shall be considered in open Executive session, the Senate Chamber shall be cleared of all persons except the Secretary, the Chief Clerk, the Principal Legislative Clerk, the Executive Clerk, the Minute and Journal Clerk, the Sergeant at Arms, the Assistant Doorkeeper, and such other officers as the Presiding Officer shall think necessary; and all such officers shall be sworn to secrecy.

On May 2, 1892, the Senate agreed to the following:
Resolved, That until otherwise ordered there shall be admitted to the floor of the Senate during Executive sessions such clerks, not exceeding three in number, as may be assigned by the Secretary of the Senate to Executive duties. (S. Ex. Jour. 225, vol. 28, 52-1, May 2, 1892.)

3. All confidential communications made by the Presi- [36.3] dent of the United States to the Senate shall be by the Senators and the officers of the Senate kept secret; and all treaties which may be laid before the Senate, and all remarks, votes, and proceedings thereon shall also be kept secret, until the Senate shall, by their resolution, take off the injunction of secrecy, or unless the same shall be considered in open Executive session. [Jefferson's Manual, Sec. LII.]

On Mar. 21, 1885, the Senate agreed to the following:
Ordered, That the injunction of secrecy be removed from the following report from the Committee on Rules, viz:
The Committee on Rules, to which was referred a question of order raised by the Senator from Maine (Mr. Frye) as to the operation of clause 3, Rule XXXVI, reported that it extends the injunction of secrecy to each step in the consideration of treaties, including the

fact of ratification; that no modification of this clause of the rules ought to be made; that the secrecy as to the fact or ratification of a treaty may be of the utmost importance, and ought not to be removed except by order of the Senate, or until it has been made public by proclamation by the President. (S. Ex. Jour. 20, 49 special, Mar. 21, 1885.)

On Feb. 8, 1900, the Senate agreed to the following:
Ordered, Whenever the injunction of secrecy shall be removed from any part of the proceedings of the Senate in Executive session, or secret legislative session, the order of the Senate removing the same shall be entered by the Secretary in the Legislative Journal as well as in the Executive Journal, and shall be published in the Record. (S. Jour. 131, 56–1, Feb. 8, 1900.)

[36.4] 4. Any Senator or officer of the Senate who shall disclose the secret or confidential business or proceedings of the Senate shall be liable, if a Senator, to suffer expulsion from the body; and if an officer, to dismissal from the service of the Senate, and to punishment for contempt.

[36.5] 5.[1] Whenever, by the request of the Senate or any committee thereof, any documents or papers shall be communicated to the Senate by the President or the head of any department relating to any matter pending in the Senate the proceedings in regard to which are secret or confidential under the rules, said documents and papers shall be considered as confidential, and shall not be disclosed without leave of the Senate.

[37]
RULE XXXVII

EXECUTIVE SESSION—PROCEEDINGS ON TREATIES

[37.1] 1. When a treaty shall be laid before the Senate for ratification, it shall be read a first time; and no motion in respect to it shall be in order, except to refer it to a committee,[2] to print it in confidence for the use of the Senate,[2] to remove the injunction of secrecy, or to consider it in open executive session.

When a treaty is reported from a committee with or without amendment, it shall, unless the Senate unanimously otherwise direct, lie one day for consideration; after which it may be read a second time and considered as in Committee of the Whole, when it shall be proceeded with by articles, and the amendments reported by the committee shall be first acted upon, after which other amendments may be proposed; and when through with, the proceedings had as in Committee of the Whole shall be reported to the Senate, when the question shall be, if the treaty be amended, "Will the Senate concur in the amendments made in Committee of the Whole?" And the amendments may be taken separately, or in gross, if no Senator shall object; after which new amendments may be proposed.[1] At any stage of such proceedings the Senate may remove the injunction of secrecy from the treaty, or proceed with its consideration in open executive session.

The decisions thus made shall be reduced to the form of a resolution of ratification, with or without amendments, as the case may be, which shall be proposed on a subsequent day, unless, by unanimous consent, the Senate determine otherwise; at which stage no amendment shall be received unless by unanimous consent.

On the final question to advise and consent to the ratification in the form agreed to, the concurrence of two-thirds of the Senators present shall be necessary to determine it in the affirmative; but all other motions and questions upon a treaty shall be decided by a majority vote, except a motion to postpone indefinitely, which shall be decided by a vote of two-thirds.

2. Treaties transmitted by the President to the Senate for ratification shall be resumed at the second or any subsequent session of the same Congress at the stage in which they were left at the final adjournment of the session at which they were transmitted; but all proceedings on treaties shall terminate with the Congress, and they shall be resumed at the commencement of the next Congress as if no proceedings had previously been had thereon. [37.2]

3. All treaties concluded with Indian tribes shall be considered and acted upon by the Senate in its open or legislative session, unless the same shall be transmitted by the [37.3]

President to the Senate in confidence, in which case they shall be acted upon with closed doors. [Jefferson's Manual, Sec. LII.

[38]
RULE XXXVIII
EXECUTIVE SESSION—PROCEEDINGS ON NOMINATIONS

[38.1] 1. When nominations shall be made by the President of the United States to the Senate, they shall, unless otherwise ordered, be referred to appropriate committees; and the final question on every nomination shall be, "Will the Senate advise and consent to this nomination?" which question shall not be put on the same day on which the nomination is received, nor on the day on which it may be reported by a committee, unless by unanimous consent.

[38.2] 2.[1] Hereafter all business in the Senate shall be transacted in open session, unless the Senate in closed session by a majority vote shall determine that a particular nomination, treaty, or other matter shall be considered in closed executive session, in which case all subsequent proceedings with respect to said nomination, treaty, or other matter shall be kept secret: *Provided*, That the injunction of secrecy as to the whole or any part of proceedings in closed executive session may be removed on motion adopted by a majority vote of the Senate in closed executive session: *Provided further*, That rule XXXV shall apply to open executive session: *And provided further*, That any Senator may make public his vote in closed executive session.

Anything in the rules of the Senate inconsistent with the foregoing is hereby repealed.

[38.3] 3. When a nomination is confirmed or rejected, any Senator voting in the majority may move for a reconsideration on the same day on which the vote was taken, or on either of the next two days of actual executive session of the Senate; but if a notification of the confirmation or rejection of a nomination shall have been sent to the President before the expiration of the time within which a motion to reconsider may be made, the motion to reconsider shall be accom-

STANDING RULES OF THE SENATE—94TH CONGRESS 183

panied by a motion to request the President to return such notification to the Senate. Any motion to reconsider the vote on a nomination may be laid on the table without prejudice to the nomination, and shall be a final disposition of such motion.

4. Nominations confirmed or rejected by the Senate shall not be returned by the Secretary to the President until the expiration of the time limited for making a motion to reconsider the same, or while a motion to reconsider is pending unless otherwise ordered by the Senate. [38.4]

5. When the Senate shall adjourn or take a recess for more than thirty days, all motions to reconsider a vote upon a nomination which has been confirmed or rejected by the Senate, which shall be pending at the time of taking such adjournment or recess, shall fall; and the Secretary shall return all such nominations to the President as confirmed or rejected by the Senate, as the case may be. [38.5]

6. Nominations neither confirmed nor rejected during the session at which they are made shall not be acted upon at any succeeding session without being again made to the Senate by the President; and if the Senate shall adjourn or take a recess for more than thirty days, all nominations pending and not finally acted upon at the time of taking such adjournment or recess shall be returned by the Secretary to the President, and shall not again be considered unless they shall again be made to the Senate by the President. [38.6]

On Dec. 16, 1885, the Senate agreed to the following:
Resolved, All nominations to office shall be prepared for the printer by the Official Reporter, and printed in the Record, after the proceedings of the day in which they are received, also nominations recalled, and confirmed. (S. Ex. Jour., vol. 25, 197, 49–1, Dec. 16, 1885.)

On Dec. 17, 1885, the Senate agreed to the following:
Ordered, The Secretary shall furnish the Official Reporters with a list of nominations to office after the proceedings of the day on which they are received, and a like list of all confirmations and rejections. (S. Ex. Jour., vol. 25, 237, 49–1, Dec. 17, 1885.)

On May 2, 1894, the Senate agreed to the following:
Resolved, The Secretary shall furnish to the press, and to the public upon request, the names of nominees confirmed or rejected on the day on which a final vote shall be had, except when otherwise ordered by the Senate. (S. Ex. Jour. 629, vol. 29, part 1, 53-2, May 2, 1894.)

[39]
RULE XXXIX

THE PRESIDENT FURNISHED WITH COPIES OF RECORDS OF EXECUTIVE SESSIONS

The President of the United States shall, from time to time, be furnished with an authenticated transcript of the executive records of the Senate, but no further extract from the Executive Journal shall be furnished by the Secretary, except by special order of the Senate; and no paper, except original treaties transmitted to the Senate by the President of the United States, and finally acted upon by the Senate, shall be delivered from the office of the Secretary without an order of the Senate for that purpose.

[40]
RULE XL

SUSPENSION AND AMENDMENT OF THE RULES

No motion to suspend, modify, or amend any rule, or any part thereof, shall be in order, except on one day's notice in writing, specifying precisely the rule or part proposed to be suspended, modified, or amended, and the purpose thereof. Any rule may be suspended without notice by the unanimous consent of the Senate, except as otherwise provided in clause 1, Rule XII.

[41]
RULE XLI [1]

OUTSIDE BUSINESS OR PROFESSIONAL ACTIVITY OR EMPLOYMENT BY OFFICERS OR EMPLOYEES

[41.1] 1. No officer or employee whose salary is paid by the Senate may engage in any business or professional activity or employment for compensation unless—

(a) the activity or employment is not inconsistent

nor in conflict with the conscientious performance of his official duties; and

(b) he has reported in writing when this rule takes effect or when his office or employment starts and on the 15th day of May in each year thereafter the nature of any personal service activity or employment to his supervisor. The supervisor shall then, in the discharge of his duties, take such action as he considers necessary for the avoidance of conflict of interest or interference with duties to the Senate.

2. For the purpose of this rule— [41.2]

(a) a Senator or the Vice President is the supervisor of his administrative, clerical, or other assistants;

(b) a Senator who is the chairman of a committee is the supervisor of the professional, clerical, or other assistants to the committee except that minority staff members shall be under the supervision of the ranking minority Senator on the committee;

(c) a Senator who is a chairman of a subcommittee which has its own staff and financial authorization is the supervisor of the professional, clerical, or other assistants to the subcommittee except that minority staff members shall be under the supervision of the ranking minority Senator on the subcommittee;

(d) the President pro tempore is the supervisor of the Secretary of the Senate, Sergeant at Arms and Doorkeeper, the Chaplain, and the employees of the Office of the Legislative Counsel;

(e) the Secretary of the Senate is the supervisor of the employees of his office;

(f) the Sergeant at Arms and Doorkeeper is the supervisor of the employees of his office;

(g) the Majority and Minority Leaders and the Majority and Minority Whips are the supervisors of the research, clerical, or other assistants assigned to their respective offices;

(h) the Majority Leader is the supervisor of the Secretary for the Majority. The Secretary for the Majority is the supervisor of the employees of his office; and

(i) the Minority Leader is the supervisor of the Secretary for the Minority. The Secretary for the Minority is the supervisor of the employees of his office.

[41.3] 3. This rule shall take effect ninety days after adoption.

[42]   RULE XLII [1]

                       CONTRIBUTIONS

[42.1] 1. A Senator or person who has declared or otherwise made known his intention to seek nomination or election, or who has filed papers or petitions for nomination or election, or on whose behalf a declaration or nominating paper or petition has been made or filed, or who has otherwise, directly or indirectly, manifested his intention to seek nomination or election, pursuant to State law, to the office of United States Senator, may accept a contribution from—

(a) a fundraising event organized and held primarily in his behalf, provided—

(1) he has expressly given his approval of the fundraising event to the sponsors before any funds were raised; and

(2) he receives a complete and accurate accounting of the source, amounts, and disposition of the funds raised; or

(b) an individual or an organization, provided the Senator makes a complete and accurate accounting of the source, amount, and disposition of the funds received; or

(c) his political party when such contributions were from a fundraising event sponsored by his party, without giving his express approval for such fundraising event when such fundraising event is for the purpose of providing contributions for candidates of

STANDING RULES OF THE SENATE—94TH CONGRESS   187

his party and such contributions are reported by the
Senator or candidate for Senator as provided in
paragraph (b).

2. The Senator may use the contribution only to influence [42.2]
his nomination for election, or his election, and shall not use,
directly or indirectly, any part of any contribution for any
other purpose, except as otherwise provided herein.

3. Nothing in this rule shall preclude the use of contri- [42.3]
butions to defray expenses for travel to and from each
Senator's home State; for printing and other expenses in
connection with the mailing of speeches, newsletters, and
reports to a Senator's constituents; for expenses of radio,
television, and news media methods of reporting to a
Senator's constituents; for telephone, telegraph, postage, and
stationery expenses in excess of allowance; and for newspaper
subscriptions from his home State.

4. All gifts in the aggregate amount or value of $50 or [42.4]
more received by a Senator from any single source during a
year, except a gift from his spouse, child, or parent, and
except a contribution under sections 1 and 2, shall be reported
under rule XLIV.

5. This rule shall take effect ninety days after adoption. [42.5]

RULE XLIII [1] [43]

POLITICAL FUND ACTIVITY BY OFFICERS AND EMPLOYEES

1. No officer or employee whose salary is paid by the [43.1]
Senate may receive, solicit, be the custodian of, or distribute
any funds in connection with any campaign for the nomination for election, or the election of any individual to be a
Member of the Senate or to any other Federal office. This
prohibition does not apply to any assistant to a Senator
who has been designated by that Senator to perform any of
the functions described in the first sentence of this paragraph
and who is compensated at a rate in excess of $10,000 per
annum if such designation has been made in writing and
filed with the Secretary of the Senate. The Secretary of the

188   APPENDIX 3

Senate shall make the designation available for public inspection.

[43.2]   2. This rule shall take effect sixty days after adoption.

[44]   RULE XLIV [1]

DISCLOSURE OF FINANCIAL INTERESTS

[44.1]   1. Each Senator or person who has declared or otherwise made known his intention to seek nomination or election, or who has filed papers or petitions for nomination or election, or on whose behalf a declaration or nominating paper or petition has been made or filed, or who has otherwise, directly or indirectly, manifested his intention to seek nomination or election, pursuant to State law, to the office of United States Senator, and each officer or employee of the Senate who is compensated at a rate in excess of $15,000 a year, shall file with the Comptroller General of the United States, in a sealed envelope marked "Confidential Personal Financial Disclosure of _____
(Name)
_____", before the 15th day of May in each year, the following reports of his personal financial interests:

(a) a copy of the returns of taxes, declarations, statements, or other documents which he, or he and his spouse jointly, made for the preceding year in compliance with the income tax provisions of the Internal Revenue Code;

(b) the amount or value and source of each fee or compensation of $1,000 or more received by him during the preceding year from a client;

(c) the name and address of each business or professional corporation, firm, or enterprise in which he was an officer, director, partner, proprietor, or employee who received compensation during the preceding year and the amount of such compensation;

(d) the identity of each interest in real or personal property having a value of $10,000 or more which he

STANDING RULES OF THE SENATE—94TH CONGRESS 189

owned at any time during the preceding year;

(e) the identity of each trust or other fiduciary relation in which he held a beneficial interest having a value of $10,000 or more, and the identity if known of each interest of the trust or other fiduciary relation in real or personal property in which the Senator, officer, or employee held a beneficial interest having a value of $10,000 or more, at any time during the preceding year. If he cannot obtain the identity of the fiduciary interests, the Senator, officer, or employee shall request the fiduciary to report that information to the Comptroller General in the same manner that reports are filed under this rule;

(f) the identity of each liability of $5,000 or more owed by him, or by him and his spouse jointly, at any time during the preceding year; and

(g) the source and value of all gifts in the aggregate amount or value of $50 or more from any single source received by him during the preceding year.

2. Except as otherwise provided by this section, all papers [44.2] filed under section 1 of this rule shall be kept by the Comptroller General for not less than seven years, and while so kept shall remain sealed. Upon receipt of a resolution of the Select Committee on Standards and Conduct, adopted by a recorded majority vote of the full committee, requesting the transmission to the committee of any of the reports filed by any individual under section 1 of this rule, the Comptroller General shall transmit to the committee the envelopes containing such reports. Within a reasonable time after such recorded vote has been taken, the individual concerned shall be informed of the vote to examine and audit, and shall be advised of the nature and scope of such examination. When any sealed envelope containing any such report is received by the committee, such envelope may be opened and the contents thereof may be examined only by members of the committee in executive session. If, upon such examination,

the committee determines that further consideration by the committee is warranted and is within the jurisdiction of the committee, it may make the contents of any such envelope available for any use by any member of the committee, or any member of the staff of the committee, which is required for the discharge of his official duties. The committee may receive the papers as evidence, after giving to the individual concerned due notice and opportunity for hearing in a closed session. The Comptroller General shall report to the Select Committee on Standards and Conduct not later than the 1st day of June in each year the names of Senators, officers, and employees who have filed a report. Any paper which has been filed with the Comptroller General for longer than seven years, in accordance with the provisions of this section, shall be returned to the individual concerned or his legal representative. In the event of the death or termination of service of a Member of the Senate, an officer or employee, such papers shall be returned unopened to such individual, or to the surviving spouse or legal representative of such individual within one year of such death or termination of service.

[44.3]   3. Each Senator or person who has declared or otherwise made known his intention to seek nomination or election, or who has filed papers or petitions for nomination or election, or on whose behalf a declaration or nominating paper or petition has been made or filed, or who has otherwise, directly or indirectly, manifested his intention to seek nomination or election, pursuant to State law, to the office of United States Senator, and each officer or employee of the Senate wl o is compensated at a rate in excess of $15,000 a year, shall file with the Secretary of the Senate, before the 15th day of May in each year, the following reports of his personal financial interests:

> (a) the accounting required by rule XLII for all contributions received by him during the preceding year, except that contributions in the aggregate amount or

value of less than $50 received from any single source during the reporting period may be totaled without further itemization; and

(b) the amount or value and source of each honorarium of $300 or more received by him during the preceding year.

4. All papers filed under section 3 of this rule shall be kept by the Secretary of the Senate for not less than three years and shall be made available promptly for public inspection and copying. **[44.4]**

5. This rule shall take effect on July 1, 1968. No reports shall be filed for any period before office or employment was held with the Senate, or during a period of office or employment with the Senate of less than ninety days in a year; except that the Senator, or officer or employee of the Senate, may file a copy of the return of taxes for the year 1968, or a report of substantially equivalent information for only the effective part of the year 1968. **[44.5]**

APPENDIX 4

Rules of the House of Representatives

1st Sess., 94th Cong.

RULE I
DUTIES OF THE SPEAKER

1. The Speaker shall take the chair on every legislative day precisely at the hour to which the House shall have adjourned at the last sitting and immediately call the Members to order. On the appearance of a quorum, the Speaker, having examined the Journal of the proceedings of the last day's sitting and approved the same, shall announce to the House his approval of the Journal; whereupon, unless the Speaker, in his discretion, orders the reading of the Journal, the Journal shall be considered as read. However, it shall then be in order to offer one motion that the Journal be read and such motion is of the highest privilege and shall be determined without debate.

2. He shall preserve order and decorum, and, in case of disturbances or disorderly conduct in the galleries, or in the lobby, may cause the same to be cleared.

3. He shall have general control, except as provided by rule or law, of the Hall of the House, and of the corridors and passages and the disposal of the unappropriated rooms in the part of the Capitol assigned to the use of the House, until further order.

4. He shall sign all acts, addresses, joint resolutions, writs, warrants, and subpenas of, or issued by order of, the House, and decide all questions of order, subject to an appeal by any Member, on which appeal no Member shall speak more than once, unless by permission of the House.

5. He shall rise to put a question, but may state it sitting; and shall put questions in this form, to wit: "As many as are in favor (as the question may be), say 'Aye'."; and after the affirmative voice is expressed. "As many as are opposed, say 'No'."; if he doubts, or a division is called for, the House shall divide; those in the affirmative of the question shall first rise from their seats, and then those in the negative; if he still doubts, or a count is required by at least one-fifth of a quorum, he shall name one or more from each side of the question to tell the Members in the affirmative and negative; which being reported, he shall rise and state the decision. However, if any Member requests a recorded vote and that request is supported by at least one-fifth of a quorm, such vote shall be taken by electronic device, unless the Speaker in his discretion orders clerks to tell the names of those voting on each side of the question, and such names shall be recorded by electronic device or by clerks, as the case may be, and shall be entered in the Journal, together with the names of those not voting. Members shall have not less than fifteen minutes to be counted from the ordering of the recorded vote or the ordering of clerks to tell the vote.

6. He shall not be required to vote in ordinary legislative proceedings, except where his vote would be decisive, or where the House is engaged in voting by ballot; and in cases of a tie vote the question shall be lost.

7. He shall have the right to name any Member to perform the duties of the Chair, but such substitution shall not extend beyond three legislative days: *Provided, however,* That in case of illness, he may make such appointment for a period not exceeding ten days, with the approval of the House at the time the same is made; and in his absence and omission to make such appointment, the House shall proceed to elect a Speaker pro tempore to act during his absence.

8. He shall have the authority to designate any Member, officer or employee of

the House of Representatives to travel on the business of the House of Representatives, as determined by him, within or without the United States, whether the House is meeting, has recessed or has adjourned, and all expenses for such travel may be paid for from the contingent fund of the House on vouchers solely approved and signed by the Speaker.

RULE II

ELECTION OF OFFICERS

There shall be elected by a viva voce vote, at the commencement of each Congress, to continue in office until their successors are chosen and qualified, a Clerk, Sergeant-at-Arms, Doorkeeper, Postmaster, and Chaplain, each of whom shall take an oath to support the Constitution of the United States, and for the true and faithful discharge of the duties of his office to the best of his knowledge and ability, and to keep the secrets of the House; and each shall appoint all of the employees of his department provided for by law.

RULE III

DUTIES OF THE CLERK

1. The Clerk shall, at the commencement of the first session of each Congress, call the Members to order, proceed to call the roll of Members by State in alphabetical order, and, pending the election of a Speaker or Speaker pro tempore, preserve order and decorum, and decide all questions of order subject to appeal by any Member.

2. He shall make and cause to be printed and delivered to each Member, or mailed to his address, at the commencement of every regular session of Congress, a list of the reports which it is the duty of any officer or Department to make to Congress, referring to the act or resolution and page of the volume of the laws or Journal in which it may be contained, and placing under the name of each officer the list of reports required of him to be made.

3. He shall note all questions or order, with the decisions thereon, the record of which shall be printed as an appendix to the Journal of each session; and complete, as soon after the close of the session as possible, the printing and distribution to Members, Delegates, and the Resident Commissioner from Puerto Rico of the Journal of the House, together with an accurate and complete index; retain in the library at his office, for the use of the Members, Delegates, the Resident Commissioner from Puerto Rico and officers of the House, and not to be withdrawn therefrom, two copies of all the books and printed documents deposited there; send, at the end of each session, a printed copy of the Journal thereof to the executive and to each branch of the legislature of every State; deliver or mail to any Member, Delegate or the Resident Commissioner from Puerto Rico an extra copy, in binding of good quality, of each document requested by that Member, Delegate, or the Resident Commissioner which has been printed, by order of either House of the Congress, in any Congress in which he served; attest and affix the seal of the House to all writs, warrants, and subpenas issued by order of the House, certify to the passage of all bills and joint resolutions, make or approve all contracts, bargains, or agreements relative to furnishing any matter or thing, or for the performance of any labor for the House of Representatives, in pursuance of law or order of the House, keep full and accurate accounts of the disbursements out of the contingent fund of the House, keep the stationary account of Members, Delegates, and the Resident Commissioner from Puerto Rico, and pay them as provided by law. He shall pay to the officers and employees of the House of Representatives the amount of their salaries that shall be due them.

4. He shall, in case of temporary absence or disability, designate an official in his office to sign all papers that may require the official signature of the Clerk of the House, and to do all other acts except such as are provided for by statute, that may be required under the rules and practice of the House to be done by the Clerk. Such official acts, when so done by the designated officials, shall be under the name of the Clerk of the House. The said designation shall be in writing, and shall be laid before the House and entered on the Journal.

RULE IV

DUTIES OF THE SERGEANT-AT-ARMS

1. It shall be the duty of the Sergeant-at-Arms to attend the House during its sittings, to maintain order under the direction of the Speaker or Chairman and, pending the election of a Speaker or Speaker pro tempore, under the direction of the Clerk, execute the commands of the House, and all processes issued by authority thereof, directed to him by the Speaker; and keep the accounts for the pay and mileage of Members, Delegate, and the Resident Commissioner from Puerto Rico, and pay them as provided by law.

2. The symbol of his office shall be the mace, which shall be borne by him while enforcing order on the floor.

Rule V
DUTIES OF THE DOORKEEPER

1. The Doorkeeper shall enforce strictly the rules relating to the privileges of the Hall and be responsible to the House for the official conduct of his employees.

2. He shall allow no person to enter the room over the Hall of the House during its sittings; and fifteen minutes before the hour of the meeting of the House each day he shall see that the floor is cleared of all persons except those privileged to remain, and kept so until ten minutes after adjournment.

Rule VI
DUTIES OF THE POSTMASTER

The Postmaster shall superintend the post office in the Capitol and in the respective office buildings of the House for the accommodation of Representatives, Delegates, the Resident Commissioner from Puerto Rico, and officers of the House and shall be held responsible for the prompt and safe delivery of their mail.

Rule VII
DUTIES OF THE CHAPLAIN

The Chaplain shall attend at the commencement of each day's sitting of the House and open the same with prayer.

Rule VIII
DUTIES OF THE MEMBERS

1. Every Member shall be present within the Hall of the House during its sittings, unless excused or necessarily prevented; and shall vote on each question put, unless he has a direct personal or pecuniary interest in the event of such question.

2. Pairs shall be announced by the Clerk immediately before the announcement by the Chair of the result of the vote, by the House or Committee of the Whole from a written list furnished him, and signed by the Member making the statement to the Clerk, which list shall be published in the Record as a part of the proceedings, immediately following the names of those not voting. However, pairs shall be announced but once during the same legislative day.

Rule IX
QUESTIONS OF PRIVILEGE

Questions of privilege shall be, first those affecting the rights of the House collectively, its safety, dignity, and the integrity of its proceedings; second, the rights, reputation, and conduct of Members, individually, in their representative capacity only; and shall have precedence of all other questions, except motion to adjourn.

Rule X
ESTABLISHMENT AND JURISDICTION OF STANDING COMMITTEES

The Committees and Their Jurisdiction

1. There shall be in the House the following standing committees, each of which shall have the jurisdiction and related functions assigned to it by this clause and clauses 2, 3, and 4; and all bills, resolutions, and other matters relating to subjects within the jurisdiction of any standing committee as listed in this clause shall (in accordance with and subject to clause 5) be referred to such committees, as follows:

(a) Committee on Agriculture.
(1) Adulteration of seeds, insect pests, and protection of birds and animals in forest reserves.
(2) Agriculture generally.
(3) Agricultural and industrial chemistry.
(4) Agricultural colleges and experiment stations.
(5) Agricultural economics and research.
(6) Agricultural education extension services.
(7) Agricultural production and marketing and stabilization of prices of agricultural products, and commodities (not including distribution outside of the United States).
(8) Animal industry and diseases of animals.
(9) Crop insurance and soil conservation.
(10) Dairy industry.
(11) Entomology and plant quarantine.
(12) Extension of farm credit and farm security.
(13) Forestry in general, and forest reserves other than those created from the public domain.
(14) Human nutrition and home economics.
(15) Inspection of livestock and meat products.
(16) Plant industry, soils, and agricultural engineering.
(17) Rural electrification.
(18) Commodities exchanges.
(19) Rural development.

(b) Committee on Appropriations.
(1) Appropriation of the revenue for the support of the Government.
(2) Rescissions of appropriations contained in appropriation Acts.
(3) Transfers of unexpended balances.
(4) The amount of new spending authority (as described in the Congressional Budget Act of 1974) which is to be effective for a fiscal year, including bills and resolutions (reported by other com-

mittees) which provide new spending authority and are referred to the committee under clause 4(a).

The committee shall include separate headings for "Rescissions" and "Transfers of Unexpended Balances" in any bill or resolution as reported from the committee under its jurisdiction specified in subparagraph (2) or (3), with all proposed rescissions and proposed transfers listed therein; and shall include a separate section with respect to such rescissions or transfers in the accompanying committee report. In addition to its jurisdiction under the preceding provisions of this paragraph, the committee shall have the fiscal oversight function provided for in clause 2(b)(3) and the budget hearing function provided for in clause 4(a).

(c) Committee on Armed Services.

(1) Common defense generally.

(2) The Department of Defense generally, including the Departments of the Army, Navy, and Air Force generally.

(3) Ammunition depots; forts; arsenals; Army, Navy, and Air Force reservations and establishments.

(4) Conservation, development, and use of naval petroleum and oil shale reserves.

(5) Pay, promotion, retirement, and other benefits and privileges of members of the armed forces.

(6) Scientific research and development in support of the armed services.

(7) Selective service.

(8) Size and composition of the Army, Navy, and Air Force.

(9) Soldiers' and sailors' homes.

(10) Strategic and critical materials necessary for the common defense.

In addition to its legislative jurisdiction under the preceding provisions of this paragraph (and its general oversight function under clause 2(b)(1)), the committee shall have the special oversight function provided for in clause 3(a) with respect to international arms control and disarmament, and military dependents education.

(d) Committee on Banking, Currency and Housing.

(1) Banks and banking, including deposit insurance and Federal monetary policy.

(2) Money and credit, including currency and the issuance of notes and redemption thereof; gold and silver, including the coinage thereof; valuation and revaluation of the dollar.

(3) Urban development.

(4) Public and private housing.

(5) Economic stabilization, defense production, renegotiation, and control of the price of commodities rents, and services.

(6) International finance.

(7) Financial aid to commerce and industry (other than transportation).

(8) International Financial and Monetary organizations.

(e)(1) Committee on the Budget, to consist of twenty-five Members as follows:

(A) five Members who are members of the Committee on Appropriations;

(B) five Members who are members of the Committee on Ways and Means;

(C) thirteen Members who are members of other standing committees;

(D) one Member from the leadership of the majority party; and

(E) one Member from the leadership of the minority party.

No member shall serve as a member of the Committee on the Budget during more than two Congresses in any period of five successive Congresses beginning after 1974 (disregarding for this purpose any service performed as a member of such committee for less than a full session in any Congress). All selections of Members to serve on the committee shall be made without regard to seniority.

(2) All concurrent resolutions on the budget (as defined in section 3(a)(4) of the Congressional Budget Act of 1974) and other matters required to be referred to the committee under titles III and IV of that Act.

(3) The committee shall have the duty—

(A) to report the matters required to be reported by it under titles III and IV of the Congressional Budget Act of 1974;

(B) to make continuing studies of the effect on budget outlays of relevant existing and proposed legislation and to report the results of such studies to the House on a recurring basis;

(C) to request and evaluate continuing studies of tax expenditures, to devise methods of coordinating tax expenditures, policies, and programs with direct budget outlays, and to report the results of such studies to the House on a recurring basis; and

(D) to review, on a continuing basis, the conduct by the Congressional Budget Office of its functions and duties.

(f) Committee on the District of Columbia.

(1) All measures relating to the municipal affairs of the District of Columbia in general, other than appropriations therefor, including—

(2) Adulteration of foods and drugs.
(3) Incorporation and organization of societies.
(4) Insurance, executors, administrators, wills, and divorce.
(5) Municipal code and amendments to the criminal and corporation laws.
(6) Municipal and juvenile courts.
(7) Public health and safety, sanitation, and quarantine regulations.
(8) Regulation of sale of intoxicating liquors.
(9) Taxes and tax sales.
(10) Saint Elizabeth's hospital.

(g) Committee on Education and Labor.
(1) Measures relating to education or labor generally.
(2) Child labor.
(3) Columbia Institution for the Deaf, Dumb, and Blind; Howard University; Freedman's Hospital.
(4) Convict labor and the entry of goods made by convicts into interstate commerce.
(5) Labor standards.
(6) Labor statistics.
(7) Mediation and arbitration of labor disputes.
(8) Regulation or prevention of importation of foreign laborers under contract.
(9) Food programs for children in schools.
(10) United States Employees' Compensation Commission.
(11) Vocational rehabilitation.
(12) Wages and hours of labor.
(13) Welfare of miners.
(14) Work incentive programs.

In addition to its legislative jurisdiction under the preceding provisions of this paragraph (and its general oversight function under clause 2(b)(1)), the committee shall have the special oversight function provided for in clause 3(c) with respect to domestic educational programs and institutions, and programs of student assistance, which are within the jurisdiction of other committees.

(h) Committee on Government Operations.
(1) Budget and accounting measures, other than appropriations.
(2) The overall economy and efficiency of Government operations and activities, including Federal procurement.
(3) Reorganizations in the executive branch of the Government.
(4) Intergovernmental relationships between the United States and the States and municipalities, and general revenue sharing.
(5) National archives.

In addition to its legislative jurisdiction under the preceding provisions of this paragraph (and its oversight functions under clause 2(b)(1) and (2)), the committee shall have the function of performing the activities and conducting the studies which are provided for in clause 4(c).

(i) Committee on House Administration.
(1) Appropriations from the contingent fund.
(2) Auditing and settling of all accounts which may be charged to the contingent fund.
(3) Employment of persons by the House, including clerks for Members and committees, and reporters of debates.
(4) Except as provided in clause 1(p)(4), matters relating to the Library of Congress and the House Library; statuary and pictures; acceptance or purchase of works of art for the Capitol; the Botanic Gardens; management of the Library of Congress; purchase of books and manuscripts; erection of monuments to the memory of individuals.
(5) Except as provided in clause 1(p)(4), matters relating to the Smithsonian Institution and the incorporation of similar institutions.
(6) Expenditure of contingent fund of the House.
(7) Matters relating to printing and correction of the Congressional Record.
(8) Measures relating to accounts of the House generally.
(9) Measures relating to assignment of office space for Members and committees.
(10) Measures relating to the disposition of useless executive papers.
(11) Measures relating to the election of the President, Vice President, or Members of Congress; corrupt practices; contested elections; credentials and qualifications; and Federal elections generally.
(12) Measures relating to services to the House, including the House Restaurant, parking facilities and administration of the House Office Buildings and of the House wing of the Capitol.
(13) Measures relating to the travel of Members of the House.
(14) Measures relating to the raising, reporting and use of campaign contributions for candidates for office of Representative in the House of Representatives and of Resident Commissioner to the United States from Puerto Rico.
(15) Measures relating to the compensation, retirement and other benefits of the Members, officers, and employees of the Congress.

In addition to its legislative jurisdiction under the preceding provisions of this paragraph (and its general oversight function under clause 2(b)(1)), the committee shall have the function of performing the duties which are provided for in clause 4(d).

(j) Committee on Interior and Insular Affairs.

(1) Forest reserves and national parks created from the public domain.

(2) Forfeiture of land grants and alien ownership, including alien ownership of mineral lands.

(3) Geological Survey.

(4) Interstate compacts relating to apportionment of waters for irrigation purposes.

(5) Irrigation and reclamation, including water supply for reclamation projects, and easements of public lands for irrigation projects, and acquisition of private lands when necessary to complete irrigation projects.

(6) Measures relating to the care and management of Indians, including the care and allotment of Indian lands and general and special measures relating to claims which are paid out of Indian funds.

(7) Measures relating generally to the insular possessions of the United States, except those affecting the revenue and appropriations.

(8) Military parks and battlefields; national cemeteries administered by the Secretary of the Interior, and parks within the District of Columbia.

(9) Mineral land laws and claims and entries thereunder.

(10) Mineral resources of the public lands.

(11) Mining interests generally.

(12) Mining schools and experimental stations.

(13) Petroleum conservation on the public lands and conservation of the radium supply in the United States.

(14) Preservation of prehistoric ruins and objects of interest on the public domain.

(15) Public lands generally, including entry, easements, and grazing thereon.

(16) Relations of the United States with the Indians and the Indian tribes.

In addition to its legislative jurisdiction under the preceding provisions of this paragraph (and its general oversight function under clause 2(b)(1)), the committee shall have the special oversight functions provided for in clause 3(e) with respect to all programs affecting Indians and nonmilitary nuclear energy and research and development including the disposal of nuclear waste.

(k) Committee on International Relations.

(1) Relations of the United States with foreign nations generally.

(2) Acquisition of land and buildings for embassies and legations in foreign countries.

(3) Establishment of boundary lines between the United States and foreign nations.

(4) Foreign loans.

(5) International conferences and congresses.

(6) Intervention abroad and declarations of war.

(7) Measures relating to the diplomatic service.

(8) Measures to foster commercial intercourse with foreign nations and to safeguard American business interests abroad.

(9) Neutrality.

(10) Protection of American citizens abroad and expatriation.

(11) The American National Red Cross.

(12) United Nations Organizations.

(13) Measures relating to international economic policy.

(14) Export controls.

(15) International commodity agreements (other than those involving sugar).

(16) Trading with the enemy.

(17) International education.

In addition to its legislative jurisdiction under the preceding provisions of this paragraph (and its general oversight function under clause 2(b)(1)), the committee shall have the special oversight functions provided for in clause 3(d) with respect to customs administration, intelligence activities relating to foreign policy, international financial and monetary organizations, and international fishing agreements.

(l) Committee on Interstate and Foreign Commerce.

(1) Interstate and foreign commerce generally

(2) Inland waterways.

(3) Interstate oil compacts and petroleum and natural gas, except on the public lands.

(4) Railroads, including railroad labor, railroad retirement and unemployment, except revenue measures related thereto.

(5) Regulation of interstate and foreign communications.

(6) Regulation of interstate transmission of power, except the installation of connections between Government waterpower projects.

(7) Securities and exchanges.

(8) Consumer affairs and consumer protection.

(9) Travel and tourism.
(10) Public health and quarantine.
(11) Health and health facilities, except health care supported by payroll deductions.
(12) Biomedical research and development.
  (m) Committee on the Judiciary.
(1) Judicial proceedings, civil and criminal generally.
(2) Apportionment of Representatives.
(3) Bankruptcy, mutiny, espionage, and counterfeiting.
(4) Civil liberties.
(5) Constitutional amendments.
(6) Federal courts and judges.
(7) Immigration and naturalization.
(8) Interstate compacts generally.
(9) Local courts in the Territories and possessions.
(10) Measures relating to claims against the United States.
(11) Meetings of Congress, attendance of Members and their acceptance of incompatible offices.
(12) National penitentiaries.
(13) Patent Office.
(14) Patents, copyrights, and trademarks.
(15) Presidential succession.
(16) Protection of trade and commerce against unlawful restraints and monopolies.
(17) Revision and codification of the Statutes of the United States.
(18) State and territorial boundary lines.
(19) Communist and other subversive activities affecting the internal security of the United States.

All property and records of the Committee on Internal Security are hereby transferred to the Committee on the Judiciary and shall be available for use by the latter committee to the same extent as if such property and records were originally that of the Committee on the Judiciary.

Such staff members of the Committee on Internal Security as the chairman of that committee for the 93rd Congress may designate after consultation and agreement with the chairman of the Committee on the Judiciary shall, without reduction in compensation, be transferred and appointed to the Committee on the Judiciary as additional members of the staff of the Committee on the Judiciary for the period of the 94th Congress, and shall be paid from the contingent fund of the House.

  (n) Committee on Merchant Marine and Fisheries.

(1) Merchant marine generally.
(2) Oceanography and Marine Affairs, including coastal zone management.
(3) Coast Guard, including lifesaving service, lighthouses, lightships, and ocean derelicts.
(4) Fisheries and wildlife, including research, restoration, refuges, and conservation.
(5) Measures relating to the regulation of common carriers by water (except matters subject to the jurisdiction of the Interstate Commerce Commission) and to the inspection of merchant marine vessels, lights and signals, lifesaving equipment, and fire protection on such vessels.
(6) Merchant marine officers and seamen.
(7) Navigation and the laws relating thereto, including pilotage.
(8) Panama Canal and the maintenance and operation of the Panama Canal, including the administration, sanitation, and government of the Canal Zone; and interoceanic canals generally.
(9) Registering and licensing of vessels and small boats.
(10) Rules and international arrangements to prevent collisions at sea.
(11) United States Coast Guard and Merchant Marine Academies, and State Maritime Academies.
(12) International fishing agreements.
  (o) Committee on Post Office and Civil Service.
(1) Census and the collection of statistics generally.
(2) All Federal Civil Service, including intergovernmental personnel.
(3) Postal-savings banks.
(4) Postal service generally, including the railway mail service, and measures relating to ocean mail and pneumatic-tube service; but excluding post roads.
(5) Status of officers and employees of the United States, including their compensation, classification, and retirement.
(6) Hatch Act.
(7) Holidays and celebrations.
(8) Population and demography.
  (p) Committee on Public Works and Transportation.
(1) Flood control and improvement of rivers and harbors.
(2) Measures relating to the Capitol Building and the Senate and House Office Buildings.
(3) Measures relating to the construction or maintenance of roads and post roads, other than appropriations therefor; but it shall not be in order for any bill providing general legislation in relation to roads to contain any provision

HOUSE RULES—94TH CONGRESS

for any specific road, nor for any bill in relation to a specific road to embrace a provision in relation to any other specific road.

(4) Measures relating to the construction or reconstruction, maintenance, and care of the buildings and grounds of the Botanic Gardens, the Library of Congress, and the Smithsonian Institute.

(5) Measures relating to the purchase of sites and construction of post offices, customhouses, Federal courthouses, and Government buildings within the District of Columbia.

(6) Oil and other pollution of navigable waters.

(7) Public buildings and occupied or improved grounds of the United States generally.

(8) Public works for the benefit of navigation, including bridges and dams (other than international bridges and dams).

(9) Water power.

(10) Transportation, including civil aviation except railroads, railroad labor and pensions.

(11) Roads and the safety thereof.

(12) Water transportation subject to the jurisdiction of the Interstate Commerce Commission.

(13) Related transportation regulatory agencies, except (A) the Interstate Commerce Commission as it relates to railroads; (B) Federal Railroad Administration; and (C) Amtrak.

(q) Committee on Rules.

"(1) The rules and joint rules (other than rules or joint rules relating to the Code of Official Conduct or relating to financial disclosure by a Member, officer, or employee of the House of Representatives), and order of business of the House.

(2) Emergency waivers (under the Congressional Budget Act of 1974) of the required reporting date for bills and resolutions authorizing new budget authority.

(3) Recesses and final adjournments of Congress.

(4) The Committee on Rules is authorized to sit and act whether or not the House is in session.

(r) Committee on Science and Technology.

(1) Astronautical research and development, including resources, personnel, equipment, and facilities.

(2) Bureau of Standards, standardization of weights and measures and the metric system.

(3) National Aeronautics and Space Administration.

(4) National Aeronautics and Space Council.

(5) National Science Foundation.

(6) Outer space, including exploration and control thereof.

(7) Science Scholarships.

(8) Scientific research and development.

(9) Civil aviation research and development.

(10) Environmental research and development.

(11) All energy research and development except nuclear research and development.

(12) National Weather Service.

In addition to its legislative jurisdiction under the preceding provisions of this paragraph (and its general oversight function under clause 2(b)(1)), the committee shall have the special oversight functions provided for in clause 3(f) with respect to all non-military research and development.

(s) Committee on Small Business.

(1) Assistance to and protection of small business, including financial aid.

(2) Participation of small-business enterprises in Federal procurement and Government contracts.

In addition to its legislative jurisdiction under the preceding provisions of this paragraph (and its general oversight function under clause 2(b)(1)), the committee shall have the special oversight function provided for in clause 3(g) with respect to the problems of small business.

(t) Committee on Standards of Official Conduct.

(1) Measures relating to the Code of Official Conduct.

(2) Measures relating to financial disclosure by Members, officers, and employees of the House of Representatives.

(3) Measures relating to activities designed to (1) assist in defeating, passing, or amending any legislation by the House or (2) influence, directly or indirectly, the passage or defeat of any legislation by the House.

In addition to its legislative jurisdiction under the preceding provisons of this paragraph (and its general oversight function under clause 2(b)(1)), the committee shall have the functions with respect to recommendations, studies, investigations, and reports which are provided for in clause 4(e).

(u) Committee on Veterans' Affairs.

(1) Veterans' measures generally.

(2) Cemeteries of the United States in which veterans of any war or conflict are or may be buried, whether in the United States or abroad, except cemeteries administered by the Secretary of the Interior.

(3) Compensation, vocational rehabilitation, and education of veterans.
(4) Life insurance issued by the Government on account of service in the Armed Forces.
(5) Pensions of all the wars of the United States, general and special.
(6) Readjustment of servicemen to civil life.
(7) Soldiers' and sailors' civil relief.
(8) Veterans' hospitals, medical care, and treatment of veterans.
(v) Committee on Ways and Means.
(1) Customs, collection districts, and ports of entry and delivery.
(2) Reciprocal trade agreements.
(3) Revenue measures generally.
(4) Revenue measures relating to the insular possessions.
(5) The bonded debt of the United States.
(6) The deposit of public moneys.
(7) Transportation of dutiable goods.
(8) Tax exempt foundations and charitable trusts.
(9) National social security, except (A) health care and facilities programs that are supported from general revenues as opposed to payroll deductions and (B) work incentive programs.

General Oversight Responsibilities

2. (a) In order to assist the House in—
(1) its analysis, appraisal, and evaluation of (A) the application, administration, execution, and effectiveness of the laws enacted by the Congress, or (B) conditions and circumstances which may indicate the necessity or desirability of enacting new or additional legislation, and
(2) its formulation, consideration, and enactment of such modifications of or changes in those laws, and of such additional legislation, as may be necessary or appropriate,
the various standing committees shall have oversight responsibilities as provided in paragraph (b).

(b)(1) Each standing committee (other than the Committee on Appropriations and the Committee on the Budget) shall review and study, on a continuing basis, the application, administration, execution, and effectiveness of those laws, or parts of laws, the subject matter of which is within the jurisdiction of that committee, and the organization and operation of the Federal agencies and entities having responsibilities in or for the administration and execution thereof, in order to determine whether such laws and the programs thereunder are being implemented and carried out in accordance with the intent of the Congress and whether such programs should be continued, curtailed, or eliminated. In addition, each such committee shall review and study any conditions or circumstances which may indicate the necessity or desirability of enacting new or additional legislation within the jurisdiction of that committee (whether or not any bill or resolution has been introduced with respect thereto), and shall on a continuing basis undertake futures research and forecasting on matters within the jurisdiction of that committee. Each such committee having more than twenty members shall establish an oversight subcommittee, or require its subcommittees, if any, to conduct oversight in the area of their respective jurisdiction, to assist in carrying out its responsibilities under this subparagraph.

The establishment of oversight subcommittees shall in no way limit the responsibility of the subcommittees with legislative jurisdiction from carrying out their oversight responsibilities.

(2) The Committee on Government Operations shall review and study, on a continuing basis, the operation of Government activities at all levels with a view to determining their economy and efficiency.

(3) The Committee on Appropriations shall conduct such studies and examinations of the organization and operation of executive departments and other executive agencies (including any agency the majority of the stock of which is owned by the Government of the United States) as it may deem necessary to assist it in the determination of matters within its jurisdiction.

(c) At the beginning of each Congress, an appropriate representative of the Committee on Government Operations shall meet with appropriate representatives of each of the other committees of the House to discuss the oversight plans of such committees and to assist in coordinating all of the oversight activities of the House during such Congress. Within 60 days after the Congress convenes, the Committee on Government Operations shall report to the House the results of such meetings and discussions, and any recommendations which it may have to assure the most effective coordination of such activities and otherwise achieve the objectives of this clause.

(d) Each standing committee of the House shall have the function of reviewing and studying on a continuing basis the impact or probable impact of tax policies affecting subjects within its jurisdiction as described in clauses 1 and 3.

SPECIAL OVERSIGHT FUNCTIONS

3. (a) The Committee on Armed Services shall have the function of reviewing and studying, on a continuing basis, all laws, programs, and Government activities dealing with or involving international arms control and disarmament and the education of military dependents in schools.

(b) The Committee on the Budget shall have the function of—

(1) making continuing studies of the effect on budget outlays of relevant existing and proposed legislation, and reporting the results of such studies to the House on a recurring basis; and

(2) requesting and evaluating continuing studies of tax expenditures, devising methods of coordinating tax expenditures, policies, and programs with direct budget outlays, and reporting the results of such studies to the House on a recurring basis.

(c) The Committee on Education and Labor shall have the function of reviewing, studying, and coordinating, on a continuing basis, all laws, programs, and Government activities dealing with or involving domestic educational programs and institutions and programs of student assistance, which are within the jurisdiction of other committees.

(d) The Committee on International Relations shall have the function of reviewing and studying, on a continuing basis, all laws, programs and Government activities dealing with or involving customs administration, intelligence activities relating to foreign policy, international financial and monetary organizations, and international fishing agreements.

(e) The Committee on Interior and Insular Affairs shall have the function of reviewing and studying, on a continuing basis, all laws, programs, and Government activities dealing with Indians and nonmilitary nuclear energy and research and development including the disposal of nuclear waste.

(f) The Committee on Science and Technology shall have the function of reviewing and studying, on a continuing basis, all laws, programs, and Government activities dealing with or involving nonmilitary research and development.

(g) The Committee on Small Business shall have the function of studying and investigating, on a continuing basis, the problems of all types of small business.

Additional Functions of Committees

4. (a)(1)(A) The Committee on Appropriations shall, within thirty days after the transmittal of the Budget to the Congress each year, hold hearings on the Budget as a whole with particular reference to—

(i) the basic recommendations and budgetary policies of the President in the presentation of the Budget; and

(ii) the fiscal, financial, and economic assumptions used as bases in arriving at total estimated expenditures and receipts.

(B) In holding hearings pursuant to subdivision (A), the committee shall receive testimony from the Secretary of the Treasury, the Director of the Office of Management and Budget, the Chairman of the Council of Economic Advisers, and such other persons as the committee may desire.

(C) Hearings pursuant to subdivision (A), or any part thereof, shall be held in open session, except when the committee, in open session and with a quorum present, determines by rollcall vote that the testimony to be taken at that hearing on that day may be related to a matter of national security: *Provided, however,* That the committee may by the same procedure close one subsequent day of hearing. A transcript of all such hearings shall be printed and a copy thereof furnished to each Member, Delegate, and the Resident Commissioner from Puerto Rico.

(D) Hearings pursuant to subdivision (A), or any part thereof, may be held before joint meetings of the committee and the Committee on Appropriations of the Senate in accordance with such procedures as the two committees jointly may determine.

(2) Whenever any bill or resolution which provides new spending authority described in section 401(c)(2)(C) of the Congressional Budget Act of 1974 is reported by a committee of the House and the amount of new budget authority which will be required for the fiscal year involved if such bill or resolution is enacted as so reported exceeds the appropriate allocation of new budget authority reported as described in clause 5(j) in connection with the most recently agreed to concurrent resolution on the budget for such fiscal year, such bill or resolution shall then be referred to the Committee on Appropriations with instructions to report it, with the committee's recommendations and (if the committee deems it desirable) with an amendment limiting the total amount of new spending authority provided in the bill or resolution, within 15 calendar days (not counting any day on which the House is not in session) beginning with the day following the day on which it is

so referred. If the Committee on Appropriations fails to report the bill or resolution within such 15-day period, the committee shall be automatically discharged from further consideration of the bill or resolution and the bill or resolution shall be placed on the appropriate calendar.

(3) In addition, the Committee on Appropriations shall study on a continuing basis those provisions of law which (on the first day of the first fiscal year for which the congressional budget process is effective) provide spending authority or permanent budget authority, and shall report to the House from time to time its recommendations for terminating or modifying such provisions.

(b) The Committee on the Budget shall have the duty—

(1) to review on a continuing basis the conduct by the Congressional Budget Office of its functions and duties;

(2) to hold hearings, and receive testimony from Members of Congress and such appropriate representatives of Federal departments and agencies, the general public, and national organizations as it deems desirable, in developing the first concurrent resolution on the budget for each fiscal year;

(3) to make all reports required of it by the Congressional Budget Act of 1974, including the reporting of reconciliation bills and resolutions when so required;

(4) to study on a continuing basis those provisions of law which exempt Federal agencies or any of their activities or outlays from inclusion in the Budget of the United States Government, and to report to the House from time to time its recommendations for terminating or modifying such provisions; and

(5) to study on a continuing basis proposals designed to improve and facilitate methods of congressional budget-making, and to report to the House from time to time the results of such study together with its recommendations.

(c)(1) The Committee on Government Operations shall have the general function of—

(A) receiving and examining reports of the Comptroller General of the United States and of submitting such recommendations to the House as it deems necessary or desirable in connection with the subject matter of such reports;

(B) evaluating the effects of laws enacted to reorganize the legislative and executive branches of the Government; and

(C) studying intergovernmental relationships between the United States and the States and municipalities, and between the United States and international organizations of which the United States is a member.

(2) In addition to its duties under subparagraph (1), the Committee on Government Operations may at any time conduct investigations of any matter without regard to the provisions of clause 1, 2, or 3 (or this clause) conferring jurisdiction over such matter upon another standing committee. The committee's findings and recommendations in any such investigation shall be made available to the other standing committee or committees having jurisdiction over the matter involved (and included in the report of any such other committee when required by clause 2(l)(3) of Rule XI).

(d) The Committee on House Administration shall have the function of—

(1) examining all bills, amendments, and joint resolutions after passage by the House and, in cooperation with the Senate, examining all bills and joint resolutions which shall have passed both Houses to see that they are correctly enrolled, forthwith presenting those which originated in the House to the President of the United States in person after their signature by the Speaker of the House and the President of the Senate and reporting the fact and date of such presentation to the House;

(2) reporting to the Sergeant-at-Arms of the House concerning the travel of Members of the House; and

(3) providing, through the House Information Systems a scheduling service which may be used by all the committees and subcommittees of the House to eliminate, insofar as possible, any meeting and scheduling conflicts.

(e)(1) The Committee on Standards of Official Conduct is authorized; (A) to recommend to the House from time to time such administrative actions as it may deem appropriate to establish or enforce standards of official conduct for Members, officers, and employees of the House; (B) to investigate, subject to subparagraph (2) of this paragraph, any alleged violation, by a Member, officer, or employee of the House, of the Code of Official Conduct or of any law, rule, regulation, or other standard of conduct applicable to the conduct of such Member, officer, or employee in the performance of his duties or the discharge of his responsibilities, and, after notice and hearing, to recommend to the House by resolution or otherwise, such action as the committee may deem appropriate in the circumstances; (C) to report to the appropriate Federal or State authorities, with the approval of the House, any substantial evidence of a violation, by a Member, officer, or employee of the House, of any law applicable to the performance of his duties or the discharge of his responsibilities, which may have been disclosed in a committee investigation; and (D) to give consideration to the request of any Member, officer, or employee of the House for an advisory opinion with respect to the general propriety of any current or proposed conduct of such Member, officer, or employee and, with appropriate deletions to assure the privacy of the individual concerned, to publish such opinion for the guidance of other Members, officers, and employees of the House.

(2) (A) No resolution, report, recommendation, or advisory opinion relating to the official conduct of a Member, officer, or employee of the House shall be made by the Committee on Standards of Official Conduct, and no investigation of such conduct shall be undertaken by such committee, unless approved by the affirmative vote of a majority of the members of the committee.

(B) Except in the case of an investigation undertaken by the committee on its own initiative, the committee may undertake an investigation relating to the official conduct of an individual Member, officer, or employee of the House of Representatives only—

(i) upon receipt of a complaint, in writing and under oath, made by or submitted to a Member of the House and transmitted to the committee by such Member, or

(ii) upon receipt of a complaint, in writing and under oath, directly from an individual not a Member of the House if the committee finds that such complaint has been submitted by such individual to not less than three Members of the House who have refused, in writing, to transmit such complaint to the committee.

(C) No investigation shall be undertaken by the committee of any alleged violation of a law, rule, regulation, or standard of conduct not in effect at the time of the alleged violation.

(D) A member of the committee shall be ineligible to participate, as a member of the committee, in any committee proceeding relating to his or her official conduct. In any case in which a member of the committee is ineligible to act as a member of the committee under the preceding sentence, the Speaker of the House shall designate a Member of the House from the same political party as the ineligible member of the committee to act as a member of the committee in any committee proceeding relating to the official conduct of such ineligible member.

(f) (1) Each standing committee of the House shall, in its consideration of all bills and joint resolutions of a public character within its jurisdiction, insure that appropriations for continuing program and activities of the Federal Government and the District of Columbia government will be made annually to the maximum extent feasible and consistent wth the nature, requirements, and objectives of the programs and activities involved. For the purposes of this paragraph a Government agency includes the organizational units of government listed in clause 7(d) of Rule XIII.

(2) Each standing committee of the House shall review, from time to time, each continuing program within its jurisdiction for which appropriations are not made annually in order to ascertain whether such program could be modified so that appropriations therefor would be made annually.

(g) Each standing committee of the House shall, on or before March 15 of each year, submit to the Committee on the Budget (1) its views and estimates with respect to all matters to be set forth in the concurrent resolution on the budget for the ensuing fiscal year which are within its jurisdiction or functions, and (2) an estimate of the total amounts of new budget authority, and budget outlays resulting therefrom, to be provided or authorized in all bills and resolutions within its jurisdiction which it intends to be effective during that fiscal year.

(h) As soon as practicable after a concurrent resolution on the budget for any fiscal year is agreed to, each standing Committee of the House (after consulting with the appropriate committee or committees of the Senate) shall subdivide any allocations made to it in the joint explanatory statement accompanying the conference report on such resolution, and promptly report such subdivisions to the House, in the manner provided by section 302 of the Congressional Budget Act of 1974.

(i) "Each standing committee of the House which is directed in a concurrent resolution on the budget to determine and recommend changes in laws, bills, or resolutions under the reconciliation process shall promptly make such determinations and recommendations, and report a reconciliation bill or resolution (or both) to the House or submit such recommendations to the Committee on the Budget, in accordance with the Congressional Budget Act of 1974.

Referral of Bills, Resolutions, and Other Matters to Committees

5. (a) Each bill, resolution, or other matter which relates to a subject listed under any standing committee named in clause 1 shall be referred by the Speaker in accordance with the provisions of this clause.

(b) Every referral of any matter under paragraph (a) shall be made in such manner as to assure to the maximum extent feasible that each committee which has jurisdiction under clause 1 over the subject matter of any provision thereof will have responsibility for considering such provision and reporting to the House with respect thereto. Any precedents, rulings, and procedures in effect prior to the Ninety-Fourth Congress shall be applied with respect to referrals under this clause only to the extent that they will contribute to the achievement of the objectives of this clause.

(c) In carrying out paragraph (a) and (b) with respect to any matter, the Speaker may refer the matter simultaneously to two or more committees for concurrent consideration or for consideration in sequence (subject to appropriate time limitations in the case of any committee after the first), or divide the matter into two or more parts (reflecting different subjects and jurisdictions) and refer each such part to a different committee, or refer the matter to a special ad hoc committee appointed by the Speaker with the approval of the House (from the members of the committees having legislative jurisdiction) for the specific purpose of considering that matter and reporting to the House thereon, or make such other provision as may be considered appropriate.

(d) After the introduction in the House of each bill or resolution the Congressional Research Service of the Library of Congress shall prepare a factual description of the subject involved therein not to exceed one hundred words; such description shall be published in the Congressional Record and the Digest of Public General Bills and Resolutions as soon as possible after introduction.

Election and Membership of Committees; Chairmen; Vacancies; Select and Conference Committees

6. (a)(1) The standing committees specified in clause 1 shall be elected by the House at the commencement of each Congress, from nominations submitted by the respective party caucuses.

(2) One-half of the members of the Committee on Standards of Official Conduct shall be from the majority party and one-half shall be from the minority party.

(b) One of the Members of each standing committee shall be elected by the House from nominations submitted by the majority party caucus, at the commencement of each Congress, as chairman thereof. In the temporary absence of the chairman, the Member next in rank in the order named in the election of the committee, and so on, as often as the case shall happen, shall act as chairman; and in case of a permanent vacancy in the chairmanship of any such committee the House shall elect another chairman.

(c) Each standing committee of the House of Representatives, except the Committee on the Budget, that has more than twenty members shall establish at least four subcommittees.

(d) All vacancies in standing committees shall be filled by election by the House.

(e) The Speaker shall appoint all select and conference committees which shall be ordered by the House from time to time. In appointing members to conference committees the Speaker shall appoint no less than a majority of members who generally supported the House position as determined by the Speaker.

(f) The Speaker may appoint the Resident Commissioner from Puerto Rico and the Delegate from the District of Columbia, Virgin Islands, and Guam to any conference committee that is considering legislation reported from a committee on which they serve.

(g) There shall be in the House the permanent Select Committee on Aging, which shall not have legislative jurisdiction but which shall have jurisdiction—

(1) to conduct a continuing comprehensive study and review of the problems of the older American, including but not limited to income maintenance, housing, health (including medical research), welfare, employment, education, recreation, and participation in family and community life as self-respecting citizens;

(2) to study the use of all practicable means and methods of encouraging the development of public and private programs and policies which will assist the older American in taking a

full part in national life and which will encourage the utilization of the knowledge, skills, special aptitudes, and abilities of older Americans to contribute to a better quality of life for all Americans;

(3) to develop policies that would encourage the coordination of both governmental and private programs designed to deal with problems of aging; and

(4) to review any recommendations made by the President or by the White House Conference on Aging relating to programs or policies affecting older Americans.

RULE XI

RULES OF PROCEDURE FOR COMMITTEES

In General

1. (a)(1) The Rules of the House are the rules of its committees and subcommittees so far as applicable, except that a motion to recess from day to day is a motion of high privilege in committees and subcommittees.

(2) Each subcommittee of a committee is a part of that committee, and is subject to the authority and direction of that committee and to its rules so far as applicable.

(b) Each committee is authorized at any time to consider such investigations and studies as it may consider necessary or appropriate in the exercise of its responsibilities under Rule X, and (subject to the adoption of expense resolutions as required by clause 5) to incur expenses (including travel expenses) in connection therewith.

(c) Each committee is authorized to have printed and bound testimony and other data presented at hearings held by the committee. All costs of stenographic services and transcripts in connection with any meeting or hearing of a committee shall be paid from the contingent fund of the House.

(d) Each committee shall submit to the House, not later than January 2 of each odd-numbered year, a report on the activities of that committee under this rule and Rule X during the Congress ending at noon on January 3 of such year.

Committee Rules

Adoption of written rules

2. (a) Each standing committee of the House shall adopt written rules governing its procedure. Such rules—

(1) shall be adopted in a meeting which is open to the public unless the committee, in open session and with a quorum present, determines by rollcall vote that all or part of the meeting on that day is to be closed to the public.

(2) shall be not inconsistent with the Rules of the House or with those provisions of law having the force and effect of Rules of the House; and

(3) shall in any event incorporate all of the succeeding provisions of this clause to the extent applicable.

Each committee's rules specifying its regular meeting days, and any other rules of a committee which are in addition to the provisions of this clause, shall be published in the Congressional Record not later than thirty days after the Congress convenes in each odd-numbered year. Each select or joint committee shall comply with the provisions of this paragraph unless specifically prohibited by law.

Regular meeting days

(b) Each standing committee of the House shall adopt regular meeting days, which shall be not less frequent than monthly, for the conduct of its business. Each such committee shall meet, for the consideration of any bill or resolution pending before the committee or for the transaction of other committee business, on all regular meeting days fixed by the committee, unless otherwise provided by written rule adopted by the committee.

Additional and special meetings

(c)(1) The chairman of each standing committee may call and convene, as he or she considers necessary, additional meetings of the committee for the consideration of any bill or resolution pending before the committee or for the conduct of other committee business. The committee shall meet for such purpose pursuant to that call of the chairman.

(2) If at least three members of any standing committee desire that a special meeting of the committee be called by the chairman, those members may file in the offices of the committee their written request to the chairman for that special meeting. Such request shall specify the measure or matter to be considered. Immediately upon the filing of the request, the clerk of the committee shall notify the chairman of the filing of the request. If, within three calendar days after the filing of the request, the chairman does not call the requested special meeting, to be held within seven calendar days after the filing of the request, a majority of the members of the committee may file in the offices of the committee their written notice that a special meeting of the committee will be held, specifying the date and hour of, and the measure or matter to be considered at, that special meeting. The Committee shall meet on that date and hour. Immediately upon the filing of the notice, the

clerk of the committee shall notify all members of the committee that such special meeting will be held and inform them of its date and hour and the measure or matter to be considered; and only the measure or matter specified in that notice may be considered at that special meeting.

Ranking majority Member to preside in absence of chairman

(d) If the chairman of any standing committee is not present at any meeting of the committee, the ranking member of the majority party on the committee who is present shall preside at that meeting.

Committee records

(e)(1) Each committee shall keep a complete record of all committee action which shall include a record of the votes on any question on which a rollcall vote is demanded. The result of each such rollcall vote shall be made available by the committee for inspection by the public at reasonable times in the offices of the committee. Information so available for public inspection shall include a description of the amendment, motion, order or other proposition and the name of each Member voting for and each Member voting against such amendment, motion, order, or proposition, and whether by proxy or in person, and the names of those Members present but not voting.

(2) All committee hearings, records, data, charts, and files shall be kept separate and distinct from the congressional office records of the Member serving as chairman of the committee; and such records shall be the property of the House and all Members of the House shall have access thereto.

Proxies

(f) No vote by any Member of any Committee or subcommittee with respect to any measure or matter may be cast by proxy unless such committee, by written rule adopted by the committee, permits voting by proxy and requires that the proxy authorization shall be in writing, shall assert that the Member is absent on official business or is otherwise unable to be present at the meeting of the committee, shall designate the person who is to execute the proxy authorization, and shall be limited to a specific measure or matter and any amendments or motions pertaining thereto; except that a member may authorize a general proxy only for motions to recess, adjourn or other procedural matters. Each proxy to be effective shall be signed by the Member assigning his or her vote and shall contain the date and time of day that the proxy is signed. Proxies may not be counted for a quorum.

Open meetings and hearings

(g)(1) Each meeting for the transaction of business, including the markup of legislation, of each standing committee or subcommittee thereof shall be open to the public except when the committee or subcommittee, in open session and with a quorum present, determines by rollcall vote that all or part of the remainder of the meeting on that day shall be closed to the public. *Provided, however,* That no person other than members of the committee and such congressional staff and such departmental representatives as they may authorize shall be present at any business or markup session which has been closed to the public. This paragraph does not apply to open committee hearings which are provided for by clause 4(a)(3) of Rule X or by subparagraph (2) of this paragraph, or to any meeting that relates solely to internal budget or personnel matters.

(2) Each hearing conducted by each committee or subcommittee thereof shall be open to the public except when the committee or subcommittee, in open session and with a quorum present, determines by rollcall vote that all or part of the remainder of that hearing on that day shall be closed to the public because disclosure of testimony, evidence, or other matters to be considered would endanger the national security or would violate any law or rule of the House of Representatives: *Provided, however,* That the committee or subcommittee may by the same procedure vote to close one subsequent day of hearing.

(3) Each committee of the House (except the Committee on Rules) shall make public announcement of the date, place and subject matter of any committee hearing at least one week before the commencement of the hearing. If the committee determines that there is good cause to begin the hearing sooner, it shall make the announcement at the earliest possible date. Any announcement made under his subparagraph shall be promptly published in the Daily Digest.

(4) Each committee shall, insofar as is practicable, require each witness who is to appear before it to file with the committee (in advance of his or her appearance) a written statement of the proposed testimony and to limit the oral presentation at such appearance to a brief summary of his or her argument.

(5) No point of order shall lie with

respect to any measure reported by any committee on the ground that hearings on such measure were not conducted in accordance with the provisions of this clause; except that a point of order on that ground may be made by any member of the committee which reported the measure if, in the committee, such point of order was (A) timely made and (B) improperly overruled or not properly considered.

(6) The preceding provisions of this paragraph do not apply to the committee hearings which are provided for by clause 4(a)(1) of Rule X.

Quorum for taking testimony

(h) Each committee may fix the number of its members to constitute a quorum for taking testimony and receiving evidence, which shall be not less than two.

Prohibition against committee meetings during five-minute rule

(i) No committee of the House (except the Committee on Appropriations, the Committee on the Budget, and the Committee on Rules) may sit, without special leave, while the House is reading a measure for amendment under the five-minute rule.

Calling and interrogation of witnesses

(j)(1) Whenever any hearing is conducted by any committee upon any measure or matter, the minority party Members on the committee shall be entitled, upon request to the chairman by a majority of them before the completion of the hearing, to call witnesses selected by the minority to testify with respect to that measure or matter during at least one day of hearing thereon.

(2) Each committee shall apply the five-minute rule in the interrogation of witnesses in any hearing until such time as each Member of the committee who so desires has had an opportunity to question each witness.

Investigative hearing procedures

(k)(1) The chairman at an investigative hearing shall announce in an opening statement the subject of the investigation.

(2) A copy of the committee rules and this clause shall be made available to each witness.

(3) Witnesses at investigative hearings may be accompanied by their own counsel for the purpose of advising them concerning their constitutional rights.

(4) The chairman may punish breaches of order and decorum, and of professional ethics on the part of counsel, by censure and exclusion from the hearings; and the committee may cite the offender to the House for contempt.

(5) If the committee determines that evidence or testimony at an investigative hearing may tend to defame, degrade, or incriminate any person, it shall—

(A) receive such evidence or testimony in executive session;

(B) afford such person an opportunity voluntarily to appear as a witness; and

(C) receive and dispose of requests from such person to subpena additional witnesses.

(6) Except as provided in subparagraph (5), the chairman shall receive and the committee shall dispose of requests to subpena additional witnesses.

(7) No evidence or testimony taken in executive session may be released or used in public sessions without the consent of the committee.

(8) In the discretion of the committee, witnesses may submit brief and pertinent sworn statements in writing for inclusion in the record. The committee is the sole judge of the pertinency of testimony and evidence adduced at its hearing.

(9) A witness may obtain a transcript copy of his testimony given at a public session or, if given at an executive session, when authorized by the committee.

Committee procedures for reporting bills and resolutions

(l)(1)(A) It shall be the duty of the chairman of each committee (except as provided in subdivision (C)) to report or cause to be reported promptly to the House any measure approved by the committee and to take or cause to be taken necessary steps to bring the matter to a vote.

(B) In any event, the report of any committee on a measure which has been approved by the committee shall be filed within seven calendar days (exclusive of days on which the House is not in session) after the day on which there has been filed with the clerk of the committee a written request, signed by a majority of the members of the committee, for the reporting of that measure. Upon the filing of any such request, the clerk of the committee shall transmit immediately to the chairman of the committee notice of the filing of that request. This subdivision does not apply to the reporting of a regular appropriation bill by the Committee on Appropriations prior to compliance with subdivision (C) and does not apply to a report of the Committee on Rules with respect to the rules, joint rules, or order of business of the House or to the reporting of a resolution of inquiry addressed to the head of an executive department.

(C) Before reporting the first regular appropriation bill for each fiscal year, the Committee on Appropriations shall, to the extent practicable and in accordance with section 307 of the Congressional Budget Act of 1974, complete subcommittee markup and full committee action on all regular appropriation bills for that year and submit to the House a summary report comparing the committee's recommendations with the appropriate levels of budget outlays and new budget authority as set forth in the most recently agreed to current resolution on the budget for that year.

(2)(A) No measure or recommendation shall be reported from any committee unless a majority of the committee was actually present.

(B) With respect to each rollcall vote on a motion to report any bill or resolution of a public character, the total number of votes cast for, and the total number of votes cast against, the reporting of such bill or resolution shall be included in the committee report.

(3) The report of any committee on a measure which has been approved by the committee (A) shall include the oversight findings and recommendations required pursuant to the last sentence of clause 2(b)(1) of Rule X separately set out and clearly identified; (B) the statement required by section 308(a) of the Congressional Budget Act of 1974, separately set out and clearly identified, if the measure provides new budget authority or new or increased tax expenditures; (C) the estimate and comparison prepared by the Director of the Congressional Budget Office under section 403 of such Act, separately set out and clearly identified, whenever the Director (if timely submitted prior to the filing of the report) has submitted such estimate and comparison to the committee; and (D) a summary of the oversight findings and recommendations made by the Committee on Government Operations under clause 2(b)(2) of Rule X separately set out and clearly identified whenever such findings and recommendations have been submitted to the legislative committee in a timely fashion to allow an opportunity to consider such findings and recommendations during the committee's deliberations on the measure.

(4) Each report of a committee on each bill or joint resolution of a public character reported by such committee shall contain a detailed analytical statement as to whether the enactment of such bill or joint resolution into law may have an inflationary impact on prices and costs in the operation of the national economy.

(5) If, at the time of approval of any measure or matter by any committee, other than the Committee on Rules, any member of the committee gives notice of intention to file supplemental, minority, or additional views, that member shall be entitled to not less than three calendar days (excluding Saturdays, Sundays, and legal holidays) in which to file such views, in writing and signed by that member, with the clerk of the committee. All such views so filed by one or more members of the committee shall be included within, and shall be a part of, the report filed by the committee with respect to that measure or matter. The report of the committee upon that measure or matter shall be printed in a single volume which—

(A) shall include all supplemental, minority, or additional views which have been submitted by the time of the filing of the report, and

(B) shall bear upon its cover a recital that any such supplemental, minority, or additional views (and any material submitted under subdivisions (C) and (D) of subparagraph (3)) are included as part of the report.

This subparagraph does not preclude—

(i) the immediate filing or printing of a committee report unless timely request for the opportunity to file supplemental, minority, or additional views has been made as provided by this subparagraph; or

(ii) the filing by any such committee of any supplemental report upon any measure or matter which may be required for the correction of any technical error in a previous report made by that committee upon that measure or matter.

(6) A measure or matter reported by any committee (except the Committee on Rules in the case of a resolution making in order the consideration of a bill, resolution, or other order of business), shall not be considered in the House until the third calendar day (or the tenth calendar day in the case of a concurrent resolution on the budget), excluding Saturdays, Sundays, and legal holidays following the day on which the report of that committee upon that measure or matter has been available to the Members of the House. If hearings have been held on any such measure or matter so reported, the committee reporting the measure or matter shall make every rea-

sonable effort to have such hearings printed and available for distribution to the Members of the House prior to the consideration of such measure or matter in the House. This subparagraph shall not apply to—
(A) any measure for the declaration of war, or the declaration of a national emergency, by the Congress; or
(B) any executive decision, determination, or action which would become, or continue to be, effective unless disapproved or otherwise invalidated by one or both Houses of Congress.

(7) If, within seven calendar days after a measure has, by resolution, been made in order for consideration by the House, no motion has been offered that the House consider that measure, any member of the committee which reported that measure may be recognized in the discretion of the Speaker to offer a motion that the House shall consider that measure, if that committee has duly authorized that member to offer that motion.

Power to sit and act; subpoena power

(m)(1) For the purpose of carrying out any of its functions and duties under this rule and Rule X (including any matters referred to it under clause 5 of Rule X), any committee, or any subcommittee thereof, is authorized (subject to subparagraph (2)(A) of this paragraph)—
(A) to sit and act at such times and places within the United States, whether the House is in session, has recessed, or has adjourned, and to hold such hearings, and
(B) to require, by subpoena or otherwise, the attendance and testimony of such witnesses and the production of such books, records, correspondence, memorandums, papers, and documents as it deems necessary. The chairman of the committee, or any member designated by such chairman, may administer oaths to any witness.

(2)(A) A subpoena may be issued by a committee or subcommittee under subparagraph (1)(B) in the conduct of any investigation or activity or series of investigations or activities, only when authorized by a majority of the members of the committee, and authorized subpoenas shall be signed by the chairman of the committee or by any member designated by the committee.

(B) Compliance with any subpoena issued by a committee or subcommittee under subparagraph (1)(B) may be enforced only as authorized or directed by the House.

Use of committee funds for travel

(n) Funds authorized for a committee under clause 5 are for expenses incurred in the committee's activities within the United States; however, local currencies owned by the United States shall be made available to the committee and its employees engaged in carrying out their official duties outside the United States. No appropriated funds shall be expended for the purpose of defraying expenses of members of the committee or its employees in any country where local currencies are available for this purpose; and the following conditions shall apply with respect to their use of such currencies:

(1) No Member or employee of the committee shall receive or expend local currencies for subsistence in any country at a rate in excess of the maximum per diem rate set forth in applicable Federal law.

(2) Each Member or employee of the committee shall make to the chairman of the committee an itemized report showing the number of days visited in each country whose local currencies were spent, the amount of per diem furnished, and the cost of transportation if furnished by public carrier, or, if such transportation is furnished by an agency of the United States Government, the cost of such transportation and the identification of the agency. All such individual reports shall be filed by the chairman with the Committee on House Administration and shall be open to public inspection.

BROADCASTING OF COMMITTEE HEARINGS

3. (a) It is the purpose of this clause to provide a means, in conformity with acceptable standards of dignity, propriety, and decorum, by which committee hearings, or committee meetings, which are open to the public may be covered, by television broadcast, radio broadcast, and still photography, or by any of such methods of coverage
(1) for the education, enlightenment, and information of the general public, on the basis of accurate and impartial news coverage, regarding the operations, procedures, and practices of the House as a legislative and representative body and regarding the measures, public issues, and other matters before the House and its committees, the consideration thereof, and the action taken thereon; and
(2) for the development of the perspective and understanding of the general public with respect to the role and function of the House under the

Constitution of the United States as an organ of the Federal Government.

(b) In addition, it is the intent of this clause that radio and television tapes and television film of any coverage under this clause shall not be used, or more available for use, as partisan political campaign material to promote or oppose the candidacy of any person for elective public offce.

(c) It is, further, the intent of this clause that the general conduct of each meeting (whether of a hearing or otherwise) covered, under authority of this clause, by television broadcast, radio broadcast, and still photograph, or by any of such methods of coverage, and the personal behavior of the committee members and staff, other Government officials and personnel, witnesses, television, radio, and press media personnel, and the general public at the hearing or other meeting shall be in strict conformity with and observance of the acceptable standards of dignity, propriety, courtesy, and decorum traditionally observed by the House in its operations and shall not be such as to—

(1) distort the objects and purposes of the hearing or other meeting or the activities of committee members in connection with that hearing or meeting or in connection with the general work of the committee or of the House; or

(2) cast discredit or dishonor on the House, the committee, or any Member or bring the House, the committee, or any Member into disrepute.

(d) The coverage of committee hearings and meetings by television broadcast, radio broadcast, or still photography is a privilege made available by the House and shall be permitted and conducted only in strict conformity with the purposes, provisions, and requirements of this clause.

(e) Whenever any hearing or meeting conducted by any committee of the House is open to the public, that committee may permit, by majority vote of the committee, that hearing or meeting to be covered, in whole or in part, by television broadcast, radio broadcast, and still photography, or by any of such methods of coverage, but only under such written rules as the committee may adopt in accordance with the purposes, provisions, and requirements of this clause.

(f) The written rules which may be adopted by a committee under paragraph (e) of this clause shall contain provisions to the following effect:

(1) If the television or radio coverage of the hearing or meeting is to be presented to the public as live coverage, that coverage shall be conducted and presented without commercial sponsorship.

(2) No witness served with a subpena by the committee shall be required against his or her will to be photographed at any hearing or to give evidence or testimony while the broadcasting of that hearing, by radio or television, is being conducted. At the request of any such witness who does not wish to be subjected to radio, television, or still photography coverage, all lenses shall be covered and all microphones used for coverage turned off. This subparagraph is supplementary to clause 2(k)(5) of this rule, relating to the protection of the rights of witnesses.

(3) Not more than four television cameras, operating from fixed positions, shall be permitted in a hearing or meeting room. The allocation among the television media of the positions of the number of television cameras permitted in a hearing or meeting room shall be in accordance with fair and equitable procedures devised by the Executive Committee of the Radio and Television Correspondents' Galleries.

(4) Television cameras shall be placed so as not to obstruct in any way the space between any witness giving evidence or testimony and any member of the committee or the visibility of that witness and that member to each other.

(5) Television cameras shall not be placed in positions which obstruct unnecessarily the coverage of the hearing or meeting by the other media.

(6) Equipment necessary for coverage by the television and radio media shall not be installed in, or removed from, the hearing or meeting room while the committee is in session.

(7) Floodlights, spotlights, strobelights, and flashguns shall not be used in providing any method of coverage of the hearing or meeting, except that the television media may install additional lighting in the hearing or meeting room, without cost to the Government, in order to raise the ambient lighting level in the hearing or meeting room to the lowest level necessary to provide adequate television coverage of the hearing or meeting at the then current state of the art of television coverage.

(8) Not more than five press photographers shall be permitted to cover a hearing or meeting by still photography. In the selection of these photographers, preference shall be given to photographers from Associated Press Photos and United Press International Newspictures. If request is made by more than five of the media for coverage of the hearing or

meeting by still photography, that coverage shall be made on the basis of a fair and equitable pool arrangement devised by the Standing Committee of Press Photographers.

(9) Photographers shall not position themselves, at any time during the course of the hearing or meeting, between the witness table and the members of the committee.

(10) Photographers shall not place themselves in positions which obstruct unnecessarily the coverage of the hearing by the other media.

(11) Personnel providing coverage by the television and radio media shall be then currently accredited to the Radio and Television Correspondents' Galleries.

(12) Personnel providing coverage by still photography shall be then currently accredited to the Press Photographers' Gallery.

(13) Personnel providing coverage by the television and radio media and by still photography shall conduct themselves and their coverage activities in an orderly and unobtrusive manner.

Privileged Reports and Amendments

4. (a) The following committees shall have leave to report at any time on the matters herein stated, namely: The Committee on Appropriations—on general appropriation bills; the Committee on the Budget—on the matters required to be reported by such committee under Titles III and IV of the Congressional Budget Act of 1974; the Committee on House Administration—on enrolled bills, contested elections, and all matters referred to it of printing for the use of the House or the two Houses, and on all matters of expenditure of the contingent fund of the House; the Committee on Rules—on rules, joint rules, and the order of business; and the Committee on Standards of Official Conduct—on resolutions recommending action by the House of Representatives with respect to an individual Member, officer, or employee of the House of Representatives.

(b) It shall always be in order to call up for consideration a report from the Committee on Rules on a rule, joint rule, or the order of business (except it shall not be called up for consideration on the same day it is presented to the House, unless so determined by a vote of not less than two-thirds of the Members voting, but this provision shall not apply during the last three days of the session), and, pending the consideration thereof, the Speaker may entertain one motion that the House adjourn; but after the result is announced the Speaker shall not entertain any other dilatory motion until the report shall have been fully disposed of. The Committee on Rules shall not report any rule or order which provides that business under clause 7 of Rule XXIV shall be set aside by a vote of less than two-thirds of the Members present; nor shall it report any rule or order which would prevent the motion to recommit from being made as provided in clause 4 of Rule XVI.

(c) The Committee on Rules shall present to the House reports concerning rules, joint rules, and order of business, within three legislative days of the time when the bill or resolution involved is ordered reported by the committee. If any such rule or order is not considered immediately, it shall be referred to the calendar and, if not called up by the Member making the report within seven legislative days thereafter, any member of the Rules Committee may call it up as a question of privilege and the Speaker shall recognize any member of the Rules Committee seeking recognition for that purpose. If the Committee on Rules makes an adverse report on any resolution pending before the committee, providing for an order of business for the consideration by the House of any public bill or joint resolution, on days when it shall be in order to call up motions to discharge committees it shall be in order for any Member of the House to call up for consideration by the House such adverse report, and it shall be in order to move the adoption by the House of such resolution adversely reported notwithstanding the adverse report of the Committee on Rules, and the Speaker shall recognize the Member seeking recognition for that purpose as a question of the highest privilege.

(d) Whenever the Committee on Rules reports a resolution repealing or amending any of the Rules of the House of Representatives or part thereof it shall include in its report or in an accompanying document—

(1) the text of any part of the Rules of the House of Representatives which is proposed to be repealed; and

(2) a comparative print of any part of the resolution making such an amendment and of any part of the Rules of the House of Representatives to be amended, showing by an appropriate typographical device the omissions and insertions proposed to be made.

COMMITTEE EXPENSES

5. (a) Whenever any standing committee (except the Committee on Appropriations and the Committee on the Budget) is to be granted authorization

for the payment, from the contingent fund of the House, of its expenses in any year, other than those expenses to be paid from appropriations provided by statute, such authorization initially shall be procured by one primary expense resolution for that committee providing funds for the payment of the expenses of the committee for that year from the contingent fund of the House. Any such primary expense resolution reported to the House shall not be considered in the House unless a printed report on that resolution has been available to the Members of the House for at least one calendar day prior to the consideration of that resolution in the House. Such report shall, for the information of the House—

(1) state the total amount of the funds to be provided to the committee under the primary expense resolution for all anticipated activities and programs of the committee; and

(2) to the extent practicable, contain such general statements regarding the estimated foreseeable expenditures for the respective anticipated activities and programs of the committee as may be appropriate to provide the House with basic estimates with respect to the expenditure generally of the funds to be provided to the committee under the primary expense resolution.

(b) After the date of adoption by the House of any such primary expense resolution for any such standing committee for any year, authorization for the payment from the contingent fund of additional expenses of such committee in that year, other than those expenses to be paid from appropriations provided by statute, may be procured by one or more additional expense resolutions for that committee, as necessary. Any such additional expense resolution reported to the House shall not be considered in the House unless a printed report on that resolution has been available to the Members of the House for at least one calendar day prior to the consideration of that resolution in the House. Such report shall, for the information of the House—

(1) state the total amount of additional funds to be provided to the committee under the additional expense resolution and the purpose or purposes for which those additional funds are to be used by the committee; and

(2) state the reason or reasons for the failure to procure the additional funds for the committee by means of the primary expense resolution.

(c) The preceding provisions of this clause do not apply to—

(1) any resolution providing for the payment from the contingent fund of the House of sums necessary to pay compensation for staff services performed for, or to pay other expenses of, any standing committee at any time from and after the beginning of any year and before the date of adoption by the House of the primary expense resolution providing funds to pay the expenses of that committee for that year; or

(2) any resolution providing in any Congress, for all of the standing committees of the House, additional office equipment, airmail and special delivery postage stamps, supplies, staff personnel, or any other specific item for the operation of the standing committees, and containing an authorization for the payment from the contingent fund of the House of the expenses of any foregoing items provided by that resolution, subject to and until enactment of the provisions of the resolution as permanent law.

(d) From the funds provided for the appointment of committee staff pursuant to primary and additional expense resolutions—

(1) The chairman of each standing subcommittee of a standing committee of the House is authorized to appoint one staff member who shall serve at the pleasure of the subcommittee chairman.

(2) The ranking minority party member of each standing subcommittee on each standing committee of the House is authorized to appoint one staff person who shall serve at the pleasure of the ranking minority party member.

(3) The staff members appointed pursuant to the provisions of subparagraphs (1) and (2) shall be compensated at a rate determined by the subcommittee chairman not to exceed (A) 75 per centum of the maximum established in paragraph (c) of clause 6 or (B) the rate paid the staff member appointed pursuant to subparagraph (1) of this paragraph.

(4) For the purpose of this paragraph, (A) there shall be no more than six standing subcommittees of each standing committee of the House, except for the Committee on Appropriations, and (B) no member shall appoint more than one person pursuant to the above provisions.

(5) The staff positions made available to the subcommittee chairman and ranking minority party members pursuant to subparagraphs (1) and

(2) of this paragraph shall be made available from the staff positions provided under clause 6 of Rule XI unless such staff positions are made available pursuant to a primary or additional expense resolution.

Committee Staffs

6. (a)(1) Subject to subparagraph (2) of this paragraph and paragraph (f) of this clause, each standing committee may appoint, by majority vote of the committee, not more than eighteen professional staff members. Each professional staff member appointed under this subparagraph shall be assigned to the chairman and the ranking minority party member of such committee, as the committee considers advisable.

(2) Subject to paragraph (f) of this clause, whenever a majority of the minority party members of a standing committee (except the Committee on Standards of Official Conduct) so request, not more than six persons may be selected, by majority vote of the minority party members, for appointment by the committee as professional staff members from among the number authorized by subparagraph (1) of this paragraph. The committee shall appoint any persons so selected whose character and qualifications are acceptable to a majority of the committee. If the committee determines that the character and qualifications of any person so selected are unacceptable to the committee, a majority of the minority party members may select other persons for appointment by the committee to the professional staff until such appointment is made. Each professional staff member appointed under this subparagraph shall be assigned to such committee business as the minority party members of the committee consider advisable.

(3) The professional staff members of each standing committee—

(A) shall be appointed on a permanent basis, without regard to race, creed, sex, or age, and solely on the basis of fitness to perform the duties of their respective positions;

(B) shall not engage in any work other than committee business; and

(C) shall not be assigned any duties other than those pertaining to committee business.

(4) Services of the professional staff members of each standing committee may be terminated by majority vote of the committee.

(5) The foregoing provisions of this paragraph do not apply to the Committee on Appropriations and to the Committee on the Budget.

(b)(1) The clerical staff of each standing committee shall consist of not more than twelve clerks, to be attached to the office of the chairman, to the ranking minority party member, and to the professional staff, as the committee considers advisable. Subject to subparagraph (2) of this clause, the clerical staff shall be appointed by majority vote of the committee, without regard to race, creed, sex, or age. Except as provided by subparagraph (2) of this paragraph, the clerical staff shall handle committee correspondence and stenographic work both for the committee staff and for the chairman and the ranking minority party member on matters related to committee work.

(2) Subject to paragraph (f) of this clause, whenever a majority of the minority party members of a standing committee (except the Committee on Standards of Official Conduct) so request, four persons may be selected, by majority vote of the minority party members, for appointment by the committee to positions on the clerical staff from among the number of clerks authorized by subparagraph (1) of this paragraph. The committee shall appoint to those positions any person so selected whose character and qualifications are acceptable to a majority of the committee. If the committee determines that the character and qualifications of any person so selected are unacceptable to the committee, a majority of the minority party members may select other persons for appointment by the committee to the position involved on the clerical staff until such appointment is made. Each clerk appointed under this subparagraph shall handle committee correspondence and stenographic work for the minority party members of the committee and for any members of the professional staff appointed under subparagraph (2) of paragraph (a) of this clause on matters related to committee work.

(3) Services of the clerical staff members of each standing committee may be terminated by majority vote of the committee.

(4) The foregoing provisions of this paragraph do not apply to the **Committee on Appropriations** and to the **Committee on the Budget.**

(c) Each employee on the **professional staff,** and each employee on the **clerical staff,** of each standing committee, is entitled to pay at a single per annum gross rate, to be fixed by the chairman, which does not exceed the highest rate of basic pay, as in effect from time to time, of level V of the Executive Schedule in section 5316 of title 5, United States Code.

(d) Subject to appropriations hereby authorized, the Committee on Appropriations and the Committee on the Budget may appoint such staff, in addition to the clerk thereof and assistants for the minority, as it determines by majority vote to be necessary, such personnel, other than minority assistants, to possess such qualifications as the committee may prescribe.

(e) No committee shall appoint to its staff any experts or other personnel detailed or assigned from any department or agency of the Government, except with the written permission of the Committee on House Administration.

(f) If a request for the appointment of a minority professional staff member under paragraph (a), or a minority clerical staff member under paragraph (b), is made when no vacancy exists to which that appointment may be made, the committee nevertheless shall appoint, under paragraph (a) or paragraph (b), as applicable, the person selected by the minority and acceptable to the committee. The person so appointed shall serve as an additional member of the professional staff or the clerical staff, as the case may be, of the committee, and shall be paid from the contingent fund, until such a vacancy (other than a vacancy in the position of head of the professional staff, by whatever title designated) occurs, at which time that person shall be deemed to have been appointed to that vacancy. If such vacancy occurs on the professional staff when seven or more persons have been so appointed who are eligible to fill that vacancy, a majority of the minority party members shall designate which of those persons shall fill that vacancy.

(g) Each staff member appointed pursuant to a request by minority party members under paragraph (a) or (b) of this clause, and each staff member appointed to assist minority party members of a committee pursuant to an expense resolution described in paragraph (a) or (b) of clause 5, shall be accorded equitable treatment with respect to the fixing of his or her rate of pay, the assignment to him or her of work facilities, and the accessibility to him or her of committee records.

(h) Paragraphs (a) and (b) of this clause shall not be construed to authorize the appointment of additional professional or clerical staff members of a committee pursuant to a request under either of such paragraphs by the minority party members of that committee if six or more professional staff members or four or more clerical staff members, provided for in paragraph (a)(1) or paragraph (b)(1) of this clause, as the case may be, who are satisfactory to a majority of the minority party members, are otherwise assigned to assist the minority party members.

(i) Notwithstanding paragraphs (a)(2) and (b)(2), a committee may employ nonpartisan staff, in lieu of or in addition to committee staff designated exclusively for the majority or minority party, upon an affirmative vote of a majority of the members of the majority party and a majority of the members of the minority party.

(j) Each committee shall report to the Clerk of the House within fifteen days after December 31 and June 30 of each year the name, profession, and total salary of each person employed by such committee or any subcommittee thereof during the period covered by such report, and shall make an accounting of funds made available to and expended by such committee or subcommittee during such period; and such information when reported shall be published in the Congressional Record.

RULE XII

RESIDENT COMMISSIONER FROM PUERTO RICO, AND DELEGATE FROM THE DISTRICT OF COLUMBIA

1. The Resident Commissioner to the United States from Puerto Rico shall be elected to serve on standing committees in the same manner as Members of the House and shall possess in such committees the same powers and privileges as the other Members.

2. The Delegate from the District of Columbia shall be elected to serve as a member of the Committee on the District of Columbia and each Delegate to the House shall be elected to serve on standing committees of the House in the same manner as Members of the House and shall possess in all committees on which he serves the same powers and privileges as the other Members.

RULE XIII

CALENDARS AND REPORTS OF COMMITTEES

1. There shall be three calendars to which all business reported from committees shall be referred, viz.:

First. A Calendar of the Committee of the Whole House on the State of the Union, to which shall be referred bills raising revenues, general appropriation bills, and bills of a public character directly or indirectly appropriating money or property.

Second. A House Calendar, to which shall be referred all bills of a public character not raising revenue nor directly or indirectly appropriating money or property.

Third. A Calendar of the Committee of the Whole House, to which shall be referred all bills of a private character.

2. All reports of committees, except as provided in clause 4(a) of Rule XI, together with the views of the minority, shall be delivered to the Clerk for printing and reference to the proper calendar under the direction of the Speaker, in accordance with the foregoing clause, and the titles or subject thereof shall be entered on the Journal and printed in the Record: *Provided,* That bills reported adversely shall be laid on the table, unless the committee reporting a bill, at the time, or any Member within three days thereafter, shall request its reference to the calendar, when it shall be referred, as provided in clause 1 of the rule.

3. Whenever a committee reports a bill or a joint resolution repealing or amending any statute or part thereof it shall include in its report or in an accompanying document—

(1) The text of the statute or part thereof which is proposed to be repealed; and

(2) A comparative print of that part of the bill or joint resolution making the amendment and of the statute or part thereof proposed to be amended. showing by stricken-through type and italics, parallel columns, other appropriate typographical devices the omissions and insertions proposed to be made: *Provided, however,* That if a committee reports such a bill or joint resolution with amendments or an amendment in the nature of a substitute for the entire bill, such report shall include a comparative print showing any changes in existing law proposed by the amendment or substitute instead of as in the bill as introduced.

4. After a bill has been favorably reported and shall be upon either the House or Union Calendar any Member may file with the Clerk a notice that he desires such bill placed upon a special calendar to be known as the "Consent Calendar." On the first and third Mondays of each month immediately after the reading of the Journal, the Speaker shall direct the Clerk to call the bills in numerical order, which have been for three legislative days upon the "Consent Calendar." Should objection be made to the consideration of any bill so called it shall be carried over on the calendar without prejudice to the next day when the "Consent Calendar" is again called. and if objected to by three or more Members it shall immediately be stricken from the calendar, and shall not thereafter during the same session of that Congress be placed again thereon: *Provided,* That no bill shall be called twice on the same legislative day.

5. There shall also be a Calendar of Motions to Discharge Committees, as provided in clause 4 of Rule XXVII.

6. Calendars shall be printed daily.

7. (a) The report accompanying each bill or joint resolution of a public character reported by any committee shall contain—

(1) an estimate, made by such committee, of the costs which would be incurred in carrying out such bill or joint resolution in the fiscal year in which it is reported and in each of the five fiscal years following such fiscal year (or for the authorized duration of any program authorized by such bill or joint resolution, if less than five years), except that, in the case of measures affecting the revenues, such reports shall require only an estimate of the gain or loss in revenues for a one-year period; and

(2) a comparison of the estimate of costs described in subparagraphs (1) of this paragraph made by such committee with any estimate of such costs made by any Government agency and submitted to such committee.

(b) It shall not be in order to consider any such bill or joint resolution in the House if the report of the committee which reported that bill or joint resolution does not comply with paragraph (a) of this clause.

(c) For the purposes of this clause, the members of the Joint Committee on Atomic Energy who are Members of the House shall be deemed to be a committee of the House.

(d) For the purposes of subparagraph (2) of paragraph (a) of this clause, a Government agency includes any department, agency, establishment, wholly owned Government corporation, or instrumentality of the Federal Government or the government of the District of Columbia.

(e) The preceding provisions of this clause do not apply to the Committee on Appropriations, the Committee on House Administration, the Committee on Rules, and the Committee on Standards of Official Conduct.

RULE XIV

OF DECORUM AND DEBATE

1. When any Member desires to speak or deliver any matter to the House, he shall rise and respectfully address him-

self to "Mr. Speaker," and, on being recognized, may address the House from any place on the floor or from the Clerk's desk, and shall confine himself to the question under debate, avoiding personality.

2. When two or more Members rise at once, the Speaker shall name the Member who is first to speak; and no Member shall occupy more than one hour in debate on any question in the House or in committee, except as further provided in this rule.

3. The Member reporting the measure under consideration from a committee may open and close, where general debate has been had thereon; and if it shall extend beyond one day, he shall be entitled to one hour to close, notwithstanding he may have used an hour in opening.

4. If any Members, in speaking or otherwise, transgress the rules of the House, the Speaker shall, or any Member may, call him to order; in which case he shall immediately sit down, unless permitted, on motion of another Member, to explain, and the House shall, if appealed to, decide on the case without debate; if the decision is in favor of the Member called to order, he shall be at liberty to proceed, but not otherwise; and, if the case requires it, he shall be liable to censure or such punishment as the House may deem proper.

5. If a Member is called to order for words spoken in debate, the Member calling him to order shall indicate the words excepted to, and they shall be taken down in writing at the Clerk's desk and read aloud to the House; but he shall not be held to answer, nor be subject to the censure of the House therefor, if further debate or other business has intervened.

6. No Member shall speak more than once to the same question without leave of the House, unless he be the mover, proposer, or introducer of the matter pending, in which case he shall be permitted to speak in reply, but not until every Member choosing to speak shall have spoken.

7. While the Speaker is putting a question or addressing the House no Member shall walk out of or across the hall, nor, when a Member is speaking, pass between him and the Chair; and during the session of the House no Member shall wear his hat, or remain by the Clerk's desk during the call of the roll or the counting of ballots or smoke upon the floor of the House; and the Sergeant-at-Arms and Doorkeeper are charged with the strict enforcement of this clause. Neither shall any person be allowed to smoke upon the floor of the House at any time.

8. It shall not be in order for any Member to introduce to or to bring to the attention of the House during its sessions any occupant in the galleries of the House; nor may the Speaker entertain a request for the suspension of this rule by unanimous consent or otherwise.

RULE XV
ON CALLS OF THE ROLL AND HOUSE

1. Subject to clause 5 of this Rule, upon every roll call the names of the Members shall be called alphabetically by surname, except when two or more have the same surname, in which case the name of the State shall be added; and if there be two such Members from the same State, the whole name shall be called, and after the roll has been once called, the Clerk shall call in their alphabetical order the names of those not voting. Member appearing after the second call, but before the result is announced, may vote or announce a pair.

2. (a) In the absence of a quorum, fifteen Members, including the Speaker, if there is one, shall be authorized to compel the attendance of absent Members; and those for whom no sufficient excuse is made may, by order of a majority of those present, be sent for and arrested, wherever they may be found, by officers to be appointed by the Sergeant-at-Arms for that purpose, and their attendance secured and retained; and the House shall determine upon what condition they shall be discharged. Members who voluntarily appear shall, unless the House otherwise direct, be immediately admitted to the Hall of the House, and they shall report their names to the Clerk to be entered upon the Journal as present.

(b) Subject to clause 5 of this Rule, when a call of the House in the absence of a quorum is ordered, the Speaker shall name one or more clerks to tell the Members who are present. The names of those present shall be recorded by such clerks, and shall be entered in the Journal and the absentees noted, but the doors shall not be closed except when so ordered by the Speaker. Members shall have not less than fifteen minutes from the ordering of a call of the House to have their presence recorded.

3. On the demand of any Member, or at the suggestion of the Speaker, the names of Members sufficient to make a quorum in the Hall of the House who do not vote shall be noted by the Clerk and recorded in the Journal, and reported

to the Speaker with the names of the Members voting, and be counted and announced in determining the presence of a quorum to do business.

4. Subject to clause 5 of this Rule, whenever a quorum fails to vote on any question, and a quorum is not present and objection is made for that cause, unless the House shall adjourn there shall be a call of the House, and the Sergeant-at-Arms shall forthwith proceed to bring in absent Members; and the yeas and nays on the pending question shall at the same time be considered as ordered. The Clerk shall call the roll, and each Member as he answers to his name may vote on the pending question, and, after the roll call is completed, each Member arrested shall be brought by the Sergeant-at-Arms before the House, whereupon he shall be noted as present, discharged from arrest, and given an opportunity to vote and his vote shall be recorded. If those voting on the question and those who are present and decline to vote shall together make a majority of the House, the Speaker shall declare that a quorum is constituted, and the pending question shall be decided as the majority of those voting shall appear. And thereupon further proceedings under the call shall be considered as dispensed with. At any time after the roll call has been completed, the Speaker may entertain a motion to adjourn, if seconded by a majority of those present, to be ascertained by actual count by the Speaker; and if the House adjourns, all proceedings under this clause shall be vacated.

"5. Unless, in his discretion, the Speaker orders the calling of the names of Members in the manner provided for under the preceding provisions of this rule, upon any roll call or quorum call the names of such Members voting or present shall be recorded by electronic device. In any such case, the Clerk shall enter in the Journal and publish in the Congressional Record, in alphabetical order in each category, a list of names of those Members recorded as voting in the affirmative, of these Members recorded as voting in the negative, and of those Members answering present, as the case may be, as if their names had been called in the manner provided for under such preceding provisions. Members shall have not less than fifteen minutes from the ordering of the roll call or quorum call to have their vote or presence recorded.

"6. (a) It shall not be in order to make or entertain a point of order that a quorum is not present—

"(1) before or during the offering of prayer;

"(2) during the administration of the oath of office to the Speaker or Speaker pro tempore or a Member, Delegate, or Resident Commissioner;

"(3) during the reception of any message from the President of the United States or the United States Senate, and

"(4) during the offering, consideration, and disposition of any motion incidental to a call of the House.

"(b) A quorum shall not be required in Committee of the Whole for agreement to a motion that the Committee rise.

"(c) After the presence of a quorum is once ascertained on any day on which the House is meeting, a point of order of no quorum may not be made or entertained—

"(1) during the reading of the Journal;

"(2) during the period after a Committee of the Whole has risen after completing its consideration of a bill or resolution and before the Chairman of the Committee has reported the bill or resolution back to the House; and

"(3) during any period of a legislative day when the Speaker is recognizing Members (including a Delegate or Resident Commissioner) to address the House under special orders, with no measure or matter then under consideration for disposition by the House.

"(d) When the presence of a quorum is ascertained, a further point of order that a quorum is not present may not thereafter be made or entertained until additional business intervenes. For purposes of this paragraph, the term 'business' does not include any matter, proceeding, or period referred to in paragraph (a), (b), or (c) of this clause for which a quorum is not required or a point of order of no quorum may not be made or entertained.".

RULE XVI

ON MOTIONS, THEIR PRECEDENCE, ETC.

1. Every motion made to the House and entertained by the Speaker shall be reduced to writing on the demand of any Member, and shall be entered on the Journal with the name of the Member making it, unless it is withdrawn the same day.

2. When a motion has been made, the Speaker shall state it or (if it be in writing) cause it to be read aloud by the Clerk before being debated, and it shall then be in possession of the House, but

may be withdrawn at any time before a decision or amendment.

3. When any motion or proposition is made, the question, Will the House now consider it? Shall not be put unless demanded by a Member.

4. When a question is under debate, no motion shall be received but to adjourn, to lay on the table, for the previous question (which motions shall be decided without debate), to postpone to a day certain, to refer, or to amend, or postpone indefinitely; which several motions shall have precedence in the foregoing order; and no motion to postpone to a day certain, to refer, or to postpone indefinitely, being decided, shall be again allowed on the same day at the same stage of the question. After the previous question shall have been ordered on the passage of a bill or joint resolution one motion to recommit shall be in order, and the Speaker shall give preference in recognition for such purpose to a Member who is opposed to the bill or joint resolution. However, with respect to any motion to recommit with instructions after the previous question shall have been ordered, it always shall be in order to debate such motion for ten minutes before the vote is taken on that motion, one half of such time to be given to debate by the mover of the motion and one half to debate in opposition to the motion. It shall be in order at any time during a day for the Speaker, in his discretion, to entertain a motion that when the House adjourns it stand adjourned to a day and time certain. Such a motion shall be of equal privilege with the motion to adjourn provided for in this clause and shall be determined without debate.

5. The hour at which the House adjourns shall be entered on the Journal.

6. On the demand of any Member, before the question is put, a question shall be divided if it includes propositions so distinct in substance that one being taken away a substantive proposition shall remain: *Provided,* That any motion or resolution to elect the members or any portion of the members of the standing committees of the House and the joint standing committees shall not be divisible, nor shall any resolution or order reported by the Committee on Rules, providing a special order of business be divisible.

7. A motion to strike out and insert is indivisible, but a motion to strike out being lost shall neither preclude amendment nor motion to strike out and insert; and no motion or proposition on a subject different from that under consideration shall be admitted under color of amendment.

8. Pending a motion to suspend the rules, the Speaker may entertain one motion that the House adjourn; but after the result thereon is announced he shall not entertain any other motion till the vote is taken on suspension.

9. At any time after the reading of the Journal it shall be in order, by direction of the appropriate committees, to move that the House resolve itself into the Committee of the Whole House on the State of the Union for the purpose of considering bills raising revenue, or general appropriation bills.

10. No dilatory motion shall be entertained by the Speaker.

Rule XVII
PREVIOUS QUESTION

1. There shall be a motion for the previous question, which, being ordered by a majority of Members voting, if a quorum be present, shall have the effect to cut off all debate and bring the House to a direct vote upon the immediate question or questions on which it has been asked and ordered. The previous question may be asked and ordered upon a single motion, a series of motions allowable under the rules, or an amendment or amendments, or may be made to embrace all authorized motions or amendments and include the bill to its passage or rejection. It shall be in order, pending the motion for, or after the previous question shall have been ordered on its passage, for the Speaker to entertain and submit a motion to commit, with or without instructions, to a standing or select committee.

2. A call of the House shall not be in order after the previous question is ordered, unless it shall appear upon an actual count by the Speaker that a quorum is not present.

3. All incidental questions of order arising after a motion is made for the previous question, and pending such motion, shall be decided, whether on appeal or otherwise, without debate.

Rule XVIII
RECONSIDERATION

1. When a motion has been made and carried or lost, it shall be in order for any member of the majority, on the same or succeeding day, to move for the reconsideration thereof, and such motion shall take precedence of all other question except the consideration of a conference report or a motion to adjourn, and shall not be withdrawn after the said succeeding day without the consent of

the House, and thereafter any Member may call it up for consideration: *Provided*, That such motion, if made during the last 6 days of a session, shall be disposed of when made.

2. No bill, petition, memorial, or resolution referred to a committee, or reported therefrom for printing and recommitment, shall be brought back into the House on a motion to reconsider; and all bills, petitions, memorials, or resolutions reported from a committee shall be accompanied by reports in writing, which shall be printed.

RULE XIX
OF AMENDMENTS

When a motion or proposition is under consideration a motion to amend and a motion to amend that amendment shall be in order, and it shall also be in order to offer a further amendment by way of substitute, to which one amendment may be offered, but which shall not be voted on until the original matter is perfected, but either may be withdrawn before amendment or decision is had thereon. Amendments to the title of a bill or resolution shall not be in order until after its passage, and shall be decided without debate.

RULE XX
OF AMENDMENTS OF THE SENATE

1. Any amendment of the Senate to any House bill shall be subject to the point of order that it shall first be considered in the Committee of the Whole House on the State of the Union, if, originating in the House, it would be subject to that point: *Provided, however,* That a motion to disagree with the amendments of the Senate to a House bill or resolution and request or agree to a conference with the Senate, or a motion to insist on the House amendments to a Senate bill or resolution and request or agree to a conference with the Senate, shall always be in order if the Speaker, in his discretion, recognizes for that purpose and if the motion is made by direction of the committee having jurisdiction of the subject matter of the bill or resolution.

2. No amendment of the Senate to a general appropriation bill which would be in violation of the provisions of clause 2 of Rule XXI, if said amendment had originated in the House, nor any amendment of the Senate providing for an appropriation upon any bill other than a general appropriation bill, shall be agreed to by the managers on the part of the House unless specific authority to agree to such amendment shall be first given by the House by a separate vote on every such amendment.

RULE XXI
ON BILLS

1. Bills and joint resolutions on their passage shall be read the first time by title and the second time in full, when if the previous question is ordered, the Speaker shall state, the question to be: Shall the bill be engrossed and read a third time and, if decided in the affirmative, it shall be read the third time by title, and the question shall then be put upon its passage.

2. No appropriation shall be reported in any general appropriation bill, or be in order as an amendment thereto, for any expenditure not previously authorized by law, unless in continuation of appropriations for such public works and objects as are already in progress. Nor shall any provision in any such bill or amendment thereto changing existing law be in order, except such as being germane to the subject matter of the bill shall retrench expenditures by the reduction of the number and salary of the officers of the United States, by the reduction of the compensation of any person paid out of the Treasury of the United States, or by the reduction of amounts of money covered by the bill: *Provided,* That it shall be in order further to amend such bill upon the report of the committee or any joint commission authorized by law or the House Members of any such commission having jurisdiction of the subject matter of such amendment, which amendment being germane to the subject matter of the bill shall retrench expenditures.

3. A report from the Committee on Appropriations accompanying any general appropriation bill making an appropriation for any purpose shall contain a concise statement describing fully the effect of any provision of the accompanying bill which directly or indirectly changes the application of existing law.

4. No bill for the payment or adjudication of any private claim against the Government shall be referred, except by unanimous consent, to any other than the following committees, namely: To the Committee on Foreign Affairs or to the Committee on the Judiciary.

5. No bill or joint resolution carrying appropriations shall be reported by any committee not having jurisdiction to report appropriations, nor shall an amendment proposing an appropriation be in order during the consideration of a bill or joint resolution reported by a committee not having that jurisdiction. A

question of order on an appropriation in any such bill, joint resolution, or amendment thereto may be raised at any time.

6. No general appropriation bill or amendment thereto shall be received or considered if it contains a provision reappropriating unexpended balances of appropriations; except that this provision shall not apply to appropriations in continuation of appropriations for public works on which work has commenced.

7. No general appropriation bill shall be considered in the House until printed committee hearings and a committee report thereon have been available for the Members of the House for at least three calendar days (excluding Saturdays, Sundays, and legal holidays).

Rule XXII
OF PETITIONS, MEMORIALS, BILLS, AND RESOLUTIONS

1. Members having petitions or memorials or bills of a private nature to present may deliver them to the Clerk indorsing their names and reference or disposition to be made thereof; and said petitions and memorials and bills of a private nature, except such as, in the judgment of the Speaker, are of an obscene or insulting character, shall be entered on the Journal, with the names of the Members presenting them, and the Clerk shall furnish a transcript of such entry to the official reporters of debates for publication in the Record.

2. No private bill or resolution (including so-called omnibus claims or pension bills), and no amendment to any bill or resolution, authorizing or directing (1) the payment of money for property damages, for personal injuries or death for which suit may be instituted under the Tort Claims Procedure as provided in Title 28, United States Code, or for a pension (other than to carry out a provision of law or treaty stipulation); (2) the construction of a bridge across a navigable stream; or (3) the correction of a military or naval record, shall be received or considered in the House.

3. Any petition or memorial or private bill excluded under this rule shall be returned to the Member from whom it was received; and petitions and private bills which have been inappropriately referred may, by the direction of the committee having possession of the same, be properly referred in the manner originally presented; and an erroneous reference of a petition or private bill under this clause shall not confer jurisdiction upon the committee to consider or report the same.

4. All other bills, memorials, and resolutions may, in like manner, be delivered, indorsed with the names of Members introducing them, to the Speaker, to be by him referred, and the titles and references thereof and of all bills, resolutions, and documents referred under the rules shall be entered on the Journal and printed in the Record of the next day, and correction in case of error of reference may be made by the House, without debate, in accordance with Rule XI, on any day immediately after the reading of the Journal, by unanimous consent, or on motion of a committee claiming jurisdiction, or on the report of the committee to which the bill has been erroneously referred. Two or more but not more than twenty-five Members may introduce jointly any bill, memorial, or resolution to which this paragraph applies.

5. All resolutions of inquiry addressed to the heads of executive departments shall be reported to the House within one week after presentation.

6. When a bill,. resolution, or memorial is introduced "by request," these words shall be entered upon the Journal and printed in the Record.

Rule XXIII
OF COMMITTEES OF THE WHOLE HOUSE

1. In all cases, in forming a Committee of the Whole House, the Speaker shall leave his chair after appointing a Chairman to preside, who shall, in case of disturbance or disorderly conduct in the galleries or lobby, have power to cause the same to be cleared.

2. Whenever a Committee of the Whole finds itself without a quorum, which shall consist of one hundred Members, the Chairman shall invoke the procedure for the call of the roll under clause 5 of Rule XV, unless, in his discretion, he orders a call of the committee to be taken by the procedure set forth in clause 2(b) of Rule XV; and thereupon the Committee shall rise, and the Chairman shall report the names of the absentees to the House, which shall be entered on the Journal; but if on such call a quorum shall appear, the Committee shall thereupon resume its sitting without further order of the House.

If, at any time during the conduct of any quorum call in the Committee of the Whole, the Chairman determines that a quorum is present, he may, in his discretion, declare that a quorum is constituted. Proceedings under the call then shall be considered as vacated, and the

Committee shall not rise but shall continue its sitting and resume its business."

3. All motions or propositions involving a tax or charge upon the people, all proceedings touching appropriations of money, or bills making appropriations of money or property, or requiring such appropriations to be made, or authorizing payments out of appropriations already made, or releasing any liability to the United States for money or property, or referring any claim to the Court of Claims, shall be first considered in a Committee of the Whole, and a point of order under this rule shall be good at any time before the consideration of a bill has commenced.

4. In Committees of the Whole House business on their calendars may be taken up in regular order, or in such order as the committee may determine unless the bill to be considered was determined by the House at the time of going into committee, but bills for raising revenue, general appropriation bills, and bills for the improvement of rivers and harbors shall have precedence.

5. When general debate is closed by order of the House, any Member shall be allowed five minutes to explain any amendment he may offer, after which the Member who shall first obtain the floor shall be allowed to speak five minutes in opposition to it, and there shall be no further debate thereon, but the same privilege of debate shall be allowed in favor of and against any amendment that may be offered to an amendment; and neither an amendment nor an amendment to an amendment shall be withdrawn by the mover thereof unless by the unanimous consent of the committee. Upon the offering of any amendment by a Member, when the House is meeting in the Committee of the Whole, the Clerk shall promptly transmit to the majority committee table five copies of the amendment and five copies to the minority committee table. Further, the Clerk shall deliver at least one copy of the amendment to the majority cloak room and at least one copy to the minority cloak room.

6. The committee may, by the vote of a majority of the members present, at any time after the five minutes' debate has begun upon proposed amendments to any section or paragraph of a bill, close all debate upon such section or paragraph or, at its election, upon the pending amendments only (which motion shall be decided without debate); but this shall not preclude further amendment, to be decided without debate. However, if debate is closed on any section or paragraph under this clause before there has been debate on any amendment which any Member shall have caused to be printed in the Congressional Record after the reporting of the bill by the comittee but at least one day prior to floor consideration of such amendment, the Member who caused such amendment to be printed in the Record shall be given five minutes in which to explain such amendment, after which the first person to obtain the floor shall be given five minutes in opposition to it, and there shall be no further debate thereon; but such time for debate shall not be allowed when the offering of such amendment is dilatory. Material placed in the Record pursuant to this provision shall indicate the full text of the proposed amendment, the name of the proponent Member, the number of the bill to which it will be offered and the point in the bill or amendment thereto where the amendment is intended to be offered, and shall appear in a portion of the Record designated for that purpose.

7. A motion to strike out the enacting words of a bill shall have precedence of a motion to amend, and, if carried, shall be considered equivalent to its rejection. Whenever a bill is reported from a Committee of the Whole with an adverse recommendation and such recommendation is disagreed to by the House, the bill shall stand recommitted to the said committee without further action by the House, but before the question of concurrence is submitted it is in order to entertain a motion to refer the bill to any committee, with or without instructions, and when the same is again reported to the House it shall be referred to the Committee of the Whole without debate.

8. The rules of proceeding in the House shall be observed in Committee of the Whole House so far as they may be applicable.

RULE XXIV

ORDER OF BUSINESS

1. The daily order of business shall be as follows:
First. Prayer by the Chaplain.
Second. Reading and approval of the Journal.
Third. Correction of reference of public bills.
Fourth. Disposal of business on the Speaker's table.
Fifth. Unfinished business.
Sixth. The morning hour for the consideration of bills called up by committee.
Seventh. Motions to go into Committee of the Whole House on the State of the Union.

Eighth. Orders of the day.

2. Business on the Speaker's table shall be disposed of as follows:

Messages from the President shall be referred to the appropriate committees without debate. Reports and communications from heads of departments, and other communications addressed to the House, and bills, resolutions, and messages from the Senate may be referred to the appropriate committees in the same manner and with the same right of correction as public bills presented by Members; but House bills with Senate amendments which do not require consideration in a Committee of the Whole may be at once disposed of as the House may determine, as may also Senate bills substantially the same as House bills already favorably reported by a committee of the House, and not required to be considered in Committee of the Whole, be disposed of in the same manner on motion directed to be made by such committee.

3. The consideration of the unfinished business in which the House may be engaged at an adjournment, except business in the morning hour shall be resumed as soon as the business on the Speaker's table is finished, and at the same time each day thereafter until disposed of, and the consideration of all other unfinished business shall be resumed whenever the class of business to which it belongs shall be in order under the rules.

4. After the unfinished business has been disposed of, the Speaker shall call each standing committee in regular order, and then select committees, and each committee when named may call up for consideration any bill reported by it on a previous day and on the House Calendar, and if the Speaker shall not complete the call of the Committee before the House passes to other business, he shall resume the next call where he left off, giving preference to the last bill under consideration: *Provided,* That whenever any committee shall have occupied the morning hour on two days, it shall not be in order to call up any other bill until the other committees have been called in their turn.

5. After one hour shall have been devoted to the consideration of bills called up by committees, it shall be in order, pending consideration or discussion thereof, to entertain a motion to go into Committee of the Whole House on the State of the Union, or, when authorized by a committee, to go into the Committee of the Whole House on the State of the Union to consider a particular bill, to which motion one amendment only, designating another bill, may be made; and if either motion be determined in the negative, it shall not be in order to make either motion again until the disposal of the matter under consideration or discussion.

6. On the first Tuesday of each month after disposal of such business on the Speaker's table as requires reference only, the Speaker shall direct the Clerk to call the bills and resolutions on the Private Calendar. Should objection be made by two or more Members to the consideration of any bill or resolution so called, it shall be recommitted to the committee which reported the bill or resolution, and no reservation of objection shall be entertained by the Speaker. Such bills and resolutions, if considered, shall be considered in the House as in the Committee of the Whole. No other business shall be in order on this day unless the House, by two-thirds vote on motion to dispense therewith, shall otherwise determine. On such motion debate shall be limited to five minutes for and five minutes against said motion.

On the third Tuesday of each month after the disposal of such business on the Speaker's table as requires reference only, the Speaker may direct the Clerk to call the bills and resolutions on the Private Calendar, preference to be given to omnibus bills containing bills or resolutions which have previously been objected to on a call of the Private Calendar. All bills and resolutions on the Private Calendar so called, if considered, shall be considered in the House as in the Committee of the Whole. Should objection be made by two or more Members to the consideration of any bill or resolution other than an omnibus bill, it shall be recommitted to the committee which reported the bill or resolution and no reservation of objection shall be entertained by the Speaker.

Omnibus bills shall be read for amendment by paragraph, and no amendment shall be in order except to strike out or to reduce amounts of money stated or to provide limitations. Any item or matter stricken from an omnibus bill shall not thereafter during the same session of Congress be included in any omnibus bill.

Upon passage of any such omnibus bill, said bill shall be resolved into the several bills and resolutions of which it is composed, and such original bills and resolutions, with any amendments adopted by the House, shall be engrossed, where necessary, and proceedings thereon had as if said bills and resolutions had been passed in the House severally.

In the consideration of any omnibus bill the proceedings as set forth above shall have the same force and effect as if each Senate and House bill or resolution therein contained or referred to were considered by the House as a separate and distinct bill or resolution.

7. On Wednesday of each week no business shall be in order except as provided by clause 4 of this rule unless the House by a two-thirds vote on motion to dispense therewith shall otherwise determine. On such a motion there may be debate not to exceed five minutes for and against. On a call of committees under this rule bills may be called up from either the House or the Union Calendar, excepting bills which are privileged under the rules; but bills called up from the Union Calendar shall be considered in Committee of the Whole House on the State of the Union. This rule shall not apply during the last 2 weeks of the session. It shall not be in order for the Speaker to entertain a motion for a recess on any Wednesday except during the last 2 weeks of the session: *Provided,* That no more than 2 hours of general debate shall be permitted on any measure called up on Calendar Wednesday, and all debate must be confined to the subject matter of the bill, the time to be equally divided between those for and against the bill: *Provided further,* That whenever any committee shall have occupied one Wednesday it shall not be in order, unless the House by a two-thirds vote shall otherwise determine, to consider any unfinished business previously called up by such committee, unless the previous question had been ordered thereon, upon any succeeding Wednesday until the other committees have been called in their turn under this rule; *Provided,* That when, during any one session of Congress, all of the committees of the House are not called under the Calendar Wednesday rule, at the next session of Congress the call shall commence where it left off at the end of the preceding session.

8. The second and fourth Mondays in each month, after the disposition of motions to discharge committees and after the disposal of such business on the Speaker's table as requires reference only, shall, when claimed by the Committee on the District of Columbia, be set apart for the consideration of such business as may be presented by said committee.

Rule XXV

PRIORITY OF BUSINESS

All questions relating to the priority of business shall be decided by a majority without debate.

Rule XXVI

UNFINISHED BUSINESS OF THE SESSION

All business before committees of the House at the end of one session shall be resumed at the commencement of the next session of the same Congress in the same manner as if no adjournment had taken place.

Rule XXVII

CHANGE OR SUSPENSION OF RULES

1. No rule shall be suspended except by a vote of two-thirds of the Members voting, a quorum being present; nor shall the Speaker entertain a motion to suspend the rules except on the first and third Mondays of each month, and on the Tuesdays immediately following those days and during the last six days of a session.

2. All motions to suspend the rules shall, before being submitted to the House, be seconded by a majority by tellers, if demanded.

3. (a) When a motion to suspend the rules has been seconded, it shall be in order, before the final vote is taken thereon, to debate the proposition to be voted upon for forty minutes, one-half of such time to be given to debate in favor, and one-half to debate in opposition to, such proposition; and the same right of debate shall be allowed whenever the previous question has been ordered on any proposition on which there has been no debate.

"(b)(1) On any legislative day (other than during the last six days of a session) on which the Speaker is authorized to entertain motions to suspend the Rules and pass bills or resolutions, he may announce to the house, in his discretion, before entertaining the first such motion, that he will postpone further proceedings on each of such motions on which a recorded vote or the yeas and nays is ordered or on which the vote is objected to under clause 4 of Rule XV, until all of such motions on that legislative day have been entertained and any debate thereon concluded, with the question having been put and determined on each such motion on which the taking of the vote will not be postponed.

"(2) When the last of all motions on that legislative day to suspend the Rules and pass bills or resolutions has been entertained and any debate thereon concluded, with the question put and determined on each such motion on which further proceedings were not postponed, the Speaker shall put the question on each motion, on which further proceedings were postponed, in the order in which that motion was entertained.

"(3) At any time after the vote on the question has been taken on the first motion on which the Speaker has postponed further proceedings under this paragraph, the Speaker may, in his discretion, reduce to not less than five minutes the period of time within which a recorded vote on the question may be taken on any or all of the additional motions on which the Speaker has postponed further proceedings under this paragraph.

"(4) If the House adjourns before the question is put and determined on all motions on which further proceedings were postponed under this paragraph, then, on the next following legislative day on which the Speaker is authorized to entertain motions to suspend the Rules and pass bills or resolutions, the first order of legislative business after the call of bills and resolutions on the Private Calendar as provided in clause 6 of Rule XXIV shall be the disposition of all such motions, previously undisposed of, in the order in which those motions were entertained."

4. A Member may present to the Clerk a motion in writing to discharge a committee from the consideration of a public bill or resolution which has been referred to it thirty days prior thereto (but only one motion may be present for each bill or resolution). Under this rule it shall also be in order for a Member to file a motion to discharge the Committee on Rules from further consideration of any resolution providing either a special order of business, or a special rule for the consideration of any public bill or resolution favoraby reported by a standing committee, or a special rule for the consideration of a public bill or resolution which has remained in a standing committee thirty or more days without action: *Provided,* That said resolution from which it is moved to discharge the Committee on Rules has been referred to that committee at least seven days prior to the filing of the motion to discharge. The motion shall be placed in the custody of the Clerk, who shall arrange some convenient place for the signature of Members. A signature may be withdrawn by a Member in writing at any time before the motion is entered on the Journal. When a majority of the total membership of the House shall have signed the motion, it shall be entered on the Journal, printed with the signatures thereto in the Congressional Record, and referred to the Calendar of Motions to Discharge Committees.

On the second and fourth Mondays of each month, except during the last six days of any session of Congress, immediately after the approval of the Journal, any Member who has signed a motion to discharge which has been on the calendar at least seven days prior thereto, and seeks recognition, shall be recognized for the purpose of calling up the motion, and the House shall proceed to its consideration in the manner herein provided without intervening motion except one motion to adjourn. Recognition for the motions shall be in the order in which they have been entered on the Journal.

When any motion under this rule shall be called up, the bill or resolution shall be read by title only. After twenty minutes' debate, one-half in favor of the proposition and one-half in opposition thereto, the House shall proceed to vote on the motion to discharge. If the motion prevails to discharge the Committee on Rules from any resolution pending before the committee, the House shall immediately vote on the adoption of said resolution, the Speaker not entertaining any dilatory or other intervening motion except one motion to adjourn, and, if said resolution is adopted, then the House shall immediately proceed to its execution. If the motion prevails to discharge one of the standing committees of the House from any public bill or resolution pending before the committee, it shall then be in order for any Member who signed the motion to move that the House proceed to the immediate consideration of such bill or resolution (such motion not being debatable), and such motion is hereby made of high privilege; and if it shall be decided in the affirmative, the bill shall be immediately considered under the general rules of the House, and if unfinished before adjournment of the day on which it is called up it shall remain the unfinished business until it is fully disposed of. Should the House by vote decide against the immediate consideration of such bill or resolution, it shall be referred to its proper calendar and be entitled to the same rights and privileges that it would have had had the committee to which it was referred duly reported same to the House for its consideration: *Provided,* That when any perfected motion to discharge a committee from the consideration of any public bill or resolution has once been acted upon by the House it shall not be in order to entertain during the same session of Congress any other motion for the discharge from that committee of said measure, or from any other committee of any other bill or resolution substantially the same, relating in substance to or dealing with the same subject matter, or from the Committee on Rules of a resolution providing a special order of business for the consideration of any other such bill or resolution, in order that such action by the House on a motion to discharge shall be res adjudicata for the remainder of that session; *Provided further,* That if before any one motion to discharge a committee has been acted upon by the House there are on the Calendar of Motions to Discharge Committees other motions to discharge committees from the consideration of bills or resolutions substantially the same, relating in substance to or dealing with the same subject matter, after the House shall have acted on one motion to discharge, the remaining said motions shall be stricken from the Calendar of Motions to Discharge Committees and not acted on during the remainder of that session of Congress.

RULE XXVIII

CONFERENCE REPORTS

1. (a) The presentation of reports of committees of conference shall always be in order, except when the Journal is being read, while the roll is being called, or the House is dividing on any proposition.

(b) After House conferees on any bill or resolution in conference between the House and Senate shall have been appointed for twenty calendar days and shall have failed to make a report, it is hereby declared to be a motion of the highest privilege to move to discharge said House conferees and to appoint new conferees, or to instruct said House conferees; and, further, during the last six days of any session of Congress, it shall be a privileged motion to move to discharge, appoint, or instruct, House conferees after House conferees shall have been appointed thirty-six hours without having made a report.

(c) Each report made by a committee of conference to the House shall be printed as a report of the House. As so printed, such report shall be accompanied by an explanatory statement prepared jointly by the conferees on the part of the House and the conferees on the part of the Senate. Such statement shall be sufficiently detailed and explicit to inform the House as to the effect which the amendments or propositions contained in such report will have upon the measure to which those amendments or propositions relate.

2. (a) It shall not be in order to consider the report of a committee of conference until the third calendar day (excluding any Saturday, Sunday, or legal holiday) after such report and the accompanying statement shall have been filed in the House, and such consideration then shall be in order only if such report and accompanying statement shall have been printed in the daily edition of the Congressional Record for the day on which such report and statement shall have been filed; but the preceding provisions of this sentence do not apply during the last six days of the session. Nor shall it be in order to consider any conference report unless copies of the report and accompanying statement are then available on the floor. The time allotted for debate in the consideration of any such report shall be equally divided between the majority party and the minority party.

(b) It shall not be in order to consider any amendment (including an amendment in the nature of a substitute) proposed by the Senate to any measure reported in disagreement between the two Houses by a report of a committee of conference that the committee has been unable to agree, until the third calendar day (excluding any Saturday, Sunday, or legal holiday) after such report and accompanying statement shall have been filed in the House, and such consideration then shall be in order only if such report and accompanying statement shall have been printed in the daily edition of the Congressional Record for the day on which such report and statement shall have been filed; but the preceding provisions of this sentence do not apply during the last six days of the session. Nor shall it be in order to consider any such amendment unless copies of the report and accompanying statement, together with the text of such amendment, are then available on the floor. The time allotted for debate on any such amendment shall be equally divided between the majority party and the minority party.

3. Whenever a disagreement to an amendment in the nature of a substitute has been committed to a conference committee it shall be in order for the Managers on the part of the House to propose a substitute which is a germane modification of the matter in disagreement, but the introduction of any language in that substitute presenting a specific additional topic, question, issue, or proposition not committed to the conference committee by either House shall not constitute a germane modification of the matter in disagreement. Moreover, their report shall not include matter not com-

mitted to the conference committee by either House, nor shall their report include a modification of any specific topic, question, issue, or proposition committed to the conference committee by either or both Houses if that modification is beyond the scope of that specific topic, question, issue, or proposition as so committed to the conference committee.

4. (a) With respect to any report of a committee of conference called up before the House containing any matter which would be in violation of the provisions of clause 7 of Rule XVI if such matter had been offered as an amendment in the House, and which—

(1) is contained in any Senate amendment to that measure (including a substitute for the text of that measure as passed by the House) accepted by the House conferees or agreed to by the conference committee with modification; or

(2) is contained in any substitute agreed to by the conference committee; it shall be in order, at any time after the reading of the report has been completed or dispensed with and before the reading of the statement, to make a point of order that such nongermane matter, as described above, which shall be specified in the point of order, is contained in the report.

For the purposes of this clause, matter which—

(A) is contained in any substitute agreed to by the conference committee;

(B) is not proposed by the House to be included in the measure concerned as passed by the House; and

(C) would be in violation of clause 7 of Rule XVI if such matter had been offered in the House as an amendment to the provisions of that measure as so proposed in the form passed by the House;

shall be considered in violation of such clause 7.

(b) If such point of order is sustained, it then shall be in order for the Chair to entertain a motion, which is of high privilege, that the House reject the nongermane matter covered by the point of order. It shall be in order to debate such motion for forty minutes, one-half of such time to be given to debate in favor of, and one-half in opposition to, the motion.

(c) Notwithstanding the final disposition of any point of order made under paragraph (a), or of any motion to reject made pursuant to a point of order under paragraph (b), of this clause, it shall be in order to make further points of order on the ground stated in such paragraph (a), and motions to reject pursuant thereto under such paragraph (b), with respect to other nongermane matter in the report of the committee of conference not covered by any previous point of order which has been sustained.

(d) If any such motion to reject has been adopted, after final disposition of all points of order and motions to reject under the preceding provisions of this clause, the conference report shall be considered as rejected and the question then pending before the House shall be—

(1) whether to recede and concur in the Senate amendment with an amendment which shall consist of that portion of the conference report not rejected; or

(2) if the last sentence of paragraph (a) of this clause applies, whether to insist further on the House amendment.

If all such motions to reject are defeated, then, after the allocation of time for debate on the conference report as provided in clause 2(a) of this Rule, it shall be in order to move the previous question on the adoption of the conference report.

5. (a) (1) With respect to any amendment (including an amendment in the nature of a substitute) which—

(A) is proposed by the Senate to any measure and thereafter—

(i) is reported in disagreement between the two Houses by a committee of conference; or

(ii) is before the House, the stage of disagreement having been reached; and

(B) contains any matter which would be in violation of the provisions of clause 7 of Rule XVI if such matter had been offered as an amendment in the House;

it shall be in order, immediately after a motion is offered that the House recede from its disagreement to such amendment proposed by the Senate and concur therein and before debate is commenced on such motion, to make a point of order that such nongermane matter, as described above, which shall be specified in the point of order, is contained in such amendment proposed by the Senate.

(2) If such point of order is sustained, it then shall be in order for the Chair to entertain a motion, which is of high privilege, that the House reject the nongermane matter covered by the point of order. It shall be in order to debate such motion for forty minutes, one-half of such time to be given to debate in favor of, and one-half in opposition to, the motion.

(3) Notwithstanding the final disposition of any point of order made under subparagraph (1), or of any motion to reject made pursuant to a point of order under subparagraph (2), of this paragraph, it shall be in order to make further points of order on the ground stated in such subparagraph (1), and motions to reject pursuant thereto under such subparagraph (2), with respect to other nongermane matter in the amendment proposed by the Senate not covered by any previous point of order which has been sustained.

(4) If any such motion to reject has been adopted, after final disposition of all points of order and motions to reject under the preceding provisions of this clause, the motion to recede and concur shall be considered as rejected, and further motions—

(A) to recede and concur in the Senate amendment with an amendment, where appropriate (but the offering of which is not in order unless copies of the language of the Senate amendment, as proposed to be amended by such motion, are then available on the floor when such motion is offered and is under consideration);

(B) to insist upon disagreement to the Senate amendment and request a further conference with the Senate; and

(C) to insist upon disagreement to the Senate amendment;

shall remain of high privilege for consideration by the House. If all such motions to reject are defeated, then, after the allocation of time for debate on the motion to recede and concur as provided in clause 2(b) of this Rule, it shall be in order to move the previous question on such motion.

(b)(1) With respect to any such amendment proposed by the Senate as described in paragraph (a) of this clause, it shall not be in order to offer any motion that the House recede from its disagreement to such Senate amendment and concur therein with an amendment, unless copies of the language of the Senate amendment, as proposed to be amended by such motion, are then available on the floor when such motion is offered and is under consideration.

(2) Immediately after any such motion is offered and is in order and before debate is commenced on such motion, it shall be in order to make a point of order that nongermane matter, as described in subparagraph (1) of paragraph (a) of this clause, which shall be specified in the point of order, is contained in the language of the Senate amendment, as proposed to be amended by such motion, copies of which are then available on the floor.

(3) If such point of order is sustained, it then shall be in order for the Chair to entertain a motion, which is of high privilege, that the House reject the nongermane matter covered by the point of order. It shall be in order to debate such motion for forty minutes, one-half of such time to be given to debate in favor of, and one-half in opposition to, the motion.

(4) Notwithstanding the final disposition of any point of order under subparagraph (2), or of any motion to reject made pursuant to a point of order under subparagraph (3), of this paragraph, it shall be in order to make further points of order on the ground stated in subparagraph (1) of paragraph (a) of this clause, and motions to reject pursuant thereto under subparagraph (3) of this paragraph, with respect to other nongermane matter in the language of the Senate amendment, as proposed to be amended by the motion described in subparagraph (1) of this paragraph, not covered by any previous point of order which has been sustained.

(5) If any such motion to reject has been adopted, after final disposition of all points of order and motions to reject under the preceding provisions of this paragraph, the motion to recede and concur in the Senate amendment with an amendment shall be considered as rejected, and further motions—

(A) to recede and concur in the Senate amendment with an amendment, where appropriate (but the offering of which is not in order unless copies of the language of the Senate amendment, as proposed to be amended by such motion, are then available on the floor when such motion is offered and is under consideration);

(B) to insist upon disagreement to the Senate amendment and request a further conference with the Senate; and

(C) to insist upon disagreement to the Senate amendment;

shall remain of high privilege for consideration by the House. If all such motions to reject are defeated, then, after the allocation of time for debate on the motion to recede and concur in the Senate amendment with an amendment as provided in clause 2(b) of this Rule, it shall be in order to move the previous question on such motion.

(c) If, on a division of a motion that the House recede and concur, with or without amendment, from its disagreement to any such Senate amendment as described in paragraph (a)(1) of this clause, the House agrees to recede, then before debate is commenced on concurring in such Senate amendment, or on concurring therein with an amendment it shall be in order to make and dispose of points of order and motions to reject with respect to such Senate amendment in accordance with applicable provisions of this clause and to effect final determination of these matters in accordance with such provisions.

6. Open Conference Meetings

Each conference committee meeting between the House and Senate shall be open to the public except when the managers of either the House or Senate, in open session, determine by a rollcall vote of a majority of those managers present, that all or part of the remainder of the meeting on the day of the vote shall be closed to the public: *Provided,* That this provision shall not become effective until a similar rule is adopted by the Senate.

RULE XXIX

SECRET SESSION

Whenever confidential communications are received from the President of the United States, or whenever the Speaker or any Member shall inform the House that he has communications which he believes ought to be kept secret for the present, the House shall be cleared of all persons except the Members and officers thereof, and so continue during the reading of such communications, the debates and proceedings thereon, unless otherwise ordered by the House.

RULE XXX

READING OF PAPERS

When the reading of a paper other than one upon which the House is called to give a final vote is demanded, and the same is objected to by any Member, it shall be determined without debate by a vote of the House.

RULE XXXI

HALL OF THE HOUSE

The Hall of the House shall be used only for the legislative business of the House and for the caucus meetings of its Members, except upon occasions where the House by resolution agrees to take part in any ceremonies to be observed therein; and the Speaker shall not entertain a motion for the suspension of this rule.

RULE XXXII

OF ADMISSION TO THE FLOOR

1. The persons hereinafter named, and none other, shall be admitted to the Hall of the House or rooms leading thereto, viz: The President and Vice President of the United States and their private secretaries, judges of the Supreme Court, Members of Congress and Members-elect, contestants in election cases during the pendency of their cases in the House, the Secretary and Sergeants-at-Arms of the Senate, heads of departments, foreign ministers, governors of States, the Architect of the Capitol, the Librarian of Congress and his assistant in charge of the Law Library, the Resident Commissioner to the United States from Puerto Rico, each Delegate to the House, such persons as have, by name, received the thanks of Congress, ex-Members of the House of Representatives who are not interested in any claim or directly in any bill pending before Congress, elected officers and elected minority employees of the House (other than Members), the Parliamentarian and former Parliamentarians of the House, former elected officers and former elected minority employees of the House (other than ex-Members) who are not interested in any claim or directly in any bill pending before Congress, and clerks of committees when business from their committee is under consideration; and it shall not be in order for the Speaker to entertain a request for the suspension of this rule or to present from the chair the request of any Member for unanimous consent.

2. There shall be excluded at all times from the Hall of the House of Representatives and the cloakrooms all persons not entitled to the privilege of the floor during the session, except that until fifteen minutes of the hour of the meeting of the House persons employed in its service, accredited members of the press entitled to admission to the press gallery, and other persons on request of Members, by card or in writing may be admitted.

RULE XXXIII

OF ADMISSION TO THE GALLERIES

The Speaker shall set aside a portion of the west gallery for the use of the President of the United States, the members of his Cabinet, justices of the Supreme Court, foreign ministers and suites, and the members of their respective families, and shall also set aside another portion of the same gallery for the accommodation of persons to be admitted on the card of Members. The southerly half of the east gallery shall be assigned exclusively for the use of the families of Members of Congress, in which the Speaker shall control one bench, and on request of a Member the Speaker shall issue a card of admission

Rule XXXIV

OFFICIAL AND OTHER REPORTERS

1. The appointment and removal, for cause, of the official reporters of the House, including stenographers of committees, and the manner of the execution of their duties shall be vested in the Speaker.

2. Such portion of the gallery over the Speaker's chair as may be necessary to accommodate representatives of the press wishing to report debates and proceedings shall be set aside for their use, and reputable reporters and correspondents shall be admitted thereto under such regulations as the Speaker may from time to time prescribe; and the supervision of such gallery, including the designation of its employees, shall be vested in the standing committee of correspondents, subject to the direction and control of the Speaker; and the Speaker may assign one seat on the floor to Associated Press reporters and one to United Press International, and regulate the occupation of the same. And the Speaker may admit to the floor, under such regulations as he may prescribe, one additional representative of each press association.

3. Such portion of the gallery of the House of Representatives as may be necessary to accommodate reporters of news to be disseminated by radio, television, and similar means of transmission, wishing to report debates and proceedings, shall be set aside for their use, and reputable reporters thus engaged shall be admitted thereto under such regulations as the Speaker may from time to time prescribe; and the supervision of such gallery, including the designation of its employees, shall be vested in the Executive Committee of the Radio and Television Correspondents' Galleries, subject to the direction and control of the Speaker; and the Speaker may admit to the floor, under such regulations as he may prescribe, one representative of the National Broadcasting Company, one of the Columbia Broadcasting System, one of the Mutual Broadcasting System, and one of the American Broadcasting Company.

Rule XXXV

PAY OF WITNESSES

The rule for paying witnesses subpenaed to appear before the House or any of its committees shall be as follows: For each day a witness shall attend, the sum of twenty dollars; and actual expenses of travel in coming to or going from the place of examination, not to exceed twelve cents per mile; but nothing shall be paid for travel when the witness has been summoned at the place of examination.

Rule XXXVI

PAPERS

1. The clerks of the several committees of the House shall, within three days after the final adjournment of a Congress, deliver to the Clerk of the House all bills, joint resolutions, petitions, and other papers referred to the committee, together with all evidence taken by such committee under the order of the House during the said Congress and not reported to the House; and in the event of the failure or neglect of any clerk of a committee to comply with this rule the Clerk of the House shall, within three days thereafter, take into his keeping all such papers and testimony.

2. At the close of each Congress the Clerk of the House shall obtain all noncurrent records of the House and each committee thereof and transfer them to the General Services Administration for preservation subject to the order of the House. In making the transfer, the Clerk may act jointly with the Secretary of the Senate.

Rule XXXVII

WITHDRAWAL OF PAPERS

No memorial or other paper presented to the House shall be withdrawn from its files without its leave, and if withdrawn therefrom certified copies thereof shall be left in the office of the Clerk; but when an act may pass for the settlement of a claim, the Clerk is authorized to transmit to the officer in charge with the settlement thereof the papers on file in his office relating to such claim, or may loan temporarily to an officer or bureau of the executive departments any papers on file in his office relating to any matter pending before such officer or bureau. taking proper receipt therefor.

Rule XXXVIII

BALLOT

In all cases of ballot a majority of the votes given shall be necessary to an election, and where there shall not be such a majority on the first ballot the ballots shall be repeated until a majority be obtained; and in all balloting blanks shall be rejected and not taken into the count in enumeration of votes or reported by the tellers.

Rule XXXIX
MESSAGES

Messages received from the Senate and the President of the United States, giving notice of bills passed or approved, shall be entered in the Journal and published in the Record of that day's proceedings.

Rule XL
EXECUTIVE COMMUNICATIONS

Estimates, or appropriations and all other communications from the executive departments, intended for the consideration of any committees of the House, shall be addressed to the Speaker, and by him referred as provided by clause 2 of Rule XXIV.

Rule XLI
QUALIFICATIONS OF OFFICERS AND EMPLOYEES

No person shall be an officer of the House, or continue in its employment, who shall be an agent for the prosecution of any claim against the Government, or be interested in such claim otherwise than as an original claimant; and it shall be the duty of the Committee on House Administration to inquire into and report to the House any violation of this rule.

Rule XLII
GENERAL PROVISIONS

The rules of parliamentary practice comprised in Jefferson's Manual and the provisions of the Legislative Reorganization Act of 1946, as amended, shall govern the House in all cases to which they are applicable, and in which they are not inconsistent with the standing rules and orders of the House and joint rules of the Senate and House of Representatives.

Rule XLIII
CODE OF OFFICIAL CONDUCT

There is hereby established by and for the House of Representatives the following code of conduct, to be known as the "Code of Official Conduct";

1. A Member, officer, or employee of the House of Representatives shall conduct himself at all times in a manner which shall reflect creditably on the House of Representatives.

2. A Member, officer, or employee of the House of Representatives shall adhere to the spirit and the letter of the Rules of the House of Representatives and to the rules of duly constituted committees thereof.

3. A Member, officer, or employee of the House of Representatives shall receive no compensation nor shall he permit any compensation to accrue to his beneficial interest from any source, the receipt of which would occur by virtue or influence improperly exerted from his position in the Congress.

4. A Member, officer, or employee of the House of Representatives shall accept no gift of substantial value, directly or indirectly, from any person, organization, or corporation having a direct interest in legislation before the Congress.

5. A Member, officer, or employee of the House of Representatives shall accept no honorarium for a speech, writing for publication, or other similar activity, from any person, organization, or corporation in excess of the usual and customary value for such services.

6. A Member of the House of Representatives shall keep his campaign funds separate from his personal funds. Unless specifically provided by law, he shall convert no campaign funds to personal use in excess of reimbursement for legitimate and verifiable prior campaign expenditures and he shall expend no funds from his campaign account not attributable to bona fide campaign purposes.

7. A Member of the House of Representatives shall treat as campaign contributions all proceeds from testimonial dinners or other fund raising events if the sponsors of such affairs do not give clear notice in advance to the donors or participants that the proceeds are intended for other purposes.

8. A Member of the House of Representatives shall retain no one from his clerk hire allowance who does not perform duties commensurate with the compensation he receives.

9. A Member, officer or employee of the House of Representatives shall not discharge or refuse to hire any individual or otherwise discriminate against any individual with respect to compensation, terms, conditions, or privileges of employment, because of such individual's race, color, religion, sex, or national origin.

10. A Member of the House of Representatives who has been convicted by a court of record for the commission of a crime for which a sentence of two or more years' imprisonment may be imposed should refrain from participation in the business of each committee of which he is a member and should refrain from voting on any question at a meeting of the House, or of the Committee of the Whole House, unless or until judicial or executive proceedings result in reinstatement of the presumption of his innocence or until he is reelected to the

House after the date of such conviction. As used in this Code of Official Conduct of the House of Representatives— (a) the terms "Member" and "Member of the House of Representatives" include the Resident Commissioner from Puerto Rico and each Delegate to the House and (b) the term "officer or employee of the House of Representatives" means any individual whose compensation is disbursed by the Clerk of the House of Representatives.

Rule XLIV

Financial Disclosure

Members, officers, principal assistants to Members and officers, and professional staff members of committees shall not later than April 30, 1969, and by April 30 of each year thereafter, file with the Committee on Standards of Official Conduct a report disclosing certain financial interests as provided in this rule. The interest of a spouse or any other party, if constructively controlled by the person reporting, shall be considered to be the same as the interest of the person reporting. The report shall be in two parts as follows:

Part A

1. List the name, instrument of ownership, and any position of management held in any business entity doing a substantial business with the Federal Government or subject to Federal regulatory agencies, in which the ownership is in excess of $5,000 fair market value as of the date of filing or from which income or $1,000 or more was derived during the preceding calendar year. Do not list any time or demand deposit in a financial institution, or any debt instrument having a fixed yield unless it is convertible to an equity instrument.

2. List the name, address, and type of practice of any professional organization in which the person reporting, or his spouse, is an officer, director, or partner, or serves in any advisory capacity, from which income of $1,000 or more was derived during the preceding calendar year.

3. List the source of each of the following items received during the preceding calendar year: (a) Any income for services rendered (other than from the United States Government) exceeding $5,000. (b) Any capital gain from a single source exceeding $5,000, other than from the sale of a residence occupied by the person reporting. (c) Reimbursement for expenditures (other than from the United States Government) exceeding $1,000 in each instance.

(d) Honorariums from a single source aggregating $300 or more.

4. List each creditor to whom the person reporting was indebted for a period of ninety consecutive days or more during the preceding calendar year in an aggregate amount in excess of $10,000, excluding any indebtedness specifically secured by the pledge of assets of the person reporting of appropriate value.

Campaign receipts shall not be included in this report.

Information filed under part A shall be maintained by the committee on Standards of Official Conduct and made available at reasonable hours to responsible public inquiry, subject to such regulations as the committee may prescribe including, but not limited to, regulations requiring identification by name, occupation, address, and telephone number of each person examining information filed under part A, and the reason for each such inquiry.

The committee shall promptly notify each person required to file a report under this rule of each instance of an examination of his report. The committee shall also promptly notify a Member of each examination of the reports filed by his principal assistants and of each examination of the reports of professional staff members of committees who are responsible to such Member.

Part B

1. List the fair market value (as of the date of filing) of each item listed under paragraph 1 of part A and the income derived therefrom during the preceding calendar year.

2. List the amount of income derived from each item listed under paragraphs 2 and 3 of part A, and the amount of indebtedness owed to each creditor listed under paragraph 4 of part A.

The information filed under this part B shall be sealed by the person filing and shall remain sealed unless the Committee on Standards of Official Conduct, pursuant to its investigative authority, determines by a vote of not less than seven members of the committee that the examination of such information is essential in an official investigation by the committee and promptly notifies the Members concerned of any such determination. The committee may, by a vote of not less than seven members of the committee, make public any portion of the information unsealed by the committee under the preceding sentence and which the committee deems to be in the public interest.

Any person required to file a report under this rule who has no interests covered by any of the provisions of this rule shall file a report, under part A only of this rule, as stating.

In any case in which a person required to file a sealed report under part B of this rule is no longer required to file such a report, the committee shall return to such person, or his legal representative, all sealed reports filed by such person under part B and remaining in the possession of the committee.

As used in this rule—(1) the term "Members" includes the Resident Commissioner from Puerto Rico and each Delegate to the House; and (2) the term "committees" includes any committee or subcommittee of the House of Representatives and any joint committee of Congress, the expenses of which are paid from the contingent fund of the House of Representatives.

APPENDIX 5

Model Committee Caucus and Committee Rules
Special Report of the Democratic Study Group
*U.S. House of Representatives**

This DSG Special Report is designed to assist Members and committees in meeting House and Democratic Caucus requirements regarding committee rules.

The report contains a set of model rules for committee Democratic caucuses, and a set of model rules for House committees.

The report contains the following sections:
            I. Introduction
          II. Model Committee *Caucus* Rules
          III. Model Committee Rules

SECTION I

INTRODUCTION

Committee Democratic Caucuses

House Democratic Caucus Rules (M III A) require the Chairman of each standing committee or other committee with legislative jurisdiction to call a meeting of the committee's Democrats. Three days notice is required for the meeting, which must take place after the Democratic Caucus approves the committee membership lists and elects the chairmen, but before the organizational meeting of the full committee.

Section II of this report sets forth a model set of rules to govern meetings of committee Democratic caucuses. These rules conform fully to House Democratic Caucus Rules.

House Democratic Caucus Rules (M III A) only require an organizational meeting of a committee's Democratic caucus. However, House Democratic Caucus Rules (M IV) do provide that any 10, or a majority, whichever is less, of a committee's Democrats may call the committee Democratic caucus into session. House Democrats Caucus Rule M IV, entitled "Periodic Committee Caucuses," clearly anticipates use of the caucus beyond the organizing session. Thus, committee

---
* Special Report No. 94-1, January 20, 1975, Washington, D. C.

Democratic caucuses could usefully adopt a set of rules to govern such meetings.

Whether or not a committee's Democrats decide to adopt committee Democratic caucus rules, the model rules for a committee Democratic caucus set forth in Section II provide an outline of what House Democratic Caucus Rules require of the organizational meeting of the committee's Democrats. These requirements can be summed up as follows:

* Adoption of the full committee's rules, which must meet five minimum standards set forth by the House Democratic Caucus (see Rule 2(a) of model committee caucus rules).
* Filling of subcommittee chairmanships (see Rule 6 of model committee caucus rules).
* Filling of subcommitee positions (see Rule 7 of model committee caucus rules).

Model House Committee Rules

Section III of this Special Report sets forth a set of model rules for governing the organization, operation, and procedures of House committees. These model rules conform to House Rules for most standing committees. The model rules meet all requirements of House Democratic Caucus Rules for all committees and subcommittees. These Caucus-related rules appear as Rule Nos. XV, XVI, XVII, XVIII, and XIII of the model rules.

93rd Congress House Committees

The Agriculture, Armed Services, Appropriations, Banking & Currency, Government Operations, House Administration, Interstate & Foreign Commerce, Judiciary, Merchant Marine & Fisheries, Public Works, Veterans' Affairs, and Ways & Means Committees had written rules in the 93rd Congress which do not comply with the following Democratic Caucus Rules:

M III A(1)—Model Committee Rule No. XV
M III A(2)—Model Committee Rule No. XVI
M III A(3)—Model Committee Rule No. XVII
M III A(4)—Model Committee Rule No. XVIII
M II B and M III A(5)—Model Committee Rule No. XIII

The District and Foreign Affairs Committees had written rules in the 93rd Congress which do not comply with the following Democratic Caucus Rules:

M III A(1)—Model Committee Rule No. XV
M III A(2)—Model Committee Rule No. XVI

The Education & Labor, Foreign Affairs, Interior & Insular Affairs, and Post Office & Civil Service Committees had written rules in the 93rd Congress which do not comply with the following Democratic Caucus Rule:

M III A(3)—Model Committee Rule No. XVII

The District and Post Office & Civil Service Committees had written rules in the 93rd Congress which do not comply with the following Democratic Caucus Rule:

M III A(4)—Model Committee Rule No. XVIII

SECTION II

MODEL COMMITTEE DEMOCRATIC CAUCUS RULES

Attached are model rules for the operation of committee Democratic caucuses. House Democratic Caucus Rules (M III A) only require an organizational caucus of a committee's Democrats at the beginning of a Congress. However, the Rules (M IV) also set forth procedures for further periodic caucuses of a committee's Democrats, on the call of any 10 committee Democrats or a majority of committee Democrats, whichever is less.

Thus, Democratic members of committee may find it useful to adopt a set of rules to govern that caucus. The attached model rules are entirely consistent with House Democratic Caucus Rules, and meet the intent of those Rules.

Following are the contents of the model caucus rules:

- Rule 1. Membership
- Rule 2. Meetings
- Rule 3. Presiding Officer
- Rule 4. Quorum
- Rule 5. Rules
- Rule 6. Subcommittee Chairmanships
- Rule 7. Subcommittee Assignments

DEMOCRATIC CAUCUS RULES FOR THE COMMITTEE ON_____

RULE 1. *Membership*

All Democratic members of the Committee shall be *prima facie* members of the Democratic Caucus of the Committee.

RULE 2. *Meetings*

(a) At the start of each Congress, the Chairman of the full committee shall call an organizational meeting of the Caucus, giving at least 3 days notice to all members of the Caucus. Said meeting shall be called subsequent to the House Democratic Caucus approval of the committee list, but prior to any organizational meeting of the full committee.

(b) The first order of business of such Caucus meeting shall be the election of a member to serve as chairman of the Democratic Caucus of the Committee. Nominees for the position of committee caucus chairman need not follow seniority.

(c) Such Caucus shall approve and secure adoption of committee rules incorporating the following principles:

(1) *Jurisdiction and number of subcommittees.* The Caucus shall establish the number of subcommittees and shall fix the jurisdiction of each subcommittee.

(2) *Powers and duties of subcommittees.* Each subcommittee is authorized to meet, hold hearings, receive evidence and report

to the committee on all matters referred to it. Subcommittee chairmen shall set meeting dates after consultation with the chairmen and other subcommittee chairmen with a view toward avoiding simultaneous scheduling of committee and subcommittee meetings or hearings wherever possible.

(3) *Reference of legislation and other matters.* All legislation and other matters referred to the committee shall be referred to the subcommittee of appropriate jurisdiction within 2 weeks unless, by majority vote of the Caucus, consideration is to be by the full committee.

(4) *Party ratios.* The Caucus shall determine an appropriate ratio of Democratic to minority party members for each subcommittee and shall authorize a Member or Members to negotiate that ratio with the minority party; *Provided, however,* That party representation on each subcommittee, including any ex-officio members, shall be no less favorable to the Democratic Party than the ratio for the full committee. *Provided, further,* That Democratic Party representation on conference committees also shall be no less favorable to the Democratic Party than the ratio for the full House Committee.

(5) *Subcommittee budget and staffing.* Subject to overall control of a majority of the Caucus, each subcommittee shall have an adequate budget to discharge its responsibilities for legislation and oversight. Each subcommittee chairman shall be entitled to select and designate at least one staff member for said subcommittee, subject to the approval of a majority of the Caucus. Said staff member shall be compensated at a salary commensurate with the responsibilities prescribed by said subcommittee chairman. The staff members' compensation shall be provided out of appropriated amounts, if any, rather than statutory amounts allowed each committee.

(d) Such Caucus shall fill the positions of subcommittee chairman in accordance with Rule 6, and the positions of subcommittee members in accordance with Rule 7.

(e) Meetings of the Caucus shall be called by the Chairman of the committee Caucus or a majority of the members of the Caucus with due notice to all Caucus members. Members of the Caucus shall not schedule committee or subcommittee meetings or hearings at times when the Caucus is to be in session.

(f) The committee Caucus chairman shall call a meeting of the Caucus for purposes of acting upon any changes in subcommittee number, jurisdiction, chairmanship, or membership proposed subsequent to the organizational meeting of the Caucus.

(g) Upon written request of 10 members of the Caucus or upon written request of a majority of members, whichever is less, addressed to the committee Caucus chairman, said Chairman shall call a Caucus within 10 days of such request. Said request shall contain the subject matter for discussion at such Caucus.

RULE 3. *Presiding Officer*

The Committee Caucus Chairman shall have the right to name any member of the Caucus to perform the duties of the Chair during the temporary absence of the Chairman.

DSG Model Committee and Caucus Rules

RULE 4. *Quorum*

A quorum of the Caucus shall consist of a majority of the Democratic members of the Committee. If the absence of a quorum is established, the Committee Caucus Chairman may continue the meeting for purposes of discussion only, but no motion of any kind, except a motion to adjourn, shall be in order at such continued meeting.

RULE 5. *Rules*

General parliamentary law, with such special rules as may be adopted, shall govern the meetings of the Caucus. The five-minute rule that governs the House of Representatives shall govern debate in the Democratic Caucus, unless suspended by a vote of the Caucus.

RULE 6. *Subcommittee Chairmanships*

At the Democratic Caucus described in Rule 2(a) Democratic members shall have the right, in order of full committee seniority or subcommittee seniority, as the Democratic Caucus on the committee shall determine *, to bid for subcommittee chairmanships. Any such bid shall be subject to approval by a majority of those present and voting in the Democratic Caucus on the committee. Such vote shall be by secret ballot. / Such vote shall be by secret ballot at the request of one-fifth of those present in the Democratic Caucus on the Committee. If the Committee Caucus rejects a subcommittee chairmanship bid, the next senior Democratic member may bid for the position as in the first instance.

RULE 7. *Subcommittee Assignments*

All Democratic subcommittee positions on the committee shall be filled at the Democratic Committee Caucus described in Rule 2(a) in the following manner:

(a) Step One—members who served on the committee in the preceding Congress shall be entitled to retain not more than two subcommittee assignments held on that committee in the preceding Congress. Members chosen as subcommittee chairmen in accord with the procedure set forth in Rule 6 shall be entitled to only one other subcommittee assignment held on that committee in the preceding Congress.

(b) Step Two—Members (other than subcommittee chairmen **) who retain no subcommittee assignments in Step One and new Members shall be entitled, in order of their ranking on the full committee, to select one subcommittee position each.

(c) Step Three—Members who have selected only one subcommittee assignment shall be entitled, in order of their ranking on the full

---

* With the sole exception of the Appropriations Committee, all committees select subcommittee chairmen in order of full committee seniority. The Appropriations Committee proceeds by subcommittee seniority and Democratic Caucus Rules provide that in that instance the ranking of Members on subcommittees is determined by the order in which they elect to go on the subcommittees.

** The intent of the rules is that the election to a subcommittee chairmanship is deemed to be equivalent to retaining a subcommittee assignment even if the Member did not hold that particular subcommittee chairmanship in the preceding Congress.

committee, to select a second subcommittee assignment, to the extent that subcommittee size permits.

(d) Step Four—Any remaining subcommittee vacancies shall be filled by additional rounds of selection in order of Members' ranking on the full committee.

SECTION III

MODEL COMMITTEE RULES

Attached are model rules for governing the procedures and operation of House Committees and Subcommittees. These model rules adapt existing House Rules which apply to committees,* and also include existing committee rules where appropriate.

In addition, model rules XIV through XVIII contain those provisions which committees will need in order to comply with House Democratic Caucus Rules. House Democratic Caucus Rules require a committee's Democrats "to approve and secure adoption of committee rules incorporating" the principles set forth in model rules XIV through XVIII.

Following are the contents of the model committee rules:

 Rule No. I—General Provisions
 Rule No. II—Regular and Special Meetings;
  Open Committee Meetings
 Rule No. III—Records & Roll Calls
 Rule No. IV—Proxies
 Rule No. V—Power to Sit & Act;
  Subpoena Power
 Rule No. VI—Quorums
 Rule No. VII—Hearing Procedures
 Rule No. VIII—Procedures for Reporting
  Bills & Resolutions
 Rule No. IX—Oversight
 Rule No. X—Review of Continuing Programs;
  Budget Act Provisions
 Rule No. XI—Broadcasting of Committee Hearings
 Rule No. XII—Committee & Subcommittee Budgets
 Rule No. XIII—Committee & Subcommittee Staff
 Rule No. XIV—Travel of Members & Staff
 Rule No. XV—Number & Jurisdiction of Subcommittees
 Rule No. XVI—Powers & Duties of Subcommittees
 Rule No. XVII—Referral of Legislation to
  Subcommittees
 Rule No. XVIII—Sizes & Party Ratios on
  Subcommittees & Conference
  Committees

---

* In some instances House Rules apply solely to one House committee. These rules have not beee included in the model committee rules, which apply to all committees. Committees having such special rule requirements are: Appropriations, Budget, Government Operations, House Administration, Standards of Official Conduct, and Rules.

RULES FOR THE COMMITTEE ON _____

Rule No. I*

GENERAL PROVISIONS

(a) The Rules of the House are the rules of the committee and subcommittees so far as applicable, except that a motion to recess from day to day is a motion of high privilege in committees and subcommittees. Each subcommittee of the committee is a part of the committee, and is subject to the authority and direction of the committee and to its rules as far as applicable.

(b) The committee is authorized at any time to conduct such investigations and studies as it may consider necessary or appropriate in the exercise of its responsibilities under Rule X of House Rules and (subject to the adoption of expense resolutions as required by Rule XI, clause 5 of House Rules) to incur expenses (including travel expenses) in connection therewith.

(c) The committee is authorized to have printed and bound testimony and other data presented at hearings held by the committee. All costs of stenographic services and transcripts in connection with any meeting or hearing of the committee shall be paid from the contingent fund of the House.

(d) The committee shall submit to the House, not later than January 2 of each odd-numbered year, a report on the activities of the committee under Rule X and XI of House Rules during the Congress ending at noon on January 3 of such year.

(e) The committee's rules shall be published in the Congressional Record not later than thirty days after the Congress convenes in each odd-numbered year.

Rule No. II**

REGULAR & SPECIAL MEETINGS; OPEN COMMITTEE MEETINGS

(a) Regular meetings of the committee shall be held on (specify at least one monthly day and time) while the Congress is in session. When the Chairman believes that the committee will not be considering any bill or resolution before the full committee and that there is no other business to be transacted at a regular meeting, he will give each member of the committee, as far in advance of the day of the regular meeting as the circumstances make practicable, a written notice to that effect and no committee meeting shall be held on that day.

---

* This is House Rule XI, clause 1, and clause 2(a)(3), with technical adjustments to make it applicable to a single committee rather than all committees.

** This is House Rule XI, clauses 2(b), 2(c), 2(d), 2(g), and 2(i), with technical adjustments to make it applicable to a single committee rather than all committees.

(b) The Chairman may call and convene, as he considers necessary, additional meetings of the committee for the consideration of any bill or resolution pending before the committee or for the conduct of other committee business. The committee shall meet for such purpose pursuant to that call of the Chairman.

(c) If at least three members of the committee desire that a special meeting of the committee be called by the Chairman, those members may file in the offices of the committee their written request to the Chairman for that special meeting. Such request shall specify the measure or matter to be considered. Immediately upon the filing of the request, the clerk of the committee shall notify the Chairman of the filing of the request. If, within three calendar days after the filing of the request, the Chairman does not call the requested special meeting to be held within seven calendar days after the filing of the request, a majority of the members of the committee may file in the offices of the committee their written notice that a special meeting of the committee will be held, specifying the date and hour thereof, and the measure or matter to be considered at that special meeting. The committee shall meet on that date and hour. Immediately upon the filing of the notice, the clerk of the committee shall notify all members of the committee that such meeting will be held and inform them of its date and hour and the measure or matter to be considered; and only the measure or matter specified in that notice may be considered at that special meeting.

(d) If the chairman of the committee or subcommittee is not present at any meeting of the committee or subcommittee the ranking member of the majority party on the committee or subcommittee who is present shall preside at that meeting.

(e) The committee may not sit, without special leave, while the House is reading a measure for amendment under the five-minute rule.

(f) (1) Each meeting for the transaction of business, including the markup of legislation, of the committe or each subcommittee thereof shall be open to the public except when the committee or subcommittee, in open session and with a quorum present, determines by roll call vote that all or part of the remainder of the meeting on that day shall be closed to the public: Provided, however, That no person other than members of the committee and such congressional staff and such departmental representatives as they may authorize shall be present at any business or markup session which has been closed to the public. This paragraph does not apply to open committee hearings which are provided for by clause 4(a)(3) of House Rule X or by subparagraph (2) of this paragraph, or to any meeting that relates solely to internal budget or personnel matters.

(2) Each hearing conducted by the committee or each subcommittee thereafter shall be open to the public except when the committee or subcommittee, in open session and with a quorum present, determines by roll call vote that all or part of the remainder of that hearing on that day shall be closed to the public because disclosure of testimony, evidence, or other matters to be considered would endanger the national security or would violate any law or rule of the House of Representatives; Provided, however, that the committee or subcommittee may by the same procedure vote to close one subsequent day of hearing.

RULE No. III*

RECORDS AND ROLL CALLS

(a) There shall be kept in writing a record of the proceedings of the committee and of each subcommittee, including a record of the votes on any question on which a roll call is demanded. The result of each such roll call vote shall be made available by the committee for inspection by the public at reasonable times in the offices of the committee. Information so available for public inspection shall include a description of the amendment, motion, order or other proposition and the name of each Member voting for and each Member voting against such amendment, motion, order, or proposition, and whether by proxy or in person, and the names of those Members present but not voting. A record vote may be demanded by one-fifth of the Members present or, in the apparent absence of a quorum, by any one member. With respect to each record vote by the committee to report any bill or resolution, the total number of votes cast for and the total number of votes cast against the reporting of such bill or such resolution shall be included in the committee report.

(b) All committee hearings, records, data, charts, and files shall be kept separate and distinct from the congressional office records of the Member serving as chairman of the committee; and such records shall be the property of the House and all Members of the House shall have access thereto.

RULE No. IV**

PROXIES

(a) A vote by any member in the committee or in any subcommittee may be cast by proxy, but such proxy must be in writing and in the hands of the chief clerk of the committee or the clerk of the subcommittee,, as the case may be, during each roll call in which they are to be voted. Each proxy shall designate the member who is to execute the proxy authorization and shall be limited to a specific measure or matter and any amendments or motions pertaining thereto; except that a member may authorize a general proxy only for motions to recess, adjourn or other procedural matters. Each proxy to be effective shall be signed by the member assigning his vote and shall contain the date and time of day that the proxy is signed. Proxies may not be counted for a quorum.

(b) Proxies shall be in the following form:

Hon. _____,
House of Representatives,
Washington, D.C.

---

* Conforms to House Rule XI, clause 2(e)
** Conforms to House Rule XI, clause 2(f). Committees are required to adopt a proxy rule only if they authorize the use of proxies.

Dear _____: Anticipating that I will be absent on official business/ or otherwise unable to be present, I hereby authorize you to vote in my place and stead in the consideration of _____ and any amendments or motions pertaining thereto.

_____,
Member of Congress

Executed this the _____ day of _____, 19__, at the time of _____ p.m./a.m.

Rule No. V*

POWER TO SIT AND ACT; SUBPOENA POWER

(a) For the purpose of carrying out any of its functions and duties under House Rules X and XI the committee, or any subcommittee thereof, is authorized (subject to subparagraph (b)(1) of this paragraph)—

(1) to sit and act at such times and places within the United States, whether the House is in session, has recessed, or has adjourned, and to hold such hearings, and

(2) to require, by subpoena or otherwise, the attendance and testimony of such witnesses and the production of such books, records, correspondence, memorandums, papers, and documents as it deems necessary. The chairman of the committee, or any member designated by the chairman, may administer oaths to any witness.

(b)(1) A subpoena may be issued by the committee or subcommittee under subparagraph (a)(2) in the conduct of any investigation or activity or series of investigations or activities, only when authorized by a majority of the members of the committee and authorized subpoenas shall be signed by the chairman of the committee or by any member designated by the committee.

(2) Compliance with any subpoena issued by the committee or subcommittee under subparagraph (a) (2) may be enforced only as authorized or directed by the House.

(c) Each witness who has been subpoenaed, upon the completion of his testimony before the committee or any subcommittee, may report to the office of counsel of the committee, and there sign appropriate vouchers for travel allowances and attendance fees. If hearings are held in cities other than Washington, D.C., the witness may contact the counsel of the committee, or his representative, prior to leaving the hearing room.

Rule No. VI**

QUORUMS

A majority of the members of the committee shall constitute a

---

* This is House Rule XI, clause 2(m), with technical adjustments to make it applicable to a single committee rather than all committees.

** Conforms to House Rule XI, clause 2(h).

quorum of the committee for business and a majority of the members of any subcommittee shall constitute a quorum thereof for business: *Provided,* That any two members shall constitute a quorum for the purpose of taking testimony and receiving evidence.

RULE No. VII*

HEARING PROCEDURES

(a) The Chairman, in the case of hearings to be conducted by the committee, and the appropriate subcommittee chairman, in the case of hearings to be conducted by a subcommittee, shall make public announcement of the date, place, and subject matter of any hearing to be conducted on any measure or matter at least one week before the commencement of that hearing unless the committee determines that there is good cause to begin such hearing at an earlier date. In the latter event the chairman or the subcommittee chairman whichever the case may be shall make such public announcement at the earliest possible date. The clerk of the committee shall promptly notify the Daily Digest Clerk of the Congressional Record as soon as possible after such public announcement is made.

(b) So far as practicable, each witness who is to appear before the committee or a subcommittee shall file with the clerk of the committee, at least 24 hours in advance of his appearance, a written statement of his proposed testimony and shall limit his oral presentation to a summary of his statement.

(c) When any hearing is conducted by the committee or any subcommittee upon any measure or matter, the minority party members on the committee shall be entitled, upon request to the Chairman by a majority of those minority members before the completion of such hearing, to call witnesses selected by the minority to testify with respect to that measure or matter during at least one day of hearing thereon.

(d) Upon announcement of a hearing, the Clerk and Staff Director shall cause to be prepared a concise summary of the subject matter (including legislative reports and other material) under consideration which shall be made available immediately to all members of the committee. In addition, upon announcement of a hearing and subsequently as they are received, the chairman shall make available to the members of the committee any official reports from departments and agencies on such matter.

(e) All other members of the committee may have the privilege of sitting with any subcommittee during its hearing or deliberations and may participate in such hearings or deliberations, but no such member who is not a member of the subcommittee shall vote on any matter before such subcommittee.

(f) Committee members may question witnesses only when they have been recognized by the chairman for that purpose, and only for a 5-minute period until all members present have had an opportunity to question a witness. The 5-minute period for questioning a witness by any one member can be extended only with the unanimous consent of

---

* Conforms to House Rule XI, clause 2(g), 2(j), and 2(k).

all members present. The questioning of witness in both full and subcommittee hearings shall be initiated by the chairman, followed by the ranking minority party member and all other members alternating between the majority and minority. In recognizing members to question witnesses in this fashion, the chairman shall take into consideration the ratio of the majority to minority members present and shall establish the order of recognition for questioning in such a manner as not to disadvantage the members of the majority. The chairman may accomplish this by recognizing two majority members for each minority member recognized.

(g) The following additional rules shall apply to investigative hearings:

(1) The chairman at an investigative hearing shall announce in an opening statement the subject of the investigation.

(2) A copy of the committee rules and this clause shall be made available to each witness.

(3) Witnesses at investigative hearings may be accompanied by their own counsel for the purpose of advising them concerning their constitutional rights.

(4) The chairman may punish breaches of order and decorum and of professional ethics on the part of counsel, by censure and exclusion from the hearings; and the committee may cite the offender to the House for contempt.

(5) If the committee determines that evidence or testimony at an investigative hearing may tend to defame, degrade, or incriminate any person, it shall—

(A) receive such evidence or testimony in executive session;

(B) afford such person an opportunity voluntarily to appear as a witness; and

(C) receive and dispose of requests from such person to subpoena additional witnesses.

(6) Except as provided in subparagraph (5), the chairman shall receive and the committee shall dispose of requests to subpoena additional witnesses.

(7) No evidence or testimony taken in executive session may be released or used in public sessions without the consent of the committee.

(8) In the discretion of the committee, witnesses may submit brief and pertinent sworn statements in writing for inclusion in the record. The committee is the sole judge of the pertinency of testimony and evidence adduced at its hearing.

(9) A witness may obtain a transcript copy of his testimony given at a public session or, if given at an executive session, when authorized by the committee.

Rule No. VIII*

PROCEDURES FOR REPORTING BILLS AND RESOLUTIONS

(a)(1) It shall be the duty of the chairman of the committee to

---

*This is House Rule XI, clause 2(l), with technical adjustments to make it applicable to a single committee rather than all committees.

report or cause to be reported promptly to the House any measure approved by the committee and to take or cause to be taken necessary steps to bring the matter to a vote.

(2) In any event, the report of the committee on a measure which has been approved by the committee shall be filed within seven calendar days (exclusive of days on which the House is not in session) after the day on which there has been filed with the clerk of the committee a written request, signed by a majority of the members of the committee, for the reporting of that measure. Upon the filing of any such request, the clerk of the committee shall transmit immediately to the chairman of the committee notice of the filing of that request.

(b)(1) No measure or recommendation shall be reported from the committee unless a majority of the committee was actually present.

(2) With respect to each roll call vote on a motion to report any bill or resolution of a public character, the total number of votes cast for, and the total number of votes cast against, the reporting of such bill or resolution shall be included in the committee report.

(c) The report of the committee on a measure which has been approved by the committee shall include

(1) the oversight findings and recommendations required pursuant to the last sentence of clause 2(b)(1) of Rule X of the House separately set out and clearly identified;

(2) the statement required by section 308(a) of the Congressional Budget Act of 1974, separately set out and clearly identified, if the measure provides new budget authority or new or increased tax expenditures;

(3) the estimate and comparison prepared by the Director of the Congressional Budget Office under section 403 of such Act, separately set out and clearly identified, whenever the Director (if timely submitted prior to the filing of the report) has submitted such estimate and comparison to the committee; and

(4) a summary of the oversight findings and recommendations made by the Committee on Government Operations under clause 2(b)(2) of Rule X of the House separately set out and clearly identified whenever such findings and recommendations have been submitted to the legislative committee in a timely fashion to allow an opportunity to consider such findings and recommendations during the committee's deliberations on the measure.

(d) Each report of the committee on each bill or joint resolution of a public character reported by the committee shall contain a detailed analytical statement as to whether the enactment of such bill or joint resolution into law may have an inflationary impact on prices and costs in the operation of the national economy.

(e) If, at the time of approval of any measure or matter by the committee, any member of the committee gives notice of intention to file supplemental, minority, or additional views, that member shall be entitled to not less than three calendar days (excluding Saturdays, Sundays, and legal holidays) in which to file such views, in writing and signed by that member, with the clerk of the committee. All such views so filed by one or more members of the committee shall be included within, and shall be a part of, the report filed by the committee with respect to that measure or matter. The report of the committee upon that measure or matter shall be printed in a single volume which—

(1) shall include all supplemental, minority, or additional views which have been submitted by the time of the filing of the report, and

(2) shall bear upon its cover a recital that any such supplemental, minority, or additional views (and any material submitted under subdivisions (3) and (4) of subparagraph (c) are included as part of the report. This subparagraph does not preclude—

(A) the immediate filing or printing of a committee report unless timely request for the opportunity to file supplemental, minority, or additional views has been made as provided by this subparagraph; or

(B) the filing by any such committee of any supplemental report upon any measure or matter which may be required for the correction of any technical error in a previous report made by that committee upon that measure or matter.

(f) If hearings have been held on any such measure or matter so reported, the committee shall make every reasonable effort to have such hearings printed and available for distribution to the Members of the House prior to the consideration of such measure or matter in the House. This subparagraph shall not apply to—

(1) any measure for the declaration of war, or the declaration of a national emergency, by the Congress; or

(2) any executive decision, determination, or action which would become, or continue to be, effective unless disapproved or otherwise invalidated by one or both Houses of Congress.

RULE NO. IX *

OVERSIGHT

NOTE: House Rules (Rule X, clause 2(a) and (b)(1) place certain general oversight responsibilities on House committees with more than 20 members, and require them to meet these responsibilities either by establishment of an Oversight Subcommittee or by requiring the subcommittees to conduct oversight in their jurisdictions. House Rules (Rule X, clause 3) also give certain House committees special oversight functions.

Two possible versions of Model Rule IX are set forth. The first version is for committees which opt for establishment of an Oversight Subcommittee. The second is for committees which opt for conducting oversight through their regular subcommittees.

FIRST OPTION—OVERSIGHT SUBCOMMITTEE

(a) In order to assist the House in:

(1) its analysis, appraisal, and evaluation of (A) the application, administration, execution, and effectiveness of the laws enacted by the Congress, or (B) conditions and circumstances

---

* This is House Rule X, clause 2 and clause 3 with technical adjustments to make it applicable to a single committee rather than all committees.

which may indicate the necessity or desirability of enacting new or additional legislation, and

(2) its formulation, consideration, and enactment of such modifications or changes in those laws, and of such additional legislation, as may be necessary or appropriate, there shall in conformity with Rule XV there shall [sic] be established an Oversight Subcommittee.

(b) The Oversight Subcommittee shall review and study, on a continuing basis, the application, administration, execution, and effectiveness of those laws, or parts of laws, the subject matter of which is within the jurisdiction of the committee, and the organization and operation of the Federal agencies and entities having responsibilities in or for the administration and execution thereof, in order to determine whether such laws and the programs thereunder are being implemented and carried out in accordance with the intent of the Congress and whether such programs should be continued, curtailed, or eliminated. In addition, the Oversight Subcommittee shall review and study any conditions or circumstances which may indicate the necessity or desirability of enacting new or additional legislation within the jurisdiction of the committee (whether or not any bill or resolution has been introduced with respect thereto), and shall on a continuing basis undertake futures research and forecasting on matters within the jurisdiction of the committee. The Oversight Subcommittee shall in no way limit the responsibility of the subcommittees from carrying out their oversight responsibilities.

(c) The Oversight Subcommittee shall review and study on a continuing basis the impact or probable impact of tax policies affecting subjects within the jurisdiction of the committee.

(d) The Oversight Subcommittee, in order to fulfill the committee's responsibility under Rule X, clause (3) of the Rules of the House of Representatives, shall have the function of reviewing and studying, on a continuing basis, all laws, programs, and Government activities dealing with or involving _____. (Provision (d) is necessary only for those six committees with special oversight functions under House Rule X, clause 3. Following is the language for each such committee, to follow the word "involving," above:

Armed Services

"international arms control and disarmament and the education of military dependents in schools."

Education & Labor

"domestic educational programs and institutions, and programs of student assistance, which are within the jurisdiction of other committees."

Foreign Affairs

"customs administration, intelligence activities relating to foreign policy, international financial and monetary organizations, and international fishing agreements."

Interior and Insular Affairs

"Indians and non-military nuclear energy and research and development including the disposal of nuclear waste."

Science & Technology

"non-military research and development."

Small Business

"the problems of all types of small business."

SECOND OPTION—SUBCOMMITTEE OVERSIGHT

(a) In order to assist the House in:

(1) its analysis, appraisal, and evaluation of (A) the application, administration, execution, and effectiveness of the laws enacted by the Congress, or (B) conditions and circumstances which may indicate the necessity or desirability of enacting new or additional legislation, and

(2) its formulation, consideration, and enactment of such modifications or changes in those laws, and of such additional legislation, as may be necessary or appropriate, the various subcommittees, consistent with their jurisdictions as set forth in Rule XV, shall have oversight responsibilities as provided in paragraph (b).

(b) Each subcommittee shall review and study, on a continuing basis, the application, administration, execution, and effectiveness of those laws, or parts of laws, the subject matter of which is within the jurisdiction of that subcommittee, and the organization and operation of the Federal agencies and entities having responsibilities in or for the administration and execution thereof, in order to determine whether such laws and the programs thereunder are being implemented and carried out in accordance with the intent of the Congress and whether such programs should be continued, curtailed, or eliminated. In addition, each such subcommittee shall review and study any conditions or circumstances which may indicate the necessity or desirability of enacting new or additional legislation within the jurisdiction of that subcommittee (whether or not any bill or resolution has been introduced with respect thereto), and shall on a continuing basis undertake futures research and forecasting on matters within the jurisdiction of that subcommittee.

(c) Each subcommittee shall review and study on a continuing basis the impact or probable impact of tax policies affecting subjects within its jurisdictions.

(d) The chairman of the committee, consistent with Rule XV and Rule XVII in order to fulfill the committee's responsibility under Rule X, clause (3) of the Rules of the House of Representatives, shall assign matters to subcommittees for reviewing, studying, and coordinating, on a continuing basis, all laws, programs, and Government activities dealing with or involving _____ (Provision (d) is necessary only for those six committees with special oversight functions under House Rule X, clause 3. Following is the language for each such committee, to follow the word "involving," above:

DSG MODEL COMMITTEE AND CAUCUS RULES

Armed Services

"international arms control and disarmament and the education of military dependents in schools."

Education & Labor

"domestic educational programs and institutions, and programs of student assistance, which are within the jurisdiction of other committees."

Foreign Affairs

"customs administration, intelligence activities relating to foreign policy, international financial and monetary organizations, and international fishing agreements."

Interior and Insular Affairs

"Indians and non-military nuclear energy and research and development including the disposal of nuclear waste."

Science and Technology

"non-military research and development."

Small Business

"the problems of all types of small business."

RULE No. X *
REVIEW OF CONTINUING PROGRAMS;
BUDGET ACT PROVISIONS

(a) The committee shall, in its consideration of all bills and joint resolutions of a public character within its jurisdiction, insure that appropriations for continuing program and activities of the Federal Government and the District of Columbia government will be made annually to the maximum extent feasible and consistent with the nature, requirements, and objectives of the programs and activities involved. For the purposes of this paragraph a Government agency includes the organizational units of government listed in clause 7(d) of Rule XIII of House Rules.

(b) The committee shall review, from time to time, each continuing program within its jurisdictions for which appropriations are not made annually in order to ascertain whether such program could be modified so that appropriations therefor would be made annually.

(c) The committee shall, on or before March 15 of each year, submit to the Committee on the Budget (1) its views and estimates with respect to all matters to be set forth in the concurrent resolution

---

* This is House Rule X, clause 4(f), 4(g), 4(h), and 4(i), with technical adjustments to make it applicable to a single committee rather than all committees.

on the budget for the ensuing fiscal year which are within its jurisdiction or functions, and (2) an estimate of the total amounts of new budget authority, and budget outlays resulting therefrom, to be provided or authorized in all bills and resolutions within its jurisdiction which it intends to be effective during that fiscal year.

(d) As soon as practicable after a concurrent resolution on the budget for any fiscal year is agreed to, the committee (after consulting with the appropriate committee or commitees of the Senate) shall subdivide any allocations made to it in the joint explanatory statement accompanying the conference report on such resolutions, and promptly report such subdivisions to the House, in the manner provided by section 302 of the Congressional Budget Act of 1974.

(e) Whenever the committee is directed in a concurrent resolution on the budget to determine and recommend changes in laws, bills, or resolutions under the reconciliation process it shall promptly make such determination and recommendations, and report a reconcilation bill or resolution (or both) to the House or submit such recommendations to the Committee on the Budget, in accordance with the Congressional Budget Act of 1974.

RULE No. XI *

BROADCASTING OF COMMITTEE HEARINGS

(a) It is the purpose of this clause to provide a means, in conformity with acceptable standards of dignity, propriety, and decorum, by which committee hearings, or committee meetings, which are open to the public may be covered, by television broadcast, radio broadcast, and still photography, or by any of such methods of coverage—

(1) for the education, enlightenment, and information of the general public, on the basis of accurate and impartial news coverage, regarding the operations, procedures, and practices of the House as a legislative and representative body and regarding the measures, public issues, and other matters before the House and its committees, the consideration thereof, and the action taken thereon; and

(2) for the development of the perspective and understanding of the general public with respect to the role and function of the House under the Constitution of the United States as an organ of the Federal Government.

(b) In addition, it is the intent of this clause that radio and television tapes and television film of any coverage under this clause shall not be used, or made available for use, as partisan political campaign material to promote or oppose the candidacy of any person for elective public office.

(c) It is, further, the intent of this clause that the general conduct of each meeting (whether of a hearing or otherwise) covered, under authority of this clause, by television broadcast, radio broadcast, and still photography, or by any of such methods of coverage, and the per-

---

* This is House Rule XI, clause 3, with technical adjustments to make it applicable to a single committee rather than all committees.

sonal behavior of the committee members and staff, other Government officials and personnel, witnesses, television, radio, and press media personnel, and the general public at the hearing or other meeting shall be in strict conformity with and observance of the acceptable standards of dignity, propriety, courtesy, and decorum traditionally observed by the House in its operations and shall not be such as to—

(1) distort the objects and purposes of the hearings or other meeting or the activities of committee members in connection with that hearing or meeting or in connection with the general work of the committee or of the House; or

(2) cast discredit or dishonor on the House, the committee, or any member or bring the House, the committee, or any member into disrepute.

(d) The coverage of committee hearings and meetings by television broadcast, radio broadcast, or still photography is a privilege made available by the House and shall be permitted and conducted only in strict conformity with the purposes, provisions, and requirements of this clause.

(e) Whenever any hearing or meeting conducted by any committee of the House is open to the public, that committee may permit, by majority vote of the committee, that hearing or meeting to be covered, in whole or in part, by television broadcast, and still photography, or by any of such methods of coverage, but only under such written rules as the committee may adopt in accordance with the purposes, provisions, and requirements of this clause.

(f) The written rules which may be adopted by a committee under paragraph (e) of this clause shall contain provisions to the following effect:

(1) If the television or radio coverage of the hearing or meeting is to be presented to the public as live coverage, that coverage shall be conducted and presented without commercial sponsorship.

(2) No witness served with a subpoena by the committee shall be required against his or her will to be photographed at any hearing or to give evidence or testimony while the broadcasting of that hearing, by radio or television, is being conducted. At the request of any such witness who does not wish to be subjected to radio, television, or still photography coverage, all lenses shall be covered and all microphones used for coverage turned off. This subparagraph is supplementary to clause 2(k) (5) of this rule, relating to the protection of the rights of witnesses.

(3) Not more than four television cameras, operating from fixed positions, shall be permitted in a hearing or meeting room. The allocation among the television media of the positions of the number of television cameras permitted in a hearing or meeting room shall be in accordance with fair and equitable procedures devised by the Executive Committee of the Radio and Television Correspondents' Galleries.

(4) Television cameras shall be placed so as not to obstruct in any way the space between any witness giving evidence or testimony and any member of the committee or the visibility of that witness and that member to each other.

(5) Television cameras shall not be placed in positions which obstruct unnecessarily the coverage of the hearings or meeting by the other media.

(6) Equipment necessary for coverage by the television and radio media shall not be installed in, or removed from, the hearing or meeting room while the committee is in session.

(7) Floodlights, spotlights, strobelights, and flashguns shall not be used in providing any method of coverage of the hearing or meeting, except that the television media may install additional lighting in the hearing or meeting room, without cost to the Government, in order to raise the ambient lighting level necessary to provide adequate television coverage of the hearing or meeting at the then current state of the art of television coverage.

(8) Not more than five press photographers shall be permitted to cover a hearing or meeting by still photography. In the selection of these photographers, preference shall be given to photographers from Associated Press Photos and United Press International Newspictures. If request is made by more than five of the media for coverage of the hearing or meeting by still photography, that coverage shall be made on the basis of a fair and equitable pool arrangement devised by the Standing Committee of Press Photographers.

(9) Photographers shall not position themselves, at any time during the course of the hearing or meeting, between the witness table and the members of the committee.

(10) Photographers shall not place themselves in positions which obstruct unnecessarily the coverage of the hearing by the other media.

(11) Personnel providing coverage by the television and radio media shall be then currently accredited to the Radio and Television Correspondent's Galleries.

(12) Personnel providing coverage by still photography shall be then currently accredited to the Press Photographers' Gallery.

(13) Personnel providing coverage by the television and radio media and by still photography shall conduct themselves and their coverage activities in an orderly and unobstrusive manner.

RULE No. XII *

COMMITTEE AND SUBCOMMITTEE BUDGETS

(a) The Chairman, in consultation with the majority members of the commmittee shall, for each session of the Congress, prepare a preliminary budget. Such budget shall include necessary amounts for staff personnel, for necessary travel, investigation, and other expenses of the full committee, and after consultation with the minority membership, the chairman shall include amounts budgeted to the minority members for staff personnel to be under the direction and supervision of the minority, travel expenses of minority members and staff, and minority office expenses. All travel expenses of minority members and staff shall be paid for out of the amounts so set aside and budgeted.

(b) (1) The chairman of each subcommittee, in consultation with the majority members thereof, shall prepare a budget to include funds

---
* Conforms to Caucus Rule M II B and M III A(5).

for staff, travel, investigations, and miscellaneous expenses as may be required for the work of the subcommittee.

(2) The chairman of each subcommittee shall control the funds provided for in the subcommittee budget.

(c) The chairman shall combine the proposals of each subcommittee with the preliminary budget of the full committee into a consolidated committee budget, and shall present the same to the committee for its approval. The chairman shall then take all action necessary to bring about its approval by the Committee on House Administration and by the House.

(d) Authorization for the payment of additional or unforseen committee and subcommittees' expenses may be procured by one or more additional expense resolutions processed in the same manner as set out herein.

(e) The Chairman or any chairman of a subcommittee may initiate necessary travel requests as provided in Rule XIV within the limits of their portion of the consolidated budget as approved by the House and the Chairman may execute necessary vouchers thereof.

(f) Once monthly, at the regularly scheduled meetings, the Chairman shall submit to the committee, in writing, for its approval, or other action, a full and detailed accounting of all expenditures made during the period since the last such accounting from the amount budgeted to the full committee. Such report shall show the amount and purpose of each expenditure and the budget to which such expenditure is attributed.

Rule No. XIII *

COMMITTEE AND SUBCOMMITTEE STAFF

(a) The professional and clerical staff assigned to the minority shall be appointed and their remuneration determined in such manner as the minority members or the committee shall determine within the budget approved for such purposes by the committee; Provided, however, that no minority staff person shall be compensated at a rate which exceeds that paid his or her majority party staff counterpart.

(b) The professional and clerical employees of the committee not assigned to a subcommittee or to the minority under the above provision shall be appointed, and may be removed, and their remuneration determined by the Chairman in consultation with and with the approval of the majority members of the committee within the budget approved for such purposes by the committee.

(c) The professional and clerical staff assigned to the minority shall be under the general supervision and direction of the minority members of the committee who may delegate such authority as they determine appropriate.

(d) The professional and clerical staff of the committee not assigned to a subcommittee or to the minority shall be under the general supervision and direction of the chairman, who shall establish and assign the duties and responsibilities of such staff members and delegate such authority as he determines appropriate.

---

* Conforms to House Rule XI, clause 5 and clause 6; Caucus Rule M II B and M III A(5).

(e) It is intended that the skills and experience of all members of the committee staff shall be available to all members of the committee.

(f)(1) The chairman of each standing subcommittee of this committee is authorized to appoint one staff member who shall serve at the pleasure of the subcommittee chairman.

(2) The ranking minority member of each standing subcommittee on this committee is authorized to appoint one staff person who shall serve at the pleasure of the ranking minority party member.

(3) The staff members appointed pursuant to the provisions of subparagraphs (1) and (2) shall be compensated at a rate determined by the subcommittee chairman not to exceed (A) 75 per centum of the maximum established in paragraph (c) of clause 6 of House Rule XI; Provided, however, a staff person appointed by a ranking minority member shall be compensated at a rate not to exceed that paid his or her majority party staff counterpart.

(4) Subparagraphs (1) (2) and (3) shall apply to six subcommittees only * and no member shall appoint more than one person pursuant to the above provisions.

(5) The staff positions made available to the subcommittee chairmen and ranking minority party members pursuant to subparagraphs (1) and (2) shall be made available from the staff positions provided under clause 6 of House Rule XI unless such staff positions are made available pursuant to a primary or additional expense resolution.

(6) Except as provided by the above provisions, the professional and clerical members of the subcommittee staffs shall be appointed, and may be removed, and their remuneration determined by the subcommittee chairman in consultation with and with the approval of a majority of the majority members of the subcommittee, and with the approval of a majority of the majority members of the full committee, within the budget approved for the subcommittee.

(7) The professional and clerical staff of a subcommittee shall be under the supervision and direction of the chairman of that subcommittee.

RULE NO. XIV**

TRAVEL OF MEMBERS AND STAFF

(a) Consistent with the primary expense resolution and such additional expense resolutions as may have been approved, the provisions of this rule shall govern travel of committee members and staff. Travel to be reimbursed from funds set aside for the full committee for any member or any staff member shall be paid only upon the prior authorization of the chairman. Travel may be authorized by the chairman for any member and any staff member in connection with the attendance

---
* Limit does not apply to the Appropriations Committee.
** Conforms to House Rule XI, clause 2(n).

of hearings conducted by the committee of any subcommittee thereof and meetings, conferences, and investigations which involve activities or subject matter under the general jurisdiction of the committee. Before such authorization is given there shall be submitted to the chairman in writing the following:

(1) The purpose of the travel;
(2) The dates during which the travel is to be made and the date or dates of the event for which the travel is being made;
(3) The location of the event for which the travel is to be made;
(4) The names of members and staff seeking authorization.

(b) In the case of travel of members and staff of a subcommittee to hearings, meetings, conferences, and investigations involving activities or subject matter under the legislative assignment of such subcommittee to be paid for out of funds allocated to such subcommittee, prior authorization must be obtained from the subcommittee chairman and the Chairman. Such prior authorization shall be given by the Chairman only upon the representation by the applicable chairman of the subcommittee in writing setting forth those items enumerated in (1), (2), (3), and (4) of paragraph (a) and in addition thereto setting forth that subcommittee funds are available to cover the expenses of the persons being authorized by the subcommittee chairman to undertake the travel and that there has been a compliance where applicable with Rule VII of the committee..

(c)(1) In the case of travel outside the United States of members and staff of the committee or of a subcommittee for the purpose of conducting hearings, investigations, studies, or attending meetings and conferences involving activities or subject matter under the legislative assignment of the committee or pertinent subcommittee, prior authorization must be obtained from the Chairman, or, in the case of a subcommittee from the subcommittee chairman and the Chairman. Before such authorization is given, there shall be submitted to the Chairman, in writing, a request for such authorization. Each request, which shall be filed in a manner that allows for a reasonable period of time for review before such travel is scheduled to begin, shall include the following:

(A) the purpose of the travel;
(B) the dates during which the travel will occur;
(C) the names of the countries to be visited and the length of time to be spent in each;
(D) an agenda of anticipated activities for each country for which travel is authorized together with a description of the purpose to be served and the areas of committee jurisdiction involved; and
(E) the names of members and staff for whom authorization is sought.

(2) Requests for travel outside the United States may be initiated by the Chairman or the chairman of a subcommittee (except that individuals may submit a request to the Chairman for the purpose of attending a conference or meeting) and shall be limited to members and permanent employees of the committee.

(3) At the conclusion of any hearing, investigation, study, meeting or conference for which travel outside the United States has been authorized pursuant to this rule, each subcommittee (or members and

staff attending meetings or conferences) shall submit a written report to the Chairman covering the activities and other pertinent observations or information gained as a result of such travel.

(d) Members and staff of the committee performing authorized travel on official business shall be governed by applicable laws, resolutions, or regulations of the House and of the Committee on House Administration pertaining to such travel.

RULE No. XV *

NUMBER AND JURISDICTION OF SUBCOMMITTEES

(a) There shall be _____ standing subcommittees as follows: (list names of all standing subcommittees). All proposed legislation and other matters related to the subcommittees listed under standing subcommittees named below shall be referred to such subcommittees, respectively:

(1) Subcommittee on _____: (Specify jurisdiction)
(2) Subcommittee on _____: (Specify jurisdiction)
(3) Subcommittee on _____: (Specify jurisdiction)
(4) Subcommittee on _____: (Specify jurisdiction)
(5) Subcommittee on _____: (Specify jurisdiction)
(6) Subcommittee on _____: (Specify jurisdiction)

(b) There shall be _____(as needed) additional subcommittees as follows: (list names of all special, select, *ad hoc*, investigative, or other subcommittees).

(7) Select Subcommittee on _____: (Specify jurisdiction)
(8) Special Subcommittee on _____: (Specify jurisdiction
(9) Ad Hoc Subcommittee on _____: (Specify jurisdiction)
(10) Investigations Subcommittee: (Specify jurisdiction)
(11) Oversight Subcommittee: (Specify jurisdiction)

(c) The committee may provide for such additional subcommittees as determined to be appropriate; Provided, however, that such additional subcommittees are approved by a majority of the majority members on the committee.

(d) A member serving as chairman of any subcommittee on this committee shall not also serve as the chairman of a subcommittee on any other standing committee; Provided, however, that this provision shall not apply to members serving as subcommittee chairmen on the Budget Committee; House Administration Committee; Joint Committees; or on the Small Business Committee who served as a subcommittee chairman on the Select Committee on Small Business as of October 8, 1974.

RULE No. XVI **

POWERS AND DUTIES OF SUBCOMMITTEES

(a) Each subcommittee is authorized to meet, hold hearings, re-

---
* Conforms to Caucus Rule M III A(1).
** Conforms to Caucus Rule M III 2.

ceive evidence, and report to the full committee on all matters referred to it or under its jurisdiction. Subcommittee chairmen shall set dates for hearings and meetings of their respective subcommittees after consultation with the chairman and other subcommittee chairmen with a view toward avoiding simultaneous scheduling of full committee and subcommittee meetings or hearings wherever possible.

(b) Whenever a subcommittee has ordered a bill, resolution, or other matter to be reported to the committee, the chairman of the subcommittee reporting the bill, resolution, or matter to the full committee, or any member authorized by the subcommittee to do so, may report such bill, resolution, or matter to the committee. It shall be the duty of the chairman of the subcommittee to report or cause to be reported promptly such bill, resolution, or matter, and to take or cause to be taken the necessary steps to bring such bill, resolution, or matter to a vote.

(c) In any event, the report of any subcommittee on a measure which has been approved by the subcommitte shall be filed within seven calendar days (exclusive of days on which the House is not in session) after the day on which there has been filed with the clerk of the committee a written request, signed by a majority of the members of the subcommittee, for the reporting of that measure. Upon the filing of any request, the clerk of the committee shall transmit immediately to the chairman of the subcommittee notice of the filing of that request.

(d) All committee or subcommittee reports printed pursuant to legislative study or investigation and not approved by a majority vote of the committee or subcommittee, as appropriate, shall contain the following disclaimer on the cover of such report:

"This report has not been officially adopted by the Committee on (or pertinent subcommittee thereof) and may not therefore necessarily reflect the views of its members."

(e) Bills, resolutions, or other matters favorably reported by a subcommittee shall automatically be placed upon the agenda of the committee as of the time they are reported and shall be considered by the full committee in the order in which they were reported unless the committee shall by majority vote otherwise direct: Provided, That no bill reported by a subcommittee shall be considered by the full committee unless it has been in the hands of all members at least 48 hours prior to the meeting, together with a comparison with present law and a section-by-section analysis of the proposed change, and a section-by-section justification.

RULE No. XVII *

REFERRAL OF LEGISLATION TO SUBCOMMITTEES

(a) Each bill, resolution, investigation, or other matter which relates to a subject listed under the jurisdiction of any subcommittee named in Rule XV referred to or initiated by the full committee shall be referred to the subcommittee of appropriate jurisdiction within (one week) (ten days) (two weeks) unless, by majority vote of the majority members of the full committee, consideration is to be by the full committee.

* Conforms to Caucus Rule M III A(3).

(b) Referral to a subcommittee shall not be made until three days shall have elapsed after written notification of such proposed referral to all subcommittee chairmen, at which time such proposed referral shall be made unless one or more subcommittee chairmen shall have given written notice to each subcommittee that he intends to question such proposed referral at the next regularly scheduled meeting of the committee, or at a special meeting of the committee called for that purpose at which time referral shall be made by the majority members of the committee. All bills shall be referred under this rule to the subcommittee of proper jurisdiction without regard to whether the author is or is not a member of the subcommittee. A bill, resolution, or other matter referred to a subcommittee in accordance with this rule may be recalled therefrom at any time by a vote of the majority members of the committee for the committee's direct consideration or for reference to another subcommittee.

(c) No committee report shall be filed until copies of the proposed report have been available to all members at least 36 hours prior. No material change shall be made in the report distributed to members unless agreed to by majority vote: Provided, That any member or members of the committee may file, as part of the printed report, individal, minority, or dissenting views, without reference to the preceding provision of this rule.

(d) In carrying out Rule XVII with respect to any matter, the chairman may refer the matter simultaneously to two or more subcommittees, consistent with Rule XV, for concurrent consideration or for consideration in sequence (subject to appropriate time limitations in the case of any subcommittee after the first), or divide the matter into two or more parts (reflecting different subjects and jurisdictions) and refer each such part to a different subcommittee, or refer the matter pursuant to Rule X to a special ad hoc committee appointed by the chairman (from the members of the subcommittee having legislative jurisdiction) for the specific purpose of considering that matter and reporting to the full committee thereon, or make such other provisions as may be considered appropriate.

RULE No. XVIII*

SIZES & PARTY RATIOS ON SUBCOMMITTEES
AND CONFERENCE COMMITTEES

(a) To the extent that the number of subcommittees and their party ratios permit, the size of all subcommittees shall be established so that the majority party members of the committee have an equal number of subcommittee assignments; Provided, however, that a member may waive his or her right to an equal number of subcommittee assignments on the committee; and provided further, that the majority party members may limit the number of subcommittee assignments of the chairman and the subcommittee chairmen and the minority party members may limit the number of subcommittee assignments of ranking minority party members in order to equalize committee workloads.

---

* Conforms to Caucus Rule M III A(4).

(b) On each subcommittee there shall be a ratio of at least two majority party members for each minority party member, plus one majority party member. In calculating the ratio of majority party members to minority party members, there shall be included all *ex officio* voting members of the subcommittees.

(c) Following shall be the sizes and majority/minority ratios for subcommittees:

(1) Subcommittee on _____: (size) (____majority; ____minority)

(2) Subcommittee on _____: (size) (____majority; ____minority)

(3) Subcommittee on _____: (size) (____majority; ____minority)

(4) Subcommittee on _____: (size) (____majority; ____minority)

(5) Subcommittee on _____: (size) (____majority; ____minority)

(6) Subcommittee on _____: (size) (____majority; ____minority)

(7) Select Subcommittee on _____: (size) (____majority; ____minority)

(8) Special Subcommittee on _____: (size) (____majority; ____minority)

(9) Ad Hoc Subcommittee on _____: (size) (____majority; ____minority)

(10) Investigations Subcommittee: (size) ____majority; ____minority)

(11) Oversight Subcommittee: (size) (____majority; ____minority)

(d) The full committee chairman, or a member designated by a majority of the majority members on the committee, shall recommend to the Speaker as conferees the names of those members (1) selected by the majority party members of the committee in a manner determined by them, and (2) selected by the minority party members of the committee in a manner determined by them. Provided, however, that recommendations of conferees to the Speaker shall provide a ratio of at least two majority party members for each minority party member, plus one majority party member.

APPENDIX 6

House Democratic Caucus Rules and Manual

PREAMBLE

In adopting the following rules for the Democratic Caucus, we affirm and declare that the following cardinal principles should control Democratic action:
    a. In essentials of Democratic principles and doctrine, unity.
    b. In nonessentials, and in all things not involving fidelity to party principles, entire individual independence.
    c. Party alignment only upon matters of party faith or party policy.
    d. Friendly conference and, whenever reasonably possible, party cooperation.

STANDING RULES

R 1. Membership
    a. All Democratic Members of the House of Representatives and the Resident Commissioner from Puerto Rico, the Delegate from the District of Columbia, the Delegate from Guam and the Delegate from the Virgin Islands who are members of the Democratic Party shall be prima facie members of the Democratic Caucus.
    b. Any member of the Democratic Caucus of the House of Representatives failing to abide by the rules governing the same shall thereby automatically cease to be a member of the Caucus.

R 2. Meeting Dates
    Meetings of the Democratic Caucus shall be called by the chairman upon his own motion or at the request of the Party Leader. Whenever fifty (50) members of the Caucus request the chairman, in writing, to hold a special meeting the chairman shall set the time and place of such special meeting and provide the members with the order of business of such special meeting at least 5 calendar days before the hour of convening; however, when the purpose of such special meeting is to consider a veto override or legislation that has been reported to the House, the chairman may waive the 5-day-notice requirement. In every instance, the chairman shall provide the members with reasonable notice of the time, place and order of business of all meetings. While the House is in session, the Democratic Caucus shall meet regularly at a time and place to be determined by the chairman, on the 3d Wednesday of each month, except January of odd numbered years. If the House not be in session on the 3d Wednesday, the monthly Caucus shall be held on the next succeeding Wednesday on which the House is in session. The chairman may cancel any monthly Caucus, but not two consecutive monthly Caucuses, provided members are given reasonable notice of such cancellation. Members of the Caucus shall not schedule committee meetings or hearings at times when the Caucus is to be in session.

R 3. Presiding Officer
    The chairman shall have the right to name any member of the Caucus to perform the duties of the Chair during the temporary absence of the chairman.

R 4. Quorum
    A quorum of the Caucus shall consist of a majority of the Democratic Members of the House. If the absence of a quorum is established, the chairman may continue the meeting for purposes of discussion only, but no motion of any kind, except a motion to adjourn, shall be in order at such continued meeting.

R 5. Agenda
    At each such monthly Caucus, Members shall have the right to place before the Caucus any question, provided written notice of such intention is (1) delivered to the office of the chairman, and (2) transmitted to all members of the Caucus not later than 5 p.m. on the 9th day immediately preceding the day of such Caucus. The chairman shall prescribe the order of business and shall provide members with an agenda at least 5 days before the Caucus. Amendments to the agenda shall be in order only if submitted to Caucus members at least 48 hours before the hour of convening and if supported in writing by 50 members.

HOUSE DEMOCRATIC CAUCUS RULES AND MANUAL

R 6. Rules

General parliamentary law, with such special rules as may be adopted, shall govern the meetings of the Caucus. The five-minute rule that governs the House of Representatives shall govern debate in the Democratic Caucus, unless suspended by a vote of the Caucus.

R 7. Elections

No Member shall be elected to serve as Chairman, Secretary, or Assistant Secretary of the Democratic Caucus for more than two consecutive terms.

With respect to voting in the House for Speaker and other officers of the House, for each committee chairman, and for membership of committees, a majority vote of those present and voting at a Democratic Caucus meeting shall bind all members of the Caucus.

R 8. Admittance to Caucus Meetings

All that portion of any Caucus meeting, regular or special, that involves action by the Caucus with respect to proposed legislation shall be open to the public, except when a majority determines by a rollcall vote, a quorum being present, that the portion of the Caucus meeting involving action by the Caucus with respect to proposed legislation shall be closed.

During the closed portion of any Caucus meeting, no persons, except Democratic Members of the House of Representatives, a Caucus Journal Clerk, and other necessary employees, shall be admitted to the meeting of the Caucus without the express permission of the chairman.

R 9. Journal and Notification of Policy Actions

The Caucus shall keep a journal of its proceedings, which shall be published after each meeting, and which shall be available for inspection by any member of the Caucus upon request. The yeas and nays on any question shall, at the desire of one-fifth of those present, be entered on the Journal, and a copy of each record vote shall be distributed to each Member of the Caucus. *Provided, however,* that a question shall be decided by secret ballot or other non-record vote if a majority so demand. *Provided, further,* that all votes involving the nomination or election of Members for office in the Caucus or in the House, including committee chairmanships, shall be by secret ballot unless a majority decide otherwise.

R 10. Manual of the House Democratic Caucus

There shall be a Manual of the House Democratic Caucus which shall contain all resolutions of continuing force and effect. Said Manual shall be kept current. Topical resolutions need not be included in the Manual but shall be published in the Journal. All matter included in the Manual shall have the same effect as if it were included in the Standing Rules.

MANUAL

M I. Standing Committee Memberships

A. *Committee Ratios.* Committee ratios should be established to create firm working majorities on each committee. In determining the ratio on the respective standing committees, the Speaker should provide for a *minimum* of three Democrats for each two Republicans.

B. *Seniority.* The Committee on Committees shall recommend to the Caucus nominees for chairman and membership of each committee other than the Committee on Rules for which the Democratic nominee for Speaker or Speaker as the case may be shall have exclusive nominating authority. Recommendations for committee posts need not necessarily follow seniority.

C. *Nominations for Committee Membership.* Upon a letter from a Member, signed by 50 percent or more of said Member's State Democratic Delegation, including said Member, said Member shall automatically be considered for nomination by the Committee on Committees for the committee membership position to which said Member aspires. The Chairman of the Committee on Committees shall see that such Member's name is placed in nomination. The provisions of this paragraph shall not apply with respect to nominations for the Committee on Rules.

D. *Procedures for Electing Committee Chairmen and Members.* The Democratic nominee for Speaker or Speaker as the case may be shall recommend to the Caucus nominees for chairman and membership of the Committee on Rules. Debate and balloting on any such nomination shall be subject to the same provisions as apply to the nominations of chairmen or Members of other committees. If a majority of those present and voting reject any nominee for chairman or membership of the Committee on Rules, the Democratic nominee for Speaker or Speaker as the case may be shall be entitled to submit new nominations until any such positions are filled. Chairmen: The Committee on Committees shall nominate one Member of each committee, other than the Committee on Rules, for the position of chairman and such nominations need not necessarily follow seniority. The Caucus shall vote on each nominee. If a secret ballot is demanded on any chairman nominated by the Committee on Committees, such vote will be taken by secret ballot if the demand for the same is supported by one-fifth of those present. No debate shall be allowed unless requested by a nominee or a Member who wishes to speak in opposition to a nomination provided that the request to speak in opposition is supported by three or more Members. Debate on any nomination shall be limited to 30 minutes equally divided between proponents and opponents of that nominee, such time to be further extended only by majority vote of the Caucus. If a majority of those present and voting reject its nominee for chairman, the Committee on Committees shall make a new nomination within 5 days. Five to ten days after the Committee on Committees reports such new nominations, the Caucus shall meet to consider the new nominee of the Committee on Committees and any additional nominations offered from the floor. Only Members who have been recommended for membership on the committee shall be eligible for nomination as chairman. Should additional nominations be made from the floor, debate shall be limited to 15 minutes per nominee, unless extended by majority vote of the Caucus; election shall be by secret ballot; and a majority of those present and voting a quorum being present, shall be required to elect.

The Committee on Committees shall make recommendations to the Caucus regarding the assignment of Members to each committee other than the Committee on Rules, one committee at a time. Upon a demand supported by 10 or more Members, a separate vote shall be had on any member of the committee. If any such motion prevails, the committee list of that particular committee shall be considered recommitted to the Committee on Committees for the sole purpose of implementing the direction of the Caucus. Also, such demand, if made and properly supported, shall be debated for no more than 30 minutes with the time equally divided between proponents and opponents. If the Caucus and the Committee on Committees be in disagreement after completion of the procedure herein provided, the Caucus may make final and complete disposition of the matter.

Appendix 6

In making nominations for committee assignments the Committee on Committees shall not discriminate on the basis of prior occupation or profession in making such nominations.

E. *Rules for Making Committee Assignments.* For the purposes of this section the following committee designations shall apply:

(1) Appropriations; Ways and Means; and Rules Committee shall be "exclusive" committees.

(2) Agriculture; Armed Services; Banking, Currency and Housing; Education and Labor; International Relations; Interstate and Foreign Commerce; Judiciary; and Public Works and Transportation shall be considered "major" committees.

(3) Budget; District of Columbia; Government Operations; House Administration; Interior and Insular Affairs; Merchant Marine and Fisheries; Post Office and Civil Service; Science and Technology; Small Business; and Veterans' Affairs shall be considered "nonmajor" committees.

a. No Democratic Member of an exclusive committee shall also serve on another exclusive, major, or nonmajor committee.

b. Each Democratic Member shall be entitled to serve on one but only one exclusive or one major committee.

c. No Democratic Member shall serve on more than one major and one nonmajor committee or two nonmajor committees.

d. No chairman of an exclusive or major committee may serve on another exclusive, major or nonmajor committee.

e. Members who served as members of the Select Committee on Small Business or the Small Business Subcommittee of the Committee on Banking and Currency on October 8, 1974, shall not be deemed to be in violation of the provisions of this clause by reason of membership on the Small Business Committee.

f. Members of the Budget Committee as of December 1, 1974, shall not be deemed to be in violation of the provisions of this clause by reason of their Budget Committee membership and Members of the Appropriations and Ways and Means Committees shall be eligible for membership on the Budget Committee as provided by law, not withstanding the provisions of subsection a. Any Member of the Budget Committee shall be entitled to take a leave of absence from service on any committee or subcommittee during the period he or she serves on the Budget Committee and seniority rights of such Member on such committee and on each subcommittee to which such Member was assigned at the time shall be fully protected as if such Member had continued to so serve during the period of the leave of absence. Any Member on such leave of absence shall not be deemed to be in violation of the provisions of this clause by reason of their membership on the committee from which they are on a leave of absence.

M II. Standing Full Committee and Subcommittee Chairmanships

A. The chairman of a full committee shall not be the chairman of more than one subcommittee on such full committee and shall insofar as practicable permit subcommittee chairman of other subcommittees to handle legislation on the floor which has been reported by their subcommittee.

B. No Member shall be chairman of more than one legislative subcommittee. A subcommittee chairman shall be entitled to select and designate at least one staff member for said subcommittee, subject to the approval of a majority of the Democratic Members of said full committee. Said staff member shall be compensated at a salary commensurate with the responsibilities prescribed by said subcommittee chairman. The staff members' compensation shall be provided out of appropriated amounts, if any, rather than statutory amounts allowed each committee.

C. No Member shall be a member of more than two committees with legislative jurisdiction.

D. The following committees shall be exempt from the three immediately preceding provisions: House Administration; Standards of Official Conduct; House Recording; House Beauty Shop; and Joint Committees.

E. A Member who served as chairman or subcommittee chairman of the Select Committee on Small Business or as subcommittee chairman of the Small Business Subcommittee of the Banking and Currency Committee as of October 8, 1974, shall not be deemed to be in violation of the provisions of this clause because of service as chairman or subcommittee chairman on the Small Business Committee. The chairman of a major or exclusive full committee shall not serve simultaneously as the chairman of any other full, select or joint committee; *Provided, however,* the chairman of the Way and Means Committee may also serve as chairman of the Joint Committee on Internal Revenue Taxation.

F. Members of the Budget Committee shall be eligible for subcommittee chairmanships on such committee without regard to the first sentence of section B.

M III. Committee and Subcommittee Organization and Procedure

A. At the start of each Congress, the chairman of each standing committee or other committee with legislative jurisdiction shall call a meeting of all of the Democratic Members of the committee, giving at least 3 days notice to all Democratic Members of the committee. Said meeting shall be called subsequent to the House Democratic Caucus approval of the committee lists but prior to any organizational meeting of the full committee. Such Caucus shall fill the positions of subcommittee chairmen and subcommittee members in accordance with procedures described in sections M. V. A and M. V. B and shall approve and secure adoption of committee rules incorporating the following principles:

(1) *Jurisdiction and number of subcommittees.* The Democratic Caucus of each committee shall establish the number of subcommittees and shall fix the jurisdiction of each subcommittee.

(2) *Powers and duties of subcommittees.* Each subcommittee is authorized to meet, hold hearings, receive evidence and report to the committee on all matters referred to it. Subcommittee chairmen shall set meeting dates after consultation with the chairman and other subcommittee chairmen with a view toward avoiding simultaneous scheduling of committee and subcommittee meetings or hearings wherever possible.

(3) *Reference of legislation and other matters.* All legislation and other matters referred to a committee shall be referred to the subcommittee of appropriate jurisdiction within 2 weeks unless, by majority vote of the Democratic Members of the full committee, consideration is to be by the full committee.

(4) *Party ratios.* The Democratic Caucus of each committee shall determine an appropriate ratio of Democratic to minority party members for each subcommittee and shall authorize a Member or Members to negotiate that ratio with the minority party; *Provided, however,* That party representation on each subcommittee, including any ex-officio members, shall be no less favorable to the Democratic Party than the ratio for the full committee. *Provided, further,* That Democratic Party representation on conference committees also shall be no less favorable to the Democratic Party than the ratio for the full House committee.

(5) *Subcommittee budget and staffing.* Subject to overall control of a majority of the Democratic Caucus on the committee, each subcommittee shall have an adequate budget to discharge its responsibilities for legislation and oversight. All subcommittee staff shall be selected in the manner provided in M II. B of this Manual.

M IV. Periodic Committee Caucuses

A. There shall be a Democratic Caucus of each standing committee and any other committee with legislative jurisdiction consisting of all Democratic Members of the committee. Meetings of the Caucus may be called by the chairman or a majority of the Democratic Members of the committee with due notice to all Caucus Members. A quorum of the

Democratic Caucus on each committee shall consist of a majority of the Democratic Members assigned thereto. All actions by the Democratic Caucus of said committees shall require a majority of those voting, a quorum being present. Upon written request of 10 Democratic Members of any committee or upon the written request of a majority of the Democratic Members, whichever is less, addressed to the chairman thereof to hold a Caucus of the Democratic Members, said chairman shall call such Caucus within 10 days of such request. Said request shall contain the subject matter for discussion at such Caucus.

M V. Rules for Making Subcommittee Assignments

A. *Subcommittee Chairmen.* At the Democratic Caucus described in section M III. A, Democratic Members of the committee shall have the right, in order of full committee seniority, or seniority on the subcommittee concerned, as the Democratic Caucus on the committee may determine, to bid for subcommittee chairmanships. Any such request shall be subject to approval by a majority of those present and voting in the Democratic Caucus on the committee. If the committee Caucus rejects a subcommittee chairmanship bid, the next senior Democratic Member may bid for the position as in the first instance. *Provided however*, That the full Democratic Caucus also shall vote on each Member nominated to serve as chairman of an Appropriations subcommittee following the same procedure set forth in Caucus Rules for the election of standing committee chairmen.

B. *Subcommittee Membership.* All Democratic subcommittee positions on House standing committees shall be filled at the Democratic Committee Caucus described in section M III. A in the following manner:

(1) Step One—Members who served on the committee in the preceding Congress shall be entitled to retain not more than two subcommittee assignments held on that committee in the preceding Congress. Members chosen as subcommittee chairmen in accord with the procedure set forth in section M V. A shall be entitled to retain only one other subcommittee assignment held on that committee in the preceding Congress.

(2) Step Two—Members who retain no subcommittee assignments in Step One and new Members shall be entitled, in order of their ranking on the full committee, to select one subcommittee position each.

(3) Step Three—Members who have selected only one subcommittee assignment shall be entitled, in order of their ranking on the full committee, to select a second subcommittee assignment, to the extent that subcommittee size permits.

(4) Step Four—Any remaining subcommittee vacancies shall be filled by additional rounds of selection in order of Members' ranking on the full committee.

(5) If a committee Caucus determines, as described in section M V. A, that Members may bid for subcommittee chairmanships by subcommittee rather than full committee seniority, the ranking Members on each subcommittee shall be determined by the order in which Members elect to go on the subcommittee.

M VI. Appointments to Joint and Select Committees, Boards, and Commissions

In those instances where the Speaker has the power to appoint Members to joint and select committees, boards, and commissions, due consideration should be given to sharing the workload and responsibility among qualified Members of the House who have indicated an interest in the subject matter of the committee, board, or commission, and have expressed a willingness to actively participate in its deliberations and operations. All Members serving on joint and select committees, boards, and commissions by virtue of appointment by the Speaker shall be considered to have completed their tenure and their positions deemed to be vacant until filled by appointment or reappointment by the Speaker.

M VII. House Democratic Policy and Steering Committee

There should be a House Democratic Steering and Policy Committee constituted as follows:

a. *Membership.* The Democratic Steering and Policy Committee shall consist of the elected Democratic leadership (the Speaker, Majority Leader, and Caucus Chairman), 12 Members who shall be elected from 12 equal regions as set forth below, and not to exceed eight Members who shall be appointed by the Speaker. (*Provided*, that in the 93d and 94th Congresses, five of the eight appointees shall be the Whip and the four Deputy Whips) and the Speaker is authorized to appoint one additional Member for the 94th Congress only. The size of the committee shall be reviewed at the start of the 94th Congress and consideration shall be given to reducing the number of appointive Members thereto.

b. *Organization and Procedure.* The Speaker shall serve as Chairman of the committee, the Majority Leader as Vice Chairman, and the Caucus Chairman as Second Vice Chairman. The committee shall adopt its own rules which shall be in writing; shall keep a journal of its proceedings; and shall meet at least once each month while the House is in session and upon the call of the Chairman or whenever requested in writing by four of its Members. In addition, the committee may authorize the Chairman to appoint ad hoc committees from among the entire membership of the Caucus to conduct special studies or investigations whenever necessary.

c. *Functions.* The committee shall make recommendations regarding party policy, legislative priorities, scheduling of matters for House or Caucus action, and other matters as appropriate to further Democratic programs and policies.

d. *Regions.* The 50 States (and other areas represented in the House) shall be divided into 12 compact and contiguous regions, each containing approximately one-twelfth of the Members of the Democratic Caucus. At the beginning of each Congress, the Speaker (or Minority Leader if Democrats are in the minority) shall submit to the Caucus for its approval changes necessary to maintain, as near as practicable, an equal number of Members in each region. The proposed changes and a list of Members in each region indicating the total years of service for each as of the start of that Congress shall be made available to Members of the Caucus at least 10 days before a Caucus which shall meet no later than March 1 of odd-numbered years to approve or amend the regions.

e. *Regional Elections.* Each region shall meet no later than March 30 in odd-numbered years to elect its representatives to the committee. Such regional elections shall be held at a time determined by the Chairman of the Steering and Policy Committee and announced by written notice at least 10 days in advance. The Chairman shall also designate a Member from each region to call that region's election meeting to order and to preside until a permanent presiding officer is elected, which shall be the first order of business. If at such meeting, the election of a Member to the Steering and Policy Committee does not take place due to lack of a quorum, the Chairman shall reschedule the meeting as soon as practicable, provided Members are given at least 48 hours notice in writing of when and where the rescheduled meeting will be held. Nominations may be made from the floor or in advance of the election meeting by written notice signed by two Members from the region other than the nominee. Written nominations must be delivered to the Steering and Policy Committee office not later than 5 p.m. on the second day immediately preceding the day of the election meeting and mailed to all Members of the Caucus in that region not later than midnight of the second day immediately preceding the day of the election meeting. Following the close of advance nominations, a ballot shall be prepared for each region containing the names of candidates nominated in advance for election from the region.

Candidates shall be listed in alphabetical order and all ballots shall contain space to write in the names of Members nominated from the floor. One-half of the Members of a region shall constitute a quorum for an election and a majority of those present and voting shall be required to elect. If more than one ballot be required, the candidate receiving the fewest votes on each ballot shall be eliminated from all succeeding votes until one candidate receives a majority of the votes cast. If a region's representative in the preceding Congress had completed 12 or more years service at the start of said Congress, he or she shall be succeeded by a Member who has less than 12 years service. This provision shall not apply to the re-election of an incumbent Member of the committee who is entitled to seek another term.

    f. *Terms of Service.* Each regionally elected Member of the committee shall serve for a term of two years, or until his successor is elected. In the event of a vacancy the region shall elect a successor to fill the unexpired term. No Member shall be elected or appointed to more than two consecutive full terms. However, six of the 12 members elected in the 93d Congress—as determined by lot at the first meeting of the committee—shall not be eligible for re-election in the 94th Congress.

M VIII. Committee on Organization, Study and Review

    The Caucus Chairman shall appoint a committee on Organization, Study and Review for the purposes of review of the Caucus Rules and Manual as circumstances may indicate, with no powers other than those recommending action to the Caucus.

M IX. Closed Rule Restriction

    (a) It shall be the policy of the Democratic Caucus that no committee chairman or designee shall seek, and the Democratic Members of the Rules Committee shall not support, any rule or order prohibiting any germane amendment to any bill reported from committee until four (4) legislative days have elapsed following notice in the Congressional Record of an intention to do so.

    (b) If, within the four (4) legislative days following said notice in the Congressional Record, 50 or more Democratic Members give written notice to the chairman of the committee seeking the rule and to the chairman of the Rules Committee that they wish to offer a particular germane amendment, the chairman or designee shall not seek and the Democratic Members of the Rules Committee shall not support, any rule or order relating to the bill or resolution involved until the Democratic Caucus has met and decided whether the proposed amendment should be allowed to be considered in the House.

    (c) If 50 or more Democratic Members give notice as provided in subsection (b) above, then, notwithstanding the provisions of Caucus Rule No. 5, the Caucus shall meet for such purpose within three (3) legislative days following a request for such a Caucus to the Speaker and the chairman of the Democratic Caucus by said committee chairman or designee.

    (d) *Provided, further,* that notices referred to above also shall be submitted to the Speaker, the Majority Leader, and the chairman of the Democratic Caucus.

M X. Budget Committee

    The Democratic Caucus shall elect the Democratic Members of the Budget Committee at the start of each Congress in accord with the following provisions:

    A. *Party Ratio.* The party ratio on the Budget Committee shall be determined by the Caucus at the start of each Congress; *Provided, however,* that the ratio shall not be less than three Democrats for each two Republicans.

    B. *Leadership Member.* The Speaker shall appoint the leadership member of the committee.

    C. *Nomination of Other Members.* The chairman of the Appropriations Committee shall nominate three of the Democratic Members of that committee, the chairman of the Ways and Means Committee shall nominate three of the Democratic Members of that committee, and the chairman of the Steering and Policy Committee shall nominate Members from other committees to fill all remaining vacancies. A list of said nominees shall be distributed to all Members of the Caucus at least 9 days prior to the election meeting. Members shall then have at least 7 days to nominate additional candidates by written notice signed by five Members other than the nominee. Written nominations must be delivered to the offices of the Caucus chairman and the Caucus secretary not later than noon on the second day immediately preceding the election meeting, and the Caucus chairman or secretary shall mail a list of all nominees to Members of the Caucus that same day.

    D. *Election Procedure.* Election shall be by ballot which lists all candidates by category (Appropriations, Ways and Means, other committees) in the order they were nominated, and a majority shall be required to elect.

    E. *Election of Chairman.* Following election of all Democratic Members, the Caucus shall elect one of said Members to serve as chairman. Nominating speeches shall not exceed 3 minutes per nominee and seconding speeches shall not exceed 1 minute and shall be limited to two per nominee. Election shall be by ballot and a majority shall be required to elect.

    F. *Service Limitations.* The following limitations shall apply to Members of the Budget Committee:

        (1) The Democratic Members elected in 1974 shall serve on an interim basis for the remainder of the 93d Congress only. A new election shall be held at the start of the 94th Congress and half of the Members elected at that time (to be determined by lot at the first meeting following that election) shall not be eligible for reelection at the start of the 95th Congress.

        (2) The chairman of the Budget Committee shall not serve simultaneously as chairman of any other standing committee.

        (3) No Member shall serve as a Member of the Committee on the Budget during more than two Congresses in any period of five successive Congresses beginning after 1974 (disregarding for this purpose any service performed as a Member of such committee for less than a full session in any Congress). All selections of Members to serve on the committee shall be made without regard to seniority.

M XI. Election Procedure for Ways and Means Vacancies

    Resolved, That for the 94th Congress the Democratic Caucus shall elect Democratic Members to fill vacancies on the Ways and Means Committee in accord with the following procedure:

        (1) *Nominations.* The Democratic Committee on Committees shall nominate one Member for each Democratic vacancy to be filled on the Ways and Means Committee and shall distribute the name(s) of such nominee(s) to all Members of the Democratic Caucus at least 9 days prior to the election meeting. Members shall then have 7 days to nominate additional candidates by written notice signed by 5 Democratic Members other than the nominee. Written nominations must be delivered to the offices of the Caucus chairman and the Caucus secretary not later than noon at the second day immediately preceding the election meet-

ing, and the Caucus chairman or secretary shall mail a list of all nominees to Members of the Caucus that same day.
(2) *Election Procedure.* Election shall be by ballot which lists all candidates in the order they were nominated, and a majority shall be required to elect; *Provided, however,* that any ballot which contains votes for more or fewer candidates than there are vacancies to be filled shall not be counted.
(3) *Previous Members.* The nomination of any Member who served on the committee in the preceding Congress shall be reported by the Committee on Committees for action by the Caucus in the same manner as is provided for nomination of Members to other standing committees.

APPENDIX 7
Extracts From the Legislative Reorganization Acts of 1946 and 1970

Provisions Applicable to the Senate*

LEGISLATIVE REORGANIZATION ACT OF 1946[1] AS AMENDED THROUGH MARCH 7, 1975

SHORT TITLE

(2 U.S.C. 72a note)

That (a) this Act, divided into titles and sections according to the following table of contents, may be cited as the "Legislative Reorganization Act of 1946":

*   *   *   *   *

SEPARABILITY CLAUSE

(b) If any provision of this Act or the application thereof to any person or circumstances is held invalid, the validity of the remainder of the Act and of the application of such provision to other persons and circumstances shall not be affected thereby.

TITLE I—CHANGES IN RULES OF SENATE AND HOUSE

RULE-MAKING POWER OF THE SENATE AND HOUSE

SEC. 101. The following sections of this title are enacted by the Congress:

(a) As an exercise of the rule-making power of the Senate and the House of Representatives, respectively, and as such

---

*Selected provisions taken from U.S., Congress, Senate, Committee on Rules and Administration, STANDING RULES OF THE UNITED STATES SENATE AND PROVISIONS OF THE LEGISLATIVE REORGANIZATION ACTS OF 1946 AND 1970 RELATING TO OPERATION OF THE SENATE, March 7, 1975. In the original, footnotes are numbered beginning with 1 on each page. In the following excerpts, only substantive footnotes have been included, and while the original footnote numbering has been retained, pagination differs.

they shall be considered as part of the rules of each House, respectively, or of that House to which they specifically apply; and such rules shall supersede other rules only to the extent that they are inconsistent therewith; and

(b) With full recognition of the constitutional right of either House to change such rules (so far as relating to the procedure in such House) at any time, in the same manner and to the same extent as in the case of any other rule of such House.

* * * * *

PART 3—PROVISIONS APPLICABLE TO BOTH HOUSES

PRIVATE BILLS BANNED

(2 U.S.C. 190g)

SEC. 131. No private bill or resolution (including so-called omnibus claims or pension bills), and no amendment to any bill or resolution, authorizing or directing (1) the payment of money for property damages, for personal injuries or death for which suit may be instituted under the Federal Tort Claims Act, or for a pension (other than to carry out a provision of law or treaty stipulation); (2) the construction of a bridge across a navigable stream; or (3) the correction of a military or naval record, shall be received or considered in either the Senate or the House of Representatives.[1]

CONGRESSIONAL ADJOURNMENT

(2 U.S.C. 198)

SEC. 132. (a) Unless otherwise provided by the Congress, the two Houses shall—
 (1) adjourn sine die not later than July 31 of each year; or
 (2) in the case of an odd-numbered year, provide, not later than July 31 of such year, by concurrent resolution adopted in each House by rollcall vote, for the adjournment of the two Houses from that Friday in August which occurs at least thirty days before the first Monday in September (Labor Day) of such year to the second day after Labor Day.

(b) This section shall not be applicable in any year if on July 31 of such year a state of war exists pursuant to a declaration of war by the Congress.[2]

---

[1] This provision of law is no longer applicable to the House of Representatives. The House has included in its rules a substantially similar provision.

APPENDIX 7

COMMITTEE PROCEDURE

(2 U.S.C. 190a)

SEC. 133. (a) Each standing committee of the Senate shall fix regular weekly, biweekly, or monthly meetings days for the transaction of business before the committee and additional meetings may be called by the chairman as he may deem necessary. If at least three members of any such committee desire that a special meeting of the committee be called by the chairman, those members may file in the offices of the committee their written request to the chairman for that special meeting. Immediately upon the filing of the request, the clerk of the committee shall notify the chairman of the filing of the request. If, within three calendar days after the filing of the request, the chairman does not call the requested special meeting, to be held within seven calendar days after the filing of the request, a majority of the members of the committee may file in the offices of the committee their written notice that a special meeting of the committee will be held, specifying the date and hour of that special meeting. The committee shall meet on that date and hour. Immediately upon the filing of the notice, the clerk of the committee shall notify all members of the committee that such special meeting will be held and inform them of its date and hour. If the chairman of any such committee is not present at any regular, additional, or special meeting of the committee, the ranking member of the majority party on the committee who is present shall preside at that meeting.[1]

(b) Meetings for the transaction of business of each standing committee of the Senate, other than for the conduct of hearings, shall be open to the public except during executive sessions for marking up bills or for voting or when the committee by majority vote orders an executive session.[2] Each such committee shall keep a complete record of all committee action. Such record shall include a record of the votes on any question on which a record vote is demanded. The results of rollcall votes taken in any meeting of any such standing committee of the Senate upon any measure, or any amendment thereto, shall be announced in the committee report on that measure unless previously announced by the committee, and such announcement shall include a tabulation of the votes cast in favor of and the votes cast in opposition to each such measure and amendment by each member of the committee who was present at that meeting.[3]

(c) It shall be the duty of the chairman of each standing committee of the Senate to report or cause to be reported

---

[2] As added, Sec. 103(a) of Pub. Law 91–510, 84 Stat. 1144–1145, Oct. 26, 1970. This sentence has in effect been superseded by paragraph 7(b) of Rule XXV.

promptly to the Senate any measure approved by his committee and to take or cause to be taken necessary steps to bring the matter to a vote. In any event, the report of any such committee upon a measure which has been approved by the committee shall be filed within seven calendar days (exclusive of days on which the Senate is not in session) after the day on which there has been filed with the clerk of the committee a written and signed request of a majority of the committee for the reporting of that measure. Upon the filing of any such request, the clerk of the committee shall transmit immediately to the chairman of the committee notice of the filing of that request.[1]

(d) No measure or recommendation shall be reported from any standing committee of the Senate (including the Committee on Appropriations) unless a majority of the committee were actually present. The vote of the committee to report a measure or matter shall require the concurrence of a majority of the members of the committee who are present. No vote of any member of any such committee to report a measure or matter may be cast by proxy if rules adopted by such committee forbid the casting of votes for that purpose by proxy; however, proxies shall not be voted for such purpose except when the absent committee member has been informed of the matter on which he is being recorded and has affirmatively requested that he be so recorded. Action by any such committee in reporting any measure or matter in accordance with the requirements of this subsection shall constitute the ratification by the committee of all action theretofore taken by the committee with respect to that measure or matter, including votes taken upon the measure or matter or any amendment thereto, and no point of order shall lie with respect to that measure or matter on the ground that such previous action with respect thereto by such committee was not taken in compliance with such requirements. Whenever any such committee by rollcall vote reports any measure or matter, the report of the committee upon such measure or matter shall include a tabulation of the votes cast in favor of and the votes cast in opposition to such measure or matter by each member of the committee. Nothing contained in this subsection shall abrogate the power of any committee of the Senate to adopt rules—

    (1) providing for proxy voting on all matters other than the reporting of a measure or matter, or

    (2) providing in accordance with the rules of the Senate for a lesser number as a quorum for any action other than the reporting of a measure or matter.[2]

(e) If, at the time of approval of a measure or matter by any standing committee of the Senate, any member of the committee gives notice of intention to file supplemental, minority, or additional views, that member shall be entitled to not less than three calendar days in which to file such views, in writing, with the clerk of the committee. All such views so filed by one or more members of the committee shall be included within, and shall be a part of, the report filed by the committee with respect to that measure or matter. The report of the committee upon that measure or matter shall be printed in a single volume which—

    (1) shall include all supplemental, minority, or additional views which have been submitted by the time of the filing of the report, and

    (2) shall bear upon its cover a recital that supplemental, minority, or additional views are included as part of the report.

This subsection does not preclude—

    (A) the immediate filing and printing of a committee report unless timely request for the opportunity to file supplemental, minority, or additional views has been made as provided by this subsection; or

    (B) the filing by any such committee of any supplemental report upon any measure or matter which may be required for the correction of any technical error in a previous report made by that committee upon that measure or matter.[1]

(f) A measure or matter reported by any standing committee of the Senate (including the Committee on Appropriations) shall not be considered in the Senate unless the report of that committee upon that measure or matter has been available to the Members of the Senate for at least three calendar days (excluding Saturdays, Sundays, and legal holidays) prior to the consideration of that measure or matter in the Senate. If hearings have been held on any such measure or matter so reported, the committee reporting the measure or matter shall make every reasonable effort to have such hearings printed and available for distribution to the Members of the Senate prior to the consideration of such measure or matter in the Senate. This subsection—

    (1) may be waived by joint agreement of the majority leader and the minority leader of the Senate; and

    (2) shall not apply to—

        (A) any measure for the declaration of war, or the declaration of a national emergency, by the Congress, and

        (B) any executive decision, determination, or action which would become, or continue to be, effective unless disapproved or otherwise invalidated by one or both Houses of Congress.[1]

(g) Each standing committee of the Senate which, in any year beginning on or after January 1, 1971, requires authorization for the expenditure of funds in excess of the amount specified by section 134(a) of this Act shall offer one annual authorization resolution to procure such authorization. Each such annual authorization resolution shall include a specification of the amount of all such funds sought by such committee for expenditure by all subcommittees thereof during that year and the amount so sought for each such subcommittee. The annual authorization resolution of any such committee of the Senate for each year beginning on or after January 1, 1971, shall be offered not later than January 31 of that year, except that, whenever the designation of members of standing committees of the Senate occurs during the first session of any Congress at a date later than January 20, such resolution may be offered by any standing committee of the Senate at any time within thirty days after the date on which a majority of the members of such committee have been designated during that session. After the date on which an annual authorization resolution has been offered by any such committee in any year, or the last date on which such committee pursuant to the preceding sentence may offer such a resolution, whichever date occurs earlier, such committee in any year may procure authorization for the expenditure of funds in excess of the amount specified by section 134(a) of this Act only by offering a supplemental authorization resolution. Each such supplemental authorization resolution shall include a specification of the amount of all supplemental funds sought by that committee for expenditure by all subcommittees thereof under such resolution and the amount so sought for each such subcommittee. Each such supplemental authorization resolution shall amend the annual authorization resolution of such committee for that year unless the committee offered no annual authorization resolution for that year, in which case the committee's supplemental authorization resolution shall not be an amendment to any other resolution and any subsequent supplemental authorization resolution of such committee for the same year shall amend the first such resolution offered by the committee for that year. Each such supplemental resolution reported by such committee shall be accompanied by a report to the Senate specifying with particularity the purpose for which such authorization is sought and the reason why such authorization could not have been sought at the time of, or within the period provided for, the submission by such committee of an annual authorization resolution for that year.[1] The minority shall receive fair consideration in the appointment of staff personnel pursuant to any such annual or supplemental resolution. This subsection shall not apply to any resolution requesting funds in addition to the amount specified in such section 134(a) and which are to be expended only for the same purposes for which such amount may be expended.[2] [3]

(h) Except as otherwise specifically provided by this section, the foregoing provisions of this section do not apply to the Committee on Appropriations of the Senate.[2]

SENATE COMMITTEE HEARING PROCEDURE

(2 U.S.C. 190a-1)

SEC. 133A. (a) Each standing, select, or special committee of the Senate (except the Committee on Appropriations) shall make public announcement of the date, place, and subject matter of any hearing to be conducted by the committee on any measure or matter at least one week before the commencement of that hearing unless the committee determines that there is good cause to begin such hearing at an earlier date.

(b) [4] Each hearing conducted by each standing, select, or special committee of the Senate (except the Committee on Appropriations) shall be open to the public except when the committee determines that the testimony to be taken at that hearing may relate to a matter of national security, may tend to reflect adversely on the character or reputation of the witness or any other individual, or may divulge matters deemed confidential under other provisions of law or Government regulation. Whenever any such hearing is open to the public, that hearing may be broadcast by radio or television, or both, under such rules as the committee may adopt.

(c) Each standing, select, or special committee of the Senate (except the Committee on Appropriations) shall require each witness who is to appear before the committee in any hearing to file with the clerk of the committee, at least one day before the date of the appearance of that witness, a written statement of his proposed testimony unless the committee chairman and the ranking minority member determine that there is good cause for the failure of the witness to file such a statement in compliance with this subsection. If so requested by any such committee, the staff of the committee shall prepare for the use of the members of the committee before each day of hearing before the committee a digest of the statements which have been so filed by witnesses who are to appear before the committee on that day.

(d) After the conclusion of each day of hearing, if so requested by any such committee, the staff shall prepare for the use of the members of the committee a summary of the testimony given before the committee on that day. After approval by the chairman and the ranking minority member of the committee, each such summary may be printed as a part

---

[4] This subsection does not apply to the Committee on the Budget. Sec. 102(e) of Pub. Law 93-344, 88 Stat. 302, July 12, 1974. However, Section 102(d) of the same Act does carry special provisions relating to open or closed sessions of the Budget Committee.

of the committee hearings if such hearings are ordered by the committee to be printed.

(e) Whenever any hearing is conducted by any such committee of the Senate (except the Committee on Appropriations) upon any measure or matter, the minority on the committee shall be entitled, upon request made by a majority of the minority members to the chairman before the completion of such hearing, to call witnesses selected by the minority to testify with respect to the measure or matter during at least one day of hearing thereon.

(f) Whenever any such committee of the Senate (except the Committee on Appropriations) has reported any measure, by action taken in conformity with the requirements of section 133(d) of this Act, no point of order shall lie with respect to that measure on the ground that hearings upon that measure by the committee were not conducted in accordance with the provisions of this section.[1]

SENATE COMMITTEE RULES

(2 U.S.C. 190a-2)

SEC. 133B. Each standing, select, or special committee of the Senate shall adopt rules (not inconsistent with the Standing Rules of the Senate or with those provisions of law having the force and effect of Standing Rules of the Senate) governing the procedure of such committee. The rules of each such committee shall be published in the Congressional Record not later than March 1 of each year, except that if any such committee is established on or after February 1 of a year, the rules of that committee during the year of establishment shall be published in the Congressional Record not later than sixty days after such establishment. An amendment to the rules of any such committee shall be published in the Congressional Record not later than thirty days after the adoption of such amendment. If the Congressional Record is not published on the last day of any period during which the rules of any such committee, or an amendment to those rules, is required to be published in the Congressional Record by this section, such rules or amendment shall be published in the first daily edition of the Congressional Record published following such day.[2]

COMMITTEE POWERS

(2 U.S.C. 190b)

SEC. 134. (a) Each standing committee of the Senate, including any subcommittee of any such committee, is authorized to hold such hearings, to sit and act at such times and places during the sessions, recesses, and adjourned periods of the Senate, to require by subpena or otherwise the attendance of such witnesses and the production of such correspondence, books, papers, and documents, to take such testimony and to make such expenditures (not in excess of $10,000 for each committee during any Congress) as it deems advisable. Each such committee may make investigations into any matter within its jurisdiction, may report such hearings as may be had by it, and may employ stenographic assistance at a cost not exceeding 25 cents per hundred words.[1] The expenses of the committee shall be paid from the contingent fund of the Senate upon vouchers approved by the chairman.

(b) (Superseded by 2 U.S.C. 104a.)

(c) Except as otherwise provided in this subsection, no standing committee of the Senate shall sit, without special leave, while the Senate is in session. The prohibition contained in the preceding sentence shall not apply to the Committee on Appropriations or the Committee on the Budget of the Senate.[2] Any other standing committee of the Senate may sit for any purpose while the Senate is in session if consent therefor has been obtained from the majority leader and the minority leader of the Senate. In the event of the absence of either of such leaders, the consent of the absent leader may be given by a Senator designated by such leader for that purpose. Notwithstanding the provisions of this subsection, any standing committee of the Senate may sit without special leave for any purpose as authorized by paragraph 7 of rule XXV of the Standing Rules of the Senate.[3]

SENATE CONFERENCE REPORTS

(2 U.S.C. 190c)

SEC. 135. (a) In any case in which a disagreement to an amendment in the nature of a substitute has been referred to conferees, it shall be in order for the conferees to report a substitute on the same subject matter; but they may not include in the report matter not committed to them by either House. They may, however, include in their report in any such case matter which is a germane modification of subjects in disagreement.

---

[1] The provision of this sentence relating to compensation for stenographic assistance has been superseded by the following provision of the Act of June 27, 1956 (70 Stat. 360 ; 2 U.S.C. 68c) :

Compensation for stenographic assistance of committees paid out of the foregoing items under "Contingent Expenses of the Senate" hereafter shall be computed at such rates and in accordance with such regulations as may be prescribed by the Committee on Rules and Administration, notwithstanding, and without regard to any other provision of law.

For current rates and regulations, contact the Committee on Rules and Administration.

LEGISLATIVE REORGANIZATION ACTS—EXTRACTS 275

(b) In any case in which the conferees violate subsection (a), the conference report shall be subject to a point of order.

(c) Each report made by a committee of conference to the Senate shall be printed as a report of the Senate. As so printed, such report shall be accompanied by an explanatory statement prepared jointly by the conferees on the part of the House and the conferees on the part of the Senate. Such statement shall be sufficiently detailed and explicit to inform the Senate as to the effect which the amendments or propositions contained in such report will have upon the measure to which those amendments or propositions relate.[1]

(d) If time for debate in the consideration of any report of a committee of conference upon the floor of the Senate is limited, the time allotted for debate shall be equally divided between the majority party and the minority party.[1]

LEGISLATIVE REVIEW BY STANDING COMMITTEES OF THE SENATE AND HOUSE OF REPRESENTATIVES

(2 U.S.C. 190d)

SEC. 136. (a) In order to assist the Congress in—
 (1) its analysis, appraisal, and evaluation of the application, administration, and execution of the laws enacted by the Congress, and
 (2) its formulation, consideration, and enactment of such modifications of or changes in those laws, and of such additional legislation, as may be necessary or appropriate,
each standing committee of the Senate and the House of Representatives shall review and study, on a continuing basis, the application, administration, and execution of those laws, or parts of laws, the subject matter of which is within the jurisdiction of that committee. Such committees may carry out the required analysis, appraisal, and evaluation themselves, or by contract, or may require a Government agency to do so and furnish a report thereon to the Congress. Such committees may rely on such techniques as pilot testing, analysis of costs in comparison with benefits, or provision for evaluation after a defined period of time.[2]

(b) In each odd-numbered year beginning on or after January 1, 1973, each standing committee of the Senate shall submit, not later than March 31, to the Senate, and each standing committee of the House shall submit, not later than January 2, to the House, a report on the activities of that committee under this section during the Congress ending at noon on January 3 of such year.

(c) The preceding provisions of this section do not apply to the Committees on Appropriations and the Budget of the Senate and the Committees on Appropriations, the Budget,

House Administration, Rules, and Standards of Official Conduct of the House.[1]

DECISIONS ON QUESTIONS OF COMMITTEE JURISDICTION

(2 U.S.C. 190)

SEC. 137. In any case in which a controversy arises as to the jurisdiction of any standing committee of the Senate with respect to any proposed legislation, the question of jurisdiction shall be decided by the presiding officer of the Senate, without debate, in favor of that committee which has jurisdiction over the subject matter which predominates in such proposed legislation; but such decision shall be subject to an appeal.

LEGISLATIVE BUDGET

SEC. 138. (Repealed by section 242(b)(1) of the Legislative Reorganization Act of 1970.)

HEARINGS AND REPORTS BY APPROPRIATIONS COMMITTEES

(2 U.S.C. 190f)

SEC. 139. (a) (Repealed by section 108(d) of the Legislative Reorganization Act of 1970.)
(b) (Executed.)
(c) No general appropriation bill or amendment thereto shall be received or considered in either House if it contains a provision reappropriating unexpended balances of appropriations; except that this provision shall not apply to appropriations in continuation of appropriations for public works on which work has commenced.
(d) (Executed.)

*   *   *   *   *

TITLE III—REGULATION OF LOBBYING ACT *

SHORT TITLE

(2 U.S.C. 261 note)

SEC. 301. This title may be cited as the "Federal Regulation of Lobbying Act".

DEFINITIONS

(2 U.S.C. 261)

SEC. 302. When used in this title—
(a) The term "contribution" includes a gift, subscription, loan, advance, or deposit of money or anything of value and

---

*As this manual goes to press, Congress is considering amendments to lobbying disclosure legislation. The Senate passed S. 2477 on June 15, 1976, and the House was marking up a companion bill, H.R. 15.

includes a contract, promise, or agreement, whether or not legally enforceable, to make a contribution.

(b) The term "expenditure" includes a payment, distribution, loan, advance, deposit, or gift of money or anything of value, and includes a contract, promise, or agreement, whether or not legally enforceable, to make an expenditure.

(c) The term "person" includes an individual, partnership, committee, association, corporation, and any other organization or group of persons.

(d) The term "Clerk" means the Clerk of the House of Representatives of the United States.

(e) The term "legislation" means bills, resolutions, amendments, nominations, and other matters pending or proposed in either House of Congress, and includes any other matter which may be the subject of action by either House.

DETAILED ACCOUNTS OF CONTRIBUTIONS

(2 U.S.C. 262)

SEC. 303. (a) It shall be the duty of every person who shall in any manner solicit or receive a contribution to any organization or fund for the purposes hereinafter designated to keep a detailed and exact account of—

(1) all contributions of any amount or of any value whatsoever;

(2) the name and address of every person making any such contribution of $500 or more and the date thereof;

(3) all expenditures made by or on behalf of such organization or fund; and

(4) the name and address of every person to whom any such expenditure is made and the date thereof.

(b) It shall be the duty of such person to obtain and keep a receipted bill, stating the particulars, for every expenditure of such funds exceeding $10 in amount, and to preserve all receipted bills and accounts required to be kept by this section for a period of at least two years from the date of the filing of the statement containing such items.

RECEIPTS FOR CONTRIBUTIONS

(2 U.S.C. 263)

SEC. 304. Every individual who receives a contribution of $500 or more for any of the purposes hereinafter designated shall within five days after receipt thereof rendered to the person or organization for which such contribution was received a detailed account thereof, including the name and address of the person making such contribution and the date on which received.

STATEMENTS TO BE FILED WITH CLERK OF HOUSE

(2 U.S.C. 264)

SEC. 305. (a) Every person receiving any contributions or expending any money for the purposes designated in subparagraph (a) or (b) of section 307 shall file with the Clerk between the first and tenth day of each calendar quarter, a statement containing complete as of the day next preceding the date of filing—

(1) the name and address of each person who has made a contribution of $500 or more not mentioned in the preceding report; except that the first report filed pursuant to this title shall contain the name and address of each person who has made any contribution of $500 or more to such person since the effective date of this title;

(2) the total sum of the contributions made to or for such person during the calendar year and not stated under paragraph (1);

(3) the total sum of all contributions made to or for such person during the calendar year;

(4) the name and address of each person to whom an expenditure in one or more items of the aggregate amount or value, within the calendar year, of $10 or more has been made by or on behalf of such person, and the amount, date, and purpose of such expenditure;

(5) the total sum of all expenditures made by or on behalf of such person during the calendar year and not stated under paragraph (4);

(6) the total sum of expenditures made by or on behalf of such person during the calendar year.

(b) The statements required to be filed by subsection (a) shall be cumulative during the calendar year to which they relate, but where there has been no change in an item reported in a previous statement only the amount need be carried forward.

STATEMENT PRESERVED FOR TWO YEARS

(2 U.S.C. 265)

SEC. 306. A statement required by this title to be filed with the Clerk—

(a) shall be deemed properly filed when deposited in an established post office within the prescribed time, duly stamped, registered, and directed to the Clerk of the House of Representatives of the United States, Washington, District of Columbia, but in the event it is not received, a duplicate of such statement shall be promptly filed upon notice by the Clerk of its nonreceipt;

(b) shall be preserved by the Clerk for a period of two years from the date of filing, shall constitute part of the public records of his office, and shall be open to public inspection.

PERSONS TO WHOM APPLICABLE

(2 U.S.C. 266)

SEC. 307. The provisions of this title shall apply to any person (except a political committee as defined in the Federal Corrupt Practices Act, and duly organized State or local committees of a political party), who by himself, or through any agent or employee or other persons in any manner whatsoever, directly or indirectly, solicits, collects, or receives money or any other thing of value to be used principally to aid, or the principal purpose of which person is to aid, in the accomplishment of any of the following purposes:

(a) The passage or defeat of any legislation by the Congress of the United States.

(b) To influence, directly or indirectly, the passage or defeat of any legislation by the Congress of the United States.

REGISTRATION WITH SECRETARY OF THE SENATE AND CLERK OF THE HOUSE

(2 U.S.C. 267)

SEC. 308. (a) Any person who shall engage himself for pay or for any consideration for the purpose of attempting to influence the passage or defeat of any legislation by the Congress of the United States shall, before doing anything in furtherance of such object, register with the Clerk of the House of Representatives and the Secretary of the Senate and shall give to those officers in writing and under oath, his name and business address, the name and address of the person by whom he is employed, and in whose interest he appears or works, the duration of such employment, how much he is paid and is to receive, by whom he is paid or is to be paid, how much he is to be paid for expenses, and what expenses are to be included. Each such person so registering shall, between the first and tenth day of each calendar quarter, so long as his activity continues, file with the Clerk and Secretary a detailed report under oath of all money received and expended by him during the preceding calendar quarter in carrying on his work; to whom paid; for what purposes; and the names of any papers, periodicals, magazines, or other publications in which he has caused to be published any articles or editorials; and the proposed legislation he is employed to support or oppose. The provisions of this section shall not apply to any person who merely appears before a committee of the Congress of the United States in support of or opposition to legislation; nor to any public official acting in his official capacity; nor in the case of any newspaper or other regularly published periodical (including any individual who owns, publishes, or is employed by any such newspaper or periodical) which in the ordinary course of business publishes news items, editorials, or other comments, or paid advertisements, which directly or indirectly urge the passage or defeat of legislation, if such newspaper, periodical, or individual, engages in no further or other activities in connection with the passage or defeat of such legislation, other than to appear before a committee of the Congress of the United States in support of or in opposition to such legislation.

(b) All information required to be filed under the provisions of this section with the Clerk of the House of Representatives and the Secretary of the Senate shall be compiled by said Clerk and Secretary, acting jointly, as soon as practicable after the close of the calendar quarter with respect to which such information is filed and shall be printed in the Congressional Record.

REPORTS AND STATEMENTS TO BE MADE UNDER OATH

(2 U.S.C. 268)

SEC. 309. All reports and statements required under this title shall be made under oath, before an officer authorized by law to administer oaths.

PENALTIES

(2 U.S.C. 269)

SEC. 310. (a) Any person who violates any of the provisions of this title, shall, upon conviction, be guilty of a misdemeanor, and shall be punished by a fine of not more than $5,000 or imprisonment for not more than twelve months, or by both such fine and imprisonment.

(b) In addition to the penalties provided for in subsection (a), any person convicted of the misdemeanor specified therein is prohibited, for a period of three years from the date of such conviction, from attempting to influence, directly or indirectly, the passage or defeat of any proposed legislation or from appearing before a committee of the Congress in support of or opposition to proposed legislation; and any person who violates any provision of this subsection shall, upon conviction thereof, be guilty of a felony, and shall be punished by a fine of not more than $10,000, or imprisonment for not more than five years, or by both such fine and imprisonment.

EXEMPTION

(2 U.S.C. 270)

SEC. 311. The provisions of this title shall not apply to practices or activities regulated by the Federal Corrupt Practices Act nor be construed as repealing any portion of said Federal Corrupt Practices Act.

* * * * *

LEGISLATIVE REORGANIZATION ACT OF 1970 [1] AS AMENDED THROUGH MARCH 7, 1975

TITLE I—THE COMMITTEE SYSTEM

RULEMAKING POWER OF SENATE AND HOUSE

SEC. 101. The following sections of this title are enacted by the Congress—
  (1) insofar as applicable to the Senate, as an exercise of the rulemaking power of the Senate and, to the extent so applicable, those sections are deemed a part of the Standing Rules of the Senate, superseding other individual rules of the Senate only to the extent that those sections are inconsistent with those other individual Senate rules, subject to and with full recognition of the power of the Senate to enact or change any rule of the Senate at any time in its exercise of its constitutional right to determine the rules of its proceedings; and
  (2) insofar as applicable to the House of Representatives, as an exercise of the rulemaking power of the House of Representatives, subject to and with full recognition of the power of the House of Representatives to enact or change any rule of the House at any time in its exercise of its constitutional right to determine the rules of its proceedings.

(The remainder of this title consists of amendments to the Standing Rules of the Senate, to the Legislative Reorganization Act of 1946, and to the Rules of the House of Representatives.

* * * * *

PART 2—THE BUDGET

SUPPLEMENTAL BUDGET INFORMATION

SEC. 221. (Section 221 amended section 201 of the Budget and Accounting Act, 1921 (31 U.S.C. 11). Section 201 has sub-

sequently been further amended and now reads as follows:)
[SEC. 201. (a) The President shall transmit to Congress during the first fifteen days of each regular session, the Budget, which shall set forth his Budget message, summary data and text, and supporting detail. The Budget shall set forth in such form and detail as the President may determine—

[(1) functions and activities of the Government;

[(2) at such times as may be practicable, information on program costs and accomplishments;

[(3) any other desirable classifications of data;

[(4) a reconciliation of the summary data on expenditures with proposed appropriations;

[(5) estimated expenditures and proposed appropriations necessary in his judgment for the support of the Government for the ensuing fiscal year and projections for the four fiscal years immediately following the ensuing fiscal year, except that estimated expenditures and proposed appropriations for such years for the legislative branch of the Government and the Supreme Court of the United States shall be transmitted to the President on or before October 15 of each year, and shall be included by him in the Budget without revision;

[(6) estimated receipts of the Government during the ensuing fiscal year and projections for the four fiscal years immediately following the ensuing fiscal year, under (1) laws existing at the time the Budget is transmitted and also (2) under the revenue proposals, if any, contained in the Budget;

[(7) actual appropriations, expenditures, and receipts of the Government during the last completed fiscal year;

[(8) estimated expenditures and receipts, and actual or proposed appropriations of the Government during the fiscal year in progress;

[(9) balanced statements of (1) the condition of the Treasury at the end of the last completed fiscal year, (2) the estimated condition of the Treasury at the end of the fiscal year in progress, and (3) the estimated condition of the Treasury at the end of the ensuing fiscal year if the financial proposals contained in the Budget are adopted;

[(10) all essential facts regarding the bonded and other indebtedness of the Government;

[(11) such other financial statements and data as in his opinion are necessary or desirable in order to make known in all practicable detail the financial condition of the Government;

[(12) with respect to each proposal in the Budget for new or additional legislation which would create or expand any function, activity, or authority, in addition to those functions, activities, and authorities then existing or as then being administered and operated, a tabulation showing—

[(A) the amount proposed in the Budget for appropriation and for expenditure in the ensuing fiscal year on account of such proposal; and

[(B) the estimated appropriation required on account of such proposal in each of the four fiscal years, immediately following that ensuing fiscal year, during which such proposal is to be in effect; and

[(13) an allowance for additional estimated expenditures and proposed appropriations for the ensuing fiscal year, and an allowance for unanticipated uncontrollable expenditures for the ensuing fiscal year.

[(b) The President shall transmit to the Congress, on or before July 15 [1] of each year, a supplemental summary of the Budget for the ensuing fiscal year transmitted to the Congress by the President under subsection (a) of this section. Such supplemental summary—

[(1) shall reflect with respect to that ensuing fiscal year—

[(A) all substantial alterations in or reappraisals of estimates of expenditures and receipts, and

[(B) all substantial obligations imposed on that budget after its transmission to the Congress;

[(2) shall contain current information with respect to those matters covered by subparagraph (8) and clauses (2) and (3) of subparagraph (9) of subsection (a) of this section; and

[(3) shall contain such additional information, in summary form, as the President considers necessary or advisable to provide the Congress with a complete and current summary of information with respect to that Budget and the then currently estimated functions, obligations, requirements, and financial condition of the Government for that ensuing fiscal year.

[(c) The President shall transmit to the Congress, on or before July 15 [1] of each year, in such form and detail as he may determine—

[(1) summaries of estimated expenditures, for the first four fiscal years following the ensuing fiscal year for which the Budget was transmitted to the Congress by the President under subsection (a) of this section, which will be required under continuing programs which have a legal commitment for future years or are considered mandatory under existing law; and

[(2) summaries of estimated expenditures, in fiscal

years following such ensuing fiscal year, of balances carried over from such ensuing fiscal year.

[(d) The Budget transmitted pursuant to subsection (a) for each fiscal year shall set forth separately the items enumerated in section 301(a)(1)–(5) of the Congressional Budget Act of 1974.

[(e) The Budget transmitted pursuant to subsection (a) for each fiscal year shall set forth the levels of tax expenditures under existing law for such fiscal year (the tax expenditure budget), taking into account projected economic factors, and any changes in such existing levels based on proposals contained in such Budget. For purposes of this subsection, the terms "tax expenditures" and "tax expenditures budget" have the meanings given to them by section 3(a)(3) of the Congressional Budget Act of 1974.

[(f) The Budget transmitted pursuant to subsection (a) for each fiscal year shall contain—

[(1) a comparison, for the last completed fiscal year, of the total amount of outlays estimated in the Budget transmitted pursuant to subsection (a) for each major program involving uncontrollable or relatively uncontrollable outlays and the total amount of outlays made under each such major program during such fiscal year;

[(2) a comparison, for the last completed fiscal year, of the total amount of revenues estimated in the Budget transmitted pursuant to subsection (a) and the total amount of revenues received during such year, and, with respect to each major revenue source, the amount of revenues estimated in the Budget transmitted pursuant to subsection (a) and the amount of revenues received during such year; and

[(3) an analysis and explanation of the difference between each amount set forth pursuant to paragraphs (1) and (2) as the amount of outlays or revenues estimated in the Budget submitted under subsection (a) for such fiscal year and the corresponding amount set forth as the amount of outlays made or revenues received during such fiscal year.

[(g) The President shall transmit to the Congress, on or before April 10 and July 15 of each year, a statement of all amendments to or revisions in the budget authority requested, the estimated outlays, and the estimated receipts for the ensuing fiscal year set forth in the Budget transmitted pursuant to subsection (a) (including any previous amendments or revisions proposed on behalf of the executive branch) that he deems necessary and appropriate based on the most current information available. Such statement shall contain the effect of such amendments and revisions on the summary data submitted under subsection (a) and shall include such supporting detail as is practicable. The statement transmitted on or before July 15 of any year may be included in the supplemental summary required to be transmitted under subsection (b) during such year. The Budget transmitted to the Congress pursuant to subsection (a) for any fiscal year, or the supporting detail transmitted in connection therewith, shall include a statement of all such amendments and revisions with respect to the fiscal year in progress made before the date of transmission of such Budget.[1]

[(h) The Budget transmitted pursuant to subsection (a) for each fiscal year shall include information with respect to estimates of appropriations for the next succeeding fiscal year for grants, contracts, or other payments under any program for which there is an authorization of appropriations for such succeeding fiscal year and such appropriations are authorized to be included in an appropriation Act for the fiscal year preceding the fiscal year in which the appropriation is to be available for obligation.

[(i) The Budget transmitted pursuant to subsection (a) for each fiscal year, beginning with the fiscal year ending September 30, 1979, shall contain a presentation of budget authority, proposed budget authority, outlays, proposed outlays, and descriptive information in terms of—

    [(1) a detailed structure of national needs which shall be used to reference all agency missions and programs;

    [(2) agency missions; and

    [(3) basic programs.

To the extent practicable, each agency shall furnish information in support of its budget requests in accordance with its assigned missions in terms of Federal functions and subfunctions, including mission responsibilities of component organizations, and shall relate its programs to agency missions.[1]]

* * * * *

Part 4—The Appropriations Process

RULEMAKING POWER OF SENATE AND HOUSE

Sec. 241. The following sections of this Part are enacted by the Congress—

    (1) insofar as applicable to the Senate, as an exercise of the rulemaking power of the Senate and, to the extent so applicable, those sections are deemed a part of the Standing Rules of the Senate, superseding other indi-

---

[1] Subsection (1) is not effective until 1979.

vidual rules of the Senate only to the extent that those sections are inconsistent with those other individual Senate rules, subject to and with full recognition of the power of the Senate to enact or change any rule of the Senate at any time in its exercise of its constitutional right to determine the rules of its proceedings; and

(2) insofar as applicable to the House of Representatives, as an exercise of the rulemaking power of the House of Representatives, subject to and with full recognition of the power of the House of Representatives to enact or change any rule of the House at any time in its exercise of its constitutional right to determine the rules of its proceedings.

HEARINGS ON THE BUDGET BY COMMITTEES ON APPROPRIATIONS OF SENATE AND HOUSE

(2 U.S.C. 190h)

SEC. 242. (a) Each hearing conducted by the Committee on Appropriations of the Senate shall be open to the public except when the committee determines that the testimony to be taken at that hearing may relate to a matter of national security, may tend to reflect adversely on the character or reputation of the witness or any other individual, or may divulge matters deemed confidential under other provisions of law or Government regulation. Whenever any such hearing is open to the public, that hearing may be broadcast by radio or television, or both, under such rules as the committee may adopt.

(Subsections (b) and (c) are omitted since they consist of amendments to the 1946 Act and to the Rules of the House.)

ACTION AND PROCEDURE OF SENATE COMMITTEE ON APPROPRIATIONS

(2 U.S.C. 190i)

SEC. 243. The vote of the Committee on Appropriations of the Senate to report a measure or matter shall require the concurrence of a majority of the members of the committee who are present. No vote of any member of such committee to report a measure or matter may be cast by proxy if rules adopted by such committee forbid the casting of votes for that purpose by proxy; however, proxies shall not be voted for such purpose except when the absent committee member has been informed on the matter on which he is being recorded and has affirmatively requested that he be so recorded. Action by such committee in reporting any measure or matter in accordance with the requirements of this section shall constitute the ratification by the committee of all action theretofore taken by the committee with respect to that measure or matter, including votes taken upon the measure or matter or any amendment thereto, and no point of order shall lie with respect to that measure or matter on the ground that such previous action with respect thereto by such committee was not taken in compliance with such requirements. Whenever such committee by rollcall vote reports any measure or matter, the report of the committee upon such measure or matter shall include a tabulation of the votes cast in favor of and the votes cast in opposition to such measure or matter by each member of the committee. Nothing contained in this section shall abrogate the power of the committee to adopt rules—

(1) providing for proxy voting on all matters other than the reporting of a measure or matter, or

(2) providing in accordance with the Standing Rules of the Senate for a lesser number as a quorum for any action other than the reporting of a measure or matter.

PART 5—LEGISLATIVE COMMITTEES

RULEMAKING POWER OF SENATE AND HOUSE

SEC. 251. The following sections of this Part are enacted by the Congress—

(1) insofar as applicable to the Senate, as an exercise of the rulemaking power of the Senate and, to the extent so applicable, those sections are deemed a part of the Standing Rules of the Senate, superseding other individual rules of the Senate only to the extent that those sections are inconsistent with those other individual Senate rules, subject to and with full recognition of the power of the Senate to enact or change any rule of the Senate at any time in its exercise of its constitutional right to determine the rules of its proceedings; and

(2) insofar as applicable to the House of Representatives, as an exercise of the rulemaking power of the House of Representatives, subject to and with full recognition of the power of the House of Representatives to enact or change any rule of the House at any time in its exercise of its constitutional right to determine the rules of its proceedings.

COST ESTIMATES IN REPORTS OF SENATE AND HOUSE COMMITTEES ACCOMPANYING CERTAIN LEGISLATIVE MEASURES

(2 U.S.C. 190j)

SEC. 252. (a)(1) The report accompanying each bill or

joint resolution of a public character reported by any committee of the Senate (except the Committee on Appropriations) shall contain—

(A) an estimate, made by such committee, of the costs which would be incurred in carrying out such bill or joint resolution in the fiscal year in which it is reported and in each of the five fiscal years following such fiscal year (or for the authorized duration of any program authorized by such bill or joint resolution, if less than five years), except that, in the case of measures affecting the revenues, such reports shall require only an estimate of the gain or loss in revenues for a one-year period; and

(B) a comparison of the estimate of costs described in subparagraph (A) made by such committee with any estimate of costs made by any Federal agency; or

(C) in lieu of such estimate or comparison, or both, a statement of the reasons why compliance by the committee with the requirements of subparagraph (A) or (B), or both, is impracticable.

(2) It shall not be in order in the Senate to consider any such bill or joint resolution if such bill or joint resolution was reported in the Senate after the effective date of this subsection and the report of that committee of the Senate which reported such bill or joint resolution does not comply with the provisions of paragraph (1) of this subsection.

(3) For the purposes of this subsection, the members of the Joint Committee on Atomic Energy who are Members of the Senate shall be deemed to be a committee of the Senate.

(b) (This subsection amended the House Rules and is therefore omitted.)

APPROPRIATIONS ON ANNUAL BASIS

(2 U.S.C. 190k)

SEC. 253. (a) Each committee of the Senate (except the Committee on Appropriations), and each joint committee of the two Houses of Congress, which is authorized to receive, report, and recommend the enactment of, bills and joint resolutions shall, in its consideration of all bills and joint resolutions of a public character within its jurisdiction, endeavor to insure that—

(1) all continuing programs of the Federal Government and of the government of the District of Columbia, within the jurisdiction of such committee or joint committee, are designed; and

(2) all continuing activities of Federal agencies, within the jurisdiction of such committee or joint committee, are carried on;

so that, to the extent consistent with the nature, requirements, and objectives of those programs and activities, appropriations therefor will be made annually.

(b) Each committee of the Senate (except the Committee on Appropriations), and each joint committee of the two Houses of Congress, which is authorized to receive, report, and recommend the enactment of, bills and joint resolutions with respect to any continuing program within its jurisdiction for which appropriations are not made annually, shall review such program, from time to time, in order to ascertain whether such program could be modified so that appropriations therefor would be made annually.

(c) (This subsection amends the House Rules and is therefore omitted.)

*Provisions Applicable to the House**

[FROM THE LEGISLATIVE REORGANIZATION ACT OF 1970 (84 STAT. 1140)]

[TITLE II]

* * *

PART 3—UTILIZATION OF REPORTS AND EMPLOYEES OF GENERAL ACCOUNTING OFFICE

ASSISTANCE BY GENERAL ACCOUNTING OFFICE TO CONGRESSIONAL COMMITTEES IN CONNECTION WITH PROPOSED LEGISLATION AND COMMITTEE REVIEW OF FEDERAL PROGRAMS AND ACTIVITIES

SEC. 231. At the request of any committee of the House or Senate, or of any joint committee of the two Houses, the Comptroller General shall explain to, and discuss with, the committee or joint committee making the request, or the staff of such committee or joint committee, any report made by the General Accounting Office which would assist such committee in connection with—

§ 986.

(1) its consideration of proposed legislation, including requests for appropriations, or

(2) its review of any program, or of any activity of any Federal agency, which is within the jurisdiction of such committee or joint committee.

*Selected provisions taken from U.S., Congress, House, CONSTITUTION, JEFFERSON'S MANUAL, AND RULES OF THE HOUSE OF REPRESENTATIVES OF THE NINETY-FOURTH CONGRESS, 93rd Cong., 2d Sess., 1975, House Doc. No. 416.

DELIVERY BY GENERAL ACCOUNTING OFFICE TO CONGRESSIONAL ACCOUNTING OFFICE OF ITS REPORTS GENERALLY

SEC. 232. Whenever the General Accounting Office submits any reports to the Congress, the Comptroller General shall deliver copies of such report to—
 (1) The Committees on Appropriations of the House and Senate,
 (2) the Committees on Government Operations of the House and Senate, and
 (3) any other committee of the House or Senate, or any joint committee of the two Houses, which has requested information on any program or part thereof, or any activity of any Federal agency, which is the subject, in whole or in part, of such report.

* * *

[FROM THE LEGISLATIVE REORGANIZATION ACT OF 1946, AS AMENDED (84 STAT. 1181)]

TITLE II—MISCELLANEOUS

* * *

[FROM H. RES. 988, 93D CONGRESS—THE "COMMITTEE REFORM AMENDMENTS OF 1974", AS MADE PERMANENT LAW BY PUBLIC LAW 93–554 (88 STAT. 1777)]

EARLY ORGANIZATION OF THE HOUSE

SEC. 202. (a)(1) The majority leader or minority leader of the House of Representatives after consultation with the Speaker may at any time during any even-numbered year call a caucus or conference, to begin on or after the first day of December and conclude on or before the twentieth day of December in such year and to be attended by all incumbent Members of his or her political party who have been reelected to the ensuing Congress and all other Members-elect of such party, for the purpose of taking all steps necessary to achieve the prompt organization of the Members and Members-elect of such party for the ensuing Congress.

§ 1000.

(2) If the majority leader or minority leader calls an organizational caucus or conference under paragraph (1), he or she shall file with the Clerk of the House a written notice designating the date upon which the caucus or conference is to convene. As soon as possible after the election of Members to the ensuing Congress, the Clerk shall furnish each Member-elect of the party involved with appropriate written notification of the caucus or conference.

(3) If a vacancy occurs in the office of majority leader or minority leader during any even-numbered year (and has not been filled), the chairman of the caucus or conference of the party involved for the current Congress may call an organizational caucus or conference under paragraph (1) by filing written notice thereof as provided by paragraph (2).

(b)(1)(A) Each Member-elect (other than an incumbent Member reelected to the ensuing Congress) who attends a caucus or conference called under subsection (a), and each incumbent Member reelected to the ensuing Congress who attends any such caucus or conference convening after the adjournment sine die of the Congress in the year involved, shall be paid for one round trip between his or her place of residence in the district which he or she represents and Washington, District of Columbia, for the purpose of attending such caucus or conference. Payment shall be made through the issuance of a transportation request form to each such Member-elect or incumbent Member by the Finance Office of the House before such caucus or conference.

(B) Each Member-elect (other than an incumbent Member reelected to the ensuing Congress) who attends a caucus or conference called under subsection (a) shall in addition be reimbursed on a per diem or other basis for expenses incurred in connection with his or her attendance at such caucus or conference for a period not to exceed the shorter of the following—

(i) the period beginning with the day before the designated date upon which such caucus or conference is to convene and ending with the day after the date of the final adjournment of such caucus or conference; or

(ii) fourteen days.

(2) Payments and reimbursements to Members-elect under paragraph (1) shall be made as provided (with respect to Members) in the regulations prescribed by the Committee on House Administration with respect to travel and other expenses of committees and Members. Reimbursements shall be paid on special voucher forms prescribed by the Committee on House Administration.

(c) The contingent fund of the House is made available to carry out the purposes of this section.

[FROM THE CONGRESSIONAL BUDGET ACT OF 1974 (88 STAT. 297)]

TITLE III—CONGRESSIONAL BUDGET PROCESS

* * *

TIMETABLE

SEC. 300. The timetable with respect to the congressional

§ 1007. budget process for any fiscal year is as follows:

On or before:	Action to be completed:
November 10	President submits current services budget.
15th day after Congress meets	President submits his budget.
March 15	Committees and joint committees submit reports to Budget Committees.
April 1	Congressional Budget Office submits report to Budget Committees.
April 15	Budget Committees report first concurrent resolution on the budget to their Houses.
May 15	Committees report bills and resolutions authorizing new budget authority.
May 15	Congress completes action on first concurrent resolution on the budget.
7th day after Labor Day	Congress completes action on bills and resolutions providing new budget authority and new spending authority.
September 15	Congress completes action on second required concurrent resolution on the budget.
September 25	Congress completes action on reconciliation bill or resolution, or both, implementing second required concurrent resolution.
October 1	Fiscal year begins.

ADOPTION OF FIRST CONCURRENT RESOLUTION

SEC. 301. (a) ACTION TO BE COMPLETED BY MAY 15.—On or before May 15 of each year, the Congress shall complete action on the first concurrent resolution on the budget for the fiscal year beginning on October 1 of such year. The concurrent resolution shall set forth—

(1) the appropriate level of total budget outlays and of total new budget authority;

(2) an estimate of budget outlays and an appropriate level of new budget authority for each major functional category, for contingencies, and for undistributed intragovernmental transactions, based on allocations of the appropriate level of total budget outlays and of total new budget authority;

(3) the amount, if any, of the surplus or the deficit in the budget which is appropriate in light of economic conditions and all other relevant factors;

(4) the recommended level of Federal revenues and the amount, if any, by which the aggregate level of Federal revenues should be increased or decreased by bills and resolutions to be reported by the appropriate committees;

(5) the appropriate level of the public debt, and the amount, if any, by which the statutory limit on the public

debt should be increased or decreased by bills and resolutions to be reported by the appropriate committees; and

(6) such other matters relating to the budget as may be appropriate to carry out the purposes of this Act.

(b) ADDITIONAL MATTERS IN CONCURRENT RESOLUTION.— The first concurrent resolution on the budget may also require—

(1) a procedure under which all or certain bills and resolutions providing new budget authority or providing new spending authority described in section 401(c)(2)(C) for such fiscal year shall not be enrolled until the concurrent resolution required to be reported under section 310(a) has been agreed to, and, if a reconciliation bill or reconciliation resolution, or both, are required to be reported under section 310(c), until Congress has completed action on that bill or resolution, or both; and

(2) any other procedure which is considered appropriate to carry out the purposes of this Act.

Not later than the close of the Ninety-fifth Congress, the Committee on the Budget of each House shall report to its House on the implementation of procedures described in this subsection.

(c) VIEWS AND ESTIMATES OF OTHER COMMITTEES.—On or before March 15 of each year, each standing committee of the House of Representatives shall submit to the Committee on the Budget of the House, each standing committee of the Senate shall submit to the Committee on the Budget of the Senate, and the Joint Economic Committee and Joint Committee on Internal Revenue Taxation shall submit to the Committee on the Budget of both Houses—

(1) its views and estimates with respect to all matters set forth in subsection (a) which relate to matters within the respective jurisdiction or functions of such committee or joint committee; and

(2) except in the case of such joint committees, the estimate of the total amounts of new budget authority, and budget outlays resulting therefrom, to be provided or authorized in all bills and resolutions within the jurisdiction of such committee which such committee intends to be effective during the fiscal year beginning on October 1 of such year.

The Joint Economic Committee shall also submit to the Committees on the Budget of both Houses, its recommendations as to the fiscal policy appropriate to the goals of the Employment Act of 1946. Any other committee of the House or Senate may submit to the Committee on the Budget of its House, and any other joint committee of the Congress may submit to the Committees on the Budget of both Houses, its view and estimates with respect to all matters set forth in subsection

(a) which relate to matters within its jurisdiction or functions.

(d) HEARINGS AND REPORT.—In developing the first concurrent resolution on the budget referred to in subsection (a) for each fiscal year, the Committee on the Budget of each House shall hold hearings and shall receive testimony from Members of Congress and such appropriate representatives of Federal departments and agencies, the general public, and national organizations as the committee deems desirable. On or before April 15 of each year, the Committee on the Budget of each House shall report to its House the first concurrent resolution on the budget referred to in subsection (a) for the fiscal year beginning on October 1 of such year. The report accompanying such concurrent resolution shall include, but not be limited to—

(1) a comparison of revenues estimated by the committee with those estimated in the budget submitted by the President;

(2) a comparison of the appropriate levels of total budget outlays and total new budget authority, as set forth in such concurrent resolution, with total budget outlays estimated and total new budget authority requested in the budget submitted by the President;

(3) with respect to each major functional category, an estimate of budget outlays and an appropriate level of new budget authority for all proposed programs and for all existing programs (including renewals thereof), with the estimate and level for existing programs being divided between permanent authority and funds provided in appropriation Acts, and each such division being subdivided between controllable amounts and all other amounts;

(4) an allocation of the level of Federal revenues recommended in the concurrent resolution among the major sources of such revenues;

(5) the economic assumptions and objectives which underlie each of the matters set forth in such concurrent resolution and alternative economic assumptions and objectives which the committee considered;

(6) projections, not limited to the following, for the period of five fiscal years beginning with such fiscal year of the estimated levels of total budget outlays, total new budget outlays, total new budget authority, the estimated revenues to be received, and the estimated surplus or deficit, if any, for each fiscal year in such period, and the estimated levels of tax expenditures (the tax expenditures budget) by major functional categories;

(7) a statement of any significant changes in the proposed levels of Federal assistance to State and local governments; and

(8) information, data, and comparisons indicating the manner in which, and the basis on which, the committee determined each of the matters set forth in the concurrent resolution, and the relationship of such matters to other budget categories.

MATTERS TO BE INCLUDED IN JOINT STATEMENT OF MANAGERS; REPORTS BY COMMITTEES

SEC. 302. (a) ALLOCATION OF TOTALS.—The joint explanatory statement accompanying a conference report on a concurrent resolution on the budget shall include an estimated allocation, based upon such concurrent resolution as recommended in such conference report, of the appropriate levels of total budget outlays and total new budget authority among each committee of the House of Representatives and the Senate which has jurisdiction over bills and resolutions providing such new budget authority.

(b) REPORTS BY COMMITTEES.—As soon as practicable after a concurrent resolution on the budget is agreed to—

(1) the Committee on Appropriations of each House shall, after consulting with the Committee on Appropriations of the other House, (A) subdivide among its subcommittees the allocation of budget outlays and new budget authority allocated to it in the joint explanatory statement accompanying the conference report on such concurrent resolution, and (B) further subdivide the amount with respect to each such subcommittee between controllable amounts and all other amounts; and

(2) every other committee of the House and Senate to which an allocation was made in such joint explanatory statement shall, after consulting with the committee or committees of the other House to which all or part of its allocation was made, (A) subdivide such allocation among its subcommittees or among programs over which it has jurisdiction, and (B) further subdivide the amount with respect to each subcommittee or program between controllable amounts and all other amounts.

Each such committee shall promptly report to its House the subdivisions made by it pursuant to this subsection.

(c) SUBSEQUENT CONCURRENT RESOLUTIONS.—In the case of a concurrent resolution on the budget referred to in section 304 or 310, the allocation under subsection (a) and the subdivisions under subsection (b) shall be required only to the extent necessary to take into account revisions made in the most recently agreed to concurrent resolution on the budget.

FIRST CONCURRENT RESOLUTION ON THE BUDGET MUST BE ADOPTED BEFORE LEGISLATION PROVIDING NEW BUDGET AUTHORITY, NEW SPENDING AUTHORITY, OR CHANGES IN REVENUES OR PUBLIC DEBT LIMIT IS CONSIDERED

SEC. 303. (a) IN GENERAL.— It shall not be in order in either the House of Representatives or the Senate to consider any bill or resolution (or amendment thereto) which provides—
 (1) new budget authority for a fiscal year;
 (2) an increase or decrease in revenues to become effective during a fiscal year;
 (3) an increase or decrease in the public debt limit to become effective during a fiscal year; or
 (4) new spending authority described in section 401(c) (2) (C) to become effective during a fiscal year;
until the first concurrent resolution on the budget for such year has been agreed to pursuant to section 301.

 (b) EXCEPTIONS.—Subsection (a) does not apply to any bill or resolution—
 (1) providing new budget authority which first becomes available in a fiscal year following the fiscal year to which the concurrent resolution applies; or
 (2) increasing or decreasing revenues which first become effective in a fiscal year following the fiscal year to which the concurrent resolution applies.

 (c) WAIVER IN THE SENATE.—
 (1) the committee of the Senate which reports any bill or resolution to which subsection (a) applies may at or after the time it reports such bill or resolution, report a resolution to the Senate (A) providing for the waiver of subsection (a) with respect to such bill or resolution, and (B) stating the reasons why the waiver is necessary. The resolution shall then be referred to the Committee on the Budget of the Senate. That committee shall report the resolution to the Senate within 10 days after the resolution is referred to it (not counting any day on which the Senate is not in session) beginning with the day following the day on which it is so referred, accompanied by that committee's recommendations and reasons for such recommendations with respect to the resolution. If the committee does not report the resolution within such 10-day period, it shall automatically be discharged from further consideration of the resolution and the resolution shall be placed on the calendar.
 (2) During the consideration of any such resolution, debate shall be limited to one hour, to be equally divided between, and controlled by, the majority leader and minority leader or their designees, and the time on any debatable motion or appeal shall be limited to twenty minutes, to be equally divided between, and controlled by, the mover and

the manager of the resolution. In the event the manager of the resolution is in favor of any such motion or appeal, the time in opposition thereto shall be controlled by the minority leader or his designee. Such leaders, or either of them, may, from the time under their control in the passage of such resolution, allot additional time to any Senator during the consideration of any debatable motion or appeal. No amendment to the resolution is in order.

(3) If, after the Committee on the Budget has reported (or been discharged from further consideration of) the resolution, the Senate agrees to the resolution, then subsection (a) of this section shall not apply with respect to the bill or resolution to which the resolution so agreed to applies.

PERMISSIBLE REVISIONS OF CONCURRENT RESOLUTIONS OF THE BUDGET

SEC. 304. At any time after the first concurrent resolution on the budget for a fiscal year has been agreed to pursuant to section 301, and before the end of such fiscal year, the two Houses may adopt a concurrent resolution on the budget which revises the concurrent resolution on the budget for such fiscal year most recently agreed to.

PROVISIONS RELATING TO THE CONSIDERATION OF CONCURRENT RESOLUTIONS ON THE BUDGET

SEC. 305. (a) PROCEDURE IN HOUSE OF REPRESENTATIVES AFTER REPORT OF COMMITTEE; DEBATE.—

(1) When the Committee on the Budget of the House has reported any concurrent resolution on the budget, it is in order at any time after the tenth day (excluding Saturdays, Sundays, and legal holidays) following the day on which the report upon such resolution has been available to Members of the House (even though a previous motion to the same effect has been disagreed to) to move to proceed to the consideration of the concurrent resolution. The motion is highly privileged and is not debatable. An amendment to the motion is not in order, and it is not in order to move to reconsider the vote by which the motion is agreed to or disagreed to.

(2) General debate on any concurrent resolution on the budget in the House of Representatives shall be limited to not more than 10 hours, which shall be divided equally between the majority and minority parties. A motion further to limit debate is not debatable. A motion to recommit the concurrent resolution is not in order, and it is not in order to move to reconsider the vote by which the concurrent resolution is agreed to or disagreed to.

(3) Consideration of any concurrent resolution on the budget by the House of Representatives shall be in the Com-

mittee of the Whole, and the resolution shall be read for amendment under the five-minute rule in accordance with the applicable provisions of rule XXIII of the Rules of the House of Representatives. After the Committee rises and reports the resolution back to the House, the previous question shall be considered as ordered on the resolution and any amendments thereto to final passage without intervening motion; except that it shall be in order at any time prior to final passage (notwithstanding any other rule or provision of law) to adopt an amendment (or a series of amendments) changing any figure or figures in the resolution as so reported to the extent necessary to achieve mathematical consistency.

(4) Debate in the House of Representatives on the conference report or any concurrent resolution on the budget shall be limited to not more than 5 hours, which shall be divided equally between the majority and minority parties. A motion further to limit debate is not debatable. A motion to recommit the conference report is not in order, and it is not in order to move to reconsider the vote by which the conference report is agreed to or disagreed to.

(5) Motions to postpone, made with respect to the consideration of any concurrent resolution on the budget, and motions to proceed to the consideration of other business, shall be decided without debate.

(6) Appeals from the decisions of the Chair relating to the application of the Rules of the House of Representatives to the procedure relating to any concurrent resolution on the budget shall be decided without debate.

(b) PROCEDURE IN SENATE AFTER REPORT OF COMMITTEE; DEBATE; AMENDMENTS.—

(1) Debate in the Senate on any concurrent resolution on the budget, and all amendments thereto and debatable motions and appeals in connection therewith, shall be limited to not more than 50 hours, except that, with respect to the second required concurrent resolution referred to in section 310(a), all such debate shall be limited to not more than 15 hours. The time shall be equally divided between, and controlled by, the majority leader and the minority leader or their designees.

(2) Debate in the Senate on any amendment to a concurrent resolution on the budget shall be limited to 2 hours, to be equally divided between, and controlled by, the mover and the manager of the concurrent resolution, and debate on any amendment to an amendment, debatable motion, or appeal shall be limited to 1 hour, to be equally divided between, and controlled by, the mover and the manager of the concurrent resolution, except that in the event the manager of the concurrent resolution is in favor of any such amendment, motion, or appeal, the time in opposition thereto shall be controlled

by the minority leader or his designee. No amendment that is not germane to the provisions of such concurrent resolution shall be received. Such leaders, or either of them, may, from the time under their control on the passage of the concurrent resolution, allot additional time to any Senator during the consideration of any amendment, debatable motion, or appeal.

(3) A motion to further limit debate is not debatable. A motion to recommit (except a motion to recommit with instructions to report back within a specified number of days, not to exceed 3, not counting any day on which the Senate is not in session) is not in order. Debate on any such motion to recommit shall be limited to 1 hour, to be equally divided between, and controlled by, the mover and the manager of the concurrent resolution.

(4) Notwithstanding any other rule, an amendment, or series of amendments, to a concurrent resolution on the budget proposed in the Senate shall always be in order if such amendment or series of amendments proposes to change any figure or figures then contained in such concurrent resolution so as to make such concurrent resolution mathematically consistent or so as to maintain such consistency.

(c) ACTION ON CONFERENCE REPORTS IN THE SENATE.—

(1) The conference report on any concurrent resolution on the budget shall be in order in the Senate at any time after the third day (excluding Saturdays, Sundays, and legal holidays) following the day on which such a conference report is reported and is available to Members of the Senate. A motion to proceed to the consideration of the conference report may be made even though a previous motion to the same effect has been disagreed to.

(2) During the consideration in the Senate of the conference report on any resolution on the budget, debate shall be limited to 10 hours, to be equally divided between, and controlled by, the majority leader and minority leader or their designees. Debate on any debatable motion or appeal related to the conference report shall be limited to 1 hour, to be equally divided between, and controlled by, the mover and the manager of the conference report.

(3) Should the conference report be defeated, debate on any request for a new conference and the appointment of conferees shall be limited to 1 hour, to be equally divided between, and controlled by, the manager of the conference report and the minority leader or his designee, and should any motion be made to instruct the conferees before the conferees are named, debate on such motion shall be limited to one-half hour, to be equally divided between, and controlled by, the mover and the manager of the conference report. Debate on any amendment to any such instruction shall be

limited to 20 minutes, to be equally divided between, and controlled by, the mover and the manager of the conference report. In all cases when the manager of the conference report is in favor of any motion, appeal, or amendment, the time in opposition shall be under the control of the minority leader or his designee.

(4) In any case in which there are amendments in disagreement, time on each amendment shall be limited to 30 minutes, to be equally divided between, and controlled by, the manager of the conference report and the minority leader or his designee. No amendment that is not germane to the provisions of such amendments shall be received.

(d) REQUIRED ACTION BY CONFERENCE COMMITTEE.—If, at the end of 7 days (excluding Saturdays, Sundays, and legal holidays) after the conferees of both Houses have been appointed to a committee of conference on a concurrent resolution on the budget, the conferees are unable to reach agreement with respect to all matters in disagreement between the two Houses, then the conferees shall submit to their respective Houses, on the first day thereafter on which their House is in session—

(1) a conference report recommending those matters on which they have agreed and reporting in disagreement those matters on which they have not agreed; or

(2) a conference report in disagreement, if the matter in disagreement is an amendment which strikes out the entire text of the concurrent resolution and inserts a substitute text.

(e) CONCURRENT RESOLUTION MUST BE CONSISTENT IN THE SENATE.—It shall not be in order in the Senate to vote on the question of agreeing to—

(1) a concurrent resolution on the budget unless the figures then contained in such resolution are mathematically consistent; or

(2) a conference report on a concurrent resolution on the budget unless the figures contained in such resolution, as recommended in such conference report, are mathematically consistent.

LEGISLATION DEALING WITH CONGRESSIONAL BUDGET MUST BE HANDLED BY BUDGET COMMITTEES

SEC. 306. No bill or resolution, and no amendment to any bill or resolution, dealing with any matter which is within the jurisdiction of the Committee on the Budget of either House shall be considered in that House unless it is a bill or resolution which has been reported by the Committee on the Budget of that House (or from the consideration of which such committee has been discharged) or unless it is an amendment to such a bill or resolution.

LEGISLATIVE REORGANIZATION ACTS—EXTRACTS 301

HOUSE COMMITTEE ACTION ON ALL APPROPRIATION BILLS TO BE COMPLETED BEFORE FIRST APPROPRIATION BILL IS REPORTED

SEC. 307. Prior to reporting the first regular appropriation bill for each fiscal year, the Committee on Appropriations of the House of Representatives shall, to the extent practicable, complete subcommittee markup and full committee action on all regular appropriation bills for that year and submit to the House a summary report comparing the committee's recommendations with the appropriate levels of budget outlays and new budget authority as set forth in the most recently agreed to concurrent resolution on the budget for that year.

REPORTS, SUMMARIES, AND PROJECTIONS OF CONGRESSIONAL BUDGET ACTIONS

SEC. 308. (a) REPORTS ON LEGISLATION PROVIDING NEW BUDGET AUTHORITY OR TAX EXPENDITURES.—Whenever a committee of either House reports a bill or resolution to its House providing new budget authority (other than continuing appropriations) or new or increased tax expenditures for a fiscal year, the report accompanying that bill or resolution shall contain a statement, prepared after consultation with the Director of the Congressional Budget Office, detailing—

(1) in the case of a bill or resolution providing new budget authority—

(A) how the new budget authority provided in that bill or resolution compares with the new budget authority set forth in the most recently agreed to concurrent resolution on the budget for such fiscal year and the reports submitted under section 302;

(B) a projection for the period of 5 fiscal years beginning with such fiscal year of budget outlays, associated with the budget authority provided in that bill or resolution, in each fiscal year in such period; and

(C) the new budget authority, and budget outlays resulting therefrom, provided by that bill or resolution for financial assistance to State and local governments; and

(2) in the case of a bill or resolution providing new or increased tax expenditures—

(A) how the new or increased tax expenditures provided in that bill or resolution will affect the levels of tax expenditures under existing law as set forth in the report accompanying the first concurrent resolution on the budget for such fiscal year, or, if a report accompanying a subsequently agreed to concurrent resolution for such year sets forth such levels, then as set forth in that report; and

(B) a projection for the period of 5 fiscal years beginning with such fiscal year of the tax expenditures which will result from that bill or resolution in each fiscal year in such period.

No projection shall be required for a fiscal year under paragraph (1)(B) or (2)(B) if the committee determines that a projection for that fiscal year is impracticable and states in its report the reason for such impracticability.

(b) UP-TO-DATE TABULATION OF CONGRESSIONAL BUDGET ACTIONS.—The Director of the Congressional Budget Office shall issue periodic reports detailing and tabulating the progress of congressional action on bills and resolutions providing new budget authority and changing revenues and the public debt limit for a fiscal year. Such reports shall include, but are not limited to—

(1) an up-to-date tabulation comparing the new budget authority for such fiscal year in bills and resolutions on which Congress has completed action and estimated outlays, associated with such new budget authority, during such fiscal year to the new budget authority and estimated outlays set forth in the most recently agreed to concurrent resolution on the budget for such fiscal year and the reports submitted under section 302;

(2) an up-to-date status report on all bills and resolutions providing new budget authority and changing revenues and the public debt limit for such fiscal year in both Houses;

(3) an up-to-date comparison of the appropriate level of revenues contained in the most recently agreed to concurrent resolution on the budget for such fiscal year with the latest estimate of revenues for such year (including new revenues anticipated during such year under bills and resolutions on which the Congress has completed action); and

(4) an up-to-date comparison of the appropriate level of the public debt contained in the most recently agreed to concurrent resolution on the budget for such fiscal year with the latest estimate of the public debt during such fiscal year.

(c) FIVE-YEAR PROJECTION OF CONGRESSIONAL BUDGET ACTION.—As soon as practicable after the beginning of each fiscal year, the Director of the Congressional Budget Office shall issue a report projecting for the period of 5 fiscal years beginning with such fiscal year—

(1) total new budget authority and total budget outlays for each fiscal year in such period;

(2) revenues to be received and the major sources thereof, and the surplus or deficit, if any, for each fiscal year in such period; and

(3) tax expenditures for each fiscal year in such period.

COMPLETION OF ACTION ON BILLS PROVIDING NEW BUDGET AUTHORITY AND CERTAIN NEW SPENDING AUTHORITY

SEC. 309. Except as otherwise provided pursuant to this title, not later than the seventh day after Labor Day of each year, the Congress shall complete action on all bills and resolutions—

(1) providing new budget authority for the fiscal year beginning on October 1 of such year, other than supplemental, deficiency, and continuing appropriation bills and resolutions, and other than the reconciliation bill for such year, if required to be reported under section 310(c); and

(2) providing new spending authority described in section 401(c)(2)(C) which is to become effective during such fiscal year.

Paragraph (1) shall not apply to any bill or resolution if legislation authorizing the enactment of new budget authority to be provided in such bill or resolution has not been timely enacted.

SECOND REQUIRED CONCURRENT RESOLUTION AND RECONCILIATION PROCESS

SEC. 310. (a) REPORTING OF CONCURRENT RESOLUTION.—The Committee on the Budget of each House shall report to its House a concurrent resolution on the budget which reaffirms or revises the concurrent resolution on the budget most recently agreed to with respect to the fiscal year beginning on October 1 of such year. Any such concurrent resolution on the budget shall also, to the extent necessary—

(1) specify the total amount by which—

(A) new budget authority for such fiscal year;

(B) budget authority initially provided for prior fiscal years; and

(C) new spending authority described in section 401(a)(2)(C) which is to become effective during such fiscal year,

contained in laws, bills, and resolutions within the jurisdiction of a committee, is to be changed and direct that committee to determine and recommend changes to accomplish a change of such total amount;

(2) specify the total amount by which revenues are to be changed and direct that the committees having jurisdiction to determine and recommend changes in the revenue laws, bills, and resolutions to accomplish a change of such total amount;

(3) specify the amount by which the statutory limit on the public debt is to be changed and direct the committees having jurisdiction to recommend such change; or

(4) specify and direct any combination of the matters described in paragraphs (1), (2), and (3).

Any such concurrent resolution may be reported, and the report accompanying it may be filed, in either House notwithstanding that that House is not in session on the day on which such concurrent resolution is reported.

(b) COMPLETION OF ACTION ON CONCURRENT RESOLUTION.—Not later than September 15 of each year, the Congress shall complete action on the concurrent resolution on the budget referred to in subsection (a).

(c) RECONCILIATION PROCESS.—If a concurrent resolution is agreed to in accordance with subsection (a) containing directions to one or more committees to determine and recommend changes in laws, bills, or resolutions, and—

(1) only one committee of the House or the Senate is directed to determine and recommend changes, that committee shall promptly make such determination and recommendations and report to its House a reconciliation bill or reconciliation resolution, or both, containing such recommendations; or

(2) more than one committee of the House or the Senate is directed to determine and recommend changes, each such committee so directed shall promptly make such determination and recommendations, whether such changes are to be contained in a reconciliation bill or reconciliation resolution, and submit such recommendations to the Committee on the Budget of its House, which upon receiving all such recommendations, shall report to its House a reconciliation bill or both, carrying out all such recommendations without any substantive revision.

For purposes of this subsection, a reconciliation resolution is a concurrent resolution directing the Clerk of the House of Representatives or the Secretary of the Senate, as the case may be, to make specified changes in bills and resolutions which have not been enrolled.

(d) COMPLETION OF RECONCILIATION PROCESS.—Congress shall complete action on any reconciliation bill or reconciliation resolution reported under subsection (c) not later than September 25 of each year.

(e) PROCEDURE IN THE SENATE.—

(1) Except as provided in paragraph (2), the provisions of section 305 for the consideration in the Senate of concurrent resolutions on the budget and conference reports thereon shall also apply to the consideration in the Senate of reconciliation bills and reconciliation resolutions reported under subsection (c) and conference reports thereon.

(2) Debate in the Senate on any reconciliation bill or resolution reported under subsection (c), and all amendments thereto and debatable motions and appeals in connection

therewith, shall be limited to not more than 20 hours.

(f) CONGRESS MAY NOT ADJOURN UNTIL ACTION IS COMPLETED.—It shall not be in order in either the House of Representatives or the Senate to consider any resolution providing for the adjournment sine die of either House unless action has been completed on the concurrent resolution on the budget required to be reported under subsection (a) for the fiscal year beginning on October 1 of such year, and, if a reconciliation bill or resolution, or both, is required to be reported under subsection (c) for such fiscal year, unless the Congress has completed action on that bill or resolution, or both.

NEW BUDGET AUTHORITY, NEW SPENDING AUTHORITY AND REVENUE LEGISLATION MUST BE WITHIN APPROPRIATE LEVELS

SEC. 311. (a) LEGISLATION SUBJECT TO POINT OF ORDER.—After the Congress has completed action on the concurrent resolution on the budget required to be reported under section 310(a) for a fiscal year, and, if a reconciliation bill or resolution, or both, for such fiscal year are required to be reported under section 310(c), after that bill has been enacted into law or that resolution has been agreed to, it shall not be in order in either the House of Representatives or the Senate to consider any bill, resolution, or amendment providing additional new budget authority for such fiscal year, providing new spending authority described in section 401 (c)(2)(C) to become effective during such fiscal year, or reducing revenues for such fiscal year, or any conference report on any such bill or resolution, if—

(1) the enactment of such bill or resolution as reported;

(2) the adoption and enactment of such amendment; or

(3) the enactment of such bill or resolution in the form recommended in such conference report;

would cause the appropriate level of total new budget authority or total budget outlays set forth in the most recently agreed to concurrent resolution on the budget for such fiscal year to be exceeded, or would cause revenues to be less than the appropriate level of revenues set forth in such concurrent resolution.

(b) DETERMINATION OF OUTLAYS AND REVENUES.—For purposes of subsection (a), the budget outlays to be made during a fiscal year and revenues to be received during a fiscal year shall be determined on the basis of estimates made by the Committee on the Budget of the House of Representatives or the Senate, as the case may be.

TITLE IV—ADDITIONAL PROVISIONS TO IMPROVE FISCAL PROCEDURES

BILLS PROVIDING NEW SPENDING AUTHORITY

SEC. 401. (a) LEGISLATION PROVIDING CONTRACT OR BORROWING AUTHORITY.—It shall not be in order in either the House of Representatives or the Senate to consider any bill or resolution which provides new spending authority described in subsection (c)(2)(A) or (B) (or any amendment which provides such new spending authority), unless that bill, resolution, or amendment also provides that such new spending authority is to be effective for any fiscal year only to such extent or in such amounts as are provided in appropriation Acts.

§ 1008.

(b) LEGISLATION PROVIDING ENTITLEMENT AUTHORITY.—

(1) It shall not be in order in either the House of Representatives or the Senate to consider any bill or resolution which provides new spending authority described in subsection (c)(2)(C) (or any amendment which provides such new spending authority) which is to become effective before the first day of the fiscal year which begins during the calendar year in which such bill or resolution is reported.

(2) If any committee of the House of Representatives or the Senate reports any bill or resolution which provides new spending authority described in subsection (c)(2)(C) which is to become effective during a fiscal year and the amount of new budget authority which will be required for such fiscal year if such bill or resolution is enacted as so reported exceeds the appropriate allocation of new budget authority reported under section 302(b) in connection with the most recently agreed to concurrent resolution on the budget for such fiscal year, such bill or resolution shall then be referred to the Committee on Appropriations of that House with instructions to report it, with the committee's recommendations, within 15 calendar days (not counting any day on which that House is not in session) beginning with the day following the day on which it is so referred. If the Committee on Appropriations of either House fails to report a bill or resolution referred to it under this paragraph within such 15-day period, the committee shall automatically be discharged from further consideration of such bill or resolution and such bill or resolution shall be placed on the appropriate calendar.

(3) The Committee on Appropriations of each House shall have jurisdiction to report any bill or resolution referred to it under paragraph (2) with an amendment which limits the total amount of new spending authority provided in such bill or resolution.

(c) DEFINITIONS.—

(1) For purposes of this section, the term "new spending

authority" means spending authority not provided by law on the effective date of this section, including any increase in or addition to spending authority provided by law on such date.

(2) For purposes of paragraph (1), the term "spending authority" means authority (whether temporary or permanent)—

(A) to enter into contracts under which the United States is obligated to make outlays, the budget authority for which is not provided in advance by appropriation Acts;

(B) to incur indebtedness (other than indebtedness incurred under the Second Liberty Bond Act) for the repayment of which the United States is liable, the budget authority for which is not provided in advance by appropriation Acts; and

(C) to make payments (including loans and grants), the budget authority for which is not provided for in advance by appropriation Acts, to any person or government if, under the provisions of the law containing such authority, the United States is obligated to make such payments to persons or governments who meet the requirements established by such law.

Such term does not include authority to insure or guarantee the repayment of indebtedness incurred by another person or government.

(d) EXCEPTIONS.—

(1) Subsections (a) and (b) shall not apply to new spending authority if the budget authority for outlays which will result from such new spending authority is derived—

(A) from a trust fund established by the Social Security Act (as in effect on the date of the enactment of this Act); or

(B) from any other trust fund, 90 percent or more of the receipts of which consist or will consist of amounts transferred from the general fund of the Treasury) equivalent to amount of taxes (related to the purposes for which such outlays are or will be made) received in the Treasury under specified provisions of the Internal Revenue Code of 1954.

(2) Subsections (a) and (b) shall not apply to new spending authority which is an amendment to or extension of the State and Local Fiscal Assistance Act of 1972, or a continuation of the program of fiscal assistance to State and local governments provided by that Act, to the extent so provided in the bill or resolution providing such authority.

(3) Subsections (a) and (b) shall not apply to new spending authority to the extent that—

(A) the outlays resulting therefrom are made by an organization which is (i) a mixed-ownership Government corporation (as defined in section 201 of the Government Corporation Control Act), or (ii) a wholly owned Government corporation (as defined in section 101 of such Act) which is specifically exempted by law from compliance with any or all of the provisions of that Act; or

(B) the outlays resulting therefrom consist exclusively of the proceeds of gifts or bequests made to the United States for a specific purpose.

REPORTING OF AUTHORIZING LEGISLATION

SEC. 402. (a) REQUIRED REPORTING DATE.—Except as otherwise provided in this section, it shall not be in order in either the House of Representatives or the Senate to consider any bill or resolution which, directly or indirectly, authorizes the enactment of new budget authority for a fiscal year, unless that bill or resolution is reported in the House or the Senate, as the case may be, on or before May 15 preceding the beginning of such fiscal year.

(b) EMERGENCY WAIVER IN THE HOUSE.—If the Committee on Rules of the House of Representatives determines that emergency conditions require a waiver of subsection (a) with respect to any bill or resolution, such committee may report, and the House may consider and adopt, a resolution waiving the application of subsection (a) in the case of such bill or resolution.

(c) WAIVER IN THE SENATE.—

(1) The committee of the Senate which reports any bill or resolution may, at or after the time it reports such bill or resolution, report a resolution to the Senate (A) providing for the waiver of subsection (a) with respect to such bill or resolution, and (B) stating the reasons why the waiver is necessary. The resolution shall then be referred to the Committee on the Budget of the Senate. That committee shall report the resolution to the Senate, within 10 days after the resolution is referred to it (not counting any day on which the Senate is not in session (beginning with the day following the day on which it is so referred accompanied by that committee's recommendations and reasons for such recommendations with respect to the resolution. If the committee does not report the resolution within such 10-day period, it shall automatically be discharged from further consideration of the resolution and the resolution shall be placed on the calendar.

(2) During the consideration of any such resolution, debate shall be limited to one hour, to be equally divided between, and controlled by, the majority leader and the minority leader or their designees, and the time on any debat-

able motion or appeal shall be limited to 20 minutes, to be equally divided between, and controlled by, the mover and the manager of the resolution. In the event the manager of the resolution is in favor of any such motion or appeal, the time in opposition thereto shall be controlled by the minority leader or his designee. Such leaders, or either of them, may, from the time under their control on the passage of such resolution, allot additional time to any Senator during the consideration of any debatable motion or appeal. No amendment to the resolution is in order.

(3) If, after the Committee on the Budget has reported (or been discharged from further consideration of) the resolution, the Senate agrees to the resolution, then subsection (a) of this section shall not apply with respect to that bill or resolution referred to in the resolution.

(d) CERTAIN BILLS AND RESOLUTIONS RECEIVED FROM OTHER HOUSE.—Notwithstanding the provisions of subsection (a), if under that subsection it is in order in the House of Representatives to consider a bill or resolution of the House, then it shall be in order to consider a companion or similar bill or resolution of the Senate; and if under that subsection it is in order in the Senate to consider a bill or resolution of the Senate, then it shall be in order to consider a companion or similar bill of the House of Representatives.

(e) EXCEPTIONS.—

(1) Subsection (a) shall not apply with respect to new spending authority described in section 401(c)(2)(C).

(2) Subsection (a) shall not apply with respect to new budget authority authorized in a bill or resolution for any provision of the Social Security Act if such bill or resolution also provides new spending authority described in section 401(c)(2)(C) which, under section 401(d)(1)(A), is excluded from the application of section 401(b).

(f) STUDY OF EXISTING SPENDING AUTHORITY AND PERMANENT APPROPRIATIONS.—The Committees on Appropriations of the House of Representatives and the Senate shall study on a continuing basis those provisions of law, in effect on the effective date of this section, which provide spending authority or permanent budget authority. Each committee shall, from time to time, report to its House its recommendations for terminating or modifying such provisions.

ANALYSIS BY CONGRESSIONAL BUDGET OFFICE

SEC. 403. The Director of the Congressional Budget Office shall, to the extent practicable, prepare for each bill or resolution of a public character reported by any committee of the House of Representatives or the Senate (except the Committee on Appropriations of each House), and submit to such committee—

(1) an estimate of the costs which would be incurred in carrying out such bill or resolution in the fiscal year in which it is to become effective and in each of the 4 fiscal years following such fiscal year, together with the basis for each such estimate; and

(2) a comparison of the estimate of costs described in paragraph (1) with any available estimate of costs made by such committee or by any Federal agency.

The estimate and comparison so submitted shall be included in the report accompanying such bill or resolution if timely submitted to such committee before such report is filed.

JURISDICTION OF APPROPRIATIONS COMMITTEES

SEC. 404. (a) AMENDMENT OF HOUSE RULES.—Clause 2 of rule XI of the Rules of the House of Representatives is amended by redesignating paragraph (b) as paragraph (e) and by inserting after paragraph (a) the following paragraphs:

"(b) Rescission of appropriations contained in appropriation Acts (referred to in section 105 of title 1, United States Code).

"(c) The amount of new spending authority described in section 401(c)(2)(A) and (B) of the Congressional Budget Act of 1974 which is to be effective for a fiscal year.

"(d) New spending authority described in section 401(c)(2)(C) of the Congressional Budget Act of 1974 provided in bills and resolutions referred to the committee under section 401(b)(2) of that Act (but subject to the provisions of section 401(b)(3) of that Act)."

(b) AMENDMENT OF SENATE RULES.—Subparagraph (c) of of paragraph 1 of rule XXV of the Standing Rules of the Senate is amended to read as follows:

"(c) Committee on Appropriations, to which committee shall be referred all proposed legislation, messages, petitions, memorials, and other matters relating to the following subjects:

"1. Except as provided in subparagraph (r), appropriation of the revenue for the support of the Government.

"2. Rescission of appropriations contained in appropriation Acts (referred to in section 105 of title 1, United States Code).

"(3) The amount of new spending authority described in section 401(c)(2)(A) and (B) of the Congressional Budget Act of 1974 provided in bills and resolutions referred to the committee under section 401(b)(2) of that Act (but subject to the provisions of section 401(b)(3) of that Act).

"4. New advance spending authority described in section 401(c)(2)(C) of the Congressional Budget Act of 1974 provided in bills and resolutions referred to the committee under section 401(b)(2) of that Act (but subject to the provisions of section 401(b)(3) of that Act)."

* * * * * * *

YEAR-AHEAD REQUESTS FOR AUTHORIZATION OF NEW BUDGET AUTHORITY

§ 1009.

SEC. 607. Notwithstanding any other provision of law, any request for the enactment of legislation authorizing the enactment of new budget authority to continue a program or activity for a fiscal year (beginning with the fiscal year commencing October 1, 1976) shall be submitted to the Congress not later than May 15 of the year preceding the year in which such fiscal year begins. In the case of a request for the enactment of legislation authorizing the enactment of new budget authority for a new program or activity which is to continue for more than one fiscal year, such request shall be submitted for at least the first 2 fiscal years.

TITLE VII—PROGRAM REVIEW AND EVALUATION

REVIEW AND EVALUATION BY STANDING COMMITTEES

§ 1010.

SEC. 701. Section 136(a) of the Legislative Reorganization Act of 1946 (2 U.S.C. 190d) is amended by adding at the end thereof the following new sentences: "Such committees may carry out the required analysis, appraisal, and evaluation themselves, or by contract, or may require a Government agency to do so and furnish a report thereon to the Congress. Such committees may rely on such techniques as pilot testing, analysis of costs in comparison with benefits, or provision for evaluation after a defined period of time."

REVIEW AND EVALUATION BY THE COMPTROLLER GENERAL

SEC. 702. (a) Section 204 of the Legislative Reorganization Act of 1970 (31 U.S.C. 1154) is amended to read as follows:

"REVIEW AND EVALUATION

"SEC. 204. (a) The Comptroller General shall review and evaluate the results of Government programs and activities carried on under existing law when ordered by either House of Congress, or upon his own initiative, or when requested by any committee of the House of Representatives or the

Senate, or any joint committee of the two Houses, having jurisdiction over such programs and activities.

"(b) The Comptroller General, upon request of any committee of either House or any joint committee of the two Houses, shall—

"(1) assist such committee or joint committee in developing a statement of legislative objectives and goals and methods for assessing and reporting actual program performance in relation to such legislative objectives and goals. Such statements shall include, but are not limited to, recommendations as to methods of assessment, information to be reported, responsibility for reporting, frequency of reports, and feasibility of pilot testing; and

"(2) assist such committee or joint committee in analyzing and assessing program reviews or evaluation studies prepared by and for any Federal agency.

Upon request of any Member of either House, the Comptroller General shall furnish to such Member a copy of any statement or other material compiled in carrying out paragraphs (1) and (2) which has been released by the committee or joint committee for which it was compiled.

"(c) The Comptroller General shall develop and recommend to the Congress methods for review and evaluation of Government programs and activities carried on under existing law.

"(d) In carrying out his responsibilities under this section, the Comptroller General is authorized to establish an Office of Program Review and Evaluation within the General Accounting Office. The Comptroller General is authorized to employ not to exceed ten experts on a permanent, temporary, or intermittent basis and to obtain services as authorized by section 3109 of title 5, United States Code, but in either case at a rate (or the daily equivalent) for inidviduals not to exceed that prescribed, from time to time, for level V of the Executive Schedule under section 5316 of title 5, United States Code.

"(e) The Comptroller General shall include in his annual report to the Congress a review of his activities under this section, including his recommendations of methods for review and evaluation of Government programs and activities under subsection (c)."

(b) Item 204 in the table of contents of such Act is amended to read as follows:

"Sec. 204. Review and evaluation."

CONTINUING STUDY OF ADDITIONAL BUDGET REFORM PROPOSALS

SEC. 703. (a) The Committee on the Budget of the House of Representatives and the Senate shall study on a continuing basis proposals designed to improve and facilitate methods of congressional budget-making. The proposals to be studied shall include, but are not limited to, proposals for—

(1) improving the information base required for determining the effectiveness of new programs by such means as pilot testing, survey research, and other experimental and analytical techniques;

(2) improving analytical and systematic evaluation of the effectiveness of existing programs;

(3) establishing maximum and minimum time limitations for program authorization; and

(4) developing techniques of human resource accounting and other means of providing noneconomic as well as economic evaluation measures.

(b) The Committee on the Budget of each House shall, from time to time, report to its House the results of the study carried on by it under subsection (a), together with its recommendations.

(c) Nothing in this section shall preclude studies to improve the budgetary process by any other committee of the House of Representatives or the Senate or any joint committee of the Congress.

*　　　*　　　*　　　*　　　*

EXERCISE OF RULEMAKING POWERS

SEC. 904. (a) The provisions of this title (except section 905) and of titles I, III, and IV and the provisions of sections 606, 701, 703, and 1017 are enacted by the Congress—

(1) as an exercise of the rulemaking power of the House of Representatives and the Senate, respectively, and as such they shall be considered as part of the rules of each House, respectively, or of that House to which they specifically apply, and such rules shall supersede other rules only to the extent that they are inconsistent therewith; and

(2) with full recognition of the constitutional right of either House to change such rules (so far as relating to such House) at any time, in the same manner, and to the same extent as in the case of any other rule of such House.

(b) Any provision of title III or IV may be waived or suspended in the Senate by a majority vote of the Members voting, a quorum being present, or by the unanimous consent of the Senate.

(c) Appeals in the Senate from the decisions of the Chair relating to any provision of title III or IV or section 1017 shall, except as otherwise provided therein, be limited to 1 hour, to be equally divided between, and controlled by, the mover and the manager of the resolution, concurrent resolution, reconciliation bill, or rescission bill, as the case may be.

Pursuant to this section, and under its authority contained in clause 4(b) of Rule XI to report on rules and the order of business, the

Committee on Rules may report as privileged a resolution recommending the temporary waiver of the provisions of section 401 of the Congressional Budget Act during the consideration of designated legislation in the House (Speaker Albert, March 20, 1975, p. —).

EFFECTIVE DATES

§ 1011.

SEC. 905. (a) Except as provided in this section, the provisions of this Act shall take effect on the date of its enactment.

(b) Title II (except section 201(a), section 403, and section 502(c) shall take effect on the day on which the first Director of the Congressional Budget Office is appointed under section 201(a).

(c) Except as provided in section 906, title III and section 402 shall apply with respect to the fiscal year beginning on October 1, 1976, and succeeding fiscal years, and section 401 shall take effect on the first day of the second regular session of the Ninety-fourth Congress.

(d) The amendments to the Budget and Accounting Act, 1921, made by sections 601, 603, and 604 shall apply with respect to the fiscal year beginning on July 1, 1975, and succeeding fiscal years, except that section 201(g) of such Act (as added by section 601) shall apply with respect to the fiscal year beginning on October 1, 1976, and succeeding fiscal years and section 201(i) of such Act (as added by section 601) shall apply with respect to the fiscal year beginning on October 1, 1978, and succeeding fiscal years. The amendment to such Act made by section 602 shall apply with respect to the fiscal year beginning on October 1, 1976, and succeeding fiscal years.

APPLICATION OF CONGRESSIONAL BUDGET PROCESS TO FISCAL YEAR 1976

SEC. 906. If the Committees on the Budget of the House of Representatives and the Senate both agree that it is feasible to report and act on a concurrent resolution on the budget referred to in section 301(a), or to apply any provision of title III or section 401 or 402, for the fiscal year beginning on July 1, 1975, and submit reports of such agreement to their respective Houses, then to the extent and in the manner specified in such reports, the provisions so specified and section 202(f) shall apply with respect to such fiscal year. If any provision so specified contains a date, such reports shall also specify a substitute date.

Pursuant to this section, the Committee on the Budget reported to the House its recommendation for implementation of new Congressional budget procedures for fiscal year 1976 (H. Rept. 94-25, March 3, 1975).

GLOSSARY

Amendment: A change in a measure proposed by a congressman. An amendment may be in the first degree—that is, a change directly in a measure—or in the second degree—that is, a change in a pending amendment—but an amendment in the third degree—a proposal to amend a proposal to amend a pending amendment—would be subject to a point of order as a violation of Senate or House rules.

Bill: A measure other than a joint resolution which, if enacted by both Houses in the same form and signed by the President, becomes a law.

Christmas Tree: A nickname for a measure which begins with some central core or purpose and to which a wide variety of amendments are attached as "ornaments" until, upon final passage, there are more ornaments than there is tree.

Closed Rule: A rule or resolution from the House Rules Committee governing the conduct of debate upon a pending bill but permitting no amendment to it.

Cloture: A closing of debate in the Senate. The motion, if voted upon favorably (by a 60-percent majority), limits each member to only one hour of floor debate and then forces a vote on the pending measure.

Committee of the Whole: A device used in the House of Representatives for resolving the House into the "Committee of the Whole House on the State of the Union"—a committee in which slightly less formal rules for the conduct of debate and voting upon amendments apply.

Committees: See *standing committees, select committees,* and *joint committees.*

Concurrent Resolution: A resolution passed by both Houses of Congress, not requiring or intended for approval by the President and without the effect of law, except as it relates to the internal affairs of Congress or as otherwise provided by law.

Conference Committee: The committee consisting of House and Senate managers of a particular piece of legislation, who meet to reconcile differences between the House and Senate versions of the same measure.

Cosponsor: A person who adds his name to a measure as a sponsor, but who is not the principal sponsor or person who introduced the measure in the first place.

Floor Manager: The person in charge of a bill when it reaches the floor, who typically controls the allocation of time, the recognition of members for debate, the acceptance of amendments without rollcall votes, and related matters.

Germaneness: A rule of relevancy. In the House, amendments must be "germane" to the main subject of a bill. In the Senate, except in special circumstances or by unanimous consent agreement (see below), any amendment may be offered to any bill, whether the amendment is germane or not.

Independent Agencies: Agencies created by Congress with varying degrees of independence and/or quasi-judicial regulatory authority.

Individual Views: See *separate views*.

Introductory Remarks: The statement made by a congressman upon introduction of a measure, explaining the measure for the reader of the *Congressional Record*.

Joint Committee: A committee having members from both Houses and established for investigatory or other purposes but not ordinarily involving jurisdiction for legislative purposes—e.g., the Joint Economic Committee, the Joint Committee on Internal Revenue Taxation.

Joint Resolution: A resolution passed by both Houses of Congress and signed by the President, ordinarily limited to special circumstances but having the effect of law to the same extent as a bill that has passed both Houses of Congress and thus has become an Act of Congress.

Legislative History: The documents making up the origins of a law—the hearings, committee reports, floor debates, conference reports, and related public documents, including amendments and early versions of a bill, which trace the sources of a particular piece of legislation and to which reference can be made in finding the intent and meaning of a law.

Live Bill: A bill which ought to be taken seriously—that is, a bill which is likely to receive legislative consideration, as distinguished from the majority of bills and resolutions which are introduced, referred to committee, and never heard of again.

Minority Views: See *separate views*.

Open Rule: A "rule" or resolution from the House Rules Committee governing floor debate on a bill and permitting amendments.

Pair: Refers to an agreement between two members under which neither will vote on a particular matter. A "dead pair" or a "general pair" is a pair between two members, both of whom are absent from the chamber at the time of voting. A "live pair" is a pair between two members, one of whom is present in the chamber at the time of voting. Thus, a "dead pair" does not affect the outcome of a vote, while a "live pair" may affect the outcome if the vote is close.

Point of Order: An objection that a particular motion, amendment, bill, or other proposal is out of order, in violation of a rule. If sustained, a point of order defeats the pending motion, amendment, etc., unless the point of order itself is overruled by vote.

Political Departments: These are typically the departments of government headed by Cabinet officers, and are to be distinguished from independent agencies (see above).

The Previous Question: The issue pending before the chamber. A request for the previous question, or a motion on the previous question, brings to a vote the question of whether debate should cease and the merits of the pending issue should be voted upon. Thus, a motion on the previous question in the House of Representatives is akin to a motion for cloture (see above) in the Senate.

Primary Sponsor: See *sponsor*.

Pocket Veto: The President's failure to sign before the adjournment of Congress a bill given him within the 10-day period prior to adjournment constitutes an indirect or "pocket" veto. During a session of Congress a bill will become a law if, after 10 working days from the time it is presented to the President, the President has not signed it.

Program Legislation: This term is used to identify laws authorizing the expenditure of money for a particular purpose and should be distinguished from the term "regulatory legislation" (see below).

Regulatory Legislation: Legislation designed to govern the behavior of citizens and businesses, e.g., antitrust laws, labor laws, product safety laws, etc.

Resolution: Referring to a simple resolution, rather than a concurrent resolution or a joint resolution, this is a measure passed only in one House, and ordinarily without the effect of law, commonly used for internal business of that House or for expressing the "sense" or views of that House. See also *concurrent resolution* and *joint resolution*.

Rule: This term has many meanings. It may refer to a standing rule of either House of Congress, but in the House of Representatives, a "rule" is often a resolution from the House Rules Committee, which, if adopted by the House, sets the procedures and time limits for debate and voting on a pending measure.

Select Committee: A committee established for a specific purpose by either House of Congress—e.g., the Select Committee on Small Business. (Select committees are similar to special committees.)

Separate Views: The views of individual members or groups of members of a committee, who wish to separate their views from those set forth in the main body of a committee report. Also occasionally termed individual views, minority views, additional views, or supplemental views.

Sponsor: The person who introduces a measure and whose name is printed first on it. Also called primary sponsor.

Standing Committee: A permanent committee of either House of Congress. Standing committees have legislative jurisdiction over particular subject matter. Almost all major bills are referred to and, if favorably acted upon, will be reported from standing committees.

Supplemental Views: See *separate views*.

Unanimous Consent Agreement: An order entered in the Senate without objection by unanimous consent which limits debate, fixes a time for a vote, or otherwise establishes procedural rules for the conduct of debate upon a particular bill. It serves a purpose similar to the function of a "rule" (see above) or resolution from the House Rules Committee in the other body of Congress.

Wednesday Clubs: Informal Republican bodies in both Houses. These separate House and Senate groups of Republican congressmen, who lunch together on Wednesdays, tend to to be in the moderate or liberal wings of their party (although that is arguable in some cases) and discuss possible joint actions or policies.

TOPICAL INDEX

A

"AA" (*See* Administrative assistants)
Academic institutions, legislative drafting assistance 31
Administrative assistants 111
"Advice and Consent" power 123
AFL-CIO 26
Amendments
 appropriations bills, Senate 97
 as addition to bill without deletion 15
 bill in limbo reoffered as 41
 calendar number for 14
 committee report, discussion of 55
 committees, referral to 14
 compromise 50
 conference report 74
 degrees of 8, 50
 example 10
 executive session, focus on 49
 floor amendments, form of 35
 form for introducing in Senate 10
 germaneness under House rules 69 et seq.
 House rules, floor debate and voting 66
 introduction 34
  drafting of 15
 legislative history 50
 nongermane, separate votes on 71
 numbering 8
 perfecting 50
 reoffering of 35
  committee reporting out of bill 14
 report language in lieu of 50
 requirements 7
 second-degree amendment 8
 Senate rules, floor debate 66
 sponsor and/or cosponsor 34
 substitute amendments,
  vote on 50
 vote on, sequence 49

American Association of Retired Persons 26
American Library Association 26
American Medical Association 26
Appointment calendar of congressman 128
Appropriations bills (*See also* Appropriations committee)
 authorizations and appropriations, relationship 98, 148
 constitutional authority of the House 97
 continuing resolutions 99
 fiscal year, calendar 100
 germaneness rule 100, 149
 open-ended authorizations 99
 parliamentary restrictions 100
 point-of-order provisions 101
 Senate amendment to 97
 special parliamentary conditions applicable 100
 stated, calendars and reports 62
 substantive legislation added, point of order 101, 148
Appropriations committee (*See also* Appropriations bill) 98 et seq.
Appropriations subcommittee, chairman 81
Authorizations 98 (*See also* Appropriations bills)

B

Bill 4 (*See also* Amendment; Resolution)
 ambiguity 50
 amendments
  addition to with no deletion 15
  germaneness under House rules 69 et seq.
 bipartisan measure, cosponsorship to secure 33
 bringing a bill to the House floor, methods 59 et seq.

321

Bill, cont.
  calendars, effect 62 et seq. (*See also* Calendars)
  calling up a bill,
    Senate provisions 61
  concurrent resolution terminating, effect 7
  "conferees" on 35
  congressional post-veto reaction 74
  Congressional Record, reprint of introductory remarks 36
  cosponsors 14
  debating time, allocation 58
  enacting clause 5
  example 5, 9
  failure of, number 38
  filibuster (*See* Filibuster)
  finalizing 49, 52
  floor debate and voting 65 et seq. (*See also* Floor debate)
  floor manager (*See* Floor manager)
  form for introducing in Senate 9
  germaneness (*See* Germaneness)
  hearings (*See* Hearings)
  House referral to 15
  introducer 14
  introduction 33
    clerk, handing to 35
  introductory remarks to 35, 140
  killing of, absence of hearings 39
  labelling parts of 22
  legislative assistants, role in drafting 112
  legislative history (*See* Legislative history)
  "live bill" 40
  moving of 40
    amendment, offered as 41
  numbering of 8
  official title 14
  Presidential signature 4, 71, 74
  private bill 4
    example 6
  privileged bills 61
  publicizing 36
  referral to committee 14, 36
    Parliamentarian, role of 36, 37
    primary emphasis test 36
    referral by unanimous consent 37
    Speaker's power of dual or sequential referral 85
    target committee, choice of 38
  reoffering as amendment to another bill 41
  reporting of 51 et seq.
  requests to executive agencies 40
  requirements 4
  rules 146
  Senate referral to 15
  short title 5, 14
  splitting of
    House reform measure 80
    Speaker's power 85
  sponsor and/or cosponsor, choice of 33
  supplemental, minority, or additional views, rules 54
  title and short title 14
  veto of 74
  voting on 67 et seq. (*See also* Voting)
    executive session 49
Bill clerk 8
Black Caucus 86
Bolling resolution, substitute for 79
"Buck slip" 114
Budget (*See* Federal budget)
Budget committees 104

C

Cabinet officers, congressional relationship 120 et seq.
Calendar (*See also* Consent calendar; Floor calendar)
  amendment 14
  House calendars, purposes 62 et seq., 214
  Senate calendar, provisions 61 et seq.
Calling up a bill (*See* Bill)
Casework
  conflict of interest 121
  status of cases, congressional inquiries 120
Caseworkers 114
Caucus
  compromise process 46
  effect of system 78
  voting discipline within 77
Chairmen 39
Chamber of Commerce of the United States 26
Civil rights legislation, cloture 65
Clerk
  House 117, 193

Topical Index 323

introduction of bill 35
Cloture 65
Commerce power, drafting
    problems 20
Committee on Public Works,
    reporting of bills,
    procedure 61
Committee report
    contents of 54 et seq.
    dissenting views 51, 54, 55, 57, 208
    drafting of 53 et seq.
    steps 51
    what it is 53
Committees (*See also* Conference
    committee; Subcommittees)
    amendments
        introduction at committee or
            subcommittee level 34
        referral to 14
        voted down in, effect 34
    chairmen
        election in House without
            regard to seniority 79
        election of 78, 81
        power of 39
        procedure at hearings 42
    committee of origin, role of 35
    conference committee (*See*
        Conference committees)
    consensus, operation by 40
    executive session (*See* Executive
        sessions of committees and
        subcommittees)
    hearings (*See* Hearings)
    House 194
        chairmanship criterion,
            reform 79
        power center 81
        rules, generally 205
    joint 43
    membership
        individual influence 83
        limitation on 79
    minority members, influence 83
    oversight subcommittee (*See*
        Oversight subcommittee)
    priviliged committees, procedure
        for reporting bills 61
    proxy rules 48 (*See also*
        Proxy rules)
    quorum rules 48 (*See also*
        Quorum rules)
    referral of bills to 14, 36 et seq.
        choice of target committee 38
        Parliamentarian, role 36, 37
        unanimous consent 37
    reform measures 40
    report of (*See* Committee report)
    reporting out of bill, amendment
        reintroduced after 14
    rules, publication 47
    select 43
    Senate 156
        hold on calendar 64
        transcripts of meetings of
            Senate 88
    senior members of, role as
        "Conferees" 35
    special 43
    sponsorship of bill by entire
        committee, bipartisan
        measure 33
    staff of
        appointment of 110
        drafting assistance, as
            source of 25
        personal staff of Congressman,
            relationship to 116
    target committee 38
    vote by 51 (*See also*
        Committee report)
Common Cause 26
Comptroller General,
    budgetary power 102
Concurrent resolution 8
    example 13
    Presidential approval
        not necessary 7
    requirements 7
Conference committee (*See also*
    Conference report)
    authority of, matters of
        disagreement 73
    composition 35, 72
    conference report of 72
    open and closed conference 73, 228
    public meetings,
        Senate reform measure 88
    request for an agreement to 72
    selection of managers 73
    "strike-and-insert" technique 73
Conference report (*See also*
    Conference committee)
    amendment of 74
    calling up of, rules 70
    limits of 274
    procedure 72
    voting on 72
Conflicts of interest 121

324 TOPICAL INDEX

Congress (*See also*
    Congressional power sources)
  Congressional Research
    Service 119
  federal employment
    patronage 122
  internal affairs of, use of
    resolutions for 7
  Librarian of Congress 119
  Ninety-third, resume of activity
    of, Appendix 1 131
  officers of 117 et seq.
  offices of (*See* Congressional
    offices)
  power center of 77 et seq.
  President, working relationship
    with 28
  relationship with executive
    department and independent
    agencies 120 et seq.
  retention of power,
    drafting problems 19
  staff directory 126
  staffing (*See* Congressional
    offices)
Congressional Budget and
  Impoundment Control Act of
  1974 103 et seq., 291
Congressional Budget Office 104
Congressional findings 20
Congressional offices
  administrative assistants,
    roles of 111
  caseworkers and secretaries,
    role of 114
  conflicts of interest 121
  ethical considerations in quasi-
    judicial matters 120
  executive departments and
    independent agencies,
    relationship with 120 et seq.
  inquiries about status of case 120
  legislative assistant (LA),
    role of 112
  lobbyists (*See* Lobbyists and
    interest groups)
  ombudsman function 113
  patronage, federal
    employment 122
  personal secretary, role of 113
  press secretary, role 115
  relationship of committee staff to
    personal staff 116
  structure 109 et seq.
  staff's activities 184, 187, 213

Congressional power sources 19
  et seq.
Congressional Record
  introductory remarks to bill
    printed in 35
  rules of committees,
    publication 47
Congressional Research Service 119
Congressman, appointment
  calendar of 128
Consent calendar
  bringing a bill to House floor,
    provisions 60, 215
  House, calling only on specified
    day 63
Consent vote, Senate 67
Constitutional authority, drafting
  problems 20
Continuing resolutions 100, 215
Cordon print 55
Cosponsors 14 (*See also* Sponsors)
  choice of, importance 33 (*See
    also* Amendments; Bill)
  House limit on number 34
  Senate limit on number 34
Counsel and minority counsel 111

D

Debate (*See* Floor debate)
Definitions, development in
  drafting 16
Delegation of discretion,
  drafting techniques 17, 18
Democratic Caucus (*See
    *House Democratic Caucus)
Democratic Conference, Senate 92
Democratic Policy Committee,
  Senate, power of 93
Democratic Steering and Policy
  Committee, House
  assigning committee
    memberships 80, 84
  composition 85
  function of 85
  Speaker as Chairman of 85
Democratic Steering Committee,
  Senate, power 93
Democratic Study Group (DSG)
  function of 86
  Model Caucus and Committee
    Rules 233
District of Columbia, special days
  for calling up business
    relating to 59

Division vote 67
Drafting a measure 3
  authorizations 99
  choice of type of measure 3
  committee report 53 et seq.
    (*See also* Committee report)
  individual views 57
  congressional findings 20
  definitions, development 16
  delays because of executive
    inaction 29
  delegation of discretion 19
  effective dates 23
  findings and policy 20
  judicial review 23
  jurisdictional overlaps 22
  labelling parts of bill 22
  preemption doctrine 21
  regulatory statutes 18
  retention of congressional power
    not subject to veto 19
  sources of assistance 23 et seq.
  sources of constitutional
    authority 20
  techniques and problems 8 et seq.
  amendment, introduction
    form 10, 15
  delegation of discretion 17
  examples of forms 8 et seq.
  numbering of measure 8
  open-ended authorizations,
    problems 99
  programmatic and regulatory
    statutes 18
  specificity vs. delegation 16
    et seq.
  title of bill 14

E

Ecological organizations 26
Effective dates 23
Executive branch (*See also*
  Executive departments and
  agencies; Executive
  discretion)
  Congress, cooperation with 28
  exempting power left to 17
  veto power, retention of
    congressional power not
    subject to 19
Executive departments and agencies
  bills, requests for comments 40
  congressional offices, relationship
    with 120 et seq.
  drafting assistance, as
    source of 28
Executive discretion
  abuse of, congressional
    check on 19
  judicial review 23
Executive markup sessions
  amendments, offering of 49
  compromise process 46
  House reform measure for
    openness 79
  open vs. closed 46, 206
    Senate reform measures 87
    et seq.
  press coverage 45, 49
  proxies 48
  quorum rules 48
  vote to close, timing,
    House reform 79
  voting on bill 49

F

Farm bloc 86
Federal assistance,
  drafting of legislation 18
Federal budget
  budget committees 104
  congressional budget
    timetable 105
  congressional Budget and
    Impoundment Control
    Act of 1974 103, 291
  Congressional Budget
    Office 104, 309
  fiscal year, change in 104
  impoundment, limitation on
    President's ability 106
  President's budget,
    development 102
  Congress' pre-1974
    response to 102
  impoundment controversy 103
  timetable for submission
    106, 292
Federal Energy Administration 18
Filibuster
  cloture, effect 65
  Senate reforms 89
  techniques 64
  wearing down of 65
Findings and Policy, drafting
  problems 20
Fiscal year, dating of 104

Floor amendment (See
    Amendments)
Floor calendar, rule to remove
    bill from to floor   60
Floor debate   65 et seq.
  House rules   217 et seq.
    ending debate by majority vote
      67, 218
    position of staff members on floor
      68
    press coverage   69
  Senate rules   153
    amendments during   66
    limited debate rule   65, 66, 154
    suspension of rules by vote   67
    third reading   66
    unanimous consent agreements
      66
Floor manager
  choice of   57 et seq.
  debate time, allocation   58
  majority   58
  minority   58
  subcommittee chairman as   53, 57
Funding legislative programs (See
    Appropriations bills)

G

General Accounting Office, power
    102
Germaneness rule
  amendments, House rules, provisions   69 et seq., 219
  appropriations bills provisions   100, 219
  bill from Senate-House Conference
    69, 225
  limitations on   70
  waiver of   71
Glossary   315 et seq.
Governors' Conference   26
Grants, authorization drafting   18
Gulf of Tonkin Resolution   19

H

Hansen substitute (H. Res. 988)   43, 79
Hearings (See also Executive
    sessions)
  chairman, power of   39 et seq.
  committee members, statements
    and questions   44
  House, open hearings   45
  initiation of   39
  legislative assistants' attendance
    at   113
  non-legislative   43
  open and closed   45
  oversight (See Oversight
    hearings)
  press coverage   45 (See also Press
    coverage)
  purpose and effect of   41 et seq.
  quorum rule   42
  subject matter of   43 et seq.
  testimony at   44
    chairman's procedure   42
  timing   40
  witnesses and statements   44 et
    seq.
"Holds," Senate consent calendar   63
House Democratic Caucus
  appropriations subcommittee chairman elected by   81, 82
  chairmanship election, seniority
    disregarded   79
  chairmen of full committees, vote
    on   81
  hearings, power to call   39
  rule changes, Dec. 1974   80
  Rules and Manual, Appendix   6,
    260 et seq.
  subcommittees   82
    establishment of number and
      jurisdiction   82
    substantive issues, power on   84
House of Representatives
  appropriations bills (See Appropriations bills)
    constitutional priority   97
  bill, identification of   15
  Black caucus   86
  bringing a measure to the floor
    59 et seq. (See also Bill)
  caucus system, effect of   78
  Clerk of the House   117
  committees
    chairmen of full committees,
      selection and power of   81,
      82
    proxy rules   48 (See also Proxy,
      rules)
    rules   47
    subcommittee chairmen, selection and power of   82
  Democratic Caucus (See House
    Democratic Caucus)
  Doorkeeper of the House   118

floor debate rules 65, 217, 220
leadership of, power 85
Legislative Council, Office of 119
(*See also* Legislative Counsel, Office of)
Minority and Majority Secretary 118
open vs. closed hearings 45
Parliamentarian 119 (*See also* Parliamentarian)
power centers of 77
quorum rule 42
reform measures 78 et seq.
compromise, effect on 47
consensus, committee operations by 40
Democratic Caucus, power 84 (*See also* House Democratic Caucus)
leadership, power of 85
rules (*See also* House Rules Committee)
floor debate (*See* Floor debate)
suspension to call up bill 61
text of (Ninety-Fourth Congress, 1st Session), Appendix 4 192 et seq.
House Rules Committee
closed rule restrictions (House caucus rules) 264
floor debate 65
reform measures 84
reporting of bills, procedure 61
resolution or rule, bringing measure to floor 60
voting on bill in executive sessions, effect 51

I

Impoundment of funds 103
Independent agencies
congressional offices, relationship with 120 et seq.
identification 18
delegation by legislature 18
Interest groups (*See* Lobbyists and interest groups)
Interior Committee, reporting of bills, procedure 61
Internal Revenue Code
constitutional authorization 20
definitions, approach to development 16
Introducer of bill 14 (*See also* Sponsors)
title of bill, discretion in selection 14
Introductory remarks 35

J

Johnson, Lyndon 92
Joint committee (*See* Senate-House committee)
Joint Committee on Congressional Operations, rules, publication of 47
Joint Economic Committee, power over President's budget 102
Joint resolution
concurrent resolution terminating 7
example 12
numbering 8
Presidential signing 4
requirements 4
Judicial review, drafting problems 23
Jurisdiction, drafting problems, overlap 22

K

"Killing" a bill in committee 39

L

"LA" (*See* Legislative assistant, role of)
Labor bloc 86
"Lag dates" 23
Leadership, power in House 85
Legislation
funding of (*See* Appropriations bills)
programmatic (*See* Programmatic legislation)
regulatory statutes (*See* Regulatory statutes)
Legislative assistant, role of 112
Legislative Counsel, Office of 119
drafting assistance, as source of 24
Legislative history
amendments, compromise 50
committee report (*See* Committee report)
interpretation of language, effect 50

Legislative Reorganization Act of 1946, excerpts from, Appendix 7 266 et seq.
Legislative Reorganization Act of 1970
  committee report, drafting of minority views, printing and submission of 54
  excerpts from, Appendix 7, 266 et seq.
  rules, adoption by Senate committees 47
  Senate committee hearings 45
Librarian of Congress 119
Loans, allocation to states, drafting programmatic legislation 18
Lobbyists and interest groups
  congressional offices seeking advice 124
  drafting assistance, as source of 26
  examples 26
  expertise 125 et seq.
  legislative assistants' contact with 113
  need for 123
  pros and cons of accepting assistance from 125
  registration form, Appendix 2 133
  registration under Lobbying Act 124
  Regulation of Lobbying Act 276

M

Majority Leader of Senate 92
Majority party, sponsorship of amendment by 92
Mansfield, Mike 92
Markup sessions (*See* Executive sessions)
Measure (*See also* Amendment; Bill; Concurrent resolution; Joint resolution; Resolution)
  drafting of 3 et seq. (*See also* Drafting a measure)
  number of introduced 4
  "reference" of 14
  types of 3 et seq.
Mills, Wilbur D. 84
Minority view, committee report 54, 55
Money -bills (*See* Appropriations bills; Federal budget)

Motions to reconsider and table 68

N

Nader, Ralph 26
National Association of Manufacturers 26
National Education Association 26
National Labor Relations Board 18
National Rifle Association 26

O

Office of Management and Budget proposals
  legislative proposals, activities 28
  preparation of President's budget 102
Ombudsman function 113
Oversight subcommittee
  establishment of 43
  reform measure 80

P

Paired votes, provisions 68
Parliamentarian 119
  drafting assistance, as source of 30
  referral of bill to committee, role 36
  preintroduction conference with 37
  responsibilities 14
Party caucuses (*See* Caucuses)
Patronage
  Capitol Hill staff jobs 116
  Congress and federal jobs, guidelines for 122
Pension Reform Act, 1974
  lobbyists' activities during legislation 27
  preemption doctrine, drafting 21
  sources of constitutional authority 21
Point of order
  appropriations bills 101
  filibuster tactics 64
  Senate rules, floor debate and voting 66
  waiving of, nongermane amendments, individual rule effect 71
Policy Committee, Senate

calendar, three-day hold limitation 64
Power centers 77 et seq.
Preemption doctrine, drafting problems 21
President
  bills, action on 4, 74
  Congress, working relationship with 28
  impounding of funds by 103
  joint resolution, signing 4
  messages from 28
President Pro Tempere, Senate 92
President's budget (*See* Federal budget)
Press coverage
  executive sessions 45, 49
  floor debate 69
  galleries 69
  hearings 45
  paired votes, effect on 68
  press secretary, role of 115
Programmatic legislation, drafting of 18
Proxy, rules 206
  casting of by staff 48
  committees, misuse 48
  general, on substantive matters 48
  House reform measures, Hansen substitute 80
  model rules (DSG) for committees 241
  specific 48

Q

Quorum rules
  committees 48
  filibuster tactics 64
  hearings 42
  House voting provisions 68
  model rules (DSG) for committees 242
  Senate voting provisions 67, 137

R

Radio (*See* Press coverage)
Ramsayer print 55
Reconsider and table, motions 68, 145
Recorded vote, House 67

"Reference," insertion in drafting 14
Referral to committee 36
Reform measures (*See also* House; Senate)
  cloture, history 65
  committee operation, consensus rule 40
  executive sessions, open 46
  House reforms, procedural 78 et seq.
  Legislative Reorganization Act (*See* Legislative Reorganization Act of 1970)
  open markups 87 et seq. (*See also* Executive sessions)
  oversight subcommittees 43
  proxy, rules, misuse of 48
  Senate (*See* Senate)
  seniority disregarded, House committee chairmanship 79
Regulatory statutes, drafting 18
"Reorganization Plan" 19
Reporting a bill (*See* Bills, reporting of)
Resolution (*See also* Concurrent resolution; Joint Resolution)
  appropriations bill, continuing resolutions 99
  effect 7
  example 11
  from House Rules Committee 65, 71
  numbering 8
Rollcall vote
  filibuster tactic 64
  Senate provision 67
  Yea and nay vote, House 67
Rules
  amendments, sequence of votes on 49
  bringing a measure to floor, House Rules Committee 60
  closed rule, reform measure 84
  committee report, drafting 54 (*See also* Committee report)
  conference committee considerations (*See* Conference committee)
  House
    suspension of to call up bill 61
    text (Ninety-Fourth Congress, 1st Session) Appendix 4, 192 et seq.

Rules, cont.
  House committees 47
  House Democratic Caucus Rules and Manual, Appendix 6, 260 et seq.
  Model Committee Caucus and Committee Rules, Prepared by the Democratic Study Group, Appendix 5, 233 et seq.
  point of order, effect 62
  reform measures, effect 46
  Senate, Standing Rules (Ninety-Fourth Congress), Appendix 3, 135 et seq.
  Senate committees 47
  waiving germaneness, points of order 71
Rules Committee (*See* House Rules Committee)

S

Second-degree amendment 8
Secretaries, congressional offices 114
Secretary of the Senate 117
Senate
  "Advice and Consent" nominees 123
  appropriations bills, germaneness rule 100
  bill, identification 15
  bringing a measure to the floor 59
  calling of the regular calendar, procedure for calling up a bill 61
  closed sessions, opening by rule or majority vote of committee 87
  committees and subcommittees
    chairmen of full committees, power 90
    chairmen, selection 89
    members of, influence 91
    openness of meetings 88
    power centers, as 90
    proxy rules 48 (*See also* Proxy, rules)
    rules 47
    transcripts of meetings 88
  Democratic Conference, power 92
  Democratic Policy Committee, power 93
  Democratic Steering Committee, power 93
  floor debates, unanimous consent agreements 66
  influence groups 93
  Legislative Counsel 119 (*See also* Legislative Counsel, Office of)
  Majority and Minority Secretary 118
  majority party, Majority Leader, power 92
  open vs. closed hearings 45
  Parliamentarian 119 (*See also* Parliamentarian)
  power structure of 87
  quorum rule 42
  ranking minority members, influence 91
  reform measures 87 et seq.
    filibuster 89
    open markups 87 et seq.
    selection of committee chairmen 89
    staffing for less senior Senators 89
  rules
    floor debate, position of staff members during 68 (*See also* Floor debate)
    suspension by vote during floor debate 67
  Secretary of the Senate 117
  staff breakdown of offices 110 (*See also* Congressional offices)
  Standing Rules (Ninety-Fourth Congress), Appendix 3 135 et seq.
  subcommittees, chairman of, power 91
Senate-House committee, bill returning from, Senate amendments, germaneness provision 69
Senate-House conference 51
  compromise measures, proceedings 51
Seniority, appropriations committee membership 98
Sergeant at Arms 118, 193
Short title
  distinguished from title 14
  Section 1 of bill 15
Speaker of the House
  Democratic Steering and Policy Committee, chairmanship 85

Topical Index 331

power 85, 192
Rules Committee members nominated by 81
Sponsors (*See also* Cosponsors)
   bipartisan support shown by 33
   choice of, importance 33 et seq.
     (*See also* Amendment; Bill)
   primary sponsor, role 33
Staff directory 126
Staffing (*See* Congressional offices; Senate)
Structure of congressional office 109
Subcommittees
   amendment voted down in, effect 34
   chairmen
     drafting of committee report 53
     floor manager of bill 53, 57
     hearings called by 83
     House, limitations on power 82, 83
     sponsorship of bill by 34
   executive sessions (*See* Executive sessions (markups))
   House, power and procedures of 82
   senior members of, role as "conferees" 35
   subcommittee of origin, role of 35

T

Target committee 38
Television (*See* Press coverage)
Teller vote, House 67
Title of bill 14
Types of measures 3

U

Unanimous consent agreements, Senate 66, 87

V

Veterans' Committee, reporting of bills 61

Veto
   congressional reaction to 74
   retention of congressional power over, drafting problems 19
Vice President 92
Voice vote, House and Senate 67
Voting
   caucuses, discipline within, power 77
   conference report 72
   conflict of interest 121
   congressional override of Presidential veto 74
   consent calendar, procedure 61
   filibuster, ending of, Senate requirements 89
   House methods 67 et seq.
   motion to reconsider and table 68
   paired votes 68
   Senate methods 67
   suspension of House rule 61

W

War Powers Act 19
   congressional veto power retained 17
   constitutional authority 20
Ways and Means Committee, House
   Democratic Caucus rule changes, effect 80
   increase in size of 80
   referral of bills to, basis for 37
   reform measures, effect on power 83
   reporting of bills, procedure 61
"Wednesday Clubs" 86
Welfare and Pension Plans Disclosure Act, preemption doctrine, drafting 21

Y

Yea and nay vote, House 67

LIBRA

Books on regula